WILLIAM ARTHUR DEACON:
A CANADIAN LITERARY LIFE

CLARA THOMAS AND JOHN LENNOX

WILLIAM ARTHUR DEACON

A Canadian Literary Life

University of Toronto Press • Toronto Buffalo London

© University of Toronto Press 1982
Toronto Buffalo London
Printed in Canada

ISBN 0-8020-5593-1

The Canada Council
Conseil des Arts du Canada
1957-1982

CANADIAN CATALOGUING IN PUBLICATION DATA

Thomas, Clara, 1919–
  William Arthur Deacon: a Canadian literary life

  Bibliography: p.
  Includes index.
  ISBN 0-8020-5593-1

  1. Deacon, William Arthur, 1890–1977. 2. Critics –
  Canada – Biography. 3. Critics – Canada – Corre-
  spondence. I. Lennox, John Watt, 1945–   II. Deacon,
  William Arthur, 1890–1977. III. Title: William
  Arthur Deacon: a Canadian literary life.
  PS8025.D52T56   c818'.5209   c81-095094-4
  PN75.D52T56

This book has been published with the help of a grant from the Canadian
Federation for the Humanities, using funds provided by the Social Sciences
and Humanities Research Council of Canada, and a grant from the Andrew
W. Mellon Foundation to the University of Toronto Press. Publication was
also assisted by the Canada Council and the Ontario Arts Council under their
block grants programs.

FRONTISPIECE William Arthur Deacon, oil sketch by Charles Comfort, 1926

FOR JANE AND MORLEY

CONTENTS

ACKNOWLEDGMENTS

AT EVERY STAGE OF OUR WORK on the William Arthur Deacon Project we have had massive support from individuals, from the Thomas Fisher and the Robarts libraries at the University of Toronto, from the Social Sciences and Humanities Research Council of Canada, and from York University.

Mr Lloyd Haines, literary executor of the William Arthur Deacon estate, has been an enthusiastic and cordial supporter of the project from the beginning; to him, to Bill Deacon, William Arthur Deacon's son, and to Charity Haines and John Deacon, his grandchildren, we owe very special thanks. To Mrs Viola Pratt and Claire Pratt we owe, in no small measure, the instigation of this project, as well as the many warm reminiscences they have given us of their decades of friendship with William Arthur and Sally Deacon. Many other friends and associates of the Deacons have given us their time and encouragement: Mrs Isabel LeBourdais, Mrs Yvonne Housser, Ann Phelps, William French, Gordon Sinclair, Herman Voaden and William McMaster, George Nelson and Conn Smythe. Among our own friends and colleagues, professors Francess Halpenny, Malcolm Ross, Northrop Frye, and Robert Cluett, Jean Jamieson, former Humanities Editor of the University of Toronto Press, and William Lennox gave us strong initial support and encouragement.

Scores of Deacon's former friends and correspondents, and their descendants, have given us permission to quote from letters: Mrs Agnes Armstrong, John Aylen, Constance Beresford-Howe, Bruce Billings, Mrs Margerie Bonner, Victor Brooker, Mrs Ethel Brown, Mrs Mary Cates, Charles Comfort, Jane Edgar Conway, Susan Creighton, Dr Anne Dagg, Miss Laura Lee Davidson, Robertson Davies, Professor

Jean-Marcel Duciaume, Dorothy Dumbrille, James Eayrs, Lyman Flint, Louise Guèvremont-Gentiletti, Mrs Imogen Givens, Mrs Clare Carten Grimes, Leonard Grove, George Hardy, Philip Harrold, Molly Costain Haycraft, John W. Holmes, Bruce Hutchison, Donald Innis, Hugh Innis, Father Martin Kenney, Isabel LeBourdais, Roger Lemelin, A.R.M. Lower, Brian MacFarlane, T.M. MacInnes, Mrs Grace MacInnis, Mrs Lewis MacIsaac, Hugh MacLennan, Kenneth McNaught, Miss V. McPherson, George E. Nelson, Peter Newman, Ann Phelps, Mrs Allison Pickett, Mrs Viola Pratt, Thomas H. Raddall, Esmée de la Roche Rees, Leon M. Rhodenizer, Beth Pierce Robinson, Lady Joan Roberts, Malcolm Ross, Sinclair Ross, Gabrielle Roy, George Salverson, B.D. Sandwell, Dorothy Sisco, Conn Smythe, Mrs Dorothy Taylor, Don W. Thomson, Mrs Elizabeth Volz, Margaret Whitridge.

Our research would not have been possible without the initial assistance and unfailing encouragement of Richard Landon, Chief Librarian of the Thomas Fisher Library, and of Rachel Grover, whose meticulous work on the Deacon Collection had brought a large part of it into manageable order before we began. To Robert Blackburn, Director of Library Services, University of Toronto Libraries, we owe a very special debt of gratitude: his co-operation in allotting us spacious quarters in the Robarts Library has not only made our work infinitely easier and more pleasurable, but has also been an outstanding manifestation of inter-university cooperation.

York University and the sshrcc have been major benefactors of this extensive project. To York we owe thanks for three minor research grants and a dean's stipend, enabling us at various times to help fund the assistance we needed; for the funding and expert preparation of our computerized index of the collection (Deakdex), completed in the fall of 1981, we thank Robert Drummond, Department of Political Science, Linda Crich, Edele Van Slyke and her staff at Computer Services, and John Tibert of the Institute for Behavioural Research, all at York University. Most important of all, to York University we owe the work of Doris Brillinger, Head of Secretarial Services, and her staff. Their work for us began in the fall of 1977 with the making of a complete card index for the 18,000 items of the collection and has continued, expertly and cheerfully, through the seemingly endless drafts that have finally resulted in this biography. To say that their aid has been invaluable is an understatement!

For part-time research assistance we are indebted to Jeanette Seim, Sherri Posesorski, Helen Newell, Deborah Jepson, and Ruth Panofsky.

To the SSHRCC, John Lennox and Clara Thomas owe leave grants for 1978-9 and 1980-1 respectively, allowing them to work on the Deacon Project during sabbatical leaves. The SSHRCC also awarded Clara Thomas a research grant for the years 1979-80 and 1980-1. Of all the magnificent support that we have received, that grant has been the most valuable, enabling us to hire a full-time research assistant for two years.

Our editors at the University of Toronto Press, Gerald Hallowell and Jean Wilson, have provided constant encouragement and expert support.

Without our assistant, Michèle Lacombe, neither the biography nor our other two undertakings, a correspondence collection and a computerized index of the collection, could possibly have been completed. Her outstanding talent for research, her mastery of the contents of this large collection and of computer and indexing techniques, her management of our premises in the Robarts Library, and, above all, her unfailing commitment to and enthusiasm for all the work involved, have constantly supported us and spurred us on.

Clara Thomas and John Lennox
York University, December 1981

Sarah Annie Davies and William Henry Deacon, about 1890

Great-uncle Thomas, one of a long
line of Deacon lawyers

Grandmother Davies, about 1895

William Arthur Deacon, age ten, outside Grandfather Davies' home,
Stanstead, Quebec

Deacon in Stanstead College soccer team uniform

Thomas Russell Deacon, President,
Manitoba Bridge and Iron Works,
and Mayor of Winnipeg

Sarah Townsend Syme, about 1918

H.G. Wade, W.T. Allison, Charles G.D. Roberts, Winnipeg, 1925

Book Page logo, *Saturday Night*

Judge Emily Murphy ('Janey Canuck') reviewing police, Edmonton, 1922

Hector Charlesworth, Editor,
Saturday Night, 1926–32

Sally and Bill, jr, Fall 1923

PENS AND PIRATES

BY: WILLIAM: ARTHVR: DEACON

(Candide)

THE RYERSON PRESS · · PUBLISHERS
TORONTO · · · CANADA

F.H. Varley's drawing of 'Candide,' for frontispiece, *Pens and Pirates*

Francis Dickie ('A Letter from Paris,' *Saturday Night*), at his home in Heriot Bay, BC, 1926, with his unpublished manuscripts

Billy, Deirdre, and Mary at the cottage, about 1930

(left to right) Bliss Carman, Charles G.D. Roberts, Annie Charlotte Dalton,
Lorne Pierce, A.M. Stephen (seated), Ernest Fewster

Sarah Annie Deacon, W.A. Deacon's
mother

E.J. Pratt, 1926

Arthur Phelps, about 1922

Bliss Carman on tour in the 1920s

Mazo de la Roche

Wilson MacDonald, 1926

Annie Charlotte Dalton, 1926

Laura Goodman Salverson, 1934

Bertram Booker, by Charles Comfort, 1929

Frederick Philip Grove, by Charles Comfort, 1927

Grey Owl, about 1935

Harold Innis, 1931

Wilson's Point, Lake Couchiching

A critic's choice

John Murray Gibbon, 1939   Pelham Edgar, 1933

Stephen Leacock, Old Brewery Bay, Orillia

Hugh MacLennan, 1951

Gabrielle Roy, 1945

Gwethalyn Graham, about 1944

A relaxed moment

Living room, 48 Killdeer Crescent, Toronto

'The Reviewer,' 1959

Sally Deacon, about 1955

OVERLEAF: *The Literary Map of Canada* (section), by
William Arthur Deacon, 1936

CASSIAR
M. Conway Turton

RED WILLOWS
Constance Lindsay Skinner

THE DOWNFALL OF TEMLAHAM
Marius Barbeau

Mount Robson

NIPS
Georges B

INDIAN DAYS IN THE CANADIAN ROCKIES
Marius Barbeau

A SONG OF THE FRASER RIVER
Cecily Fox-Smith

THE CARIBOO TRAIL
Elspeth Honeyman Clarke

DAVID THOMPSON
Bliss Carman

THE SKY P
Ralph Con

NORTHLAND SONGS
John Murray Gibbon

THE TRAIL TO LILLOOET
Pauline Johnson

CATHEDRAL MOUNTAIN
Constance Davies Woodrow

BANFF

BLACK ROCK
Ralph Connor

CALG
Isabel

THE P
Fred

IN THE OKANAGAN
Bliss Carman

Arrow Lake

DRYAD IN NANAIMO
Audrey Alexandra Brown

POOR MAN'S ROCK
Bertrand W. Sinclair

EBB-TIDE
Marjorie Pickthall

VANCOUVER

CHINATOWN CHANT
Tom MacInnes

VICTORIA

VICTORIA
Bliss Carman

THE PRAIRIE STORIES
Arthur Stringer
Lake Kootenay

THE KOOTENAY RAM
Ernest Thompson Seton

MED

IN SCARLET AN
T.M.

MY VISION OF CANADA
William Arthur Deacon

THE DRAMA OF THE FORESTS
Arthur Heming

THE LIVING F...
Arthur Hem...

Anne

...TON
...NA-BUM
...Hale
...RAILS
...anuck

PRINCE ALBERT

WILD GEESE PASSING
Elsie Fry Lawrence

PELICANS IN THE SKY
Harold Baldwin

THE HOMESTEADERS
Ethel Chapman

KELVINGTON

TALES OF AN EMPTY CABIN
Grey Owl

SETTEERS OF THE MARSH
Frederick Philip Grove

...ON
...ckay
...RS

...FOOT TRAILS
...A Corbett

Saskatchewan River

YOKE OF LIFE
Frederick Philip Grove

INDIAN HEAD

CLEARING IN THE WEST
Nellie L. McClung

THINK OF THE EARTH
Bertram Brooker

NEIGHBOURS
Robert J.C. Stead

REGINA

ROD OF THE LONE PATROL
H.A. Cody

BINGO
Ernest Thompson Seton

...LOTHES

CARBERRY

PORTAGE LA...

...LOTHES

JUANA MON AIMEE
Harry Bernard

VERENDRYE
A.M. Stephen

SOWING SEEDS IN DANNY
Nellie L. McClung

WILD GEESE
Martha Ostenso

Lake Winnipeg

Cartoon by Frank Newfeld for the retirement dinner program and menu, 1961

WILLIAM ARTHUR DEACON:
A CANADIAN LITERARY LIFE

I should describe my own humble function as that of herald – an anonymous figure, existing solely for the purpose of making known the names and deeds of the new arrivals. Rhetoric however must be subordinated to truth. Much as I would like to hold a silver trumpet in a dignified manner, the fact is the clothes do not fit me. My enthusiasms far outrun what is seemly in a herald; I have within me something distantly akin to what made Walt Whitman shout: 'to you, endless announcements!'

William Arthur Deacon from 'The Showman,' 1919

HEN WILLIAM ARTHUR DEACON RETIRED as literary editor of *The Globe and Mail* in 1960, he had been a full-time literary journalist for thirty-eight years – literary editor of *Saturday Night* from 1922 to 1928, of *The Mail and Empire* from 1928 to 1936, and of *The Globe and Mail* from 1936 to 1960. Four publishers approached him to write his memoirs: Lorne Pierce of Ryerson Press, Jack McClelland of McClelland and Stewart, George Nelson of Doubleday, and John Gray of Macmillan all recognized that his life's work had been spent in nurturing a Canadian reading public and in fostering the writing and publishing of Canadian literature and that in both personal and public contexts, Deacon's memory was a unique storehouse for four decades of Canadiana. Lorne Pierce, in fact, had urged him to begin a detailed reminiscence of Canadian life and letters some years earlier. In 1953 Pierce had negotiated with him for two books, one to be a history of Canadian literature from the Confederation poets to the present, the other a volume of Deacon's own memoirs as the first full-time literary journalist in Canada and the enthusiastic impresario of Canadian literature and its writers from 1918 on.

Neither in the fifties for Pierce, nor in the sixties for George Nelson, the publisher whom he chose among the four, was Deacon able to finish the story of his life and work. In the fifties his commitments to *The Globe and Mail* were still too heavy to allow him the time he needed. In the sixties, though he contracted with George Nelson for two books, and though he wrote over two hundred pages of his 'History of Canadian Literature,' his wife's and his own failing health allowed him neither to finish that one, nor to begin the second, his literary memoirs. In 1967 he declined a Canada Council Centennial Grant to help finish his work because he was devotedly committed to the full-time care of his wife, Sally, by this time an invalid.

Deacon's final inability to write his memoirs is especially ironic because he had been planning and amassing material for them since 1922, when he left the practice of law in Winnipeg to become a full-time writer and journalist. Sporadically from 1918 to 1922, and consistently after the spring of 1922 when he began as literary editor of *Saturday Night* in Toronto, Deacon kept carbon copies of letters he sent, as well as keeping letters he received. Once he had made up his mind that literature, not law, was his life's work and mission, he had immediately begun to look ahead to his own eventual use of the collection he then began, methodically, to assemble. He was a gifted letter-writer. Early letters and late ones alike project a personality of boundless energy, candour, enthusiasm, and wit; they communicate a constant, optimistic confidence in the development of Canadian writers and in the growth of literature and a reading public in this country – and they inspired a similar optimism and enthusiasm in his correspondents.

By the sixties his correspondence had grown into a huge collection and Deacon was simply swamped by his post-retirement difficulties in using it for the memoirs he had always planned. In 1974, three years before his death, a collection of approximately 18,000 items was sold by his family to the Thomas Fisher Rare Book Library, University of Toronto. It is impossible to be authoritative about what proportion of his entire correspondence these represent. He certainly discarded, destroyed, or neglected to keep carbons of some correspondence – his letters to and from J.D. Logan of Acadia, for instance, are not in the Thomas Fisher collection. However, he certainly kept the mass of correspondence that he valued most. From the beginning he had a strong sense of the value of his collection and its ultimate purpose. He called it his 'old-age insurance' and, from the early twenties, he planned to write from it after retirement. To the letters he added scrapbooks of reviews and clippings, manuscripts of articles and speeches, and boxes of records of his long involvement with the Canadian Authors' Association, the Governor-General's Awards Board, the Leacock Awards, and the Canadian Writers' Foundation, as well as with the various newspapers and journals for which he worked – an embarrassment of riches for his biographers and for Deacon, finally, an impossible burden.

From the very beginning of his years as a journalist he had been infused with a sense of mission for the establishment of an entire, self-contained, dynamic Canadian cultural milieu – a Canadian authorship, a Canadian readership, a Canadian literature – and sometimes he called himself its prophet. The professional life of the man tallies with four decades of Canada's literary life, a cycle of sturdy and ebullient growth in the twenties, stubborn endurance in the thirties and through the war years, and a new and continuing cycle of growth since 1945. *William Arthur Deacon: A Canadian Literary Life* is written out of the collection that Deacon himself gathered; its frame of reference encompasses four decades of Canadian cultural and literary history.

CHAPTER ONE

A Man with a Mission

'**B**UT I WANTED YOU to know now – this much. You dreamed great things for me in the way of a mission. I have found my work, my mission.'[1] William Arthur Deacon was in his thirties and struggling to establish himself securely in a professional literary career when he reassured his mother with those words. He was a veteran of many false starts; most particularly and most shocking to his family, he had left a promising and secure career in law to gamble in the desperately uncertain world of literary journalism. More than four decades later he repeatedly reaffirmed his decision and the sense of mission that never deserted him as he answered the many friends who congratulated him or commiserated with him on his retirement: 'All I can say in conclusion is that, if I had my life to live over again, nothing would be changed. A nation lives by its literature and the rise of Can. Lit. since 1920 has been my pride and joy.'[2]

He was born in 1890, in Pembroke, Ontario, the son of William Henry Deacon, a lawyer, and of Sarah Annie Davies, the daughter of a Welsh printer who became a Wesleyan Methodist missionary to Canada. Colourful legends and stories of success were a proud part of his Deacon heritage, for the family had first come to Canada in 1800 and had spread into a large connection:

my ancestors were hardy folk. The first Deacon to reach Canada was an Irish boy of 16, who was that unusual specimen, eye-witness to a murder. The murderer warned my family to get the boy out of Ireland in 24 hours or he would be killed also. A ship was leaving for Canada; the family could afford the price of passage, so the lad reached Perth, Ont., in 1800, went into business and did well. His two younger brothers – one of whom was my great-grandfather – were veterans of Waterloo and both married with small families. The parental farm would not hold them all. So they wrote their elder brother in Perth, Ont.: 'Is land available in Canada?' Answer yes, 100 acres each as settlers and 100 acres each extra as veterans. So they settled at Moberley just west of Perth.[3]

His maternal great-grandfather, John Smith of Liverpool, had been a wealthy sea captain and owner of six ships. Family lore credited him with hair-raising adventures on the high seas, beating up press-gang bullies in 1812, saving his own crews from them, and being captured in mid-ocean by the Americans.[4] There was also the story, tall enough for Davy Crockett, of the hired man on the farm at Moberley who 'attacked a bear and kicked it to death with his heavy boots because the skin was worth $2.'[5]

Closer to his own time and within the memory of his boyhood were the careers of his great-uncles, Judge Thomas Deacon of Pembroke and John Deacon, also a lawyer, of Mattawa, and of his uncle, Thomas Russell Deacon of Winnipeg. Judge Thomas had sponsored Deacon's father for a law career: he made '$3,000 a year salary as judge, $17,000 a year as President of the Pembroke Lumber Company.' John Deacon combined business and legal affairs in Mattawa with 'political success as Conservative boss of the riding.'[6] Thomas Russell Deacon was owner of the Winnipeg Bridge and Iron Works and for some years mayor of the city; he in his turn sponsored William Arthur Deacon for his law training in Manitoba and remained his friend and counsellor throughout his long life.

All his life Deacon was vociferously proud of the Canadian generations of Deacons behind him and equally proud of their tradition of success in the legal profession. He had been directed towards the law from early boyhood. In later life he always considered that his legal training had been invaluable to him, if uncongenial, and he always hoped that one of his grandsons would re-establish it as an occupation in the Deacon line. Writing about 1953 to his daughter-in-law, Nora Deacon, he remarked:

I wish I could stick around long enough to see your boy put on his robes for the first time. There is no reason why he should not realize this ambition. It is almost hereditary; the Deacons have been lawyers in Canada for four generations. My father was famous when he died at 34. One of my younger cousins is now head of what I guess is the best firm in Winnipeg. Of course there is more to it than can be told a boy of 7. But I'm just as sure of your son as my great-uncle Judge Thomas Deacon was when he opened the way for my father. We Irish, you know, had a great European reputation for law in the Middle Ages. An Irishman was head of the world's great law school in Italy.[7]

Deacon's own father died suddenly, when the boy was nine months old, before he had had time to consolidate any kind of financial future for his wife and son. At this time Sarah Annie's parents lived in Stanstead, in the Eastern Townships, and their home became her headquarters. Deacon speaks of being familiar with Rock Island, an adjacent town, by the time he was five years old and of spending his boyhood 'among the Laurentians in the Eastern Townships of Quebec with the summers among my father's folk in all the towns of the Ottawa Valley to Mattawa.'[8] Sarah Annie also worked as a 'practical nurse,' a distinction made then between the relatively many, on-the-spot, practically-trained women who gave nursing care and household help as well, and the few, hospital-trained 'professional nurses.' Her sister was married to the Reverend C.R. Flanders, a Methodist minister, and when in 1893 he became principal of Stanstead College, a Methodist co-educational boarding school in the town, a place was made for Sarah Annie to be matron. Until 1907, Deacon lived in Stanstead and attended the college, in beautiful, rural countryside close to the American border, near lakes Massawippi and Memphremagog, and always in the aura of the Methodist school and the Methodist parsonage.

Stanstead College in his day was a school with a long tradition already behind it; it had been founded in 1829, one of the first two Protestant schools in the Eastern Townships.[9] Deacon and Duncan Campbell Scott, his predecessor there by a quarter-century, are among its distinguished literary graduates. His education at Stanstead included a final high school year which was the equivalent of McGill's first year; in later life he sometimes proudly included a 'one year McGill' entry in his curriculum vitae. He looked back on his years there with pleasure and loyalty, always corresponding warmly with Jessie Colby, whose ancestors had founded the school and who busied herself with various projects for its benefit. He repeatedly and romantically gave Stanstead College the credit for instigating both his Canadian nationalism and his literary career.

In 1905, Mr Harvey, a visiting clergyman from Rock Island, had read to the students from Theodore Harding Rand's *A Treasury of Canadian Verse*. 'I was so thrilled and listened so intently that I sort of blacked out at times, because this eloquent man, reading these

Canadian poems, told me what it was to be a Canadian ... A Canadian
nationalist was born 57 years ago. I am he.'[10] A year before, Mr
Thompson, the registrar, had read the students his paper, 'The
Influence of Genius upon Place.' Speaking at the college in 1948, at a
memorial for Duncan Campell Scott, Deacon described his life in
literature as having been given its first dynamic impulse by the
inspiration of these two occasions.[11] He read his own first paper to
Stanstead's literary society in 1905 and thereafter never lost the desire
to write – and to have an audience.

In two major areas, as a widow's son and as an impressionable child in
a strict Methodist environment, his early life left Deacon with an
enormous, often burdensome legacy, a compound of ambition, guilt,
and responsibility. As long as he lived he carried a burden of guilt
about his father's death: had he not, as a baby, required so much of his
mother's time, he thought, she might have been able to nurse his father
back to health. In fact, it seems more likely, from the memories of
relatives, that his father suffered from tuberculosis and that the
pneumonia that killed him was its final and deadly manifestation.
Deacon was lovingly devoted to his mother for as long as she lived and
to her memory after she died. Her life was certainly not an easy one.
When the Reverend Flanders moved to Winnipeg with his family,
Sarah Annie Deacon moved with them. Until age forced her
retirement she nursed and taught at the Indian mission at Norway
House and then at Ninette Sanatorium. For the last fifteen years of her
life she lived with the Flanders family in Winnipeg. She was eighty-six
when she died in 1948.[12]

In his adult years at least Deacon was always extremely careful to
win and keep his mother's approval. Mrs Deacon's expectations of her
son had obviously been very high and his eventual practice of law had
been their apex. Particularly in the twenties and thirties when he had
fairly recently given up law for journalism, Deacon was always anxious
to convince or reassure his mother that he would, finally, live up to her
expectations of him and to his early promise. He diverged from the
path of her expectations with a lingering sense of guilt that was an
added spur towards unremitting effort in the literary career he finally
chose.

In the years between 1913 and 1922, when he was articling for law in
Dauphin, Manitoba, and then practising in Winnipeg, he did not see his
mother often, because her work and his, and the mutual state of their
finances, precluded much visiting. From the time he came to Toronto
in 1922 until her death he saw her scarcely at all, once or twice at most.

Always, however, he maintained a letter relationship with her that was loving and often anxiously self-justificatory as well. His letters to his mother, returned to him after her death, are long, detailed and, among all his correspondence, they are the only ones that are handwritten. He drafted and redrafted each before he wrote a fair copy and sent it off.[13] His Christmas letter was always a special and lengthy effort. In 1924, riding high on his burgeoning success as literary editor of *Saturday Night*, he even enlisted his great friend and mentor, Judge Emily Murphy ('Janey Canuck'), to be his emissary and accessory in assuring his mother that his personal life was honourable, that the literary life he had chosen was a worthy calling, that he had great work to do for Canada, and that he would succeed in that work.

Now you are the champion Blarney. Will you write her and explain that I am wiser than Socrates, a greater literary artist than Shakespeare, and holier than St Paul, though a little more liberal in my views as is natural in a somewhat younger man?... She doesn't know any more about me and my work and what I've done and what it means than if she were the King of the Cannibal Isles ... I told her she'd have to ask somebody else and that I had asked you to deliver a monologue: speak it like an obituary, and don't tell such whoppers that she'll see through you, because she is a shrewd woman on most matters. It's a hell of a chore but she's my mother, Janey, and she is just yearning for somebody to tell her that her boy isn't a black disgrace entirely but that some folks like him well enough...[14]

Emily Murphy answered his appeal handsomely, sending a copy of her long letter to Deacon. She was as serious as Deacon himself about the importance of the career he had chosen and her letter must have reassured his mother, especially since Judge Murphy was both renowned and respected all across the country.[15]

Deacon entered Victoria College in Toronto from Stanstead in 1907, feeling rich in comparison to many other students because he had $300 from a summer job as a fire-ranger on Lake Temagami. He and a couple of friends lived, they thought, like young men about town, in rooms off campus instead of in residence.[16] He was in the class of 1911 with E.J. Pratt, who remained a friend for life.

Though three poems written in 1909 for *Acta Victoriana*, the student magazine, are the first of his writings to be preserved, his years at Victoria were not a success. He left at the end of his second year and he remembered his experiences there with some resentment. In particular he resented the British manner, accent, and standards of Pelham

Edgar, head of the Department of English at Victoria. Deacon liked to tell how Edgar snubbed freshmen, lecturing from his swivel chair with his back to their faces, because he could not stand to look at them. 'I know him to be an aper of the English Gentleman,' he wrote sarcastically to Emily Murphy. 'He can never forget that his mother was Lady Edgar. He considers that enthusiasm is vulgar, and the kind you and I have particularly barbarous.'[17]

Truth to tell, Deacon arrived at Victoria primed for revolt, against Methodism and, as a sideline, against any authority figure whatever. As the child of a nervous widow he had been both overprotected and overdirected: 'There were too many people bringing you up,' as an older cousin put it, years later.[18] In his maturity he learned to work in reasonable amicability with Edgar when the latter was president of the Canadian Authors' Association in the thirties. But very close to the surface there always worked in Deacon an irritable resentment against any hint of a British colonial attitude and quite often this erupted into pointed, sarcastic, and effective prose. He was never more touchy than when stung in this area and his pioneer Irish forbears were never closer to him than when he fulminated against any hint of British imperialism.

The years between leaving Victoria College and decisively embarking on the law career that had always been held up as a goal to him were drifting ones. He moved restlessly from job to job, as a grocery clerk, a filing clerk for Ontario Hydro at Niagara Falls, a real estate agent, and a time-keeper in Winnipeg for his Uncle Thomas's Manitoba Bridge and Iron Works. He lived with the debilitating sense that, to his mother and her family, he was a failure. Finally, in 1913, he married Gladys Coon of Weston, Ontario, accepted his Uncle Thomas's sponsorship and financial backing and moved to Dauphin, Manitoba, to article in law under Frank Simpson, who had offices in Dauphin and Grandview. He was bored by a great deal of the training and constantly depressed by the human tragedies involved in the frequent foreclosure of mortgages, but he and Gladys were happy in their marriage and he persevered. Gladys, a musician, led a church choir in Dauphin and gave singing lessons.

Though in later life Deacon often referred to the years between leaving Victoria and graduating in law from the University of Manitoba, in 1918, as 'the ten lost years,'[19] they were crucial in his choice of a life-long philosophy and a life's work. Sometime in 1916 he and Gladys were powerfully attracted to the teachings of theosophy. From that time, when he had his 'first important psychic experience in the night in a vile hotel in the miserable Ukrainian village of Ethelbert,'[20] to the end of his life, Deacon lived by certain theosophical doctrines, especially the notion of being fated for the work he had chosen to do and being enabled to do it through the agency of higher powers called, in theosophical terms, the 'Lords of Life': 'From 1917, when I first thought of getting out of law, what happened to me was uncanny. Long ago I came to the conclusion that I was doing a job for the gods; and they saw to it that their instrument was preserved.'[21]

Mme Helena Petrovna Blavatsky had founded the parent theosophical society in 1875, choosing Adyar, India, for its international headquarters, but herself travelling constantly back and forth to North America, England, Europe, and India, with her working headquarters in England. In the late 1880s her most powerful lieutenant was Annie Besant, already an activist for women's rights in England and notorious for her advocacy of birth control. Mrs Besant was the prime mover of the society after Mme Blavatsky's death in 1891; she became its international president in 1907, and was the controlling figure in the society until her death in 1933.[22] The beliefs of the Theosophical Society were contained in Mme Blavatsky's mystical and often mystifying work, *The Secret Doctrine*. Much simplified, its major aims were: to promote universal brotherhood between people of different creeds and religions; to promote the study of Eastern thought and mysticism (in the twentieth century this second aim is phrased 'to encourage the comparative study of religion, philosophy and science'); and to investigate the laws of nature and the universe. The horror, grief, and carnage of World War I impelled many to seek answers and meanings beyond those provided by the churches and in the decade following 1914 the Theosophical Society's membership increased dramatically.

In Canada the Toronto lodge of the Theosophical Society had existed since 1891 as a junior member of the American Theosophical Society. Then in 1919 a formal petition for the formation of an official Canadian Theosophical Society was sent to Mrs Besant. At that time there were already twelve lodges functioning unofficially in Canada. Under the subsequent official organization, Albert E. Smythe, president of the Toronto lodge, became the general secretary of the general executive, composed of presidents of local lodges. He was also the editor of *The Canadian Theosophist*, which began monthly publication in 1920.[23] In 1921 the Canadian Society had 863 members, with the Toronto lodge by far the largest, with 240 members. In the early twenties many extraordinary Canadians were theosophists, among them Augusta Stowe Gullen, a pioneer among Canadian women doctors, Flora MacDonald Denison, a powerful figure in Toronto society and in women's work of all kinds, Dr Frederick Banting, one of the discovers of insulin, Lawren Harris and Bertram Brooker, artists, and Wilson MacDonald, the poet.

The Theosophical Society was not intended to replace one's religion and many members continued to attend church services in their own faith. For some members, however, the society served as a church community. There were Sunday meetings, with lectures and readings, social activities, and even a Sunday school, the 'Lotus circle,' where children were taught theosophical doctrine. Certainly for Deacon, theosophy was an exciting, inspiring, and exotic substitute for the Methodism he wished to leave behind him, and he embraced its teachings with proselytizing enthusiasm. His sense of an important personal destiny was aroused and supported and an enormous and enthusiastic energy, until then latent and frustrated, was challenged and awakened by its doctrines, particularly by theosophy's basic beliefs in reincarnation and evolution through the ages and in the destiny of individuals and races.

He and Gladys moved from Dauphin to Winnipeg in 1917, where he became a junior employee in the Pitblado, Hoskin law firm and proceeded to study for his degree in law at the University of Manitoba. They immediately found congenial friends among the Winnipeg lodge of the Theosophical Society and before he left the city Deacon had founded and become the first president of its second lodge, the Blavatsky.[24]

Deacon's beliefs seemed eccentric in the extreme to his family and many of his friends. 'It is a great grief to my Mother that I have gone a-whoring after strange gods,'[25] he wrote to Thomas Henry Billings, a Congregationalist minister in the United States and an old friend from Stanstead days. When Emily Murphy wrote to him of her concern for his beliefs he replied at length, setting forth what he termed 'the springs of his life' as he saw them after five years of practising theosophy:

The world is governed by Law – natural so-called. It is really WILL of the Lords of Life – There is no dead matter, there are no 'natural laws' in the vulgar phrase ... There are many lines of evolution – one, the Deva is very interesting, with fairies and elfs corresponding to our animals and angels etc. corresponding to men. In our line of evolution man comes up through mineral, vegetable and animal kingdoms. Then he individualizes, becomes man, a separate being ... having now to work out his salvation through the use of his will, limited by certain laws – as e.g. the law of Cause and Effect. He can never sow barley and reap oats. Man through repeated reincarnations evolves, learning a little each time. Sooner or later he gets tired of the slow movement of the herd, awakes to wider issues, and wants to go faster. He is then taken in hand by the senior members of his brotherhood and is instructed in the larger knowledge. This is the stage you have reached... Finally in all seriousness and the priest in me is very grave at this moment – I must warn you – our way is the way of the Christ ... He [a true occultist] has not time for the rewards, he does not think of them, he has lost himself in his work and his hopes for his people. It is not cheap Christian renunciation. It comes naturally ... Don't forget though that Christina Rossetti was dead right when she wrote 'Does the Road wind up-hill all the way? Yes to the very end.'[26]

Above all, he wanted to reassure her that he was his own master, not 'under control' or any such nonsense. 'We younger members are given jobs [not by other members of the Society, but through the inspiration of the Lords of Life], and then left to make plans and devise ways and means.'[27]

At bottom, however, and despite the dynamic challenge that theosophy gave him, his Methodist orientation and training never left him, as he would admit from time to time to old and dear friends and family. Especially to Thomas Henry Billings he joked about 'what an old Methodist preacher I really am inside,'[28] and although the fundamentalism of his youth was often resented, it could never be shaken. It coloured and directed his attitudes to literature and to work. Deacon no more gave credence or respect to the notion of literature for art's sake than his Methodist forbears would have done. Though he rejected a world view that was centred exclusively on Christian doctrine, his own world view was very definitely spirit-centred, and he adhered to an unceasing work ethic that was as arduous as John Wesley's.

One of the books thought fit for Sunday reading that had made an impression on him as a boy was Egerton Ryerson Young's By Forest, Lake and Prairie, the memoirs of a Methodist minister on the plains.[29] Although he spoke jokingly of the Sabbath restrictions in his grandfather's household and of the proscription of 'profane' reading material that was enforced there, Deacon never lost a conviction that was as strong as Young's that literature's basic purpose was didactic, that good literature infused its readers, willy-nilly, with directions and patterns for the moral and ethical enhancement of living, and that Canadian literature in particular had a high and holy mission in the building of

Canada and her people. In fact, for Deacon, the didactic element in the Methodism he knew dovetailed dramatically and dynamically with the teaching and preaching responsibilities of the convinced theosophist.

He truly believed that the printed word could change the world. He held as axiomatic the belief that Canadians were a vital and dynamic people who would require, demand, and produce a correspondingly dynamic literature. He came to see himself as herald, prophet, preacher, and custodian of that literature.

I come back every time to the conclusion that the Manu or Whoever has taken charge of Canadian affairs looked at me and said, 'I can use this energetic young lunatic, who seems tough enough to take a lot of punishment and grief.' So I was taken in charge. At first I thought I was doing it and was proud of myself. As time elapsed I became more and more doubtful as to whether I was really doing any of it. I was given things to say, which sometimes astonished me as much as my readers.[30]

I am satisfied that I was intended to play nursemaid to Canadian literature from the end of the Carman-Roberts-Lampman era (1920). It ended with the W.H. Blake translation of Hémon's *Maria Chapdelaine*. To you, it may seem like a small job; but I do not think so. I regard this country as important and therefore its writers as very important...[31]

CHAPTER TWO

Apprenticeship and Choice

URING THE DAUPHIN YEARS, and concurrent with Deacon's conviction that theosophy must be the basis of his life, grew the equally strong conviction that the practice of law bored and frustrated him and that only in writing would he be happy. Furthermore, the study of theosophy convinced him that he was destined to write, that to fulfil his 'karma,' his own appointed fate, he must take on the challenges and responsibilities of a writer. By 1921, events had convinced him that he was destined to be a writer-prophet for Canada. As a teenager he had begun to write and had been, he said, 'very blasé at 17 or 18 over trifles that got into print, or even a whole column in a newspaper. I remember a 2-column article I wrote for the Sherbrooke "Daily Record" at 15...'[1] Now, ten years later, he proceeded doggedly to teach himself to be a professional.

Weekends, I would set myself specific tasks – think of anything at all as subject and then wrestle, seeing what I could make of it. At first down went the ideas without regard to order or finish. When I had said everything I could think of, I then studied it to work out a form or pattern. There would be superfluities to be thrown away at once, bits to be written in to close gaps; but the main idea was a logical but, often, tricky progress from point to point. That achieved, as well as inexperience allowed, there next came a third re-writing for style. Fourth and subsequent writings were to eliminate idiocies.

I found I could put down the damnedest nonsense, and read it without sense of violation; but as I copied and re-copied, a time came when my fingers revolted against repeating the false or inane. One piece was re-written 17 times.[2]

From the start he was devoted to the essay and his models were the greatest of the essay writers: 'I want to stand at last with the great essayists – Hazlitt, Montaigne, Lamb and St Beuve.'[3] There were a few poems written after his Victoria days, but he didn't take them seriously; as for a novel sporadically in progress in 1921, 'this is an opus in the nature of a joke. I think I shall prove to my own satisfaction that I cannot write fiction. Anyway it is a side-issue and at best part of my effort to find a public on whom I can ultimately foist my essays.'[4] Early and late in his career he repeatedly described his own talent for writing as limited, though he never denigrated his own efforts in developing that talent, nor his success in his chosen writing field. He was certainly aware of the contemporary, as well as the historic, lustre of his field, for in the first quarter of this century the essayists were a proud company: Saintsbury, Raleigh, Quiller-Couch, G.K. Chesterton and J.B. Priestley in England and the men whose work Deacon knew best in the United States, Christopher Morley, Henry Seidel Canby, and H.L. Mencken. In the twenties, however, the essay genre began noticeably to divide into two streams, popular journalism on the one hand and the burgeoning, specialized field of academic literary criticism on the other. By the thirties, the field of literature that Deacon had chosen for his own efforts had lapsed considerably in popularity. Meanwhile, however, when he began to train himself to write, he was working in a still-flourishing genre, one that commanded a wide readership and, most important for a dogged, energetic, ambitious new writer, one that was saleable in a wide range of journals and periodicals across the continent.

Winnipeg in 1917 was, for the Deacons, an exciting cultural centre after their years in Dauphin. They had always bought and treasured what books they could afford; now they speedily became the centre of a small, dedicated literary-theosophical group which met at the studio of Burton Kurth, an organist, choir master, and music teacher. Kurth and his wife, Olive, gave Deacon enthusiastic support for his literary ambitions. Kurth loved to hear him talk about literature and, from the beginning of their friendship, was so positive that Deacon would become famous as a writer, or, as theosophists put it, would 'come into his possession,' that he urged Deacon to begin saving all his correspondence. He voluntarily became his archivist, called jokingly among the group the 'Custodian of the Sacred Relics.'[5]

Physically, however, Deacon was at the end of his tether by the time he passed his law examinations and was granted an LLB degree in 1918. It was also a touchy subject with him that he had volunteered for service in World War I and had been rejected on medical grounds. Now he was gaunt and sick with tension between the conflicting demands of the career he was trained for and was expected to follow and of the career that he knew indubitably to be the only one for him. He was a tall man, but at this time his weight dropped to a skeletal 130 pounds.[6] With the Kurths, Deacon and Gladys left for New York in the spring of 1919, intending to try the restorative powers of being in the very centre of the American literary scene, but Deacon was ill, nervously and physically, the whole time. His old friend, Matt Hayes, whom they visited in Buffalo en route, was extremely alarmed by his condition, lectured him soundly and funded his subsequent medical treatment for stomach ulcers in New York.

Your physical condition, old Man, worried me and still worries me quite beyond words. I want so much to have again the husky Deak of the old days on the Nelson. You have been through a fearful struggle and it is hardly to be wondered at that you are 'all shot,' but if you would only have the good sense to put the rebuilding of your human machine first, I think you would be ever so much more valuable to yourself, your friends and the world in general ... I suggest that you neither buy nor rent a typewriter and that you cut out Dunsany, Cabell and all the rest for the time being ... and take on a physician, a trainer and a sparring partner or the like.[7]

In August, Deacon returned to Winnipeg and the Pitblado firm. His health had improved after months of enforced rest. Though the trip was a fiasco as far as literary ambitions were concerned, his determination to become a writer remained constant and total.

The works which he saved from his apprentice years, 1918-21, fill three bound volumes of double-spaced typescript, 570 pages in all. The 1918-19 volume, called *In Fame's Antechamber*, is a collection of four literary essays, on John Cowper Powys, Lord Dunsany, Edgar Lee Masters, and James Branch Cabell, with an introductory and explanatory piece called 'The Showman.' The manuscript was written with an American readership in mind and Deacon submitted it hopefully to a number of American publishers. It represented his first concerted effort to break into a writer's market and his only effort to locate himself centrally in the American literary world, though later he built up a modest success as an occasional writer for American journals. Early in his writing career he always called it 'my big work, the best,'[8] but it was never accepted as a whole for publication. By 1921 he had given up: 'I've got tired sending [it] out. I'd rather now have the M.S.

here to read to my friends , and circulate orally.' But he could also add, with a certain braggadocio: 'Someday some publisher is going to pay through the nose for that volume.'9

Meanwhile he had sent the Powys article, 'written in the heat of a first enthusiasm, and having something in it of the pent-up fires of the preceding 10 years,'10 to Dr Charles Colby of the Stanstead College family. Dr Colby submitted it to The [McGill] University Magazine and there it was printed in April 1919. It was Deacon's first appearance in print since the Acta Victoriana poems of 1909 and an essay, 'Temagami the Unspoiled,' in the Stanstead College magazine of the same year.

The essays in In Fame's Antechamber are all linked by Deacon's allegiance to Whitman as a master-model and by his demonstration of Powys's, Dunsany's, Masters', and Cabell's links to Whitman.

[Whitman] is a pyramid; symmetrical, huge, rough, incalculably strong, standing gigantic against a background of desert sand. I feel his work is a little beyond human computation. He found American poets perfecting themselves in that art of imitation which is the delight of children and monkeys. He looked with cold scorn upon their slavish faithfulness to English models, and in shaggy noble defiance of the conventional laws of poetry he made his own forms. He wrote poems with vital stuff in them, with large gestures he spanned his country up and down and embraced it. And though Longfellow's Hiawatha and such work has its place, Whitman is the man against whom the sands of the years prevail not. His was the first great poetic voice in the United States. (essay on Edgar Lee Masters)

It is an easy step from Whitman to theosophical thought and all of Deacon's chosen writers are also shown to have either explicit or implicit connections with theosophy. In particular, Dunsany's mysticism provides an appealing link to The Secret Doctrine. In Cabell, Deacon finds connections with Annie Besant and Edward Carpenter, the revered theosophical sage and reformer.

In this first collection, Deacon establishes his alliances. He also repeatedly reveals himself as he sees himself – an iconoclastic essayist and critic. In his own eyes he is a rebel against all stultifying convention and, in literature, especially a rebel against the convention of realism as he understands it.

When any art has become merely imitative that art is dead; the writer who is not a seer is not an artist ... The habit of neglecting the divine imagination has been forced on the reading public by a generation of uninspired novelists and poets, who were content to drearily reproduce the surfaces of things, quite oblivious to the Life within which alone gives them meaning. *To announce is not enough, it is necessary to shout, to hurl boisterous invitations...* ('The Showman')

Unconditional advocacy is the hallmark of these early essays. Centring on John Cowper Powys's books of criticism, *Visions and Revisions* (1915) and *Suspended Judgements* (1916), Deacon finds him a lyric poet writing literary criticism, the greatest critic since Oscar Wilde, with a style and feeling as powerful as Whitman's. By comparison, all other critics, from Hazlitt, Coleridge, and Arnold to Saintsbury, Mencken, and Arnold Bennett, are 'earnest well-instructed students of literature, not inspired critics':

the shibboleth of 'constructive criticism' must be deleted from our vocabularies before one can understand his 'comrade's signal' ...

Mr Powys will never be on the curriculum of any Canadian university in our generation. Any man who talks about 'Browning's fourth-rate Protestantism' must stay outside the sacred walls. To slash desperately at Puritanism and Philistinism is to alienate the affections of pious professors. (essay on John Cowper Powys)

It is not difficult to understand why *In Fame's Antechamber* remained unpublished as a whole. The essays on Powys and Dunsany are overbalanced by the purple prose of Deacon's own enthusiasm for his subjects. While the chapters on Masters and Cabell are more successful, written in unpretentious, informal language which does not smother, but sometimes illuminates its subjects, they are still obviously apprentice works, marred by digressions and vagueness and begging for revision and reorganization. Deacon's own comment about liking to read these essays aloud to his friends is a telling commentary on them: read aloud, with his enthusiasm and conviction, they might well be impressive; read in print, on the page, they seem inflated and pretentious.

In Fame's Antechamber, however, must have served as a kind of catharsis for Deacon. For the first time he donned the persona of the joyful crusader and wrote passionately about his literary and philosophical concerns. Each of the subjects related to some quality he felt he strove for in himself: Powys was the dynamic, iconoclastic critic; Lord Dunsany was the theosophist-mystic; Edgar Lee Masters was the lawyer-writer; James Branch Cabell displayed an enviable command of the comic and the serious. Deacon's declared admiration for these men focused and clarified his own budding view of himself as a herald, 'an anonymous figure, existing solely for the purpose of making known the names and deeds of the new arrivals.' Both his subjects and the experience of writing about them fortified his ideal of the writer-seer and his high calling: 'all great literature is Revelation coming to mankind through the finer intuitive faculties of the author' ('The Showman').

The second stage of Deacon's apprenticeship involved the reconciliation of his exuberance with the practice and discipline of regular, published literary journalism. In 1921 John Dafoe of *The Manitoba Free Press* instituted a monthly literary and book review section, edited by one of his staff journalists, Thomas B. Roberton. In turn, Roberton called in Deacon to act as contributing editor, or 'Honorary Literary Editor,' as they liked to call it. On the top left-hand corner of the four-page section appeared the following statement: 'The design of this section is to give accurate literary information. To make criticism the aid of writing. To encourage Canadian literature. To cultivate a taste for reading and sound books.' Beginning with the second literary section in May 1921, Deacon contributed along with other reviewers. His subjects were wide ranging, extending beyond the literary section to the newspaper itself. In the literary section, for instance, he published a shorter reworked version of his earlier essay on Cabell, a review of M.K. Bradby's *Psycho Analysis and Its Place in Life*, articles about the new Manitoba Parliament Buildings in Winnipeg, about the poetry of Tom MacInnes, and about a book on human heredity. Other articles included various book reviews, a description of Emily Murphy, and a critique of the painting of L.L. Fitzgerald, an artist and principal of the Winnipeg School of Art. Through the pages of the *Free Press*, Deacon had his first heady and encouraging experience in developing a readership. At the same time he had a priceless opportunity to define his field, his criteria of criticism, and his audience. His confidence grew by leaps and bounds and with it his sense of the specific focus for his literary career – the evaluation and encouragement of Canadian letters.

Given Deacon's growing enthusiasm and dedication to the profession of letters, the tide of Canadian events was also decidedly in his favour. The Canadian Authors' Association had been founded in March 1921 and, in fact, John Dafoe, as one of its founding members, had immediately thereafter begun his literary section as a considerable testimony to his own concern for Canadian letters. B.K. Sandwell, who had been a journalist with *The Montreal Star* and editor of *The*

Financial Times, was the prime mover in the foundation of the Canadian Authors' Association.[11] He became editor of *The Canadian Bookman*, 'A Quarterly devoted to Literature, the Library and the Printed Book,' late in 1918 and his first editorial, of January 1919, set forth his vision of an emergent, distinctive, and autonomous Canadian culture.

To this new interest in ideas, and in the books which convey them, there is added in the case of Canadians a new national self-consciousness, a new demand that ideas be judged not by the standards of any other nation, however closely allied by kinship or economic circumstance, but by the standards of our own country; a new output of ideas by the Canadians themselves, and a new belief in those ideas as being probably the best expression of Canadian requirements, the best solution of Canadian problems and a consequent new demand for vehicles of criticism and discussion concerning this purely Canadian output.[12]

Specifically, Sandwell addressed himself to the copyright legislation brought before Parliament in 1919. This legislation was designed to provide Canada with its first comprehensive copyright law, which would adhere to the protocol of the Revised Berne Convention and thus allow Canada to apply for admission to the Convention as a self-governing nation. Several factors were in play as Sandwell wrote his first editorial on the subject of the Copyright Bill in the July 1919 issue of *The Canadian Bookman*. First was the fact that although the United States was potentially the most lucrative market for Canadian books, the United States itself had not signed the Revised Berne Convention. Within or without the Berne Convention, therefore, Canadian copyright would mean nothing to American publishers. Furthermore, copyright in the United States was granted only to works first published in the United States, a provision that became known as the 'manufacturing clause.' Therefore, Canadian writers wishing to make money out of the large American market had to publish in the United States. In retaliation, the Canadian copyright bill sought to nullify American copyright legislation by declaring that all works published outside Canada be excluded from Canadian copyright. Under these terms, the financial potential was enormous for Canadian printers and publishers who would thus be empowered to publish immensely popular American and foreign books.

The second issue concerned the writer's ownership of his own work. The Senate Committee reviewing the bill was considering the proposal of a licensing system whereby the registrar of copyrights and *not* the writer would issue final permission to a particular Canadian publisher or printer who wished to print a non-Berne work. To many successful Canadian writers who had deliberately published in the United States to secure American copyright and markets, and to editors like Sandwell, this possibility was repugnant. Sandwell was furious at how the economics of Canadian nationalism rode roughshod over the artist. He called for a hiatus in the passage of the bill and spoke against the evils of the licensing system.

The controversy continued and grew. Sandwell spoke against the bill throughout 1919 and 1920, and when the need for concrete action on the part of the writers themselves became imperative, he met in Montreal with John Murray Gibbon, writer and director of publicity for the CPR, Pelham Edgar of Victoria College, and Stephen Leacock who, as a successful Canadian author who published outside Canada, felt that he was one of the principal targets of the proposed copyright bill. They all were agreed that a national meeting of Canadian writers was necessary. Accordingly, in early 1921, Sandwell sent an undated letter on *Canadian Bookman* stationery to hundreds of Canadian writers inviting them to attend a 'Convention of Canadian Authors, Montreal, March 11 & 12.' In addition, notices were published in newspapers throughout the country. The convention met as planned with 110 in attendance. The resolve, energy, and enthusiasm of those assembled accomplished a formidable amount of business in the two-day meeting. The group was by no means limited to English Canadians and its sense of purpose was strong enough specifically to include the writers of French Canada in its constitution and to make provision for an essentially self-governing French-Canadian section with its own president, but operating under the one national constitution. Prominent, of course, among the new constitution's objectives was the determination to procure adequate copyright legislation, but more dispersed and far-reaching was the aroused enthusiasm of the association's charter members, who proceeded to work with evangelical zeal to impress on Canadians the worth and accessibility of their literary culture.

Deacon's own sense of purpose was fortified by the formation of the CAA. He became a charter member of the Winnipeg branch and a contributor to *The Canadian Bookman*. In correspondence with W.A. Kennedy of Windsor, editor of *The National Pictorial*, he announced for the first time the sense of mission that was to be, henceforth, his life-long credo:

I think with the growth of the National Movement in Literature, not only here but in other countries as well, there is increasing need for some young man, or men, to devote themselves very seriously to this work, and I have been trying for some years to fit myself for the task. I bring to it a knowledge of literature, domestic and foreign, rather wider than the average, though not comprehensive compared with that of the great critics of England, France and the u.s. It is with some hesitancy that I consider any scheme which would deflect my energies from my self-appointed missionary work.[13]

His work for *The National Pictorial* had developed from correspondence with D.M. LeBourdais, editor of *The Canadian Nation*, whom he had successfully approached about becoming that magazine's literary editor. Though the demise of *The Canadian Nation* in the summer of 1921 killed a promising opportunity, LeBourdais suggested that he offer his services to Kennedy's new monthly. In August 1921, Deacon suggested himself to Kennedy as literary editor and was invited to submit a page of 1,200 to 1,400 words for the September issue of the magazine. Deacon contested Kennedy's offered rate of a half cent per word and asked for a cent, but he did submit an article and his first editorial.

His confidence in his literary talents and his success in publication were growing. In September, he had published an article entitled 'The Place of Keats' in *The New York Times*. This was a short, careful answer to statements made by the critic, Richard LeGallienne, and on 6 September, he wrote Emily Murphy: 'Since starting this letter I have scored 2 more bull's eyes, one of them The New York Times Book Supplement – Say, that cheque [for $10] looked better to me than a pass to Heaven!'[14] He was also successful in placing a review of Alice Chown's *The Stairway* with the New York *Evening Post*'s book review supplement, 'The Literary Review,' edited by Henry Seidel Canby. His article on Edward Carpenter was printed in *The Canadian Theosophist* (February 1921).

However, his status with *The National Pictorial* remained uncertain because of the frequent absence of its chief editor, Kennedy, and of plans to reorganize the Pictorial Publishing Company and move it from Windsor to Toronto. Nevertheless, Deacon submitted enough wordage for two pages of copy as well as editorials for the October and November issues. He was free to focus on Canadian literature in particular, and his tenacity in the face of editorial indecision about his status and his pay shows the degree to which he was anxious to consolidate his position with *The National Pictorial*. Deacon's page was called 'The Essayist' and his first editorial proclaimed his literary nationalism: 'Canadian literature can only be produced in Canada by Canadians and for Canadians.' He spoke of the need for Canadians to buy Canadian books and of the recent founding of the Canadian Authors' Association: 'The writer is a Canadian with a rather aggressive national bias. He welcomes this further opportunity of speaking to his kinsmen.'[15]

The National Pictorial, however, was not nearly as established as Kennedy had led Deacon to believe. Between December 1921 and April 1922 it went through three editors and Deacon remained unpaid. His work was published in September of 1921 and February and March 1922, though he also prepared copy for October, November, and December 1921 and May 1922. Financially disappointed though he was, by the time he had prepared copy for the December number, Deacon was displaying the initiative and commitment of a man who had found his vocation:

I have a stack of stuff here now – a sketch 'The Angels,' in a class with 'The Headpiece' – another sketch on barbers called 'The Genial Profession.' Then there is the MacInnes poem 'Zalinka,' four fine photographs of the Canadian Players Limited in different scenes at the Home Theatre, Naramata BC. I have a notice of an extraordinary book by Miss Chown formerly of Kingston. Peter McArthur is sending photo to go with his write-up &c. &c. Could I possibly get some of this stuff set up in advance so that I could correct my own proofs, and make a real dummy out of the galley impressions?[16]

By April 1922, under its third editor, T.R. Rand-McNally, *The National Pictorial* was on the brink of its final collapse. Deacon was anxious to keep his editorial connection with it if publication continued, but he was also on the brink of the most decisive professional chance and choice of his life, his engagement as literary editor of *Saturday Night* in Toronto. He never forgot the first great day of that career:

It was Roberton's suggestion that I come East. It was B.K. Sandwell who sent me with a letter of introduction to Fred Paul, the great editor of Saturday Night, who took me in hand. I was delirious with joy when I first reported to Paul for work 22 years ago yesterday, Monday, May 29, 1922 – the first full-time, professional book reviewer that Canada had ever seen.[17]

His opportunity at *Saturday Night* was doubly precious to him because of the most momentous event of his personal life, the decision to break his marriage to Gladys. In 1918 he had met Mrs Sally Townsend Syme, who was president of the Winnipeg lodge of the Theosophical Society. They were convinced that they were destined for each other and, in fact, as theosophists, they were equally convinced that they had known and loved each other in a previous incarnation. They formed a partnership in literature and in life that remained the central fact of their existence for the next fifty years.[18]

Deacon was fortunate in the women who loved him. He and Gladys had married young and had the years of their twenties together, when she had joined in the excitement of his literary ambitions and encouraged his self-training program. Long after their divorce, in fact until Gladys remarried in 1926, they continued to correspond enthusiastically about books. But she, and for years he as well, had thought of literature as his engrossing avocation, with a successful career in law as its base and support. Besides, who could have conceived of a full-time literary career in Canada at that time? The writers they knew and met had jobs or professions which provided their basic incomes – W.T. Allison of the University of Manitoba, Arthur Phelps of Wesley College, Winnipeg, and Judge Emily Murphy, for instance; a few, like Laura Goodman Salverson, squeezed out their writing time from other primary responsibilities as housewives and mothers. Sally Townsend was a remarkable woman, a passionate theosophist, very strong in herself, strongly practical as well as literary, and the kind of person who expected to put constant and enormous resources of courage, character, and energy into the support of her spouse, at the same time remaining an independent, many-talented woman in her own right. Sally's belief in Deacon's literary potential and their attraction for each other was so strong that, ultimately, no social or emotional costs and no economic risks could deter them.

Meanwhile, as the twenties began, the prospects of a man supporting his family by reviewing and writing were brighter than anyone could have imagined a few years earlier. There are no exclusively Canadian myths of 'The Roaring Twenties,' but Canadians shared in the decade's heady optimism. Ordinary people were as poor and worked as hard as they had always done, but at the same time they became mobile as they had never been before because cars were more and more within reach of their pocketbooks. They became shareholders in a continental world of entertainment and news because of the cultural revolution that came with radio. To read Frederick Lewis Allen's *Only Yesterday*, the story of the United States in the twenties, is to recognize, or remember, that Canada's social and intellectual horizons also broadened in the twenties as they never had before. As Canadians looked outside they also felt an increasing pride in what they saw inside Canada, in the country's potential for economic, political, and intellectual growth. Most important of all, in the early twenties, people had hope and faith. They believed in the peace-preserving power of the League of Nations, they believed that a war to end wars had been fought, and they knew that Canadian troops had taken a famous part in that fight. Canadian nationalism was on the upswing and literary nationalism was one of its active components.

Deacon did not spring out of the soil of the west by random chance or act of god. He had doggedly worked towards his ambition of becoming a Canadian man of letters since his articling days in Dauphin. Furthermore, in his years in the west, he had established and consolidated for himself a powerfully idealized view of Canada's destiny from which he never wavered. He had breathed the air of the Social Gospel in all his contacts in Winnipeg and though he rejected doctrinal allegiances with Christianity, the Methodist-based, optimistic, dynamic, and humanitarian ideals of the Social Gospel were entirely congenial to his temperament. Older popular writers like Ralph Connor, Emily Murphy, and Nellie McClung wrote with conviction and sincerity of Canada as the land of golden promise, the land of beginning again, the hope of the world. Deacon passionately agreed with them. His work and, in his opinion, the work of all Canadian writers, should ultimately be at the service of Canada's fulfilment. Conversely, Canada's cultural destiny depended on her writers; they must be trained, published, and above all, read by Canadians.

The break-up of two marriages, in a day when divorce was still considered a heinous social offence, caused agony and misery to everyone concerned. When Deacon resigned from the Pitblado firm and left Winnipeg early in the spring of 1922, his only firm assets were Sally's devotion and Roberton's letter of introduction to B.K. Sandwell. He and Sally were walking into a perilous situation, risking everything, but they had total confidence in each other, in Deacon's vocation as a man of letters, and in the inevitable growth of Canadian literature, and moreover they shared an essentially mystical faith in the greatness of Canada.

Lucky was I, who wanted to be a writer but had decided that I was not a creative writer, that there was this sudden opportunity for derivative writing. This sudden change was a direct result of a literary revolution in Canada ... In 1921 I rose to the dizzy height of honorary assistant literary editor of the

Winnipeg Free Press, while continuing the practice of law. It was a fair-sized job as John W. Dafoe set aside four pages for books on the first Monday of each month. A year later I had my own department on a Toronto newspaper.[19]

In May 1922, Sally joined Deacon in Toronto and they began a new personal and professional life together.

CHAPTER THREE

Saturday Night 1922-8

ILLIAM ARTHUR DEACON'S FIRST BOOK PAGES for *Saturday Night* were published on 1 July 1922. With his abundant resources of enthusiasm and energy Deacon seized the opportunity of a trial position at $35 a week offered by Fred Paul, the editor. He was equally buoyed up by his own unflagging sense of himself as a writer and by Sally's rock-solid belief in him, and goaded, of course, by their precarious social and financial situation. From the start he had a sound and undeviating sense of his job as a Canadian literary journalist, both of its opportunities and its limitations. He formulated this many times in letters, reviews, and articles, but never more succinctly than in a letter introducing himself to John Garvin, who at that time was a prominent anthologist and a power in Toronto literary circles:

I aim to be an essayist, and a very special kind of critic. I have found in my own little literary group that I have a certain power of transmitting literary enthusiasms. By reading and discussing modern works I often fire my friends with love for an author. I seek therefore to be an introducer and an interpreter, rather than a critic with a foot rule. I have discovered that many people need to be shown the excellencies of a book before they can see them for themselves.[1]

His appointment as literary editor of *Saturday Night* meant that Deacon had captured the best opportunity in Canada to fulfil his ambition of serving the Canadian literature movement as 'a very special kind of critic.' *Saturday Night* was a handsome and flourishing weekly. Its gross circulation figure for 1921 was 36,301, with 26,974 subscriptions.[2] Founded in 1887 by two Toronto newspapermen,

Edmund Sheppard and W.C. Nichol, in 1906 it was sold to Harold Gagnier, a financier who had moved from the tobacco industry to the newspaper world.[3] Most important to the *Saturday Night* of the twenties and to Deacon was the editorship of Charles Frederick Paul from 1909 until his death in 1926. Between them, Gagnier and Paul had gone a great distance towards transforming the paper into a national, not a Toronto, weekly, widening its sphere of influence across the nation though always retaining a pious element of British colonialism and, as the twenties progressed, a spice of anti-Americanism.[4] They had enlarged the paper to a 32-page weekly, increased its staff, doubled its price (from 5 to 10 cents), and increased its advertising rates and circulation, thereby becoming a lasting legend in newpaper circles as the only Canadian publisher-editor combination who ever succeeded by raising prices. They had set out to be crusaders for legitimate, conservative investments and against the stock market racketeers of their day, and had built up a reputation for working closely with the Toronto police to unmask dishonest stock promoters.[5] Under Paul's editorship the paper moved to a circulation of about 30,000, fluctuating by several thousands during the twenties and showing a gross figure of 32,000, with 24,627 subscribers in 1927, the year after his death.[6]

Next to Fred Paul, *Saturday Night*'s most important journalist in these years was Hector Charlesworth, whom Paul had hired as an associate editor in 1910 and who was finally an editor himself, from 1926 to 1932. Charlesworth was in charge of picture services, music, theatre, art criticism, and sometimes the 'Gold and Dross' columns which gave advice on business and investments. In fact, he served as a general factotum in any department as needed. He became something of a legend himself, partly for his undoubted commitment to Canadian culture, but partly for the conservatism of mind and perception which led him to repeated attacks on the Group of Seven as wild, untalented radicals, who, in his opinion, distorted the beauties of Canada in their work. Under Gagnier and Paul, Constance Marston edited the women's section, which featured columns on motoring, designs for country homes, gardens, and summer cottages as well as exercising the everlasting appeal of society gossip and weddings. Peter Donovan had edited the book section until, in 1920, Lord Beaverbrook lured him away to London's *Daily Express*. It was his place that Deacon was hired to fill. Donovan's pseudonym, PO'D, was replaced by Deacon's 'Candide.'

Saturday Night, then, was an enviable theatre for the performance of an aspiring literary journalist, certainly pre-eminent among Canadian newspapers in its coverage of literature then, or, in terms of total column space and wordage, even now. It was full newspaper size (15″ × 20″), fluctuating between 28 and 36 pages, printed on fine stock, not pulp, lavishly illustrated, elegantly designed, and printed in three parts: the general section, the financial section, and the women's section. Its masthead listed Toronto, Montreal, Winnipeg, New York, and Chicago, though the American listings must have been essentially for distribution purposes, since the contents of the paper were almost exclusively Canadian and the advertising was predominantly so.

In every issue of the twenties, *Saturday Night*'s advertising reflects the excitement and the cultural conflicts inherent in the massive life-style changes that were rapidly taking place. Advertisements for the Victor Orthophonic Victrola disappear and ads for the Rogers Batteryless Radio take their place; automobiles move into prime advertising spots – the Reo 'Flying Cloud,' the Dodge, and the Lincoln (but not Everyman's Model-T Ford or Chevrolet), and in one issue a 12″ × 15″ ad for Marvelube Motor Oil takes up half the space of one book page (7 April 1928). Hotel and travel ads suggest the Strand in Atlantic City, the Morrison in Chicago, West Indian cruises on Canadian Pacific steamships, a trip across Canada on CPR's Vancouver Express, or a round trip on the French line to Europe, in the 'friendly intimacy' of second class for $142.50. After Lindbergh flew the Atlantic, even the staid insurance companies began to enter the contemporary world of speed and mobility, with the Metropolitan Life Insurance Company featuring an airplane over the heading 'Metal Motors and Human Hearts.' In 1927 Hiram Walker's Distillers were large advertisers, but in 1928 Canada Dry Gingerale was larger.

The music and drama pages, with their photographs, ads for theatres and movie houses and reviews, tell a clear story of the last great days of live theatre in Toronto before the takeover of entertainment by movies and radio. The Royal Alexandra, Victoria, Empire, and Garrick theatres were all on the route of touring companies and Shea's Hippodrome was a vaudeville centre. The incongruities of 'culture' and 'entertainment' in Toronto society lie in the juxtapositioning of names and faces in every issue of the paper: Victor McLaglen and Dolores del Rio in *What Price Glory* and *Carmen*, Sir Martin Harvey playing Garrick, Eddie Cantor in *Make It Snappy*, Georgie Jessel in *The Jazz Singer*, and Lady Eaton, who has been 'improving her voice in Europe' and is a guest soloist with the Toronto Symphony at Massey Hall. As the decade moves on the movie ads become more numerous, more clamorous, and more confident, and the theatre ads fewer, but the performing arts in Toronto are still strong – D'Oyly Carte draws its yearly devotees, Fritz Reiner, with the Cincinnati Symphony, conducts the Mendelssohn Choir in Massey Hall, and inside of one month in the spring of 1928, Fritz Kreisler and Paderewski performed at Massey Hall, Sir Harry Lauder at the Princess Margaret Theatre, and George Arliss played Shylock in *The Merchant of Venice* at the Royal Alexandra.

Clearly, the readership that *Saturday Night* envisaged as its own either did live or could aspire to live as its contents, particularly its advertising, suggest. The paper was directed to married, professional, and business, 'upwardly mobile' readers, conservative and sedate in their standards and temperately nationalistic in thought and habit, with their values confidently and sometimes defensively centred on their own expanding, middle-class opportunities. Though there was still a very large British colonial component to this society as it is seen and remembered down a fifty-year vista, these people thought of themselves as emphatically Canadian when they were challenged by the dominance of either British or American culture. The complacent confidence of tone in Fred Paul's editorials was one aspect of the Canadian psyche; but on the other hand, Vimy Ridge had established a heroic symbol of Canada's nationhood amid the carnage of World War I and her right to vote as a sovereign nation in the League of Nations had consolidated a considerable component of national pride. Furthermore, the reactionary energy of the United States in its post-war years and its bustling, hustling economy worked its usual ambivalent way with Canadians: they enjoyed the benefits – who could resist the availability of cars, movies, and radios, to say nothing of Coca Cola, canned pineapple, Campbell's soups, and Heinz baked beans? But they also felt threatened by the overpowering lustiness of the neighbour. Some drew back into serious, introspective examinations and definitions of Canadianism, while others met one cultural and economic aggression with another, a confident and militant Canadian nationalism.

Deacon was one of the latter. In the twenties, in his years at *Saturday Night*, he was the right man in the right place at the right time. He was international in his intellectual interests and totally Canadian in his emotional loyalties. When the two came in conflict in his work he chose nationalistically and was convinced that it was in the best interests of Canada, its culture, its readers, and its writers to do so. Against the conservative cushion of *Saturday Night*, all that he wrote and his very attitude towards Canadian literature reverberated with remarkable, disarming, and sometimes deceptive freshness and authority. He was in no sense radical either in the literary or political sense, but against this backdrop he often sounded so. His personal ambitions of becoming a writer and a man of letters easily encompassed the roles of book reviewer and literary impresario for Canadian authors. His energies were prodigious: he could regularly write serious reviews of a half-dozen works weekly and brief notices of a dozen or more additional works under his 'Books Received' column. He solicited advertising both personally and through the persuasiveness of his reviews. Nothing is more striking in *Saturday Night* than the flood of publishers' advertisements that the book pages came to carry during his six-year tenure. Besides his literary work as 'Candide' he also wrote, under his own name, a syndicated weekly advice column for the financial section, called 'Law and Common Sense.' This went on for years, appearing in *The Manitoba Free Press*, among other papers, as well as in *Saturday Night*. He corresponded with increasing numbers of people: old friends and mentors from the Winnipeg days like Arthur Phelps and William Allison; old writers and new, who, recognizing his enthusiasm and drive, needed from him, and got, personal support and encouragement; readers who knew him as 'Candide' and instigated continuing literary correspondences; and publishers whose writers he promoted and whose advertising he courted. These were also the years of his own best literary productivity: *Peter McArthur, Poteen, Pens and Pirates*, and *The Four Jameses* were all published between 1922 and 1928.

Peter Donovan had established the book pages as 'The Book Shelf,' the title superimposed on a black and white sketch of a gentleman reading at leisure, feet on a table, wearing eyeglasses with a ribbon and looking rather like a sketch of one of the best-known photographs of Sir Charles G.D. Roberts. Donovan as PO'D had also established an international, but predominantly British, character for his book pages. Under Deacon as 'Candide,' the 'Book Shelf' heading remained and also, at the start, the international emphasis. In his first pages, for 8 July 1922, he gave long reviews to four works, all long forgotten and all published by Macmillan, the company which, he grumbled to William Allison, dictated *Saturday Night*'s book coverage and reviewing policies.[7] These were followed by shorter notices of eighteen books received and read that week. The entire production was quiet, informative, and without colour or evidence of flair. Only three months later, however, in the issue of 28 October 1922, an intimate, jocular, and personal flavour had been firmly established and guaranteed by Deacon's feature within 'The Book Shelf,' his column called 'Saved from the Waste-Basket.' This column, printed in smaller type than the reviews, and sometimes running to a greater length in wordage than the sum of the reviews' length, was a varying pot-pourri of letters, messages, notes, and comments between 'Candide' and his readers. Some of the columns were set up by the previous permission of the correspondent. All carry the atmosphere of a friendly, intimate club; they are briskly humorous and refreshingly irreverent of persons and institutions. He quotes Arthur Phelps, for instance:

I am enclosing the Chapbook thing [*A Bobcaygeon Chapbook*] for your private or public comment. I don't know that it has sufficient body to make it really reviewable. Except insofar as it might start something. I really meant it to be a sort of left-handed casual thing. I wish Canadian versifiers would be more left-handed and casual in a serious way – if you know what I mean. I'd like to see the Chapbook idea catch on. I think it would be fun and something more than a fad, and if a group of us could begin ragging one another, and hating and loving one another, and making fun of one another (and of ourselves) that would be fun. (28 October 1922)

To which Deacon replies that as the chapbook is not for sale he cannot review it in his 'more sedate' columns. He then proceeds at length (at least 1,000 words) with both reviewing and the 'ragging' that Phelps wished.

Now for your alleged poems ... you say in the Preface that you wrote 'Knack Rovey' in three minutes ... I like my eggs soft-boiled. Three minutes is about right ... I prefer my poems not quite so soft ... Sorry to knock 'Rovey,' but he's really too thin...

There [*Bits from Bobcaygeon*], you have written your autobiography in five lines ... that's you all over Mable. What has prevented you, heretofore, from ranking among the greatest of Canada's poets – and the only thing – is that you haven't got a sufficient grip on life ... Too much of a bystander. Too vague. Life is not real enough to you. I assure you it can be tangible. I suppose I should advise you to read 'This Freedom' and 'suffer' a bit with Mr Hutchinson – and the rest of us. Well, I'm not going to. Life is a wonderful corrective, my Boy. You'll find yourself...

You talk of our loving one another ... Well, I not only love you: I admire you; and you will understand the extreme offhandedness (which implies friendliness) of even my most uncomplimentary remarks ... I have thrown these to you negligently – as I would throw dogs to a bone – negligently, en passant, also couchant (because I am writing lying on my back) ... Hoping you are the same.

Candide

Among all the friendly nonsense, Deacon inserted a core of serious advice to aspiring writers which guaranteed him valuable follow-up correspondence. 'The duty of a writer is to get into print; it is for the public, and those insects the critics, to say how they like it; and they should say it louder. But nothing can be done till this man's work is out in some form or other. Junior writers, especially, who cannot find a tractable publisher, should spend $25.00 or $50.00 and get their work out in Chapbook or leaflet form for free distribution.' (28 October 1922)

A month later Candide gives up his own commentary in 'Saved from the Waste-Basket' to print Tom MacInnes's poem, 'Zalinka,' entire:

> Last night in a land of Triangles
> I lay in a cubicle where
> A girl in pyjamas and bangles
> Slept with her hands in my hair...

He prefaces the poem with a picture of MacInnes and an exchange of banter from their letters. This poem had previously appeared only in *The China Mail*, Hongkong, while MacInnes was working to establish a public transportation system there. He had submitted it to a Canadian literary periodical which rejected it immediately 'on moral grounds – I had not met with such an example of anti-deluvian prudery since I had heard the story of the Boston lady who kept books by male authors in one book-case and books by female authors in another.' (4 November 1922) Such schoolboy joshing and the intimacy of 'Saved from the Waste-Basket,' combined with its information, criticism, and the illusion of being party to private, friendly conversations, were irresistible to readers accustomed to a more formal and distant stance on the part of their reviewers. Soon they were corresponding with 'Candide,' often in the hope, usually implicit but unacknowledged in their words, of being quoted in 'Saved from the Waste-Basket.' Fred Paul acknowledged Deacon's success in attracting interest in the literary section when his six-month trial period ended – he raised his pay to $40 a week.

The issue of 28 October 1922 also celebrated 'Book Week' in Canada, an institution instigated in 1921, sponsored by the Canadian Authors'

Association, and the occasion of the convergence of 130 of their members on Ottawa to present a petition on fair copyright practices to the minister of Trade and Commerce. All the books reviewed that week were Canadian: Emily Murphy's *Black Candle*, Carol Cassidy Cole's *Velvet Paws and Shiny Eyes*, *Verse and Reverse*, a collection of poetry by the Toronto Women's Press Club, *Canadian Cities of Romance* by Katherine Hale, and *Neighbours* by Robert Stead. Deacon's editorial announcing Book Week and exhorting readers to buy Canadian books could be transposed without change to a press release today from the Writers' Union of Canada:

business men will be addressed at hundreds of luncheons, and have it pointed out to them that millions of copies of foreign magazines, with their advertising, poured into Canada annually, do not help Canadian business. Every foreign book is written from the author's national standpoint; it carries subtle, and generally unconscious, propaganda in its very atmosphere. Foreign influences are broadening, and beneficial provided they do not dominate. In the past we have imported the bulk of our reading matter. At one time that was necessary if there was to be any culture here at all. At present it is not only unnecessary; it is a positive danger to a healthy nationalism. Remembering that the movement is primarily patriotic, and only secondarily to help the native author, will you do your part? (28 October 1922)

From the beginning Deacon reviewed Canadian works with a special gusto that meant not only placing them front and centre and cheering their appearance, but also at times imposing on them his views of what the special qualities of Canadianism and Canadian life should be. Reviewing Robert Stead's *Neighbours*, for instance, he finds something 'fresh and homely' about it, though he deplores, with abundant examples, the forced precision of its structure. Finally, however, 'I would rather read "Neighbors" than many a cleverer book. I feel perfectly at home among these people; they are my people and real, even if Mr. Stead does order their matrimonial affairs with an eye to geometry rather than psychology.' (28 October 1922)

A retrospective look at *Robert Norwood* (1923) by Albert Durrant Watson in the 'Makers of Canadian Literature' series makes agreement with his critical estimate easy: he chides Watson for an over-cautious conservatism in the treatment of his subject.

I have only seen Dr Norwood once, but he struck me instantly as a man of tempestuous vigour, and of a delightful pugnacity that could only have had its origin in a certain green island. Now of this there is not a word in the book. There is a mild word or two about Norwood's courage – but we would never dream from Dr Watson's book that Norwood is a fighting parson who would positively die of ennui if he found himself without a scrap on his hands. This outstanding characteristic must have won the man friends and enemies, and influenced his whole career, yet of it not a word. Nor are there samples of Norwood's bubbling wit, flashing invectives and mordant satire. Surely the gravity with which Dr Norwood's books are discussed should have been laid aside for a moment or two to make room for specimens of that humour so characteristic of him and which enhances by so much our affection for the thinker and the serious literary artist. (14 July 1923)

Today, taken singly or together, the 'Makers of Canadian Literature' volumes seem thin and bland. These words on the Norwood volume follow four paragraphs of praise for the series, its conception and handsome format, and for Dr Watson's work. The entire review illustrates perfectly a major problem for Deacon, and his solution: he quickly became adept at balancing praise with blame, to the point where sometimes the effect of one was cancelled by the other. But he was, and he knew he was, nurturing the extremely tender plant of Canadian literature and he was also, by the demands of his job as well as his own missionary zeal, persuading his reluctant 'average readers' to read and *buy* Canadian books. He had no problems with what he considered the 'good' books or the 'bad' ones; on these he was very outspoken. But for the vast bland middle ground he had to and did develop a balanced line of strategy.

About *Newfoundland Verse* (1923), E.J. Pratt's first collection, however-er, Deacon could be wholly and enthusiastically his own man. The review is accompanied by a fine 3″ × 5″ photographic reproduction of the poet. It includes several quotations from the poems and the whole of 'Carlo,' the celebration of the dog who saved the lives of more than ninety persons by swimming with a line from a sinking ship to shore. The review's beginning is a triumphant start: 'A new man, with the old authentic ring to his verses! Freshness and freedom of spirit finding expression in the common and more conventionalized forms! ... Such maturity and strength and beauty are in these poems that the day of their publication is a date to be remembered.' After this ringing citation Deacon considers individual poems, particularly for their graphic and dramatic intensity – 'The Ice-Floes, a tragedy of the annual seal hunt, is exceptionally strong here' – and for their 'hearty quality of humour.' He ends by congratulating Pratt on the strength of his narrative talent:

'It is significant that the new poet is at his best in narrative. Canadian poets have been somewhat weak in that kind of sustained effort, and too often have been content with the lyrical interpretation of their own moods, and rather subjective descriptions of nature reflecting these moods.' (21 April 1923)

To fortify, and complicate, his reviewing further, Deacon had a well-developed set of beliefs and prejudices about literature and life. He set out, not only to nurture and encourage Canadian writers, but in a sense to instruct them in what and how a Canadian writer should write and in what a Canadian should and could be. He was totally at odds with the literary mode of realism when it moved towards naturalism just as he was at odds with imagism and, effectively, with the entire modernist movement in poetry. Hence, he began his review of Mazo de la Roche's *Possession* (1923) with an overall condemnation of her mode which, translated into more general terms, removes from the writer his choice of theme and method.

The epic of gloom has reached Canada via the pen of the author of 'Explorers of the Dawn,' which, last year, was read so widely with very evident enthusiasm. That someone should try something a little more serious and more ambitious than the 'glad-book' was highly praiseworthy. That Miss de la Roche should represent farm life on the shore of Lake Ontario, in the Niagara district as pervaded by the pessimism of a Siberian village is a more questionable proceeding. (31 March 1923)

This is criticism of conception, not execution, and it is rationalized by Deacon's own beliefs and perceptions of the area and its people.

Not a single character is successful or happy. All are hypnotized into futility by some subtle emanation from the ground which blankets the whole region ... Now I have lived in Niagara Falls and in Toronto, and am tolerably familiar with the places in between and the people who live in them, and I have never noticed this horizon-wide depression. In the older countries of Europe and in England, it is possible for the momentum of the past to sweep along an individual or group beyond his or their ability to break away from enervating experiences. In the country described in this book I do not think it possible. (31 March 1923)

Here is the old 'Canada, pure, strong and free' myth and though Ralph Connor and L.M. Montgomery were the only two Canadian writers Deacon consistently denigrated for their sentimental optimism, his own fantasies about Canada and Canadians, translated into deeply held beliefs, ran on the same track.

Martha Ostenso's *Wild Geese* won his high praise for what he calls her 'modified realism' and her 'knowledge of life.'

My optimism concerning the author's future rose out of a suspicion that she has a fine artistic conscience that defeated an original desire to follow the fashion in rural fiction by making the land obsess her characters inimically and wreck them ... four out of five of the chief persons achieve triumph of character over that environment. Therefore the conclusion is highly satisfying, and I feel that Miss Ostenso will continue to subordinate temporary fads to the inner dictates of her knowledge of life. (28 November 1925)

Deacon did not write fiction himself and when he read fiction, especially Canadian fiction, he preferred either romance or a treatment that he considered epic in its scope and documentary in its details. His review of Laura Goodman Salverson's *The Viking Heart* was highly favourable, because he considered it 'the epic of the large colony of Icelanders who immigrated in the early seventies, and established themselves on the shores of Lake Winnipeg at, or near, the site of the present town of Gimli':

Seldom has the Canadian public been offered such a strong and intimate piece of fiction as Mrs Salverson has made out of the records of the Icelandic people in Manitoba. Even to call it fiction is straining a point, for while I do not suppose that the characters in the book are known under these names in daily life, and while events that are accredited in the tale to such and such persons may not actually have happened to them, I believe that every portrait in the book is that of some person the author has known, and that all the happenings recorded in the story have been experienced by the author or her acquaintances ... The narrative partakes of the good qualities of both the realistic and historical novel, and is a literary achievement of distinct merit. In publishing so just, so fair, and so readable an account of the deeds, thoughts and emotions of her own people, Mrs Salverson has not only done them a lasting service, but also has given Canada a book that deserves to live long past the time of the popularity it will doubtless enjoy during the next few months. (24 November 1923)

In 1925 *Saturday Night* began publication of a separate magazine, 'The Saturday Night Literary Section,' completely devoted to reviews, special literary features, and book advertising. This was Deacon's dearest project, a testament to the popularity of his three years as literary editor, to his success in attracting advertising to the paper, and to his unflagging energy and enthusiasm. It was a separate, 10″ × 15″ fold-in supplement to *Saturday Night*, sixteen to twenty-four pages long and in format obviously based on *The Saturday Review of Literature*, founded in 1924 and edited by Henry Seidel Canby, who had four years earlier established *The Literary Review* of *The New York Evening Post*. In August 1924, having left the *Evening Post* after its sale to Cyrus Curtis, Canby published the first issue of his new literary magazine. Deacon continued to publish in *The Literary Review* but he also began to write for *The Saturday Review of Literature* and did so until 1933, contributing survey articles on Canadian literature in 1924 and 1925. As a model for his new literary section he had obviously studied its format of reviews, features such as Christopher Morley's 'Letter from Paris,' and advertising lay-out. At the beginning the enterprise was his own work entirely, from the assigning of reviews, to the soliciting of advertising, to paste-up of the pages. His papers include an entire packet on issue no. 1, 28 November 1925, including drawings for page lay-outs, advertising, photographs, and columns labelled in his hand-writing, a paste-up of the whole issue, and a set of corrected proofs. Later he had help: a presentation copy of 1 October 1927 is addressed to 'My very loyal and efficient sub-editor, May Sharples, without whom this issue would not have appeared. She saw it through from first to last.' From 1925 on, Deacon was officially designated as editor of both 'The Book Shelf' and this new 'Literary Section'; gradually he gave up using 'Candide' and a facsimile signature of William Arthur Deacon took its place.

Writing to his friend Professor W.T. Allison, on 26 October 1925, Deacon described his aims for the new supplement:

It is my idea to furnish a medium whereby the abler Canadian critics may talk with the utmost candor, and to which the reader may turn for vigorous expressions of opinion from many minds: differences of viewpoint between the several writers will be the keynote. Besides independence of thought, I am striving for tolerance, a comprehensive survey, sound criticism and good writing. I am satisfied that with proper support from authors and the trade we can turn out something as fine in its way as the International Book Review...

As president of the c.a.a. you might keep in mind that our function is national, and that the prestige and wide high class circulation of *Saturday Night* is at the disposal of the Canadian writers and book interests; and that I am having a hard time convincing our business dept. as to the wisdom of my policy and it is up to the authors to get behind me, and to everybody concerned to support us. Perhaps you might impress the Ass'n with the fact of our consistent friendliness to the native author, who has always got a show here, and who will be given a better one once the new publication is firmly on its feet.[8]

Deacon also adds that *Saturday Night* is losing five hundred dollars on this first number of the supplement despite large ads from the book trade. His plan was to make it into a quarterly in the fall of 1927, and enlarge it to a monthly supplement as soon as possible. Reviewers were to be paid one cent a word and artist illustrators approximately two dollars a drawing.

Readers and publishers greeted the new venture enthusiastically; it was an exciting extension for the literary community already devoted to 'The Book Shelf' and 'Saved from the Waste-Basket.' Hugh Eayrs, president of the Macmillan Company of Canada and a potent force on the literary scene, wrote a long letter to Deacon, pledging his support in advertising (even at higher than the accustomed rates) and applauding the enterprise. The new section, said Eayrs, would supply a unique and badly needed combination of '*book news*' and '*book views*' in Canada, comparable to *The Times Literary Supplement* and *The New York Times Book Review Supplement*. As a publisher, but above all as a bookman, genuinely interested in bringing books and readers together, Eayrs voiced his approval and support:

I respect the Canadian Forum as book views, but it is not book news. Fred Jacob, Morgan Powell, Austin Bothwell and yourself as Candide, give us weekly book views and to some extent (in your own case to a fairly large extent) book news, but all that any of you that I have named can do is done in very circumscribed space. Your own columns are larger than any of the others indeed, but from your own standpoint as critic, and mine as interested bookman, if I may say so, I think the conclusion is that although all is done that space permits, space does not permit anything like the service that the supplement idea does.

... when you consider that we have had four difficult industrial years and when you consider the incursion of the radio, the movie and the motor car into the people's time and the people's interest, the growth of interest in books (which, mark you, is a fact) is all the more remarkable. Well, you and I, neither of us from the merely business standpoint, (though it does come in a bit) are anxious to foster and nourish this growth in interest in books and above all in good books.[9]

Deacon's grand plans for a regular supplement did not materialize: there were only seven of them during his years at *Saturday Night*, on 28 November 1925, 2 October 1926, 4 December 1926, 12 March 1927, 1 October 1927, 26 November 1927, and 17 March 1928. The last three were also issued for a second week, dated 8 October 1927, 3 December 1927, and 24 March 1928. All are remarkably attractive because of *Saturday Night*'s traditional specialities: high-quality glossy stock, lavish illustrations, and elegant lay-outs. They are particularly distinguished by numbers of black and white drawings by Charles Comfort, then recently arrived in Toronto from Winnipeg, who often did not sign his drawings or signed them simply 'C,' but was gratefully identified by Deacon in his 'Saved from the Waste-Basket.' The front page carried Deacon's editorial in the left-hand column, a poem top centre (Wilson MacDonald [3], E.J. Pratt, Duncan Campbell Scott, Raymond Knister, and Annie Charlotte Dalton), a fine 4″ × 6″ photographic reproduction (Conrad, Hardy, Carman), or drawing by Comfort (Grove, William de Morgan), a table of contents, and the first column of the lead review on the right-hand side. Some twenty to thirty-five books were reviewed in each of these issues; the coverage was international, but selectively so, with the balance tipping towards Canadian books; furthermore, Deacon offered to supply on request any book reviewed in the pages (the exception was *Ulysses*, reviewed in the 'Literary Section' of 2 October 1926.) He had been using outside reviewers on 'The Book Shelf' pages from the beginning and in his first editorial in the 'Literary Section' he pointed with pride to the contributors involved:

It is as representative as it is possible to make it. Seven of the writers of the present Literary Section are on the staffs of five universities, while many of the more prominent of the newspaper reviewers have lent their aid. Several of our more prominent authors, who have heretofore done no critical writing, have also been pressed into service. Besides these are some talented juniors, the stars of the future, which it is the necessity and the privilege of every editor to seek out and encourage. (28 November 1925)

Deacon was justified in his pride. The reviews were signed by Pratt and Pelham Edgar (Victoria), MacMechan (Dalhousie), Allison (University of Manitoba), Phelps (Wesley College, Winnipeg), B.K. Sandwell (McGill and Queen's, editor of *The Canadian Bookman*), Fred Jacob (*The Mail and Empire*), Victor Lauriston (*The Chatham News*), Merrill Denison, Madge Macbeth, Katherine Hale, and Marshall Saunders (writers), and many others. In later literary sections both Morley Callaghan and Raymond Knister reviewed for him. Two of his most talented reviewers were J.L. Charlesworth, an official with the Canadian Manufacturers' Association (no relative to Hector Charlesworth), and John H. Creighton, manager of the Educational Department, Oxford Press. These two men wrote particularly fine reviews, often on contemporary work such as *Ulysses* (Creighton), or Faulkner's *Mosquitoes* (Charlesworth). Their work would be distinguished in any publication.

In the same first editorial, Deacon made a special point of *Saturday Night's* national circulation and responsibility:

There is no section of Canada, not even the Yukon, or in the far reaches of Newfoundland that is not in almost constant communication with our book department. And it is perhaps in 'the back of the beyond' that we are able to perform our greatest service. The love of books is not a matter of geography. But we are a country of vast distances, with facilities for buying books negligible except in centres of population. City dwellers can well look after their own requirements. We must serve first those who are otherwise helpless.

In these days before the CBC there was, indeed, no national communication network and Deacon's enterprise, combining reviews with literary news and gossip, was certainly devised to join together the book lovers of Canada and to give them access to books. The final pages of the November and December literary sections list 'Books for Christmas' in a lengthy and well-arranged bibliography.

Besides his usual gossipy, clubby 'Saved from the Waste-Basket' feature, Deacon initiated two new and continuing features in the supplement: Francis Dickie, a west coast writer exploring the adventure of expatriation, wrote a 'Letter from Paris' and Sheila Rand (Ruth Cohen), formerly a journalist for *The Winnipeg Telegram*, but now rather well known in England as a journalist and writer whose penname was 'Wilhelmina Stitch,' wrote a 'Letter from London.' In the first issue B.K. Sandwell wrote a nonsense sketch, 'December Afternoon in a Book Store,' and in another section 'The Disappearance of Aloysius McTurk,' a story about one of his own comic personae. He also reviewed and wrote humorous verse for further issues of the literary section. When Deacon found 'a sheltered spot from the overhanging ads,' that is, when all the advertising space was not sold, he himself contributed long and lively biographical essays – François

Villon in one supplement, Cesare Borgia and Genghis Khan in another.

Francis Dickie's Paris was a far cry from the intensely personal storm-centre of Hemingway and Fitzgerald, the Writers' Workshop of Morley Callaghan, or the hedonistic paradise and hell of John Glassco. It was, rather, a city of art and atmosphere where he strolled as observer and reported on the galleries, the book stalls, and the entertainment celebrities such as Josephine Baker, the black American whose singing there in the twenties began a Parisian jazz vogue that lasted for thirty years. Sheila Rand wrote exclusively of London's, and England's, literary circles in which she aspired to be a central figure, dropping names and spinning anecdotes around her encounters with the great (John Galsworthy) and the notoriously eccentric (Radclyffe Hall). Both features provided a pleasurable illusion of involvement in cosmopolitan glamour for readers of the literary section.

The year 1925, with the appearance of this first supplement, was one highpoint of achievement and satisfaction for William Arthur Deacon; 1927, however, was a multiple triumph for him, the apex of his career at *Saturday Night* and perhaps in retrospect the most hopeful and satisfying year of his entire literary career. Canada's bustling nationalism, already growing since the early twenties, was given added impetus by the celebration that year of the Diamond Jubilee of Confederation. The occasion functioned much as did the Centennial Year of 1967: its celebrations gave both focus and direction to numbers of groups already involved in promoting nationalism, and a coalescing enthusiasm and awareness to much larger segments of the population. *Saturday Night*'s issue of 2 July 1927 featured a front-page full-length portrait of a young Sir John A. Macdonald, and the editorials were stiff with tributes to the achievements of Canada; in the music and drama section the IODE's Confederation Pageant at Massey Hall was featured and Wilson MacDonald's lengthy 'Ode on the Diamond Jubilee of Confederation' throbbed with purple, patriotic passion:

> ...
> Arise then, O my Country this great day,
> And light your eyes with that crusading flame
> Which burns all evil obstacles away –
> The pigmies of our malice and our shame.
> We have been cowards, traitors, fools and Knaves;
> We have been fine, heroic, strong and true,

So, in this purple hour, let us renew
Our strengths and bear our hatreds to their graves –
A Kingdom, with crescendo of the sea
Sounding the golden age that is to be.

This 'Ode,' in a handsome edition with illustrations by Thoreau
Macdonald, had also been published and circulated by the CNR as a
Jubilee tribute, a move which prompted Deacon, in an editorial, to
herald a new and benign patronage of letters in Canada. In fact,
throughout the twenties Wilson MacDonald functioned as the unofficial laureate of Canada in the pages of *Saturday Night*. Many of his
poems were printed there, often enhanced by an elegantly designed
lay-out. Deacon had inherited MacDonald's popularity with *Saturday
Night*; he had then come to know him as a fellow theosophist; and
finally he had come to a temperate enthusiasm for his poetry.

I honestly believe him to be some shakes as a poet. I was not at all impressed
with his verse as I encountered it in the magazines; but he seemed to be so
highly regarded here in some quarters that I bought his book. I was not bowled
over by it, but I have had it nearly a year and like it better all the time ... And I
have seen the MS of a new collection he is bringing out in the fall; and I can't see
how, after the publication of that, it will be possible to keep his name out of the
first grade of Canadian poets.[10]

In the appropriate spirit of the Jubilee occasion, Deacon's review of
the 'Ode' was a fulsome tribute to its writer's noble sentiments, the
patriotism of its sponsor, the CNR, the skill of its designer and
illustrator, 'one of the most beautiful [books] ever made in Canada,'
and above all, to Canada and the Canadian people. By comparison the
rest of Deacon's 'Book Shelf' pages for this issue were sober, sensible,
and restrained, and all the more impressive for that. He featured a
low-keyed, intelligent, and comprehensive survey of the development
of Canadian literature with a pointed reference to the lack of official
recognition for writers, 'except for the annual gratuities of $11,000
which the Province of Quebec distributes amongst its own authors.' His
two review essays centred on Charles Mair, who at age eighty-eight was
celebrating his handsome, Radisson Society publication of *Tecumseh: A
Drama*, and Duncan Campbell Scott, who had recently been awarded
the Lorne Pierce Gold Medal and elected to the Royal Society of Britain
for his *Collected Poems*. In the case of Mair, Deacon abdicated criticism
for biography: 'Mair's fame does not rest on this book: that was

established before its publication'; for Scott he gave a short tribute, a fine photograph, and a long passage of his 'Ode to Canada,' poetry of a quieter and, in retrospect, more congenial patriotism than MacDonald's: 'And yet with all these pastoral and heroic graces, our simplest flowers wear the loveliest faces.' (2 July 1927)

The entire year's book pages and literary sections reflect a festival mood. Charles G.D. Roberts, first winner in 1926 of the Lorne Pierce Gold Medal for service to Canadian literature, in 1927 had become first holder of the Chair of Canadian Literature at the University of British Columbia. Bliss Carman, along with Scott, had been elected to the Royal Society of Literature, and Francis Dickie reported that at the annual month-long exposition of books in Paris, *Anne of Green Gables*, in a 'charming yellow and green cover,' was being offered to the French reading public for five francs, fifty. (12 March 1927) John Garvin, speaking to the Ontario Education Association, demanded a fairer representation for Canadian authors in both public and high school texts: 'Surely it is not too much to ask that at least twenty-five per cent of the *whole* be selected from the works of Canadian authors.' And Deacon's Book Week editorial shouts progress and confidence for Canadian letters: 'No more is it necessary to insist loudly that Canada has authors that merit attention and support; that fact is admitted ... Five years ago we carefully saved up Canadian books for many weeks ahead to be able to concentrate the best of them, and make a good "showing" in our issue immediately preceding Book Week. Now no such precautions are necessary. We cannot begin to give extended consideration to all Canadian books, or even all good ones.' (22 October 1927)

There were three literary sections published in 1927, on 12 March, 1 October, and 26 November, each one sixteen to twenty-four pages long, replete with publishers' advertising, and carrying between thirty and forty reviews and articles. One front page of the three is distinguished by a fine line drawing of Frederick Philip Grove by Charles Comfort (26 November), and another by 'Cherries,' a happy fantasy poem by E.J. Pratt.

There were important books from both home and abroad reviewed in 1927 – *Jalna* and *A Search for America*, *Mosquitoes*, *The Sun Also Rises* and *Elmer Gantry*, Pelham Edgar's *Henry James*, Edwin Muir's *Transition*, and Edith Sitwell's *Poetry and Criticism* among them. Deacon had already formulated his credo as a reviewer, but never more succinctly than in his review of Sitwell's *Poetry and Criticism*:

By critics, Miss Sitwell evidently means book reviewers ... and [I] have, in fact, anticipated her in the public assertion – that the bulk of book-reviewing is worthless as permanent criticism. Insofar as the reviewer can make his articles so, they should be solidly critical; and sometimes they achieve insight that is of more than ephemeral value. But if a reviewer were looking to posterity to acclaim him, his chances of reward would be infinitesimal. For the reviewer is not laboring, primarily, to perform a judicial act of appraisement, that shall satisfy creative artists through succeeding generations till the day of doom, but rather, as a typical reader, to inform the subscribers who employ him whether they would care to buy the book under review. (20 August 1927)

Despite the continuous grind of reviewing and his own caution about his 'typical reader,' and despite sporadic interference from his editor when 'the personal prejudices of His Nibs play hob with my lovely schemes,' Deacon was an indefatigably eager reader, quite often a sensitive one, and almost always alert to the writer's art and craft. He became highly skilled in informing and encouraging one group of readers without mortally offending another. For instance, his review of *The Sun Also Rises* is called 'The Perpetual Souse,' but though he deplores its cynicism, 'a despair so profound that they can only drink and forget,' he also recognizes Hemingway's strengths as a writer: 'But Mr Hemingway is forceful as well as clever. So far does he compel one to assume temporarily the outlook of amused, disinterested spectator that one forgets the tragedy and enjoys the clever and outrageous dialogue and incidents ... It is a book which authors ought to study for the technique.' (16 April 1927)

He took many opportunities to underline his conviction about the constant difference between 'important' writers and 'popular' ones: 'being to some extent outside the time spirit, and in revolt against it, they [important writers] mirror the age, as those [popular] writers who are in complete mental and emotional conformity with current conventions cannot do.' It is quite obvious, however, that he accepted as the basic fact of his journalistic life that his primary responsibility was to the mass of readers who would read only the popular writers.

Though many of his friends and his reviewers were academics, Deacon was extremely touchy about their work on behalf of his readers. His defensiveness about his own incomplete career at Victoria and about the academic study of literature in general at times grew into rifts between himself and the infant academic world of Canadian literature that produced unfortunate repercussions on either side, the first major explosion coming with A.J.M. Smith's *Forum* article, 'Wanted: Canadian Criticism,' in 1928. Deacon's review of Pelham

Edgar's *An Englishman by Choice: Henry James, Man and Author*, was a devastating dismissal of the work of the man who was then a power in the Canadian Authors' Association and head of the Department of English at Victoria College. His strictures against the book were far less than balanced by his final tribute, and on one hand he was certainly paying off an old score against the man who had turned his back in scorn on his freshman class.

Jalna and *A Search for America* were the two major Canadian works of 1927 and to these Deacon devoted lengthy reviews, both judicious and enthusiastic and, in the case of *Jalna*, incorporating handsome compensation for his earlier criticisms of Mazo de la Roche's fiction. Her winning of the *Atlantic Monthly* prize had created a furore among the literary folk of Canada and she had been honoured in Toronto by a banquet and the presentation of a silver tea service on behalf of the city. Her book was not without its detractors, however: there were those who maintained then, as now, that neither its settings nor its characters were 'typically Canadian.' Deacon defends her:

In a Country of contrast, what *is* 'typically Canadian'? - 'The Viking Heart'? 'The Kingdom of the Sun'? 'The Seats of the Mighty'? 'Salt Seas and Sailor Men'? or 'Settlers of the Marsh'? The typography of 'Jalna' is unaffectedly and recognizably exactly what it purports to be. It is true that the Whiteoaks have retained *some* English characteristics through three generations; and if it is not inevitable that they should, at least it is possible. We all know persons of Canadian birth, who are more English than Canadian; and we all know that they are in a minority; and there is no slightest hint anywhere that Miss de la Roche intended to illustrate an ethnological textbook on the typical Canadian – if he is yet really in existence. (8 October 1927)

Deacon had announced *A Search for America* in the literary section of 4 December 1926, as an 'autobiographical narrative.' Grove wrote him a letter which appeared in 'Saved from the Waste-Basket' on 8 January 1927, urging on him the fictional nature of his work.

I have half a mind to issue a denial, for I am doing my darndest to disguise the autobiographical nature of the yarn. If I were not laid up, having to dictate all things that need to be typed, with no typist but my wife, who is teaching school to provide the where-with-all for the daily bread which she cooks in her spare time, when she is not busy nursing me or bringing up two children or sewing pajamas for me or dresses for the kids, I should have rewritten the whole thing in the third person ... And now, if you are a man, print this letter to set your blunder right. The 'Search For America' is fiction man, plucked under torture out of my suffering brain. And don't you dare deny it. You may smile when you assert it; but that is all. Yours sincerely, F.P. Grove. (8 January 1927)

When he did come to review the book Deacon did not even smile. He gave it the lead review of some two to three thousand words, and Grove certainly had no valid complaint about the perception with which his work had been read or the warm critical approval which Deacon voiced in his review:

He has written as one might be expected to do a century hence, if such a writer could then command the information that Mr Grove has gathered in his own experience as an immigrant. Like the suppositious twenty-first century novelist, he treats the situation from the viewpoint of the dramatic artist. He visualizes; he makes concrete; he personifies; he tells and interprets the coming of the European as a story – the story of an individual. This is his achievement; to view the contemporary with the detachment of posterity without losing anything of the warm understanding of the contemporary.

Finally, Deacon's review climaxed with a tribute to Grove's artistry in all his works as well as in this particular work:

That Mr Grove is an artist in words was plain from his former writings. He exhibits in 'A Search for America' a new power derived from the intensity of his determination to project with utmost faithfulness the embodiment of a lifetime's experiences and the conclusions he has drawn therefrom. In creating Phil Branden, the extraordinary immigrant, he has compressed into the seemingly chance wanderings of a single character something of the attraction of all seekers for a new homeland. Phil Branden's sufferings and questionings will hereafter stare disconcertingly from the faces of foreigners. The story of the coming of the European has been written. (26 November 1927)

Writing later to Vernon Rhodenizer, an English professor at Acadia University and a pioneer in the teaching of Canadian literature, Deacon compared de la Roche and Grove. As always, he was predisposed to romance and, as always, he prized most the writers who, to him, seemed most 'Canadian' – in this case, de la Roche:

On the Roche-Grove question I offer this suggestion: Truth is more than fact; and the truth we get from a novelist is inevitably strained through his temperament. Scandinavian and most north-European literature is tragic, gloomy, sordid – not that life is much different there from other countries, but the tense creative mind of the literary artist sees it so. Grove is a Swede. He would make a description of a wedding or a circus a grave and a sad business, that is truth for him and that is artistic truth as revealed through him. And, when I am reading him I accept that view of life – absolutely.

Mazo is an Anglo-Celt, with a Gallic streak. Life to her is much brighter. Her emotions are more resilient, more mobile. She reveals through her characters a variation of mood. Mazo is Canadian.

Now, my lad, this Canadian people about whom they both write is not perhaps an exuberant people; it may be a stolid people in some respects. But by God, old man, we are a damned happy lot compared to those turgid Scandinavians ... Mazo feels us in mind and heart and this Swede cannot. In mood, regardless of what her characters do, in their moods and emotions they approximate nearer to the Canadian soul than Grove's human wrecks do.[11]

Writing to his mother at Christmas in 1927, Deacon was buoyant with optimism about his future and that of the literary section. His mail overflowed with testimonials to his work's success, none more precious to him than the approval and encouragement of Arthur Phelps, who had first encouraged him in the Winnipeg years:

Speaking broadly, you have, I think, achieved the reputation for free, frank, thoroughgoing book comment on your page. You have accustomed your readers to the idea that books are not perfect things, that a given book may have a good deal of shoddy or 'offness' about it and yet be splendidly worth while, that a book is often a kind of grab bag out of which one reader will take one thing, one another, and above all that book reviewing is the expression of opinion about books, one man's opinion, the reviewer's; the more personal, the more sincere, the more informed and competent the better ... As I understand it, you don't like ambiguity, log-rolling, or ignorance.[12]

He had just been given a young advertising manager and so was relieved of the burden of looking after all the advertising as well as the editing of the literary section. Paid advertising was up from 8,000 lines in 1924 to 40,000 in 1927, a clear indication to the management of his industry and success. He was making a salary of $65 a week. He wrote with total confidence in his 'power to create the magazine I want to build up, the magazine that will be powerful, and will be a real determining factor in the kind of nation Canada will be made into during the next twenty years.'[13] He was sadly mistaken. Deacon's last issue as book editor of *Saturday Night* came on 8 April 1928. The achievements of the golden year of 1927 masked accumulating pressures and tensions between himself and the management. First of all, he was the supporter of a family of five; he and Sally had had three children since coming to Toronto. Partly from need and certainly, also, from the combination of astonishing energy and ambition that characterized his encounters with literature, Deacon continued his freelance work in these years. Besides writing for *The New York Post*'s *Saturday Review*, he contributed to a number of other publications, *The New York Times*'s *Literary Section*, *The American Mercury*, *The Passing Show*, *The Canadian Bookman*, and *The Canadian Magazine* among them. Fred Paul, as editor of *Saturday Night*, had understood both Deacon's ambition and his financial situation. But his successor, Hector Charlesworth, prompted by Margaret R. Sutton, who ran the firm after Harold Gagnier's death in 1922,[14] harassed Deacon about his outside literary activity. Through Charlesworth Miss Sutton accused him of breaking 'unwritten laws' of journalism by writing for other publications and, in a lengthy letter to her, Deacon had to humiliate himself by describing and pleading his financial situation (though not his ambition) as his reason.[15]

The problem of advertising within *Saturday Night* and particularly in its literary sections was intermittent, sometimes acute. Until 1927 Deacon was in charge of every aspect of the supplements. Besides many letters soliciting advertising from American and British publishers, his papers include, for instance, a comparative table of advertisers between 28 November 1925 and 26 November 1927, showing a growth from 26 to 52, a gain of 100 per cent.[16] Of 36 advertisers in the 26 November 1927 literary section, 21 were publishers, with Macmillan, Irwin, and Graphic Press buying the most space – Macmillan paid 24 cents a line for 760 lines, a total of $182.40. In one advertising revenue chart for 1 October 1927, there is a commission column recorded. It would seem that Deacon was paid a 15 per cent commission by 4 out of 33 advertisers, a total of $42.57 in a revenue of $1,571.18. Advertising rates ran from a minimum of 21 cents a line, paid only by Graphic Press, to 26 cents a line, paid by McClelland and Stewart, John Britnell, and others.[17]

Of all the publishers, The Macmillan Company of Canada was almost certainly the largest consistent advertiser and, consequently, an important factor in *Saturday Night*'s and Deacon's reckoning. When he began as 'Candide,' Deacon felt that Macmillan dominated and directed the reviewing in 'The Book Shelf,' and certainly Hugh Eayrs could be extremely touchy about the treatment of his books. Though he had been enthusiastic about the literary sections from the start and eventually became a genial friend of Deacon's, he was quick to write a letter of complaint when he felt that Deacon had been 'laying for' Macmillan or 'favouring' Ryerson, or when one of his books had received a poor review or had been ignored. He expected prime space for both his books and his advertising.[18] There was also a period of some months in 1926-7 when Macmillan withdrew advertising altogether in protest against *Saturday Night*'s carrying of ads for the newly formed book club, The Literary Guild. The Macmillan Company of Canada held the agency for Alfred Knopf in New York, and joined Knopf in a move to shut out the threatening book clubs.[19]

Then there was the problem of Graphic Press, an ambitious and enthusiastically nationalistic venture in which Deacon was interested from the beginning. Graphic was a heavy advertiser, consistently holding a large, prime position on 'The Book Shelf' pages, but unfortunately as financially unstable as its enthusiasts were ambitious. When it encountered serious financial difficulties in 1927, it owed money to *Saturday Night*. Since Deacon had tried to raise Graphic's advertising in *Saturday Night* from $1,000 to $2,000 a year, the loss to the paper may have been a considerable sum. At any rate, Deacon had been under suspicion of a conflict of interest for some time: 'Eayrs is spreading it around that I am a director of Graphic and using S.N. dishonestly to promote that firm. Damned lie. Do not own or control one share in Graphic (rather wish I did – could).'[20]

All these factors complicated a situation that has been perpetuated in legend as a continuing 'personality clash' with Hector Charlesworth. The major contributing factor to Deacon's dismissal, however, was almost certainly his own personality and success in creating the community of readers and writers in Canada that he had dreamed of from the start. His ambitions were, ultimately, too individualistic to be accommodated within the structure of *Saturday Night*. His weekly 'The Book Shelf,' his 'Saved from the Waste-Basket,' and especially the literary sections which he considered uniquely his own, had fulfilled the ambition he had voiced to John Garvin in 1921. He had transmitted literary enthusiasm; he had been a very special kind of critic, announcing Canadian writers to Canadian readers; he had made a place for himself in the Canadian movement; and he had fostered Canadian writing in every possible way, certainly to the point of being told by Charlesworth that he was showing 'too much partiality for Canadian writers.'[21] He dreamed of making the literary sections into monthlies and, eventually, into an independent literary magazine.

Under pressure from Miss Sutton, Hector Charlesworth finally ordered Deacon to cut off all his outside literary connections. In the fall of 1927 he ordered Deacon to drop the 'Saved from the Waste-Basket' column; and in January 1928 his letter to Deacon was both peremptory and ominous:

Your review of 'Lawrence and the Arabs' in this week's issue is at least three times too long. I have repeatedly spoken to you as to the policy of *Saturday Night* in this matter; which is to publish as many reviews as possible of from half to two thirds of a column long, and embracing as wide a field of interest as possible.

Please understand me, once and for all. I wish the book section to contain, during ordinary conditions of space such as have been allotted to you of late, at least six reviews of which two should be of the best current fiction. A review of a column and a half is to be the outside limit for a book of exceptional moment...

I must ask you to regard these orders as final, otherwise you will compel me, much against my will, to consider a change in the direction of the department.[22]

The literary section of 17 March 1928 was Deacon's last, and 'The Book Shelf' of 7 April contained his final reviewing for *Saturday Night*. He left 'under pressure' the next week. He was replaced by Miss Sutton's nephew, Horace Sutton, a young man of twenty-three or twenty-four, who was already known to readers as 'Hal Frank' of the joke column, and who had been 'groomed to take over.' Deacon describes himself as 'dispensed with to the greater glory of God, and fatter profits – as dropping me really means a considerable saving.'[23] His answers to many letters of shock and commiseration from friends in the literary community that he had laboured prodigiously to activate are rueful, but not bitter: 'Life from Christmas till I left SN was difficult and strenuous. To see everyone I had to see on the work, and to do the work itself, kept me toiling. You see, I was doing my utmost to jump every hurdle placed in my way. Perhaps if I had had more sense, I would have taken things more coolly and spent my time looking for another job, instead of trying to dodge the inevitable.'[24]

Sir Charles G.D. Roberts's quick letter of commiseration obviously stung Deacon a little, however, for his reply is both sharp and firm: 'I am not quite as helpless, nor my prospects quite as hopeless, as is thought in certain quarters. I admit readily I am no millionaire, and I have to re-establish myself; but that, I think, is within the bounds of possibility.'[25]

His response was in part, of course, his defence against a humiliating dismissal. It was also, however, his typical and temperamental reaction to a new challenge. In the spring of 1928 he was in a far different situation, both personally and professionally, from the precarious and almost desperate urgency of his leaving Winnipeg, the practice of law, and the scandal of divorce to gamble on a personal and literary life in Toronto. Now he had a home and family, six years of successful literary journalism behind him, four books and a whole host of correspondents, all of whom wished him well and some of whom were also ready and able to make useful professional connections for him. With their help and encouragement, his energy fuelled by this professional crisis, he immediately began to develop plans for his own cross-Canada book review syndicate.

CHAPTER FOUR

A Community of Letters 1: 1920-9

IN 1922 BILL AND SALLY DEACON had set up housekeeping in Toronto in rooms on Ontario Street, moving in 1923 to Aberdeen Street, where their son Bill was born. In 1924 they bought their first home at 36 Dilworth Crescent in Leaside, at that time still outside the city limits. Deirdre was born in 1925 and Mary in 1926. In 1925, for $400 in easy instalments, they also acquired a piece of land at Bobcaygeon, in the Kawartha Lakes district near Peterborough, a part of the summer colony that included the Pratts and the Phelps. By 1928 Deacon had built a cabin there.

From his start on *Saturday Night* at $35 a week, Deacon had risen to $65 a week by the time he was dismissed. He also added a few hundred dollars a year to his income through the constant freelancing to which Miss Sutton of *Saturday Night* had objected and through his books. His first paid articles had brought him one cent a word; when Emily Murphy told him of getting 10 cents a word he considered such a fee 'riches beyond the dreams of avarice.'[1] Deacon always was and remained a good, though constantly anxious, money-manager and Sally was a splendid support in this as in every other facet of their lives. His achievements, always on a low or at best moderate salary, are impressive, especially since in the early years, until his former wife, Gladys, remarried in 1926, he was also paying towards her support. Christmas 1924, the first Christmas in their Dilworth Crescent house, was a time of special celebration, with enough money to pay the interest on the mortgage and a little of the principal, and to ensure his life for $5,000. *The New York Evening Post* had raised his rate to two cents a word and Dr Clifford Smyth of *The International Book Review*, a *Reader's Digest* affiliate, had bought five pieces and asked for more.[2] Late in life when he looked back at his financing of domestic affairs he gave credit to the training he got in the law office in Dauphin, where he had to engage in the grim work of foreclosing mortgages and of organizing and budgeting the meagre resources of many clients towards payment of their debts.

Deacon marvelled at the birth of his and Sally's children. He was thirty-three when Billy was born and considered himself old for fatherhood. He was also much ahead of his day in deciding to be with Sally and to assist the midwife at the birth. To him all three were the brightest and most brilliant of children – from babyhood he designated Billy an engineer and Deirdre a writer. Mary seems to have asserted her individuality from the beginning and was not dedicated by her father for any particular calling (in fact, she became a nurse, as Sally had been). From the beginning he invested a great weight of dream, desire, and ambition in them by the very force of his love and the conviction, partly developed from his theosophical beliefs, that theirs were high callings and special destinies. After Mary's birth he wrote to Burton Kurth, his old Winnipeg friend, a summary of his family situation that rings with happiness:

The silvery lining though, is their silvery laughter, and their love is golden. I never dreamed that babies would really love their parents – actively, positively – but these have taught me and I bask in the fond regard of a whole family, of which it gives me smug pride to be the stay and head. Yes, Sarah lets me be the Captain. She's merely the pilot 'o'er life's billers'; and you bet that I never give the helm a twist without getting her approval. God alone knows how much good sense that woman has. Of course I'm in love with her; but even if I were not it would pay me to take her into partnership. Plain fact is, old dear, that we're comfortably fixed down here – not rich, but distinctly beyond want. Besides I am no longer worried about losing my job. I have enough prestige now so I could get another job if I needed one, and to be freed of that hunger-fear that I lived with for more years that I like to remember takes away a greater burden than I can describe. We're not rich but we are on Easy Street in a modest way: the corner is distinctly turned, and things get a little smoother every month. I am amazed at the contrast between my financial position now and less than four years ago when we landed here practically penniless, with no asset but a desire to write.[3]

His time with his family was of necessity minimal, for he quickly developed a gruelling work schedule that he followed until his retirement from *The Globe and Mail* in 1960. He read works for review and wrote his own pieces until two in the morning most days of the week and quite often he was on the very edge of nervous exhaustion from overwork. Sally's solid presence always sustained him, however; she believed in his 'mission' for Canadian literature at least as strongly as he did himself, and his health never completely gave way as it had in 1918 after the ordeal of Bar examinations and the rising tensions of his marriage to Gladys. In addition to his obligatory professional work, Deacon was an inveterate joiner of clubs and, in the twenties, clubs proliferated in Toronto. There was first of all, of course, the Canadian Authors' Association; he was flattered to be elected to the Toronto Arts and Letters Club in 1923 and in 1925 to the International PEN Club (International Association of Poets, Playwrights, Editors, Essayists, and Novelists), whose president at the time was John Galsworthy. This latter seemed an enormous and unwarranted honour to him and he joked with friends about being unmasked as a fraud and expelled.[4] He was active in the Canadian Literature Club and the Whitman Fellowship, both Toronto groups, and on the Council of the Poetry Society of Canada with Pelham Edgar and Raymond Knister. He began to be known as a public speaker and though he always insisted that he had no speaking talent, he addressed such groups as Women's Canadian Clubs, local branches of the Authors' Association, and undergraduates at Victoria College, the School of Journalism, and the University of Western Ontario. Furthermore he earned the devotion of out-of-town groups by his willingness to help them find other speakers.[5]

In addition to these professional and social commitments, Deacon steadily wrote letters to scores of people, sometimes as many as ten a day. The correspondence collection which from the start he had planned to collect and which, with his copyrights, he seriously referred to as his 'old-age insurance,' proliferated. Writing letters, the kind of letters that made very disparate correspondents take up their pens to answer, was his avocation and relaxation. His correspondents covered a vast spectrum of age and occupation: among them were his mother and old friends from his youth, Thomas Henry (Josh) Billings, a Congregational minister in the United States, and Matt Hayes of Buffalo; his sponsors in literature from the Winnipeg days, Judge Emily Murphy, Arthur Phelps, and W.T. Allison; close friends from his and Gladys's Winnipeg years and their involvement with the Theosophical Society; many established and aspiring professional writers such as Charles G.D. Roberts, Mazo de la Roche, Laura Goodman Salverson, Wilson MacDonald, Tom MacInnes, Francis

Dickie, Raymond Knister; even more aspiring amateur writers; journalists from all over Canada – Laura Carten of Halifax, Evelyn Tufts of Wolfville, Ernest Harrold of Ottawa, Austin Bothwell of Regina, and Victor Lauriston of Chatham; publishers Hugh Eayrs, Lorne Pierce, and Frank Appleton; teachers and historians of Canadian literature – Archibald MacMechan of Dalhousie, and J.D. Logan and Vernon Rhodenizer of Acadia; and scores of readers who were intrigued by Deacon's reviewing, by the happy gossip of his 'Saved from the Waste-Basket' columns and by the warm feeling of community which he achieved and fostered in the book pages of *Saturday Night*.

Many of these correspondences would make monographs in themselves; certainly this is true of the letters back and forth between Emily Murphy and Deacon, from 1921 until her death in 1933. They met because he admired her work, had written of it in *The Manitoba Free Press*, and had heard her speak in Winnipeg on the need for public consciousness of Canadian literature. At that time Emily Murphy was already a judge in Edmonton, a power in the Canadian Women's Press Club, and well known for her writings, especially for *The Impressions of Janey Canuck Abroad* (1901) and *Janey Canuck in the West* (1910). She was already the prime mover in the long-drawn-out and notorious *Persons* case in which she, Nellie McClung, Irene Parlby, Henrietta Muir Edwards, and Louise McKinney organized Canadian women in support of legal action to clear the way for women to be appointed to the Bench and to other senior posts in the land, particularly the Senate. The case was lost before the Supreme Court of Canada but in an appeal, the Privy Council of Westminster reversed that decision. Emily Murphy was one of the most famous, respected, and dynamic public women in Canada in her day. Her affection for Deacon and her faith in his powers were sparked on their first meeting and never faltered. He was honestly astonished by her regard and he certainly reciprocated it warmly and with complete trust, though her belief that he could have had a great legal career as a court pleader he called her 'one delusion.'

He called her his 'Mother in the Craft,' and corresponded with her enthusiastically over a great range of topics: their common fervent nationalism, their writers' professional concerns, and also writers' gossip, Emily Murphy's political activities and her ambition to be a senator (thwarted, finally, by Mackenzie King's appointment of Cairine Wilson in 1928), her experiences on the bench, sometimes hilarious and often tragic, Deacon's growing family's progress and setbacks, and his combination of love, pride, ambition, and anxiety on their behalf. From a brief formality in their salutations to each other at the start they speedily progressed to 'My Dear William' and 'Dearest Janey' and Emily Murphy particularly enjoyed signing off as 'your affectionate old pal' or 'your old Bogey.' Their letters are unique in the whole of the collection for their complete and confiding candour on matters both public and personal:

11011-88th Ave.
Edmonton.
July 22/22.

My dear Bill Deacon:

And so you thought you'd run away from the West and never say a word! Queer boy, you are William, and past finding out. I am almost offended at you.

It was Grace E. Kennedy who told me about you, and what you were up to. She also told me that she was running 'The Study in Nom-de-Plumage' [his article on Emily Murphy] or what ever you called it, in *The National Review*. Of course, I'm preening that plumage in great style because of it, but they'll never believe you lad; everyone knows nothing good could come out of Alberta. It wouldn't be reasonable to expect such a miracle. Never mind, we'll try and fool them anyway.

I am going to be in Toronto about the first week in November and will hope to see you then.

We have had a lot of literary lights lately – E. Cora Hind (ahem!) Mrs Macbeth of Ottawa etc. Miss Laut is expected daily and also Lady Byng. I hope they will keep on coming. I get the male magistrate to take my work; put on my finest feathers, and foregather with the others on the terrace at the Macdonald Hotel where we eat chicken and tomato sandwiches, with huge slabs of ice cream (lots of fruit in them) and munch the most delectable little cakes. You can't imagine what fun it is.

I am to have an Eskimo woman in court to-morrow. She is supposed to be insane *because she beat her husband*. Now, what do you think about that? One of the Mounted Police, and a half-breed woman brought her in from someplace in the Arctic Ocean. She looks quite amiable though, and understands what you say in English. She has 8 or 10 lines tattooed on her chin – they run from her lip downward. The sergeant told me those were *her marriage lines*, and that if her husband should die, a line is run across them to show her widowhood. Paddy Doyle, up at Fort MacPherson, sent her down. He is the Dr there, and a fine Irish boy. I met him at Fort Vermilion when he was bringing the Eskimo murderers in for trial with La Nauze.

Goodbye, William. Write and tell me how it fares with you, and what you hope to do.

Always your old Bogey,
Janey Canuck.[6]

Sometimes her letters to Deacon provided a release for her from the emotional burden of tragic responsibilities as a police magistrate:

August 14, 1924 - The Police Court, Edmonton.
My dear William
I am enclosing you a snap taken in my garden on Sunday – under my own vine and birch tree. It doesn't show that 'nifty roll,' the Star speaks of, and which you declare to be an actuality.

That is all right William – just an outward and visible sign of an inward and spiritual pliability – Every P.M. who is any good should lie easy to both sides, (with just a tilt, you understand towards the Police).

I was down at the Provincial Jail to-day and the Superintendent Blythe and the Deputy Minister of Public Works were with me. I was making a report on conditions at the jail for the Social Service Council of Canada.

In the death cell, old Picarello had drawn a picture of the hangman on the wall – 'a downcast hangman who has no job' he said, but the hangman got the job alright. It must have been a grim satisfaction to that official as he bound 'Pic' up to know that he had 'Finis' up his sleeve.

At any rate, as I saw this crude attempt at authorship, it seemed that Pic reached back from outer darkness and appeared to be a very human fellow after all. There was a friend of mine who wrote a book called 'Pens and Pirates,' and he knows the ropes, if not from a mariner's standpoint, at least from that of the literary man. May he never know the hangman's !!!!!!

The Warden told me that he never expected to be executed (I mean Picarello) till that very last moment. When the Warden entered his cell, he fainted – it was a couple of hours before daylight – for he knew the hangman was right there.

The Warden tells me that the death watch is changed every four hours because the official must never take his eyes off the condemned man. If left longer the watchman's eyes get heavy and he falls asleep. Don't you think this is almost as bad as execution – to be observed for every instant? This alone, might drive a man to murder. There's a story here alright. Maybe, I'll introduce it in my book. I haven't written anything at it since last spring, being very busy and unduly inclined to festive occasions.

Superintendent Wm Blythe was born on the jail farm over 50 years ago when it was the headquarters of the Mounted Police. He was a bugler in their band, as a boy and lately was appointed the Superintendent. Yet, there are people who think this country is about 15 years old. He is a lusty, likeable fellow and has a wife who makes a wonderful dinner. Our waiter who came and stood at the dining room door with a tray upon which madam laid the dishes from the table, was a gentleman convicted for a breach of the new liquor act in Alberta, but I pretended I didn't see.

In one of the cells I talked with a man who is to die on August 30th for killing his child in a fit of rage. He wasn't a murderer to me, and I don't think he is either. I have written the Minister of Justice (but no one knows not even the prisoner) saying this should be culpable homicide under 261 of the Code, and that the sentence should be commuted to life imprisonment.

He and his wife were lovers as boy and girl and lived on adjoining farms in the States. He came here 11 years ago, and went to an arid district. In all that time, he never had a crop and I think his nerves broke under the strain, and so he destroyed what he had been trying to protect. It must be so for he is loved by his relatives, and even by his neighbours.

I didn't cry – only the men with me. It would be foolish to bid him be strong and then be weak myself. And I told him too, about all the strong young men alive to-day who would die before him – in the next 6 weeks, and of what Sir Walter Scott said,

'Come he slow, or come he fast,/It is but death that comes at last.'

He is quite a fine looking man but his hair has turned white this last month or so, and his hands were clammy as I held them in mine.

I told the Hon. the Minister of Health, at Ottawa, that I have sent two people to the Asylum because they 'waited for the rain' but that city folk could not comprehend this tragedy. I asked him to try hard to grasp it. I feel sure this is just another case, as exemplified in a man.

There are two women in the Fort awaiting trial for murder, but I could not stand any more. One is watched all the time by the girl convicts, because she has attempted suicide by hanging on two occasions, and nearly succeeded.

Do you remember those lines in *Eugene Aram*:

'A thousand times I groaned,/The dead had groaned but twice.'

Don't show this to Sarah, it would sadden her. I don't know why God lets me look into hearts like these. Maybe, He knows I needed to keep my balance true. I often feel it would otherwise be quite easy to fly without even a propellor. It must be the altitude here that causes this.

Always affectionately,
Janey Canuck[7]

Deacon's and Emily Murphy's faith in Canada and belief in the necessity for fostering the talents of Canadian writers were equally shared. When *The Canadian Bookman* became the official journal of the Canadian Authors' Association, Emily Murphy wrote with delight: 'Isn't it astonishing what a business edge Mr J. Murray Gibbon et al. are putting on literature? The first thing you know we writer folk will be able to borrow money in the bank on our manuscripts.'[8] When she was going through a low period about her writing and comparing herself unfavourably with Robert Stead, Deacon replied with heavy sarcasm:

I can understand an author committing suicide because on comparison his or her work appeared to resemble that of Robert Stead (i.e. without imagination or emotion – perfectly *wooden*) but I think no one on the preferable side of Bedlam would condemn work, much less destroy it, because it differed in tone and style from that of the late president of the Canadian Authors' Ass'n, who, in his inaugural speech as president, said (in effect): 'It is not fair to judge Canadian literature by foreign standards. That is as unfair as judging a Ford by Packard standards. Canadian books are frankly in the Ford class, cheap and serviceable and do not aim at being first class.' In other words – cut from a stock pattern and made 'to sell.' Bob is a decent fellow but he can't write. Better sober up and think a little more reasonably about it.[9]

When he wrote an essay on a 'typical' Canadian, and published it in *The Canadian Nation*, she begged him to send her a copy because she couldn't find one, and challenged him with the questions that still bedevil searchers for the 'Canadian identity':

Who is a Canadian anyway? Can there be a typical Canadian for such an enormous area? Could a man reared in a Province of the North be typical of the more Southerly ones? Is not the *habitant* the oldest Canadian, and the one who has lived closest to the soil? I think you must have had to draw on your imagination and so picture the Canadian whom you would like to consider the type. I'd like to know what fibre you gave him, and how much polish. Did you over-engine him for his beam? You see you had better send me the story. It will be easier than answering all these questions.[10]

When Lorne Pierce gave Deacon a sample Ryerson contract, preparatory to signing him up for the publication of *Pens and Pirates*, Deacon sent it to Emily Murphy for vetting. She, with business and legal acumen, and with experience behind her, responded with a three-page letter of sound contract advice, as pertinent for writers today and as necessary for them to know, as in 1923. Her climax is, as always, a statement of her confidence in his talent and his future:

I'll tell you William, the publishers are keen to get books, so don't be mealy-mouthed with them. Your position, too, on the *Saturday Night* gives them a big advantage over the works of other authors, and they will be glad to have your name on their lists. Stand pat, Boy, and make them come to scratch.

Congratulations on the decree [decree nisi in his divorce, 7 November 1922] and all the other prospects you mentioned. I am happy in your happiness. Good health, congenial work, a woman you love and a helpful ambition – what more can you want? Once, I defined the best in life as 'room to ride.' Perhaps the things I have here mentioned may be included therein.[11]

Deacon replied to her contract strictures somewhat ruefully and defensively for he was not in a strong bargaining position and knew it. Besides he was flattered by Lorne Pierce's attention to himself and his work:

Dr Lorne Pierce, head of Ryersons is a young man about my own age – a Queen's grad, and a *B.I.D.* [BD] and holder of 3 other degrees. Very brilliant, and a shrewd business head. He has just been on a year or so. That man Edward Moore whom they had before was no good. Though they were the oldest and wealthiest of Canadian publishers, they were losing in prestige terribly – Moore *gave away* the copyrights of Lampman, and about all the other worthwhile Canadian writers. Well, they got Pierce to step in as dictator and he is pursuing a much more libral policy (isn't that 'libral' Canadian though?). I think Pierce will do well with the splendid plant at his disposal. He is very broad-minded, and there will be no fool methodist or even christian complexes to resolve. I think I'll be o.k. Anyhow Pierce was the first man to be willing to publish me; everybody else had refused – so what was I to do but accept? He offered 10% royalty which is pretty good for essays by a new writer, I think. Besides they have more money to spend than anybody else and can afford to drop a couple of thousand where some of the other fellows cannot afford to gamble at all.[12]

Deacon could give firm advice too – in fact he loved to do so. When, in 1924, Emily Murphy was stuck in writing a novel about drug use and appealed to him to help her with its finish, his advice was both bracing and sound:

As I have always said, an author must write his book. It is no use for any critic to say what or how he shall write. To follow instructions is fatal: to follow instinct usually is too, but the worthwhile books are produced in that way, what there are of them. And whether by following your hunch you will produce a dud or a masterpiece only the event can teach us in its hour. Write the book and don't talk so much. (Gosh that's funny, to a magistrate and to my literary mother, and to one noted for her discretion – you never tell me a bit of juicy gossip.) Well as I was saying: I don't believe in principle on interfering with the writer. I think you can write. Maybe I'm wrong; and you can't, but I'm sure you'll write your book better in your own way than if people prompted you.

Unhappy endings are often necessary artistically; and generally fatal commercially. I don't see any way to be on both sides of the fence in this matter – nor even on it. Your own suggestion about the relapse, and the husband's triumphant love as the closing note, is the most hopeful thing I can think of. If your central figure dies in agony in the end you will by the same stroke kill your sale. If you end Pollyanna: 'The Lord God who gave you the story will know you for a louse.' What I think you must do – for art's sake no less than propaganda's – is to kill one of the other characters. Let'em die the death, right there on the 'deathless page' where everybody can see: make the agony pretty cruel, lay it on, and make it crawling horrible. Then you can have that sad-but-hopeful note mentioned in your letter for the conclusion of the drama of your principal character. I wish I were of fertile mind, but I can't think of any improvements for your book, beyond the fact that you simply must bump somebody off to show the logical end of the drug career.

With practically no exceptions I feel satisfied that the slow painful method you speak of is the only way to do first class work. I know I can do nothing else. Of course my book reviews go right onto typewriter and away to printer without revision, but it is dangerous except for my ephemeral type of journalism. I can't make time for real writing: and I feel it keenly. It takes a lot of cultivating, putting in drains, weeding, manuring, etc. etc. to raise a really good garden, especially regular crops. I have no sympathy because you write painfully. I congratulate you: I only wish I could rejoin you, and spend hours pumping out a few sentences. You were the one who first taught me that genius is 9/10th laborious work; and I believe it; and so have high hopes for your novel. Grind it out – that's a dear – and remember every minute I'll someday have to appraise it for posterity, and will want to use all my superlatives. It sounds great. Don't forget to be your charming lovable wicked self.[13]

The final note about his own work sounding in that letter recurred more and more as the involvements with his family (including one-year-old Bill's propensity for play between 6 PM and midnight) and the exigencies of his work built up. He could see his dreams of becoming a great essayist receding and this he admitted to Emily

Murphy, though to no one else: 'have not enough time for essays –
Headpieces &c., which I am scared to neglect much longer, because my
hand might forget and I'm so far, so far from the peak there; and I
can't practice daily as I should.'[14] Sometimes, however, there was also
elation in his reports on his writing, as when he reviewed May Sinclair's
Dark Night:

I satisfied my inner longing to write a review perfectly according to the
more-or-less tenuous ideals at the back of my mind. I achieve the technique I
have striven for. I'm knocked silly by it ... I may equal it again sometime – of
course, never when I want to but only when the whimsical gods see fit to
remove the obstacles in my mind and let it come through clean. I tell you all
this, Dear Heart, for the very good reason that you would pass it over
unremarked if I did not. Most readers will even be annoyed at the vague jumble
of ideas, among which I mess without apparently saying anything about the
book. But this is just what I have been trying to do for four years.[15]

To go to a consideration of the substructure of ideas in a book and the
testing of these against his own ideas – in fact to go beyond reviewing to
criticism – was Deacon's goal: 'This may not be art to anybody but me,
but I tell you it's the crown of my art as a reviewer ... Someday ...
someday ... again...'[16]

There was strong mutual support between them in personal as well
as professional matters. He was grateful for the affectionate and
explanatory letter that Emily Murphy had written to his mother about
his personal and professional decisions in leaving Winnipeg and the
law, 'though nothing anyone can say will alter mother's convictions I'm
afraid. The whole thing was most generous of you and I only fear I
have put you to a long night's work.'[17] For his part, when her brother,
Tom Ferguson, died and she was grieving, feeling 'all the sadness of
eternity' as she wrote to him, he quickly countered with the kind of
dynamic, action-directed comfort that Emily Murphy was most likely to
respond to:

Yes, I can imagine how you feel ... nothing worth while. But, do you know, I
look at it in another way? When some one near me has gone down – I mean
near me in thought and aims and affection – then, after the shock of
realization, I always find myself saying: One less soldier for our side, I'll have to
fight for us both now. And, in some instances, where I have thought the world's
loss very great, I have said: All that that man was I will be that the world may not
lose. Of course it is an ideal impossible of full realization; but within certain

limitations it works. You and I may continue that life by being what he was. Carry on, Janey. You are very like him. It will be easy. And it does not matter *where* you are being Tom Ferguson – anywhere on the earth's surface, it's just the same. It is soul quality that counts, release it anywhere and it will find its own way to its appointed goal.[18]

Deacon had no need to save face with Emily Murphy. When he was discouraged about the poor sales of *Pens and Pirates*, 'infinitesimal quantities in spite of heavy advertising,' he could tell her about it honestly: 'I doubt whether it can overcome the combined handicaps of Canadian dislike of the essay form; of its injudicious statements on controversial subjects; and of its general unevenness and immaturity.'[19] He could also set her straight from time to time about literary personalities in perfect security that his words would remain confidential, though she might well decide to take her own kind of decisive action on their message. Wilson MacDonald for instance, was touring the West in 1923, ostensibly to read his poetry, but actually spending at least equal time in complaints about his treatment by Ryerson Press and the Canadian public in general. Deacon wrote to give her his view of MacDonald and his complaining:

MacDonald is a genius. Slowly I have reached the conclusion that he is greater than Lampman – his best work being yet unpublished. But 20 years of discouragements have turned his brain, so that he suffers from in-growing egoism, and is under the perpetual illusion that he is slighted. Poor little man, such a baby! He tells me he is protesting on every platform how badly Ryersons have used him. Dear Janey, it's all myth. They are not businesslike, and Pierce seldom lives up to his agreements as a good businessman would, but they have kept MacDonald on advance royalties for a year – gave him a big cheque last Spring so that he could spend the whole summer at a swell hotel in Muskoka; and no Canadian house ever used any other author half so generously. If Ryersons had been on to the job they would have printed the Miracle Songs early last Summer; but in spite of that MacDonald is quite wrong. His woes are mostly in his own head.[20]

When he exulted over Henry Seidel Canby's acceptance of him as a contributor to *The Saturday Review of Literature*, she exulted as well. Her congratulations on that occasion sum up her constant opinion of his potential as a writer and his quality as a man.

It delights me to see how you are climbing up the hill. Presently, there will be no more fields to conquer. It is really amazing that you have come straight to the top in so short a time. This is where your love of literature, your sense of values, and your steady, faithful work have counted. Best of all, you have kept your soul. Given this, with the will and power to make it manifest through the medium of cold type – nothing, absolutely nothing, can hold you back.[21]

After Emily Murphy's sudden death in 1933, Deacon's affectionate correspondence continued with her daughter, Evelyn. Her whole family wanted him to write the biography of 'Tubbie,' as they had called their mother, and they put off all other inquirers in the hope that he would find time to do it. He wanted to do it as well, and as long as he was writing at all he collected material and planned to write a book-length portrait of Emily Murphy. But even by 1933 he knew the limitations of his time and energy and his plans for future writing were by no means as grandiose as they had been in the twenties. He urged Evelyn Murphy to give permission to the best-qualified applicant to write the biography. In 1945 Byrne Hope Saunders' *Emily Murphy* was published. Meanwhile the memorial Deacon wrote at the time of her death, published in *The Mail and Empire*, remains his final written tribute to one of the staunchest of his friends:

one had to know her to appreciate either her powers or her attractions. All that has been said of her as a judge and as a leader of movements, is true; the facts of her packed life, the list of her achievements, have been scamped in the telling. But the cause of all this bustle and resulting fame was a rich personality. She was a millionaire of the heart and the mind, and really quite poor most of the time in mere money. I think she was the heartiest person I ever knew. The West was the place for her expansive spirit.

After absence, she would greet an old friend with a boom of welcome that reminded me of the salute of a friendly battleship. She was quite short and stout, and walked with the lusty, sea-going roll of a sailor ashore. She was abundantly blessed with a love of humor. Her laughter, which was frequent, was no ladylike titter but something spontaneous and free and full-throated. She was so natural a person that, when she told of a funny incident, she didn't mind laughing at the memory of it. I never knew anyone with so keen a mind, so conscious of artistic values, to laugh so often and so loud. I used to think of her as very like Queen Victoria in appearance, only endowed with a personality resembling Harry Leon Wilson's Ma Pettingill. Oh, how fully and richly life flowed in her!

We must have made a queer pair walking up the streets of Winnipeg, I so tall and thin, she so short and stocky. She would be regaling me with tales of hilarious moments in the police court. If a sidewalk jam separated us, I could still see her over the heads of the crowd, and still hear her; for her voice would strengthen and the tale go on. Then the conclusion of the absurd tangle of events, and 'William, it was dreadful! I was on the Bench and had to keep a straight face!' On the instant she would make up for the decorous repression of the Place of Law, and there would issue peal after peal of the most intoxicating sound I ever heard out of a human throat...

Her books? Why, they are the reflexion of her radiant self. There, too, the woman of Edmonton points the way. For what we Canadian writers need most to learn is to be ourselves; and no writing done in Canada carries a more heady flavor of personality than the essays of Janey Canuck. I will set up her description of the people's representatives falling over the spitoons in the aisles of the Legislative Assembly of Minnesota as the best comic passage in any Canadian book...

A righteous judge has many enemies, and tricky ones; and many male fools would have rejoiced over a woman's incompetence. Her record is without blemish; but I often thought she was wasted hearing theft cases. Her proper place was in the Senate, where her intelligence might have functioned to wider purposes. And fancy Emily Murphy's laughter in the Senate! Perhaps that was what the politicians who kept her out really feared.

...What did she do? Why, she showed the women of Canada, I think, that the time has come for a new sort of pioneering; that the women must take hold of affairs, and use their minds, and make their wills felt, so that we can leave a better world than the man-made one into which we were born. Who will take up her challenge, follow her example? Many will, and do great things. Let them remember Emily Murphy, who blazed that broad trail to a nobler future.[22]

Arthur Phelps of Wesley College (later United College and now the University of Winnipeg) was also one of Deacon's western patrons. 'I've backed three horses, Deacon, Pratt and Grove,' he wrote to Deacon. 'Place 'em in Canadian Literature, will you?'[23] Phelps had left the Methodist ministry, spent some time at Cornell, and had come to Wesley College as a professor of English. He and Ned Pratt were close friends. Phelps was a dynamic force in Winnipeg literary circles, writing for Roberton's book pages in *The Manitoba Free Press*, writing poetry himself, presiding over Wesley College's Literary Club and always on the look-out for what he considered true talent in any writing field. He and Pratt both had 'built-by-hand' summer cottages at Bobcaygeon; when term was over in Winnipeg the Phelps family trekked east to the cottage; when the Deacons moved to Toronto they became members of the summer group. Before they could afford their own place in the little colony, both Phelps and Pratt invited them as holiday guests; later they would rent for a few weeks from either family. All three men had young children; the Pratts and the Phelps each had a daughter, Claire and Ann, and the summer intermingling of the three families included shared domestic as well as social and literary compatibility. Their letters to and fro are as warm with shared play-pens and wood-chopping as with literary gossip.

An enthusiast and, like Deacon, a nationalist, Phelps made many valuable connections for him. He had certainly advised Deacon to go to see B.K. Sandwell for a recommendation and then to apply to Fred Paul for a job on *Saturday Night*. His backing was vindicated by the success of his protégé: 'Rain on the roof and I've been moving about the cottage pipe in mouth turning your stuff over in my mind – letting its flavour give itself to me. It has flavour – I said to my wife – just this, this way - "Say, do you know, Deacon's got something of that thing called style; it's on his pages. It's there".'[24]

He introduced Deacon to Lorne Pierce and was triumphant when Pierce subsequently contracted Deacon for *Pens and Pirates* and *Peter McArthur*. The first summer after Deacon's arrival in Toronto, Phelps took him to the Arts and Letters Club, introduced him round, and put up his name for membership. By the next summer Deacon was delighted to be an elected member of the club. For his part Deacon was always quick to feature Winnipeg news in his 'Saved from the Waste-Basket' column, culling many notes from Phelps's letters for that purpose. They were contemporaries and they wrote as contemporaries and peers; very often they provided mutual support in their aims and opinions; sometimes, because each liked to give good advice and because each tended to think of the other as a willing pupil, they clashed and argued. Their friendship survived in spite of differences because its base was firm respect and because it was renewed by proximity every year when they could, as they said, argue to their hearts' content 'on the way to get the milk.'

Because they were both dynamic and somewhat iconoclastic men and because their friendship had begun out of a common concern for Canadian literature, their correspondence vibrates with energy, Phelps urging Deacon to reconsider his opinion on a certain work, or Deacon requesting ammunition for an anti-censorship crusade. In particular Phelps insisted that the development of Canadian literature should be consistent with high literary standards – he liked what he called 'grapple' in a review (American critics had no 'grapple').

Over Prairie Trails established Frederick Philip Grove as a writer very high in Phelps's esteem:

But man, man, I'm the enthusiast over Grove's *Prairie Trails* – fine prose, limpid, rhythmic – with the lure in provocation of fine writing – the fascination of that suggestion that the secret is an open secret – when it isn't – scientific observation made with the eye of a poet – things intimately and essentially Canadian embedded in the amber of good writing – Man, the thing is a Canadian event! ... I go back and back to it for that gentle refreshment which is the finest sort of intoxication.[25]

Having so committed himself, Phelps unstintingly gave both personal and professional support to Grove. In the midst of the controversy about the banning of *Settlers of the Marsh* he wrote asking Deacon about a possible speaking engagement for Grove in Toronto: 'His six feet two is compelling on a platform. He is intellectually and emotionally stimulating. He reads dramatically. Beside him many of our literary platformists seem pretty insipid. It's a vivid and almost frightening experience to sit under him for an hour.'[26] Deacon did help to arrange a speaking tour, but not until two years later; he then made up for the delay handsomely, however, by writing to Graham Spry, in charge of speakers for the Canadian Club, and to Franklin Davey McDowell of the publicity department of the CNR, requesting for Grove 'a general pass over all lines for two months,' and Grove set forth.

During the tempest over Winnipeg's threatened banning of *Settlers*, Deacon and Phelps kept the mails hot. In Winnipeg, Phelps reported that the ban was total: 'It is under ban because 1. it contains reference to abortion. 2. It deals with a prostitute. Grove himself would justify a partial ban but sees no reason for the complete ban.'[27] Deacon intended 'to raise hell in *Saturday Night*' and wanted all the facts, 'full and plenteous and free *and right*.' In the same letter he told Phelps that the Hudson's Bay Company had stopped circulation of Duncan Campbell Scott's *The Witching of Elspie: A Book of Stories* and 'high officials in Ottawa are doing everything they can underground to kill "The Land of Afternoon" (a satire on Ottawa society by Gilbert Knox, a pseudonym for Madge Macbeth).'[28] Book banning was absolute anathema to Deacon throughout his career, as his reviews, his essay 'Censorship' in *Poteen*, and his later pamphlet, *Here Comes the Censor*, demonstrate: 'you fight with me for the freedom of the press, because – among other considerations – *we're* going to win this battle.'[29] Phelps answered with a barrage of Winnipeg opinions and reviews of which his own, written in a letter to the *Free Press* because Roberton, its literary editor, had turned him down as a reviewer, uses the alleged prurience of Martha Ostenso's *Wild Geese* to draw the fire of the enemy and allow him to praise Grove as he wishes:

The Grove book is intense, uncompromising, ultimately satisfying, – one whole, with beginning, middle and inevitable conclusion. There are at least three profoundly presented characters in it. Nearly every individual mentioned can be seen walking. It is vividly three-dimensional in all its physical aspects. Sincerity and power are the solvents for such faults as it possesses. It is a book to which the artist will return for the repeated joy in good writing and powerful presentation.[30]

In the spring of 1926 Phelps wrote two letters asking Deacon's advice about possibilities for the sales of *Settlers of the Marsh*, which up to then had sold only 1,000 copies, and also about a new publisher for Grove, because Lorne Pierce, timid about the censorship storm, was hesitating over accepting his next novel. 'Can his book be moved at all so that it will help him financially? It's not a too frequent occurrence in Canada that a man serves the apprenticeship to the pen Grove has served ... I can't further boost him too obviously for awhile. The book *is* dedicated to me, you know.'[31] Just at this time Deacon was beginning to place all his publishing hopes for himself and for Canadians in general in Henry C. Miller and the Graphic Press. He quickly persuaded Phelps that Grove should become a Graphic author, took the manuscript for *A Search for America* from Phelps at Bobcaygeon and placed it with Graphic. Then, largely through Phelps, he continued to advise Grove through various crises with Graphic: 'But Grove must not get on his high horse. You tell him that I know my onions, and to follow my instructions to the letter, and he'll be alright. God, he'll lose a year's time and the best publisher in Canada if he doesn't. My instructions to the letter understand.'[32] Though in the long run Deacon's faith in Graphic was misguided, Grove's *A Search for America* appeared under its imprint in 1927.

Deacon and Phelps kept each other both entertained and instructed about the various writers who were on tour. Wilson MacDonald, Phelps reported,

came and saw – He found Winnipeg a hard nut. He wasn't known and the Ryerson Press pamphlet was super-hectic – I won't go so far as to say that to distribute the pamphlet was like pushing sub-mediocrity by super-hectic boosting. That sort of thing is often done, I believe. But MacDonald convinced a few of us that he is far from sub-mediocrity – and that puts him in the front rank of Canadians does it not?!! – But I'd better stop – I'm feeling altogether too smart. The folk who heard MacDonald – we had about 150 in Science Theatre A – felt that MacDonald is a contributor to the sum total that matters.[33]

As usual MacDonald spent a great deal of time complaining about the shabby treatment he had received from Ryerson Press, and Deacon, though he likened trying to help MacDonald to 'trying to push a ton weight uphill,' replied with an explanation of Wilson's hypersensitivity that was all too often necessary but, in his opinion, justified nonetheless, because 'he's the genius of the bunch.'

Two years later Phelps was anticipating Charles G.D. Roberts's visit to Winnipeg: 'I think we're going to give him [Roberts] a big show – our English Club is handling it – more appropriate methinks than the Presbyterian Ladies Aid who handled Carman and kept him hidden *behind* their skirts.'[34] Deacon wrote about the quality of Roberts's speeches – 'he can give you the real dope if he wants to. Some of your little gatherings will show more of the man's quality than his public lecture,' and urged a drink before speaking – 'he is fond of almost anything – but particularly old Scotch and mellow wines.'[35] Phelps assured him that a 'restorative' would be ready and after the occasion reported enthusiastically on Roberts's literary wisdom and affability.

In August 1925, Phelps and Pratt planned a gala writers' gathering at Bobcaygeon and made Deacon their agent: 'You come up for a weekend (come up yourself anyway if you can; we'd love you to see this finished house) and bring Roberts, MacDonald and Carman – *visualize it*: *Roberts, Carman, MacDonald, MacInnes, Pratt* and you and I sitting down to breakfast here on the veranda, and adjourning afterwards to the lawn or living room. It would be a news items for the nation.'[36] At the time, Tom MacInnes, who had been living with the Deacons on Dilworth Crescent because he was without funds, was already at Bobcaygeon with Phelps. Deacon tried to round up the rest of the men, but without much hope of success. Furthermore, the Deacons had already had their holiday in the Pratts' cottage and he did not want to leave Sally. The great gathering did not take place.

The friendship between Deacon and Phelps hit its greatest snag when Phelps sent an unsolicited review of Deacon's *Poteen* to him: 'Use this (1) as the regular review in the regular way (2) as a W.P.B. [Saved from the Waste-Basket] splurge (3) don't use it at all. It's my review for what it's worth. I don't think it's too bad! I believe it will bring readers to the book!'[37] Phelps admired writers, was impressed by them, and was always prepared to encourage them – in his own way. He was a gifted teacher, but essentially he was not a writer himself and, whatever the measure of his success, Deacon was all day and every day a hard-working writer. Obviously Phelps had no conception of Deacon's extreme vulnerability about his own work; his review of *Poteen* was injudicious, to say the least, in that he discussed everything he considered weak about the book first, especially the debts he saw in it to American writers and attitudes, and left his considerable critical approval to the end of the article:

I believe Mr Deacon calls his book a 'hash' book and it is true that it surprises with variety. But the comment is too modest. Amid what Mr Deacon himself and some of his readers may consider the somewhat dubious elements of its content is happily incorporated the vigour and feeling that engenders on the thirty side of fifty and the terseness and force that is rooted in experience and sincerity. No book like it has been produced in Canada. It is a presentation of Canada 'on the make.' Where the tendency of our books has been, perhaps unduly, towards careful mediocrity, *Poteen*'s apparent carelessness, sharp set independence, and occasional gayety is salutary and delightful.[38]

The correspondence that ensued is both an amusing model of restrained intensity on both sides and a great credit to both men. Deacon wrote:

I must say I admire and like your grim determination to make Poteen a Phelps book instead of a Deacon book. You didn't do it; but you made more of an impression than I like to acknowledge – for it was weakness on my part. But you did it because it was to you the finest way to serve me; and while I imagine we shall both be wary of similar snags in the future, I credit you with several marks for your stiff fight against me here. I salute the spirit!

You may be able to get this review printed in the Forum. Fred Jacob and Barker Fairley would, I think, seize on it quickly and besides it would give Fred some great suggestions for the walloping he will give me in the Mail and Empire. It will in fact save him from reading the book.[39]

Phelps closed the touchy subject with friendly grace.

Of course your section and sections is and are 'going.' Though, as you know, I beautifully, thoroughly, and mad as a Hatter, disagree with you betimes. But you still retain that power to make the sentences clang. Keep that and your head, – for heaven's sakes don't disrespect your head – and I cling to my conviction of that day when I went out to the 'island' at Bob. with the sheaf of your MS. under my arm.[40]

With W.T. Allison of the University of Manitoba, another patron of his Winnipeg days, Deacon corresponded far less intimately than with Phelps, but with equal enthusiasm for Canadian literature. Allison, who wrote for *The Winnipeg Tribune* and a group of other western newpapers under the pen-name 'Ivanhoe,' was a valued member of his guest reviewers' corps. Their correspondence was purely literary – thanks and praise for an Allison review of Pratt's *The Witches Brew*: 'Pratt is delighted with your praise, he phoned me about the review. He seriously thought you did him too much honor'; suggestions for new markets for Allison's work: 'Why don't you write for Willison's? They pay 1½¢ and are glad to get representative Canadian writers';[41] encouragement for the hope of a solidly Canadian publishing house in Winnipeg (this at the height of enthusiasm for Graphic Press); and always, Deacon's reassurances that he has not become submerged in Toronto's literary establishment or forgotten his debt to Winnipeg friends:

Yes, I know what I owe to the West. I always feel I belong to you fellows out there – until I meet some of them who insist on thinking of me as a Torontonian. Think of me please as a missionary to the East, especially to Pelham [Edgar]. The old boy, who knew me seventeen years without remembering my name or face began to cultivate me two years ago. I hardly knew what to make of it. Now I think he wants me to call him by his first name. Anyhow he's facing outwards more than he did; and this damned Balliol influence is counting for less here every year. When I am with lawyers I think of myself as a writer and when with writers – sometimes – I think of myself as a lawyer. In the east I am western, in the west most of 'em treat me and make me feel like old Daddy Ontaria. Thanks for recognizing the blizzard streak I acquired in Dauphin and Winnipeg during the 12 years that count.[42]

At the end of the decade, as a kind of summation of all their successes in expanding the consciousness of Canadian literature among the public and developing a sense of community among the writers, Deacon wrote Allison a generous tribute which he certainly would have appreciated getting himself:

At the beginning of Canadian Book Week, may I, without impertinence, congratulate you, and as a Canadian author thank you, as critic and missionary, for the noble and unselfish work you have carried on for so many years through your various papers in the West? I appreciate your patience and kindliness to emergent authors; and perhaps as I am a critic myself I know better than others the labor and worry this has often cost you ... Canadian literature is producing good ripe fruit now, with promise of better to follow. As these fine novels, poems, histories come in profusion (compared to earlier years) I would like you to know that I believe no man has done as much as you to produce these results ... I can only hope you are satisfied at realizing how successful your literary life has been, and of what importance to Canada.[43]

Allison responded to 'just about the handsomest missive that I have ever received' with the rueful account of his efforts to support – and failure to satisfy – F.P. Grove. Deacon concurred: 'If we collaborated to make a joint article "What Critics Think of Grove" we'd have so many aspiring collaborators that the resulting piece would be the size of the phone book.'[44]

Deacon's western correspondents included old friends as well as these men with whom he had speedily moved from protégé to peer. In particular he wrote to Burton Kurth without his guard up, with confidence in being appreciated and understood and sometimes with a touching faith in the fulfilment of his dreams: 'Time was when I had to have you as reader or listener because you were the only audience I had. Now there are one or two others who can substitute for you if necessary.'[45] Lorne Pierce had at first given Deacon fulsome encouragement for all his projected works and in his letters to Kurth, Deacon's imagination projected a glorious and secure writing future:

he sent for me, and we have mapped out my activities for the next two or three years, and in a general way I am married to Ryerson's for life if I want. I intend to stay here for 10 years for the education – books and learning to write, both – and then retire and write books for nine years, and after that I don't care what happens. I'll have had my chance anyway. Pierce writes me a letter almost every time a Saturday Night appears saying how he likes the stuff. It does me good to know that a man like that is watching every comma – makes me careful.[46]

He follows with a long list of projected books for the twenties, including the biographies of Emily Murphy and Tom MacInnes which forever remained unwritten.

After that there are no plans, but Pierce says he is ready to take my products and I want to take a year to do another book of leisurely essays like 'Pens and Pirates' and alternate one of these with one book of criticism until the ten years are up, when at 42 I shall retire and write first a novel – the one started in your shack, by the way. And then I shall loaf a whole year, and put in seven more years writing just as hard as I can. I will then be 51. What happens after that I don't care. I figure my royalties will keep me. I will have 15 or 16 books out, and can live modestly on the proceeds, study the great masters of prose and try to leave two or three books that will go down like Thoreau's. By this time there will be no new ideas. I shall have reached mental equilibrium, and my whole effort will be technical...

So your dream – which was more yours than mine – is starting to come true. You gave me faith Old Boy to keep trying. I wish to heaven now I had written twice as much in Winnipeg. But that will come in time. My prestige here will help sell the earlier books and the earlier books will sell the later ones. So I do not worry about Pierce dying as I did at first. If he lives to launch me I trust to the momentum to keep me going ... My effort will be to leave a certain model for the essay that will be the perfect embodiment of symmetry, balance and concision.[47]

All his life Deacon was a compulsive planner. Here, still new in Toronto and at *Saturday Night,* he was in the first flush of optimism about his future as a writer. Kurth understood and, in fact, invited and applauded the naïvely vainglorious tone. He had been and remained a leader of the cheering section for Deacon, honoured to be asked to join his team of reviewers for *Saturday Night,* thoughtfully reporting on each of Deacon's books as it came out – and he was, perhaps, the first to recognize that Deacon's prime talents lay in literary journalism and in letter-writing, not in the essay-writing so dear to his heart. When Kurth reported that Arthur Phelps believed that Deacon would indeed find success, but in the United States, Deacon confided that his efforts for American periodicals were 'to impress my fellow-countrymen ... This country will be big enough to hold me for this incarnation.'

I want to be a creative artist as well as critic; and I read so much and meet so many people that I find I must hive up – be as much of a hermit as I can – if I am to invite my (own) soul and produce the literature I desire. At first it was necessary that I get to know these birds, and that I get known. That is all over. Now I must be the recluse in what time is private; and I am cutting out meetings, ditching correspondence, and in every way trying to build up a little solitude in which I may be calm and leisured and *productive.*[48]

Deacon was also very frank with Burton Kurth about his enormous satisfaction in what he was doing:

Oh God! I'm stuffed every week with information, gossip and all that goes to make the Man of Letters. The training I am getting here is beyond anyone's power to evaluate. And I am happy Burt, in my work and my home. Happy as I never dreamed I should be. And I am not looking beyond my work and my home. At first, and for long I fretted because I had no companionship like yours; but I've got over that, and avoid rather than seek intimate friends...[49]

Deacon cherished the friends who were anchors to his past and his letters reciprocate in full measure the affection and support they gave to him. At the same time the circle of his correspondents was expanding, literally by every mail, as letters poured in from readers and writers. Writers form by far the largest category of these correspondents – aspiring, failed, or established, but all engaged in committing words to paper and all dreaming of some measure of success. As 'Candide' in *Saturday Night*, as editor of 'Saved from the Waste-Basket,' Deacon provided a public forum for their community of interest with other writers and with the whole world of literature. When they wrote to him, it soon became evident to them that he was willing to spend time and energy providing a private relationship as well.

Tom MacInnes, for instance, became one of Deacon's 'causes.' MacInnes was fifty-four when he first wrote to Deacon in 1921 after an article praising his work had appeared in *The Manitoba Free Press*. MacInnes had been an adventurer, journalist, and businessman in China for many years. The peak of his career there had been the organizing and setting up of a street railway system in Canton. His early letters to Deacon from China are full of stories of spies, smuggling, and revolutionary intrigue, the most horrendous a pair of postcards showing a group of bandits, bound and ready for execution and then, in the next postcard, executed, heads lying in the dust. When MacInnes came back to Canada in the early twenties he was disgruntled because he was not esteemed either as a writer or as an international businessman. He was frustrated beyond measure, for instance, by having suggested a British book exhibit for the Empire Conference in 1926 and then having been passed over in favour of Robert Stead as the man to take it overseas.

MacInnes suffered from ill health complicated by a touchy nature, quick to take offense, but he was tirelessly sustained by his wife and a few friends like Deacon who assembled and extended to him all the support they could muster, including giving him bed and board for weeks at a time. Lorne Pierce agreed to a MacInnes volume for the

Makers series and Deacon planned to write it; though Pierce lost interest in the volume and Deacon lost interest in writing for Pierce, he always continued to plan a book on MacInnes. For a time in the twenties he voluntarily took over the management of MacInnes's literary affairs. At some time in his life MacInnes may have been capable of reciprocal friendship, but now, disgruntled and sick, he was not. There was a stubborn loyalty in Deacon's efforts on his behalf, however, even although MacInnes testily refused to be represented in the Makers series:

I certainly have no wish now to be claimed with makers of Canadian Literature. What I have produced is world literature or else it is not worth preserving. You have done everything well for me but I am done with Canada. Perhaps I may be able to survive if I take on a line of fake oil and mine shares to sell Canadians – it is a line of activity highly honored by them – but for all the honor of it I may not care to survive. What I have written to Pierce I have written in the heat of the moment – but as it is all true . To hell with any second thoughts as to its policy. I mail it now – with this.[50]

The letter to Pierce that he speaks of is a lengthy recapitulation of the various stages in the Empire Conference controversy, climaxing with his avowed abdication of all interest in the Canadian literary scene: 'Canada has practically shoved me off the earth as far as it can; and I am now quite indifferent to any contemporary Canadian opinion. No, Doctor: this bird will not sing in that barnyard.'[51]

Wilson MacDonald was of the same ilk. Though Deacon could and did write sharply about him to others, he was tireless in his support and in the hospitality that MacDonald took for granted. Aside from the 'genius' that Deacon seriously ascribed to him, they had a common devotion to theosophy. He and Sally repeatedly fed and housed this demanding man, who was a finicky vegetarian. His propensity for long sessions of parlour magic at the level of playing disappearing tricks with coppers which enchanted little children, could hardly be said to compensate for the bother he caused in their home. When he toured Canada, reading and selling his poems as he was avidly eager to do, Deacon tried, unsuccessfully, to divert him from his notorious, hard-sell methods:

Don't stick around waiting for little third-class engagements. You go as a celebrity: everybody rushes to see the celebrity. Appear; collect your money; and disappear; so leaving the road open to return in a year or two years and repeat the whole thing with bigger crowds, etc. ... Familiarity with a good man does not breed contempt; but it takes away the burning desire to pay $1 to look at him. [52]

MacDonald was intensely jealous of his own place in the 'Star' pantheon of Canadian writers and Deacon's patience was sorely tried when, for instance, MacDonald wrote of having 'it out openly with Roberts last night' and warning him 'that he must have something to say or cease writing.'[53] Deacon's long reply counselled caution and patience. It also contained a considered opinion of Roberts's importance to Canadian literature from which he never wavered:

I was much amused at your report of talk with Roberts. I think we should not forget that our whole generation owes him a considerable debt for his pioneer work. He has done a great deal not only in setting standards but in encouraging Lampman and others, and I do think considerable respect should be shown his seniority. I truly think too that his urbanity has a very timely lesson for us younger men; and I want his visit to be as pleasant as may be.

Whether he is past his usefulness is beside the point. In his time he broke trail, and if younger men are going farther that is but natural and right and should not in any way detract from the respect we show him. I believe it would be unfortunate if you had any breach with him. He is, after all, our guest, as well as the ancient chief; and if his lordship of 45 years must end – as all reigns end – I want his retirement from the throne to be orderly and decent, and without hard feelings anywhere.[54]

Roberts, for his part, was an easier and more gracious friend than MacDonald could ever be. He certainly enjoyed the role of 'the ancient chief,' however, and he was quick, though relatively gentle, in his rebuke to Deacon for what he considered extravagant praise of MacDonald's *Out of the Wilderness*:

Your review of 'Out of the Wilderness' is a very able critique, & *in the main* I am with it. As you know, my admiration for Wilson as a *lyrist* is extreme. I class several of his poems – among them the 'Exit,' 'The Last Portage,' 'In a Wood Clearing,' 'Come Here Nevermore' – with the choicest and most exquisite lyrics in our language. And this I proclaim. But I do *not* find in his work any adequate thought, or knowledge of life; & neither do I find any command of the purely objective in art. Always, in the final analysis, he is purely subjective. This is not a defect; but it is a limitation, *n'est-ce pas?* And it seems to me inherent in his mental make-up. You touch very delicately & understandingly on his occasional lack of clear thinking!...

And just one more query. You say 'it remains to be seen whether he can maintain the supremacy he has won.' Do you mean to imply by that that, in your considered judgment, by this one volume Wilson has achieved the rank of supreme head of Canadian Poetry? If so, I should very seriously question your judgment. This ranking business, among approximate peers, is dangerous.[55]

Because they both were in Toronto and often at Bobcaygeon together, seeing each other socially as families, there is not a bulky correspondence between Pratt and Deacon. What there is has largely to do with cottage matters or the planning of gatherings at Bobcaygeon, though Pratt could and did fulminate on occasion against the editorial practices of Ryerson Press. Both Pierce and Moore, the editor before him, were notorious for changing copy (on one occasion Moore had inserted five new chapters in a book of Robert Stead's) and this exasperated even Pratt's notable good temper:

There must be telepathic affinities between us. I was on the point of writing you when your missive arrived. I have since opened up communications with the President of the Immortals inquiring why procrastination, that human failing, should also be present in the Councils of the Gods. Have not yet had a reply but certain vibrations intimate to me that Juno and Hebe are both plucking at the heart of Jove...

With regards to Moore, since reading your letter, the atmosphere of the cottage has been sulphurous. Sacré bleu! Sapristi, Ciel! Damnation Without Redemption! That fellow would alter the Codex Beza if he happened to get hold of it, on the ground of archaic lettering. I am glad the Authorized Version happened to be complete before he was born and that Hebrew vowel points were constructed before anyone thought of asking the cooperation of E.G.M. Verdammt! ... Did you ever read in cold print of such presumption. Not satisfied with altering Petrarchan Sonnet forms he must unearth the bones of the Sacred Herrick; change constructions, punctuation! He knows as much about style as the second engineer in a Kansas elevator.[56]

On one occasion though, Pratt wrote very seriously to Deacon about his own work. In answer to a request for a poem for the literary section, Pratt sent him the poem, 'Cherries,' which was duly published, and he also wrote him a lengthy discourse on his forthcoming work, 'The Iron Door':

I would like to deal with the Iron Door at some length. You remember in a couple of conversations last spring, once on a walk down to your office, and again at a dinner with Burpee, that I had in mind the construction of a poem different from anything I had ever done. The theme came to me at the time of my mother's death last December. It originated in a dream where my mother, who was a woman of the profoundest faith in the life to come, was standing before a colossal door – the door of Death – and expecting without any fear of denial whatsoever, instant and full admission into the future state where she believed other members of her family had already entered. This was the nucleus of the poem. From there I elaborated it into a general conception of the problem of Immortality, starting with the feeling of despair and apparent inevitability which faces one at a grave-side. That is, from a particular experience, I tried to universalise the idea. In front of the door are gathered a vast multitude and a number of individuals emerge to present their cases to the unseen Warders, or God or the Governor of the Universe whoever he may be, demanding some information of what is going on, the other side. All but one – the last – are drawn from persons I had known in life. The last one, to my mind, sums up the problem, partly biological, partly environmental, of injustice and inequality in the moral order, and she presents the case in its glaring enigma.

The first case is that of the naive simplicity of a child who relies upon a father to unravel the knots. The second is that of a rugged seaman who with a stark sense of justice asks the 'unknown admiral' if the great traditions of the service might be fairly assumed to prevail on the wastes of the winter sea, if such a sea might be assumed to exist. There is no cringing in this attitude whatsoever; he feels he has the right to ask and to demand it. The third – that of my own mother – represents a large number of people who believe implicitly in the essential soundness of the heart of the Universe and who impute to God only the same fair principles which they realise in their own honest natures. The next is a young man who gave up health and prime and life in a futile attempt to save an unknown life when there was not a human eye to stimulate or encourage the sacrifice. Then two more speak, one a searcher after beauty in all its forms in this life who is puzzled that Death should apparently negate the value of the quest; and another a searcher after truth – a Hardyesque type (or Bertrand Russell type) – who meets with disillusion at the end, yet exhibits a noble Stoicism when faced with what looks like extinction. Then comes the last with the most poignant and tragic appeal.

In order to make the psychological contrast as sharp as possible I put in a stanza or rather section describing the desolation of the world at this point – to give edge and relief to what follows. To my mind it would be a cardinal artistic and moral blunder to end it in complete gloom. The setting I think requires the conclusion, but I did not feel, on the other hand, that the requirements would be met by anything like a conventional heaven, harps or angels or such outworn paraphernalia. The only demand I make is that there shall be life and light with continued life effort on the other side. Hence I never see inside the door. I only judge by the reflection on the faces of human beings and by certain sounds which intermittently break through that there are vast stretches beyond. I do not aim at solutions. I only wanted to give an imaginative and emotional interpretation of what I feel myself because I have never done anything which put the same compulsion on me for expression. I do not know if I thoroughly succeeded. I simply wrote as I felt.[57]

Early in his time at *Saturday Night*, Deacon had heard from Francis Dickie of Heriot Bay, BC, a freelance writer-adventurer, much given to misfortune of his own and others' making and, like Tom MacInnes, blessed with an indomitable wife. Dickie wrote everything from novels to Sunday school stories and was published in a myriad of small magazines and papers in Canada and the United States, though he never made more than enough for bare subsistence. He was intermittently ill with tuberculosis and had built himself a wilderness retreat at Heriot Bay. When that burned down in 1925 and he and his wife lost everything, they took off for Paris in search of both health and an international literary milieu. Deacon hired him at one cent a word for 650 words, to write a Paris notebook for the new literary supplement, anxiously instructing him to make it chatty, informative – and circumspect. On occasion, he also acted as an informal agent for Dickie, dealing with straying manuscripts and reluctant publishers. In response Dickie kept him up-to-date with his continental adventures: a dinner with Scott Fitzgerald or lunch with Frank Harris or Somerset Maugham as oases in a sad but good-natured saga of ill health and hard times. This is one of the correspondences that could well be printed as an independent monograph. Deacon saluted Dickie as 'the unluckiest man since Jesus Christ' because though his adventures were many, his misadventures were even more. But he was, par excellence, a vagabond writer and whether he wrote grumpily of a strayed manuscript or elatedly of finding unknown, small, and delicious wine harvests at five francs a bottle, his letters brought a racy, exotic, international dimension to Deacon's life and correspondence:

I think I told you in my last letter about going to visit Somerset Maugham. He is one of the few authors who have not proved a disappointment. I had tea the other day with Frank Harris. And I was the guest of Gracie Fields the big musical hall artist of London. She was here visiting a very good friend of mine, and we had several trips together, finishing up at Monte Carlo day before yesterday. As for writing I pour out quite a lot that sells to the newspapers and magazines, but for the two worthwhile books that I have written (done in Canada long ago) I as yet cannot find a publisher. They are really good pieces of work, things that I wanted to do. But when one sees the Niagara of books pouring out, it brings realization of how really little it matters. As Maugham says: 'most writers are so busy writing they never have time to live,' and I don't want to be that way.

Life hasn't been very good to me. But recently I have developed a taste for good wines and food (I always had the taste for good food and cigars). Here one can get good wine, very fine vintages even, fairly cheap. And in this region, there are many little vineyards that put out small vintages peculiar to themselves. If one noses around sometimes they make marvellous discoveries. Just recently from near here I found a marvellous little wine. (It all depends on the lay of the vineyard to the sun, the soil etc. which gives the certain flavor). I have drunk up nearly the man's entire crop. He was selling it for five francs a bottle (20¢) so by raising the price an extra franc a bottle, I got it all. This may seem incredible to you. And this same wine, or its equivalent in flavor would cost in Paris about 30 francs a bottle...

Being in France (although I believe it is quite a good custom now even in Canada, or at least in the United States) I manage to find myself an agreeable mistress wherever I go, and keep her on one side of the town and my regular household on the other. One of these days I am going to write a scathing article called 'Why Girls Leave Home' symbolic of course of Canadian artists. The main point of the article will be to point out that while thousands of big companies have made fortunes out of Canada, and both native Canadians and Englishmen and Americans have become multimillionaires out of the Dominion, not one company or individual has ever given an endowment to help Canadian writers, painters or musicians.[58]

Deacon may well have spent a disproportionate amount of time and energy on his more difficult and demanding correspondents as he certainly did on Dickie and MacInnes, but he seemed to find time for all those who approached him. Letters to and from Mazo de la Roche had an unfortunate beginning, when she wrote hoping for a favourable review of *Possession*:

I see by Saturday Night that there is a probability that you will review my novel Possession. Someway, before you read it, I want to tell you that I lived on just such a farm as Grimstone for years, so that I know the life whereof I write. I have tried with all the power that is in me to depict the life on this farm, in that warm belt of Western Ontario, where on a fine day the spray of Niagara is visible. I have tried to reproduce something of the mingling of the old and new world beneath the roof of Grimstone, and to give the feeling of the sensuous fullness of the summer there.

Some of the happiest, and, by far the most tragic, years of my life were spent there, so that I have a sort of passionate sensitiveness about the book that you may understand. I gave two years to the writing of it and wish I could have given more.[59]

Deacon responded with off-putting firmness, on his high horse as an independent reviewer:

In general I very much prefer knowing as little as possible of the author and the history of his book before I commence reading. I like to judge literary work on its own merits – or rather get my impressions without the obstacle of preconceived ideas, for of course to 'judge' contemporary work is foolish. The judgments are so apt to be reversed. In this case I trust your intuition. Doubtless you were right to approach me, though nothing usually makes me quite so hostile as a request for a favourable review – no matter how subtly the appeal may be conveyed.[60]

He did not like the book and said so on his pages. After his enthusiasm for *Jalna*, however, they consolidated their interests into a friendship that lasted until Mazo de la Roche's death. She wrote intimate, charming letters about her travels and her writing to both Deacon and Sally and, of course, for three decades she was involved with him in the Canadian Authors' Association where, in keeping with her long and surpassingly successful career, she played the role of grande dame.

To Laura Goodman Salverson, a beginning writer of the 1920s, Deacon became both friend and mentor. Though he had been an enthusiastic advocate of her first novel, *The Viking Heart*, she did not write to him until after the publication of her second novel, *When Sparrows Fall*, which was based on the life of her father. As he often did in writing to authors, Deacon responded with the kind of analysis of her work that was not possible in a public review and that made him, in her case and in many others', a firm friend:

You seem to be under the delusion that my taste is all for fierce realism, the sordid; whereas I am extremely idealistic, and dote on pleasant books. What I admire most of all is what I call artistic integrity, hence my devotion to the Viking Heart. As I saw it, you achieved a great reality because these things were very real to you, and you wrote of them with passion – a restrained passion, the more powerful in its restraint. For I believe in the law of indirections (my own name for it) by which what is in a writer gets out more effectively often if he tries to hold it back. I think you tried to write V.H. with utter simplicity, and unemotionally; and it came out as intense, throbbing drama. I think that whole book vital with the finest sort of idealism ... If I may presume to give advice, always write out of your own particular knowledge, and from the heart. Do not imitate popular successes – that is if you want to create literature. Finally let me repeat what I have said so often in public, that your Viking Heart marks the beginning of a finer novel in Canadian Literature, and if you never wrote any more your place would be secure.[61]

Laura Salverson despised writing 'to please the servant maids and housewives.' She was intensely proud of her Icelandic heritage of intellectual endeavour, and especially proud of her father and his family's long tradition of writing:

My father, wrote for our weeklies, more years than I have lived. It was what kept his soul alive, in the beastly tussle to earn bread, by way of a trade he had followed merely as parttime in Iceland. Poor old Dad used to teach the three Rs to kids in the isolated places and lived I gather from the proceeds of a little scrap of land, near Mt. Hecla, – well you read the V.H. – : coming to Manitoba minus funds, without voice, one may say, no very robust health & a proud young wife whose 2 children died at sea (coming over) I fancy it rather froze the heart in her. But he lived in spirit because of the Icelander habit of reading and self expression.

My earliest memory is of father 'putting off the slave' i.e. getting into his rusty Prince Albert & grey trousers & very carefully shined boots & clean linen, to sit down to a *Sundays* bit of writing! I wish you could vision the lighting up of his kind, dear face – and the very sincere efforts of all of us to be quiet for papas sake. I never have any trouble to discover what was meant by 'the light that lighteth every man coming into the world.'[62]

Laura Salverson had been in the centre of a small tempest when Winifred Reeve (the writer, 'Onata Watanna,' whom Emily Murphy called O'Nutty Watanna), wrote to *The Canadian Bookman* accusing her of hiring an agent at fifteen per cent of the book's profits, to edit, publicize, and write favourable reviews of *The Viking Heart*. The alleged agent was the journalist, Austin Bothwell, of Regina. Though the small cauldron of gossip was well stirred by the literati, neither the issue nor the accusation was ever really clarified. Meanwhile Deacon's advice to Mrs Salverson was both reassuring and flattering:

Let this be your certificate – if you want one – that I was in no way bought, and my opinions were independently arrived at from reading 'The Viking Heart' and from my previous knowledge of literature. I consider your novel the best Canadian story of 1923; and I have already said so in Saturday Night, in the Literary Review of the New York Evening Post (for March 29, 1924) and in a public address delivered before the Canadian Literature Club, Toronto, January 10, 1924 on Canadian Literary Production of 1923. No one familiar with my writings will ever accuse me of being bribed by you to say so.

Do not worry too much about this. In the long run people are going to judge your book on its merits and quite without reference to Mrs. Reeve's charges.[63]

Laura Salverson's third book, *Lord of the Silver Dragon*, she considered her first 'real book':

it represents five years hard work in research and ancient languages. Until this story I've been sticking to character stuff just to avoid the danger of letting my plot do all the work as is so often the case in the historical romance. Now I hope to be off at last in my own field and if this falls flat I may as well fold up my wings and die for I do not intend to write sex stuff nor to do a series of Viking Hearts. My good friend Austin Bothwell tells me that at last I have done something better than V.H. so perhaps I may still hope. Sometimes I feel like a small David without a slingshot when I come up against my many enemies – mostly they are prepositions. Oh, the hateful little words! How many hours they have tormented me and how many times they have held up the whole show as it were. So you see I need time; but I mean to make good.[64]

With a very few writers Deacon approached the kind of intimate professional and personal friendship that he and Emily Murphy enjoyed. Laura Lee Davidson, a Baltimore teacher who summered in Canada on her island north of Kingston, Annie Charlotte Dalton, a poet from Vancouver, and Evelyn Tufts, a freelance journalist from Wolfville, Nova Scotia, all began life-long friendships through correspondence in the twenties. The fact that Miss Davidson was American and Mrs Dalton British by birth, though she and her husband had been in Vancouver since 1904, was important; both of these women could and did serve as sounding boards for Deacon's intense nationalism and both of them enjoyed answering back. Evelyn Tufts and he had met each other early in the twenties, probably at the Canadian Authors' Association meetings in Ottawa in 1922. She had no high ambitions as a writer, but she was an eager and intelligent reader and connoisseur of books, and she became, under Deacon's tutelage, a lively reviewer for the literary section. Most of all she was a rebel to anything that represented conventional, staid conformity. Her letters are happy, funny, witty, and malicious towards every hint of the stuffy establishment mentality that for her characterized the heads of Acadia University, where her husband was an ornithologist on the faculty. Open-handed generosity in praise, affection, and gifts characterized 'Eve': a Dunhill pipe, a smuggled copy of *Ulysses*, a Mexican birth control potion after the birth of Mary, the Deacon's third child, and an early morning, before breakfast, slightly startling visit to the Deacon household in Toronto. She was also a woman of energy and influence in the Maritimes, a combination of femme formidable and enfant terrible. Her services to 'the cause' of Canadian literature by way of her devoted friendship with Deacon ranged from her writing of reviews and drumming up of other Maritime reviewers for the literary section, through arranging engagements and entertainment for poets on tour, to providing invaluable sources of information about the life and times of James Gillis, the Cape Breton poet and one of the stars of Deacon's *The Four Jameses*. Only Evelyn Tufts and Emily Murphy shared in their correspondence with Deacon a similar irrepressible sense of fun and a similar pithy frankness of comment:

I do think he [Wilson MacDonald] should not be so violent in his dislikes. Pratt, for instance, he simply flays. And that's a mistake, for Maritime people like Pratt's stuff, without agonizing over the contention as to prose vs verse. As a poet he may be *only* a good whaler, as some English critic said, but while his verse has that fine salty tang of actuality he will always have his public down here by 'the wholesome sea,' at least. Why are poets all so confoundedly jealous of one another. It has always been a puzzle to me. Since they are all priests of beauty, in varying degrees, and presumably 'seek the one city by a million ways,' as Masefield puts it, why so much envy and heart-burning among them? Musicians, of course, are as bad or worse. Have you ever heard one opera singer giving her frank opinion of another?[65]

In comparison with Eve Tufts, Miss Davidson and Mrs Dalton were impeccably proper, but they were both articulate women of great affection, intelligence, and capacity to 'listen' to letters and reply in kind, a combination that Deacon needed and sought. Annie Charlotte

Dalton was a poet, fairly well known in the twenties, published by Ryerson Press, and selected for inclusion in John Garvin's Canadian Poets of 1926. Though Deacon became a pre-publication critic of her work as she wrote it, what he really valued was her propensity for discussion by mail. She proudly called herself a Canadian, but she was also an imperialist, always ready to defend the empire connection and arguing for it in letter after letter throughout the correspondence.

The truth is that I am intoxicated with this country. I sympathize, but I do not understand the problem which you think so important. If you knew the difference we find in it compared to the time, 27 years ago, when we arrived, you would marvel. To us, it is grown up. Another thing, in all those 27 years we have never once discovered 'the lack of self-respect, self-confidence' which you deplore in your note. On the contrary we have been fascinated, amused, & sometimes a little irritated by the average Canadian's self-importance. We found it so refreshing after so much English self-depreciation.[66]

Many times through the years Deacon was stung by her attitudes into some of his frankest and most eloquent statements of his aims and tactics:

By pure instinct at first, and later consciously and deliberately, I have tried to be an intellectual and moral brick in an invisible wall protecting this germ civilization from too great dominance by the two sizeable and proximate English-speaking nations. I strive to keep out English and American ideals, institutions and viewpoints. In a crass, practical way, my task is perfectly hopeless. It can't be done. But I go on trying. I ridicule and deride the Englishman and the American. Why? To get some idea of personal responsibility into my countrymen for our national *dharma*, which must differ from that of England and the United States; to make them stand on their own legs, face their own problems, and come to see that they are responsible to themselves and God, not to Westminister, not to Washington. *We must not be a cheap copy of Britain or the U.S.A.*[67]

He was more than a little taken aback to find that Mrs Dalton had not only made a speech quoting his words, but that *The British Columbia Monthly* had printed the speech, quoting him as 'an authority and a prophet.' However, he speedily asked for her assurance that she would quote him in public no more: 'It all hinges on the fact that friends can speak more loosely and casually than strangers, because the friends rely on what they both know to interpret what is then being said. If private letters were freely quotable you and I should have to write each other and everybody else more circumspectly: we should in fact always be addressing a public audience; and that would completely spoil the fun of letter-writing altogether.'[68] He was also quite explicit about the kind of encouragement he intended to give her in her writing, as opposed to the kind it was honest to throw before the public at large:

'Put all *your* heart into your poems and they will be great' refers to Annie Charlotte Dalton – not the poets assembled in Vancouver. Most of them have not, and will never have, the command of technique that must be present in great poetry. The world is crowded with sincere people with literary aspirations, whom I would not encourage. They can never write 'great poetry' and it is as false as false can be to tell them they can by 'putting all their heart in their poems.' A golden heart, without knowledge, doubtless gets a place in heaven; but he will never build a safe railway bridge, nor write a fine poem. One needs more than sincerity, good intentions: the 'well meaning' folk as you well know are generally the bane of the earth. Far be it from me to flatter them. I hate to think what trash will be mailed me to read as the result of this apparent subscribing to what I do *not* believe.[69]

Laura Lee Davidson introduced herself by sending Deacon the manuscript of *Winter of Content*, the story of a winter spent in her cabin in the backwoods north of Kingston in the Charbot Lake area. In his opinion her work identified her as a first-class regional writer, along with Janey Canuck for the prairies and Peter McArthur for southern Ontario farm country. He placed the manuscript for her with Ryerson Press, where Lorne Pierce was equally enthusiastic about it, and after its publication he became her literary adviser for its sequel, *Isles of Eden*. Early in the *Saturday Night* years he had begun to ask for a fee for reading and criticizing manuscripts, since numbers of aspiring writers who looked upon him as a possible agent-critic had begun to send him their work for critical appraisal. His usual charge was $5 for three or four single-spaced pages of textual criticism plus some general common sense remarks about the craft of writing. He often enclosed a copy of a pamphlet called 'The Business of Writing.' He was embarrassed by Miss Davidson's insistence on paying him $25 for a similar service, but cheerfully so. Their association ripened into an enduring friendship, Miss Davidson delighting in acting as a kind of fairy godmother for the Deacon children, and in playing the role of mother-confessor for Deacon himself. To her he felt quite free to unburden himself of concerns professional, nationalistic, and personal, and sometimes because she was an American she felt the brunt of his intense, almost obsessive, concern that Canada should work out her own destiny free of the United States.

With numbers of Canadian journalists Deacon had a special relationship. They wrote to one another as peers and fellow craftsmen in the trade, exchanging news and gossip and, sometimes, favours. E.W. Harrold of *The Ottawa Citizen* was one of these; when Deacon needed friends and connections after his dismissal from *Saturday Night*, Harrold worked successfully for him; Laura Carten of *The Halifax Herald* was another. She wrote as 'Farmer Smith' and ran a weekly children's page, 'The Rainbow Club' – 'and The Rainbows, as you know, are a not inconsiderable part of the Canadian firmament.' Deacon wrote guest editorials for her and encouraged The Rainbows to send him their own reviews of children's books with a view to developing a team of child reviewers. He had instituted a few reviews written by children in the Children's Book Week issue of *Saturday Night* as early as 1925. Victor Lauriston of *The Chatham News* was another journalist-correspondent, though he and Deacon very nearly parted company permanently over Deacon's notorious parody of Arthur Stringer's *Empty Hands*, 'What a Canadian Has Done for Canada' (1924). A personal friend of Stringer's, Lauriston was outraged by Deacon's attack. Their correspondence at this time has a hilarious cloak-and-dagger aura, with Deacon marking letters *Private Absolutely* and Lauriston marking his *Just as Personal as Yours*.

Among journalist-friends Raymond Knister was the one in whom Deacon quickly discerned a great potential for writing. Knister was at his home near Blenheim, Ontario, when he first met Deacon, working away at writing short stories and poems and sending them out to periodicals all over North America. 'I want to hail you as Dean of Canadian reviewers,' he wrote:

It may interest you to know that it was partly the spirit of emulation aroused by reading some of your work which led me into reviewing. There is no perceptible resemblance in our styles, and I fear you need be under no anxiety on that score: it will be a long time before I approach a book with the graceful ease you display. Nor do we always agree in our ratings – or beratings – of this or that author, which is refreshing ... Wasn't it Goethe in his Conversations who said that when we say what we actually think we automatically become brilliant – if it wasn't, we'll say it should have been! That must have been what I meant when I told you that your criticism was brilliant.[70]

Many people wrote to Deacon, but few in whom he immediately recognized a talent greater than his own, as he was quick to confide to Burton Kurth. His initial response to Knister was entirely free of the nationalistic bombast with which he often spoke. It was utterly sincere, as one writer to another:

Your kind words quite bowled me over, as I am not aiming at virtuosity at all, but at simplicity. From a brother reviewer, yours was high praise indeed, and I am sure quite unmerited. Between ourselves, I am very anxious to see a more free, genial and honest discussion of books than has been possible in the past. I think we have all been too much afraid of each other and ourselves; and all I want to do is to converse frankly on literary matters. If we all say what we really think right out in meeting, I believe contemporary literature will benefit more than through any other single agency.[71]

Shortly after their first meeting Knister moved to Iowa City, where he edited *The Midland*, a monthly journal carrying on its letterhead a quotation from H.L. Mencken, 'probably the most important literary magazine ever established in America.' From there the correspondence continued. Knister reviewed *Pens and Pirates* for *The Border Cities Star* (Windsor) and Deacon thanked him for his generosity, though at the same time he also issued a warning:

Don't you get it into your head that the essay precludes creative writing. Writers of fiction are apt to do this; and they are confirmed in their own minds by the use made of this form by George Saintsbury, Ernest Rhys, and the scholarly bores who use it merely as the vehicle for literary criticism. But the great essayists do not [do] so. They make something where nothing was before just as surely as novelist or poet. I have no notion of turning out book reviews and calling them essays ... I am a million miles away from the ideal essay, but that is the form I love and I hope someday when we are old I can convince you that the real essayist is not parasitical but creative.[72]

Knister sent poems and stories for possible inclusion in *Saturday Night* and Deacon regretfully returned them because he had no budget to enable him to buy either: 'I hope some day when we are older and Canada is older I'll be in a position to buy your stuff (or sell you mine as the case may be). In the meantime I will do what I can in the way of publicity.'[73] He subsequently took every opportunity to mention Knister and his work in 'Saved from the Waste-Basket' and Knister wrote several letters in thanks for the consistent publicity.

Some of Knister's work Deacon did not understand, the story,

'Elaine,' for instance, which he read 'with a great effort to understand it.' *Saturday Night*'s readers, he was sure, would understand it even less: 'They are not used to subtlety; and I have been surprised to find how frequently they miss the purport of my bluntest remarks.'[74] 'Elaine' was published in *This Quarter*, Paris. After a second story, 'The Fate of Mrs Lucier,' and a dozen poems, 'A Row of Horse Stalls,' had also appeared in *This Quarter*, then being printed in Milan, Knister reported that he had been asked to do a Canadian letter for that journal: 'The editorials are hilariously serious, and why isn't Jas. Joyce known as the Charlie Chaplin of prose? Do you know Morley Callaghan? Young Torontonian, they say, printing a story of his – a different sort of story than any other Canadian has published, meseems. I hope that you can put me in touch with him.'[75]

Deacon did not know Callaghan at this time – 'he is not in the City Directory' – and he simply did not have the taste for the kind of fiction that *This Quarter* valued. But when Knister did a piece that he could and did understand his praise was unstinting:

Far different was my reaction to your Campbell article in June Queen's Quarterly. By God, man, you've rung the bell! I am sure that the posterity of a century hence, when remembering the death of Wilfred will quote some part, and a large part, of your critical essay. It is immense, just hits the nail on the head, and is thoroughly sane, well-informed, and fair. It shows you as more mobile emotionally than anything else of yours I have seen. To the best of my memory it is the best critique by a Canadian of a Canadian that I have ever seen. Assuredly it is time for you to be the Dean – if we can pry Morgan-Powell [*Montreal Star*] loose from the job. I am not joshing: you have inaugurated a new era in Canadian criticism. I have read your article with great profit, and I agree with everything you say about his work. As I was reading, Professor Archibald MacMechan of Halifax walked into my office (he is another Dean by the way, holding sway over the Maritime Provinces for a generation). We discussed you; or rather I told him about you and we discussed the article. He was delighted...[76]

After reading and enjoying *Pens and Pirates*, Knister was equally generous about Deacon's talents as an essayist:

The whole matter of essay writing is a personal one, and I am under no delusion that it is outside true creation. On the contrary I am humble in spirit to anyone who can write an essay, as I know I assuredly can't. It is not enough to have the langwidge [sic] and the individuality – it's got to be a pleasant individuality, making the langwich [sic] perform in a fetching way. One reads a story and says, 'Powerful thing, that!' but adds with a wag of the head, 'I wouldn't care to be with the author alone on a desert island.' But an essay is likeable or it is nothing. After that it can have all the virtues of short fiction, even the greatest, characterization. Do you know Turgenieff's 'A Sportsman's Sketches'? I *like* (without at all defining a category) essays of that approach, and think you can do them. At all events, if ever you think to have approached the essay of your dreams, as the faithful in any art on occasion will do, let me see it even before book publication, if that is long delayed.[77]

This is a very attractive correspondence of mutual respect between two men whose literary personalities were highly compatible. It ends with an exchange of thanks and congratulations over Knister's Graphic Press award for *My Star Predominant*, his novel on the life of Keats, and then, sadly, with Deacon's obituary of Knister in 1931.

From the time Deacon came to Toronto, his life was completely given over to the demanding routine of his work and to the fraction of time he could spend with his family. Neither now nor later was he a traveler – the little he did was always on business or for speaking engagements. In the twenties he could not afford the time or money for trips. Even when John Murray Gibbon, chief publicity agent for the CNR, asked him to the Banff Conference of the Canadian Authors' Association as the guest of the railway, he had to refuse because he could not take the time off from *Saturday Night*. His home territory only encompassed Toronto and his beloved summer cabin and when, later in life, he could have afforded trips, he did not want them. The trip to England that he and Sally liked to plan in the twenties never came about. Movement and the excitement of others' lives came to him vicariously, but abundantly, through his correspondence with men and women who lived and worked in every part of Canada and elsewhere in the world, whose lives represented all kinds of variety in age and circumstance, and who found in him eager and constant friendship and encouragement.

CHAPTER FIVE

Writings of the Twenties:
Pens and Pirates, Poteen, and *Peter McArthur*

HE YEARS OF DEACON'S RIGOROUS and exhilarating journalistic training at *Saturday Night* were also the most productive
years of his own writing career. To Charles l'Ami, an aspiring
Winnipeg novelist, he wrote in 1927 of the 'great days' ahead for
Canadian writers,[1] and his confidence tallied with his own
experience since coming to Toronto.

In the early fall of 1922, Arthur Phelps took a number of Deacon's
manuscripts to Lorne Pierce of Ryerson Press. Pierce, as committed
and optimistic a nationalist as Deacon himself, was enthusiastic about
their quality and totally encouraging about Deacon's future as both
journalist and author: 'You have a real daring literary fist, and you will
certainly command a hearing, and some respect even from the
Calvinists and the "millionaire Methodists" you like to lambaste. To
borrow one of the quotations you make in one of the screeds I should
say that you might even now hire a painter to decorate your front door
with the legend: "Living trimly by my wit".'[2]

After what seemed to Deacon endless delays, *Pens and Pirates*
appeared in late August 1923, as did the complete edition of the poems
of Tom MacInnes, a publication for which Deacon was responsible,
having arranged for MacInnes' change in publishers from McClelland
and Stewart to Ryerson. *Pens and Pirates* is a collection of nineteen
essays, some of which had been previously published in *The Manitoba
Free Press* and in magazines like *The National Pictorial, The Canadian
Nation,* and *The Canadian Bookman.* Although diverse in range, the
essays themselves can be grouped into three general categories: comic,
literary, and nationalistic. A recurring humorous tone, however, is

common to all three, lending an attractive ease and urbanity to whatever Deacon is saying.

The classical essayist tradition of which he so often spoke – Hazlitt, Lamb, Montaigne, Sainte-Beuve – was, in his practice, secondary to the influence of the American literary scene of the late teens and twenties. He admired the techniques of essayists like Van Wyck Brooks, H.L. Mencken, Henry Seidel Canby, and Christopher Morley; Morley, in particular, who practised the art of the essay as a whimsical divertissement in collections like *Shandygaff* (1918), *Mince Pie* (1919), *Plum Pudding* (1921), and *Pipefuls* (1920), had become a valuable model for his work. In the apprentice collection, *In Fame's Antechamber*, Deacon had written with passionate advocacy based on a foundation of theosophical thought; *Pens and Pirates* demonstrates a subsequent development of the light touch, a tone and manner that were to prove congenial to his best talents as a writer.

The comic essays make effective use of occasional humour. A pig's head in a butcher shop window, a Tom Mix movie, a business sign for 'Faultless Ladies' Wear Company,' a billboard at Christmas proclaiming 'Wise Men of Today Value a Bank Account,' all provide material for satire. The personal essay, 'My Boon Companion: A Vocal Exercise on the "I" Vowel,' combines humour, intimacy, and wit in satiric praise of himself in a manner close to Leacock's 'My Financial Career.' The casual speaking style, the address to the reader, the different kinds of play on a single idea, the gentle exploitation of eccentricity, the absurdity of an Irish terrier who 'would bark for a bone but gave sign of no other ideas' (p 110) have a benign, quiet mirth which is closer to irony than satire and, ultimately, closer to Deacon's true comic métier. His essay on barbers, 'The Genial Profession,' is in the vein of what Northrop Frye has called genuine Canadian humour, the humour which is based on a vision of society and is not merely a series of wisecracks on a single theme. Its technique is, again, reminiscent of Leacock's *Sunshine Sketches*, the humour modulating into nostalgia through praise of the barber in whom Deacon celebrates the constructive qualities of small town life, the family, and the human community, which together articulate 'a vision of society': 'For now I remember hearing him [the barber] speak searching words of wisdom that I never heard repeated till, years later, I found them again in the pages of the Greek philosophers, and in the lines of the world's immortal poets. Mr Lanctot read nothing but the newspaper.' (p 23)

The techniques of this first group of essays – informality, simplicity of style, congeniality, and high spirits – also mark some of Deacon's pieces on literary topics. The title piece, 'Pens and Pirates,' was written for the book and links essayists and pirates in their common need for the qualities of courage, purpose, and a sense of humour: 'I do not mean facility in making jokes, but the ability to see them. It is not so much a matter of finding what is ridiculous in the situation of the other fellow, as an appreciation of what is absurd in our own – and how little it really matters.' (p 65) He exploits comic absurdity in 'Booze, Religion and Poetry,' mocking the shibboleth of prohibition and exalting the 'intoxicating liquors of literature.' 'Manhattan: The Book-Buyers' Heaven' shows him adept in nostalgic, evocative description, and the flippant title of 'Free Verse: What It is and What It Ain't' – masks his earnest treatment of a literary technique as well as, predictably, a eulogy of Whitman.

The last literary essay, 'My Shelves and Immortality,' is an exposition of his critical beliefs. The sober tone, the use of the authorial 'we' and the accumulation of literary allusions project his prophetic stance. In the first section, 'On Literary Immortality,' he counsels, 'Write out of your own experience; write simply. This is the law and the prophets for an author who hopes to be read in the centuries to come' (p 277). He interprets 'experience' as not only what a writer has lived, but what he can imagine living or having lived, and speaks of his own attempts to write and of his bookshelves, which provide a means of his creating an imaginary literary hierarchy in which poetry as the supreme art is followed by philosophy, by the writers of the Irish Renaissance, by books of essays and criticism, and finally by fiction.

The third group of essays in *Pens and Pirates* focuses on Canadian topics and centres on Deacon's lifelong concern with literary and cultural nationalism. 'Heritage and Destiny,' Part III of the long 'Pens and Pirates' sequence, is a vigorous attack on those who argue that Canada has no national literature; 'Local Talent' urges Canadian support of Canadian magazines; 'Local Color' praises the native qualities – colour, detail, perspective – in the paintings of W.J. Phillips; 'The National Character' is a description of the qualities Deacon feels are particular to Canadians: sense of proportion, self-reliance, generosity, candour, buoyancy. All of this group of essays echoes the preoccupations of Van Wyck Brooks and H.L. Mencken who were part of the vanguard of American authors at the time, demanding new ways of seeing the United States through a recreation and revaluation of its literature. They were Deacon's models, but between these men and Deacon lay an enormous gulf. The established audience of wide interest and knowledge, recognizing a distinctive American cultural tradition, did not exist to nearly the same degree in Canada. Mencken, Brooks, and their associates were building on a kind of structure which Deacon was still trying to erect. Their rigorous discussions of American culture symbolized the independence and community of interest for which Deacon was aiming.

In this collection and, for that matter, always, he considered himself a literary pirate and was proud to be one, a renegade who had given up a comfortable life to search for literary treasure. *Pens and Pirates* was an accomplished first collection, most successful in its comic pieces, but often showing an edge of nervous bravado which marked the still self-conscious apprentice. Although in these essays he was writing most deliberately in the spirit of his American models, Deacon was painfully aware of what he lacked in contrast to them – the confidence based on wide audience appeal and the authority based on wide academic or journalistic training.

Reviews of *Pens and Pirates* were, on the whole, positive, describing Deacon as an innovative, refreshing, and lively essayist, and were confirmed in 1924 by J.D. Logan and Donald French in their *Highways of Canadian Literature*:

The essays in this volume have novelty of theme, over which plays precisely the light of a 'whimsical' fancy and humor. They are informed, however, with the strictly literary color of allusion and quotation from the poets and prosemen of all ages to the present, but in such an incidental and light way that there is no show of pedantry. The allusion and quotation are natural to Mr Deacon's professional office as a reviewer of contemporary literature. His style is journalistic in the French sense -'style *coupé*' – as regards sentence length. But he adds a piquancy to it which makes it somewhat 'winged' and which thus pleasantly engages the sensibility.[3]

In spite of good reviews, however, the commercial success of the collection was limited, to both Deacon's and Ryerson's disappointment. By May 1924, nine months after its publication, 206 copies had been sold, and two years later, sales totalled only 276 copies. Deacon remained convinced that a more aggressive distribution and publicity policy on Ryerson's part would have resulted in greater sales. Nevertheless, *Pens and Pirates* had decisively advanced his reputation at a very early stage in his career and he remained forever grateful to Lorne Pierce for having given him such a splendid first opportunity.

When *Pens and Pirates* made its appearance in August 1923, Deacon was in the process of putting the finishing touches to his *Peter McArthur* manuscript, which he submitted to Ryerson at the end of September 1923. It was one of the 'Makers of Canadian Literature' series edited by Lorne Pierce and Victor Morin, conceived by Pierce as a sequence of monographs about Canadian writers. Each volume would contain a biography and a critical appreciation of the writer in question along with a brief representative anthology of his or her work. Like the twenty-one volume 'Makers of Canada' biographies edited by Pelham Edgar and Duncan Campbell Scott, published between 1903 and 1911, the 'Makers of Canadian Literature' series was designed to focus critical attention on outstanding Canadians. Pierce's first plans for the series were ambitious. He projected 'four introductory volumes of literary background, seven volumes in French, and twenty volumes in English.' In fact, eleven volumes were published between 1923 and 1926, six in 1923, one in 1924, three in 1925, one in 1926. Of these, three were in French. A twelfth volume appeared in 1941. *Peter McArthur* was among the first six of the Ryerson series to be published in 1923. The others were *Isabella Valancy Crawford, John Richardson, William Kirby, Robert Norwood,* and *Stephen Leacock,* the last written by McArthur himself.

For nearly twenty years, McArthur, like Deacon, had earned his living through freelance journalism, mostly in New York and London. As a student at the University of Toronto, he had contributed cartoon ideas to *Puck* and *Grip.* After leaving the university in 1889, he joined the *Globe* as a reporter for a year, during which time he also contributed humorous items to different New York newspapers. Between 1890 and 1908, he lived outside Canada, first in New York where he contributed to *Harper's, The Atlantic Monthly, The Century,* and *The Smart Set* and where he was editor of *Truth* from 1895 to 1897. In 1902, McArthur then moved to London, England, where he became a regular contributor of humorous sketches to *Punch,* the only North American besides Thomas Chandler Haliburton and Artemus Ward to be so distinguished. On his return to New York in 1904, he worked as a partner in an advertising agency until 1908 when he came home to take up farming on his family's property near Glencoe, Ontario. He continued to write for various newspapers and published six books between 1908 and 1924, the year of his death. *In Pastures Green* (1915) and *The Red Cow and Her Friends* (1919) were comprised of revised humorous columns that McArthur had written for *The Globe* and *The Farmer's Advocate.* He wrote a eulogy of Sir Wilfrid Laurier (1919) and

The Affable Stranger (1920), a book on Canadian-American relations. *Around Home* (1925) and *Friendly Acres* (1927), collections of McArthur's columns, were published posthumously.

Deacon had enthusiastically reviewed McArthur's *The Affable Stranger* for the September 1921 issue of *The Canadian Bookman* and Pierce felt that Deacon, as essayist, professional writer, and Canadian nationalist, was admirably suited to a critical understanding of McArthur's work. In 1923, McArthur was well known as a rural writer whose work was characterized by subtle shifts in mood, wit, humour and, on occasion, lively satire. He had a wide following, particularly among the readers of *The Globe* and *The Farmer's Advocate*, many of whom knew or had known farm life directly. He was consistently able to complement his rural themes and descriptions with any number of quotations from Shakespeare, Shelley, Coleridge, Tennyson, and Whitman and from Canadian poets like Bliss Carman, Archibald Lampman, and Wilfred Campbell. The subsequent informal balance of the homespun and the literary, the concrete and the figurative was immensely attractive and created a whole range of moods.

Deacon also had a great admiration for McArthur's use of humour as a means and not as an end in itself. In his description of this aspect of McArthur's style he distils much of what he himself was aiming for in comic technique: 'His humour is elusive. It plays in and out of his writing; is now felt far below the surface, too deep for guffaw or even smile, and again, unexpectedly, comes bubbling through with its cheering note of nonchalance, whimsicality or satire. It cannot be judged by itself, for the finest and most enduring of it is inextricably mixed with the matter which it leavens.' (p 149) There is praise for *The Affable Stranger*, a book about anti-American feeling in Canada; a seriously qualified review of the biography, *Sir Wilfrid Laurier*; and a brief discussion of McArthur's periodical fiction.

Deacon esteemed McArthur's independence and self-reliance and ultimately linked these Thoreauvian attributes to the transcendental concerns which have so persistently marked North American man's attitude to the natural world:

His [McArthur's] main concern is the true relationship of man to the universe; and man's relationship to things, and even to men, is a lesser problem included in the greater. Physical objects and events are, to him, mere 'shadows' of the spiritual realities; and these inner truths, with which he is quietly preoccupied, are eternal, and not subject to change or error. When he rejoices in the rest to be found in rural surroundings, it is because that rest typifies the soul at peace with the Great Heart throbbing through all nature. He loves the songs of the birds as a reminder of the harmony that should (and probably does) exist basically between all things. (p 162)

He had deliberately chosen to treat McArthur's achievements in a way that would discover to his readers, 'not the Peter McArthur of popular imagination' (p 162), but a writer who was first a poet, then a philosopher and finally a humourist. The ordering was to prove eccentric, although Deacon's evaluation of McArthur's qualities as essayist remains perceptive, articulate, and just, perhaps because of the affinity between them. Like Deacon's, McArthur's essay style was that of the conversational, spontaneous causerie. Both men were nationalists. Like his biographer, McArthur 'aimed at wakening modern Canadians to their national heritage. They did not need to bow to modern "isms" or to other nations. They only needed to see that they inherited the spirit of true democracy and the hardiness of the pioneers. Moreover, with this background Canada should stand as "a free nation within the Empire".'[4]

Before McArthur's death Deacon had spent several days with him, gathering material for his book. He found it difficult to do justice to a man he had liked and admired so much. However, he was quick to praise both McArthur for his co-operation and Pierce who had, in his opinion, devised an ideal format for the Makers series. Although he was again disappointed in sales – initially he had surrendered copyright to Ryerson and secured a ten per cent sales royalty – his financial expectations concerning *Peter McArthur* had been ambitious, for he had anticipated royalties which would have given him a year in which he would have been free to practise his writing. In the event, faced with low sales, Deacon grudgingly agreed to cancel his contract in favour of a single payment of $500. The monograph's success, however, remained consistent and three years after its publication, he was able to report the printing of a second edition, though 'I would feel very badly if I thought this was due solely to my friend's death.'[5]

The publication of *Peter McArthur* marked the end of the first stage in Deacon's career as an author-critic. He had acquired firsthand experience of the business of Canadian publishing and out of this he developed the tough, practical common sense for which he became noted, particularly his emphasis on the importance to the Canadian book business of advertising and markets. His support and sympathy for the practical problems of the writer in Canada were immeasurably strengthened. Most important, he had acquired a measure of fame and recognition within Canada, and a consequent confidence which sustained him in his desire to seek publication and exposure in New York and London literary circles. Accordingly, he solicited work with different periodicals, and between 1924 and 1926 he contributed to *The Literary Review*, the weekly supplement of *The New York Evening Post*, *The International Book Review*, *The Saturday Review of Literature*, *The American Mercury*, *The New York Times*, and *The Empire Review* in London, England. His longest association was with Henry Seidel Canby's *Saturday Review of Literature*, from 1924 to 1934, during which time he contributed seven survey articles on Canadian literature. Not only did he wish to extend the range of his reputation outside Canada, but he also knew, as he wrote to Tom MacInnes, that his fame inside Canada would be immeasurably enhanced by his publishing in the United States: 'They have no respect for literary natives here unless they have made their mark abroad.'[6]

Ten days later, he was writing MacInnes to say that he had been appointed 'Canadian correspondent for the Literary Review of the New York Post.' Much of Deacon's work in New York was as a reviewer. Initially *The International Book Review* called upon him to comment on Canadian and non-Canadian works, but soon he was producing a range of reviews, articles, and literary surveys on Canadian literature for American readers, trying to provide readers in the United States with an awareness of Canada. In 1924 his subject matter was almost exclusively Canadian, from 'What a Canadian Has Done for Canada,' the review-parody of Arthur Stringer's *Empty Hands* for *The Literary Review*, to his survey, 'rehashed from Saturday Night' of Canadian literature written for *The Saturday Review of Literature*.

The Stringer parody had given Deacon much amusement in the writing and had caused considerable subsequent excitement. In his novel, *Empty Hands*, Stringer had taken what to Deacon were unwarranted liberties with the Canadian setting and had produced a preposterous adventure story of a man and woman lost in the wilderness, a story whose gross inaccuracies demanded correction. The review first appeared in abbreviated form in *The Literary Review* on 19 July 1924, three months after it had been commissioned by Canby. Deacon's persistence in pressing for its publication resulted from his indignation at Stringer's crass falsification of facts and his shrewd recognition of the potential positive exposure stemming from its values as entertainment. Stringer was quick to respond in an incensed letter to W. Orton Tewson, the new editor of *The Literary Review*, and both author and reviewer argued with each other through Tewson. The exchange was comic, Stringer explaining why his heroine's bathing suit was ripped off in the rapids, how raspberry juice is really red and not bluish-purple, and how there is an important difference between fighting a bull moose on land and in the water. Deacon replied with the cocky confidence of his own experiences as a woodsman and with the advantage enjoyed by a belligerent who has already fired the devastating initial salvo. His aggressiveness was increased further by his dislike of what he called the prurience of *Empty Hands*, by his belief that Stringer had appropriated much of his material from the rough draft of a novel given him to read by Arthur Heming and by the fact that *Empty Hands* was being turned into a film with no credit given to Heming. In fact, Heming, soon after the publication of *Empty Hands*, was said to have demanded and received from Stringer a cheque for $7,000.[7] Stringer stood to recoup that amount and much more from the sale of the film rights. The movie was shot in the Capilano district of Vancouver in the late summer of 1924 and was released in the fall.

Deacon's piece continued to bring him much welcome publicity and was reprinted in the Philadelphia *Ledger* and in the Montreal magazine *World Wide*. He enlarged it for *Saturday Night* and wrote a parody – '"Pre-historic Honeymooning Up-to-Date" by Arthur Stringingus' – and signed it R.T. Wilson for the November 1924 number of the Montreal *Listening Post*. He told his mother that he had rewritten the piece yet again for sale to British periodicals. The whole episode had tickled his fancy and made him a centre of much flattering publicity. Although he had met and liked Stringer, he experienced no guilt over what he had done, 'as the bird fairly flew to the chopping-block, stretched out his neck and asked for the axe'[8] and, in fact, Stringer felt no lasting resentment towards him over the episode.

In 1925 Deacon prepared an article for H.L. Mencken in which he argued, contrary to Mencken's editorial request, against the American annexation of Canada. The article appeared in the November number of *The American Mercury*. He continued to write reviews in *The Literary Review* and *The International Book Review* on Canadian material as diverse as Hector Charlesworth's memoirs, *Jack Miner and the Birds*, and Arthur Heming's juvenile novel, *The Living Forest*. In the 1924-6 period, he wrote a total of eight pieces for *The International Book Review*, five for *The Literary Review* of *The New York Evening Post*, four surveys for *The Saturday Review of Literature*, a major article for *The American Mercury*, and two articles for *The New York Times*. He was delighted with the work and the exposure and gained a confidence that had a real, residual effect, particularly after Deacon had sent Mencken the annexation article written against the advocacy stand that Mencken had wanted him to take. Although he was worried about not being able to devote enough time to his own creative writing, Deacon was in his element as a spokesman for his nation, caught up in the challenge of describing, defining, and directing its cultural life.

Along with his articles in New York periodicals, Deacon was writing for Canadian markets between 1924 and 1926 – literary surveys in *The Listening Post* in 1924 and 1925, general articles on Canadian literature in *Willison's Monthly* and the Canadian edition of the *Christian Science Monitor*, pieces on Peter McArthur in *The Ontario Farmer*, and on Tom MacInnes for John Garvin's *Canadian Poets* and *The Star Weekly*. His energy and productivity were proving compatible and Deacon was very happy with the result: 'I positively lose track of what I have written, and sometimes little cheques appear by mail that cause me to consult my ledger to see what it is I am being paid for.'[9] Nevertheless he was anxious to publish another book, though his efforts in that direction were impeded by the demands of his reviewing. In 1925 he had hoped to have his 'Law and Common Sense' columns out in book form, but they never appeared. However, the contract for *Poteen*, the collection of essays which Deacon had predicted for 1927 or 1928, was signed with Graphic Press in Ottawa on 25 March 1926.

Deacon's optimism and his literary nationalism were buoyant complements to the ethos of Graphic Press, established in Ottawa in 1924 as the Canadian publisher of exclusively Canadian books. He was also happy to become one of Graphic's authors because he had been disappointed with what he considered to be the indifferent sales policy of Ryerson, and he thought that Henry Miller of Graphic was a better businessman than Lorne Pierce. His collection was scheduled to appear in August 1926; by mid-July, the new chapter on Canadian literature was written and the manuscript was completed.

Poteen, a colloquial Irish term for home-brew and a title reminiscent of Christopher Morley's *Shandygaff* (1918), is an apt title for Deacon's second essay collection. Subtitled 'A Pot-Pourri of Canadian Essays,' it is less a miscellany than a distillation of his ongoing concerns, consolidating further the three major categories of *Pens and Pirates* – humour, literature, and nationalism – with a noticeable conflation of the last two. The essays in *Poteen* are assured and authoritative, in keeping with Deacon's growing confidence in his unique professional status in Canada. Of the twelve essays in the collection, four are humorous, four are on general or non-Canadian literary topics, three are on Canadian literature, and one deals with Canadian nationalism. Three of these essays are the outstanding pieces of the collection and ensure its success: 'The Bogey of Annexation'; the long section on Canadian literature which comprises almost half the book; and 'What a Canadian Has Done for Canada,' the review-parody of *Empty Hands*. Together, these three centre the issues of political and cultural nationalism.

The anti-annexation piece which Deacon had written with some trepidation for H.L. Mencken is a reasoned defence of Canadian autonomy, consciously directed at an American audience. The thesis of Deacon's article is that Canadian national feeling 'is far less of a romantic love for the British Isles than the outcome of Canada's relations with the United States.' (p 8) His avowed adversary is Goldwin Smith, the long-dead expatriate Englishman whose *Canada and the Canadian Question* (1871) had advocated political and economic union with the United States.

Deacon's argument focuses on three major areas: colonial and constitutional history, regionalism and its discontents, and economics. His language is measured, deliberate, and pragmatic and his point of reference remains constant – the United States. His arguments continually refer his audience back to what they know best and the consistency of his technique is an effective rhetorical device. He attributes the British decision to keep Canada after 1776 to its fear of the United States. Canada's growth to independence after that is the result of British indifference to it. Recent disappointments over disputes involving boundaries and fisheries are attributable 'not so much to the shrewdness of the American negotiators as to the general willingness of Great Britain's representatives to conciliate the United States without due regard to Canadian interests.' (p 10) Canadian history is also full of anti-American sentiment, from the emigration of the Loyalists to the defeat of Sir Wilfrid Laurier by Sir Robert Borden in October 1911 over the issue of a proposed reciprocity treaty.

Deacon goes on to argue that in spite of regional differences and talk of secession in different parts of Canada, the provinces, especially Quebec, 'an area as large as several good-sized states' (p 22), with the special privileges it enjoys, would lose economically and culturally if annexation ever took place. Point by point, Deacon weights his arguments with historical facts and figures. He raises the possibility of a Canada eventually independent enough to withdraw from its partnership in the Empire in the event of sustained conflict of interest: 'As an important part of the British Empire, Canada will never consider becoming a subservient part of the United States. Should events lead to Canadian independence, some understanding with her one neighbor would naturally be a necessity, though organic union would hardly be desirable to either nation.' (p 24)He concludes by mentioning the lack of attention paid to a recent pro-annexation article in the Montreal magazine *The Listening Post*. His final sentence maintains the tone of the article – restrained, balanced, reasonable: 'So far as I can learn, no other paper even mentioned the controversy. That significant ignoring of "The Listening Post's" challenge indicates how little Canadians think of the idea of annexation.' (p 25) Deacon had argued his case carefully, with his legal training much in evidence as he makes his opening statement, presents the evidence, and reaches his conclusion. Facts are called to bear witness; forging them together are his own bedrock conviction and dedication.

The long, ambitious, multi-sectioned essay on Canadian literature was written especially as the centrepiece for *Poteen* and was meant to be the core of a later and far more complete book on the subject. The essay comprises six parts, and is nearly half the length of *Poteen*. Its intention is twofold: to provide a concise literary history of Canada and to demonstrate that justifiable pride is to be taken in an emerging literature that already has such worth and distinctiveness. 'Prelude' deals with the origins of Canadian literature and argues that 'the true test of the nationality of a literature is whether it could have originated elsewhere; and, with few exceptions, we find that never in substance, and sometimes not even in form, could the books designated as Canadian literature have emanated from any other country.' (p 146) The literature of exploration, Joseph Howe's essays, Haliburton's Sam Slick, and the work of writers like John Richardson, Susanna Moodie, Catharine Parr Traill, and Charles Sangster are all products of a distinctive Canadian experience. He concludes with Charles Mair, in whom is reflected 'every one of the distinguishing characteristics of the strong school that was to follow him – the consciousness of a land begging for expression, worship of Nature, consistent craftsmanship, the lyric note and at least a hint of the frank pantheism that was to dominate the minds of Canadian poets for more than half a century to come.' (p 155)

Deacon's treatment of the Confederation poets – 'The Group of '67' – is a clear but brief résumé of their talents, including a description of other poets who wrote or began writing in the nineteenth century: Pauline Johnson, Wilfred Campbell, Frederick George Scott, Isabella Valancy Crawford, and William Henry Drummond. He admires in all of them their powers of natural description, distinctive language, sympathy, and vitality. His admiration of the historical romances of Sir Gilbert Parker and William Kirby is lukewarm at most, and Ralph Connor he considers a gifted story-teller but a purveyor of 'dangerous half-truths.' As for the 'girls' sugary stories begun with "Anne of Green Gables" ... Canadian fiction was to go no lower.' (p 169)

'The Modern Era' provides a critical analysis of different genres of Canadian literature published from 1900 to 1925. Reviewing the poetry of Robert Service, Tom MacInnes, Marjorie Pickthall, Wilson MacDonald, and E.J. Pratt, Deacon shows an eclectic admiration for different verse forms and subjects. The romance and narrative action of Service, MacInnes, and Pratt, the romanticism of Pickthall, and the flexibility of MacDonald he sees as accompanied by an admirable mastery of technique. The abandonment of sentimentality by Canadian novelists, exemplified especially in the work of Grove and Mazo de la Roche, represents 'a new maturity for our fiction, a sterner, more austere and better balanced view of life.' (p 178) He speaks of the humour of Stephen Leacock, of Peter Donovan of *Saturday Night*, and of Peter McArthur, provides a survey of essay collections and of history and considers the animal story and the short story. At the end of his survey, he notes the need for provincial cash prizes for literature. One impassioned theme forms the leitmotif throughout: 'The politician and the business man, though they may not be fond of reading, should realize that it is a choice between a national literature and annexation.' (p 183)

The section entitled 'A Guide to the Anthologies' is a critical survey of poetry collections. Using a criterion which searches for the greatest 'quantity, variety and quality of Canadian poetry' (p 187) in a single anthology, Deacon makes a statistical inventory of each of the seven volumes he considers, from William Douw Lighthall's *Songs and Poems of the Great Dominion* (1889) to John W. Garvin's enlarged *Canadian Poets* (1926). For Deacon, 'there are two main lines an anthologist may follow: he may select poems for their literary beauty, indifferent to their authorship; or he may collect poets from an historical instinct, representing each by the best available poem.' (p 192) Ultimately, Garvin's *Canadian Poets* 'is the best from which to form a conception of the wealth and variety of Canadian poetic literature down to the present.' (p 200) However, Deacon still recognized the need for a rigorous selection 'made up solely of verse of the highest charm and merit, regardless of authorship – a book that would have no room for the passable, but only for the best.' (p 203)

'The First Histories of Canadian Literature' is essentially an evaluation of three books: J.D. Logan's and Donald G. French's *Highways of
Canadian Literature* (1924), Ray Palmer Baker's *A History of English-
Canadian Literature to the Confederation* (1920), and Archibald MacMechan's *Headwaters of Canadian Literature* (1924). They 'are not, strictly
speaking, the first histories of Canadian literature,' but they are "the
first in point of time to be printed independently – the only books ever
issued simply to satisfy curiosity about Canadian literature.' (p 209)
Deacon also has a theory he wishes to test in the course of examining
these three histories:

This more or less natural indifference of English and American critics and
readers to the state of culture in British North America has had the result of
impressing upon Canadian writers a sense of their inferiority – sometimes, but
not always, justified. It has probably deterred many authors from attempting
the more ambitious kinds of work, and it has certainly prevented native critics
from doing justice to those of their countrymen whose books are worthy to
stand beside similar productions in Great Britain and the United States. (p 208)

He finds that the apologetic tone of MacMechan's study echoes this
indifference and he questions the critic's omission of John Richardson,
Duncan Campbell Scott, Isabella Valancy Crawford, and others. While
questioning MacMechan's evaluations, especially of contemporary
writers, and his uncritical emphasis on recent best sellers, Deacon
praises his survey of French-Canadian literature. The merits of
MacMechan's *Headwaters*, however, are not enough, in his opinion, to
offset the decided superiority of *Highways of Canadian Literature*. Logan
and French offer 'an encyclopaedic quantity of particularized facts,
and have thus contributed the comprehensive source book that was
needed before any extensive weeding-out could be done safely.' (p 212)
The deficiencies in their book – its wordiness, the confining prescrip-
tiveness of its critical terminology, the surfeit of comparisons with
British and American works, which run the risk of overstatement – are
faults of method and do not eradicate the undoubted value of the
study. With its ample coverage of the Confederation poets, its
generically divided chapters, and its sound judgments, he names
Highways as 'the ranking history of Canadian literature.' (p 215) It is
also 'the safest guide for those seeking a knowledge of Canadian
literature, its characteristics and its figures and their backgrounds and
works.' (p 214)
Deacon praises Baker's *History* as 'much the best planned and best

written of the three, being a model of clarity and revealing a fine sense of proportion in its author.' (p 215) The book provides an enlightening study of the seminal contribution of the United Empire Loyalists to Canada's literature and culture, and also contains a full-length study of Thomas Haliburton. Nevertheless, Baker's study is severely limited by not going beyond 1867. Deacon concludes this section of his overview by praising Lorne Pierce's Makers of Canadian Literature series. The last two parts of the essay contain a book list organized generically and a chart-guide to the work of Canadian poets in different anthologies.

Poteen was primarily a forum for Deacon's views on the literary, cultural, and political imperatives of a self-sustaining nation. The high seriousness of much of its tone was lightened, however, by the inclusion of his ever-popular satire on Stringer's *Empty Hands*. After a hilarious send-up of some 5,000 words, 'What a Canadian Has Done for Canada' rises to this peroration:

Canadians owe a boundless debt to Mr Stringer. They have writhed for years under the misrepresentations of English and American authors, who have written absurd tales purporting to depict life in the Canadian woods. There was only one way to stop it: to tell such a 'whopper' as to elevate the myth to a place among the great imaginative classics of the world ... It is a matter for national pride that one of our native authors has made two people 'disappear' down a rapid as Lewis Carroll took Alice down the rabbit-hole, has made his hero slay a moose with the rib of a deer as an earlier fighter slew a thousand Philistines with the jaw-bone of an ass – has, in short, achieved a *tour de force* in that superlative kind of untruth we love under the name of fairy-story, and, at the same time, has erected a monument of unconscious humor. (p 62)[10]

Poteen received more consistently favourable attention from reviewers than had *Pens and Pirates*. Deacon was at once especially nervous about and pleased by the review which appeared in *Saturday Night* on 25 September 1926, written by E.W. Harrold, associate editor of *The Ottawa Citizen*. Keenly aware of the liabilities of being reviewed in his own literary section, he was overjoyed at Harrold's description of how he was 'engaged in writing and spreading the light in dark places, a task to which he brings valuable critics and essayists in Canada today.'[11]

By 9 November, Henry Miller was writing to Catherine Grove, Frederick Philip Grove's wife, that 'Deacon's "*Pens and Pirates*" sold 276 copies in three years, "*Poteen*" has sold over 1,000 copies in six weeks.'[12] Miller was exaggerating, but sales were nonetheless substantial. By February 1928, 'Poteen [had] sold something like 584 copies.'[13] Deacon had good reason to be gratified by the book's critical and popular success. He had obviously gained in confidence and authority since *Pens and Pirates*. His commitment to his role as literary prophet was strengthened and he wrote to his mother of his plans to write '*the masterpiece*': 'I felt seriously that it was a mistake to write anything ambitious at first. I needed the training, the discipline of, journalism, and to get to know all sorts of ropes, as well as to gradually prepare the public to the idea of me as a writer. There are cases of the instant success; but generally the unknown author has the dicken's own time of it for a hearing, even if he has done the greatest piece of writing on record.'[14]

Deacon's next book, *The Four Jameses*, was to be quite different from what he had planned. Nevertheless, it did prove to be his enduring achievement and a confirmation of the humorous gift he had displayed with such style in his review of *Empty Hands*. One important distinction emerged, however, for in *The Four Jameses* Deacon revealed that the satire of his Stringer review was only one note in the much richer and more resonant scale of his comic writing.

CHAPTER SIX

The Four Jameses

And there stands the Queen, in glorious regalia,
One foot on Canada and one on Australia.

James McIntyre, the Cheese Poet of Ingersoll

EACON'S STUDY OF THE FOUR POETS, James Gay of Guelph,
James McIntyre of Ingersoll, James Gillis of Cape Breton, and
James MacRae of St Mary's, Ontario, began as a light-hearted
diversion and ended as his most memorable work, the product
of the best of his writing talents. It was reprinted in the fifties
and again in the seventies, when Doug Fetherling, writing its introduction, described it as an 'underground classic.' In the Winnipeg
days W.T. Allison had introduced Deacon to the poetry of McIntyre
and Gay,[1] but from much further back he remembered his mother
telling stories of 'Nora Pembroke,' a poet who adopted the name of
his home town to do it honour and whose 'Verses and Rhymes by the
Way' was published through subscription by his father and other
businessmen of Pembroke.

In his first months at *Saturday Night* he published 'The Booby Prize,'
an article on Nora Pembroke, James McIntyre, and James Gay; like so
many of his ideas for 'The Bookshelf,' this one caught on and over the
next four years some of his most entertaining correspondence was
about other notorious and noteworthy Canadian writers. In a spirit of
good humoured raillery, Deacon had quoted the last verse of Gay's
'The Elephant and the Flea' as evidence that 'this Canadian holds the
world's championship as the worst poet who ever got his verses printed'
(*SN*, 4 November 1922). The replies he got were astutely used by

Deacon to keep the 'worst poet competition' alive in future issues of *Saturday Night*. His most sustained and fruitful correspondence on this subject was with Charles Conroy of the Reid Newfoundland Company of St John's, who, over the years, supplied him with a variety of clippings from Newfoundland newspapers. Linked by their love of nonsense, the two men became firm friends. Eventually, Conroy's best contributions became an entire chapter in *The Four Jameses*, 'Journalistic Prose in Newfoundland.'[2]

Deacon returned to the Jameses time and again during his *Saturday Night* years and Tom MacInnes even suspected him of having written an anonymous article about them in *The Toronto Sunday World*.[3] In the 28 April 1923 and 12 May 1923 numbers of *Saturday Night*, he devoted two pages to James D. Gillis's *The Cape Breton Giant*, the life of Angus MacAskill. On 13 December 1924, Gillis was once more the subject when *The Great Election* was discussed and on 19 June 1926, Deacon celebrated his discovery of James MacRae by reviewing his *An Ideal Courtship*. Ironic but steeped in affection for these versifiers, his mock-serious tone as he wrote of them remained the basic element of the book that was taking shape in his mind. The articles appeared during the busy years between 1922 and 1926 when *Pens and Pirates*, *Peter McArthur*, and *Poteen* were being written and published. Deacon had fully expected that his fourth book would be an extension of the predominant cultural and political concerns of *Poteen*, but in May 1927 he negotiated with Graphic about a book which was to be 'just straight humor.'[4] Between the beginning of June and the end of August, *The Four Jameses* was written.

Of the four poets, only MacRae and Gillis were alive in 1927. Gay had died in 1891 and McIntyre in 1906. Faced with a dearth of detailed biographical information about his proposed subjects, Deacon sought to obtain it by sending them or their heirs itemized questionnaires. Details about James MacRae, a pseudonym for John J. Macdonald, were secured from him by a friend of May Sharples, Deacon's secretary. Born in 1849, a Scottish Catholic in Glengarry County, Ontario, MacRae had received very little schooling and had worked in turn on the farm where he was born and then on the Grenville Canal. After obtaining a surveyor's certificate, he worked at this profession for two years before moving in 1875 to the outskirts of St Mary's, where he took up farming. His *Poems by J.J. Macdonald* had been published in 1877 and *An Ideal Courtship* appeared forty-six years later, in 1923.

Very limited information about James Gay, the self-styled 'Poet

Laureate of Canada,' was forthcoming from his family, who had been stung by previous, satiric comments on his poetry, especially on his masterpiece, 'The Elephant and the Flea.' Deacon did learn, however, that Gay had been born in Devonshire, England, in 1810 and had immigrated to Canada in 1834, where he settled in Guelph, Ontario, and became a gunsmith and hosteler. One of his books of poetry had been published in Guelph in 1883 and by Leadenhall Press in London, England, in 1884 or 1885. He had also at one time simultaneously exhibited a two-headed colt at fall fairs in Ontario and sold copies of his poems. Deacon delighted in this last detail, as he revelled in the letter Gay had addressed to Tennyson as a dedication to the 1883 collection of his poems:

TO DR C.L. ALFRED TENNYSON,

POET LAUREATE OF ENGLAND, BARON, &c., &c.

Dear Sir,
Now Longfellow is gone there are only two of us left. There ought to be no rivalry between us two.
    'A poet's mind is clear and bright,
      No room for hatred, malice or spite.'
To my brother poet, I affectionately dedicate these original verses not before printed. Other verses from my pen, when so inspired, have been numerously printed in Canadian and American papers:
    'Giving a few outlines of my fellow-man,
      As nigh as I can see or understand.'
Almost the first poetry I can remember is the beautiful line –
    'Satan finds some mischief still for idle hands to do';
and similar sentiments likewise occur in my own poems –
    'Up, up with your flag, let it wave where it will:
      A natural born poet his mind can't keep still.'
I do not know whether a Baron or a Poet Laureate gets any wages in England. In Canada there is no pay.
    'Ambition is a great thing, of this I must say;
      This has been proved by the poet James Gay;
      He feels like Lord Beaconsfield, and best left alone;
      Respects every man and yet cares for none.'
It is a solemn thing to reflect that I am the link connecting two great countries.
    I hope when I am gone another may raise up.
    I believe you have one boy, dear Sir, and I read in the papers the other day as

he had been play-acting somewheres. I once exhibited a two-headed colt myself at several fairs, ten cents admission, and know something about play-acting and the like.

DON'T YOU LET HIM.

I hope to be in England sometime during the present year, if spared, and shall not fail to call round, if not too far from my lodging for a man nigh upon seventy-four, which, dear Sir, is the age of
> Yours alway,
>> James Gay,
>>> (this day).
> Poet Laureate of Canada
> and Master of All Poets.

Royal City of Guelph, Ontario. (pp 24-5)

On the whole, securing facts about MacRae and Gay was relatively straightforward. By comparison, his search for information about James McIntyre, the Ingersoll cheese poet, and about James D. Gillis, the bard of Cape Breton, was appropriately picaresque. McIntyre had one surviving child, his daughter, Mrs Kate Ruttan, a retired school-teacher living in La Vallée, Rainy River District, northern Ontario, and it was to her that Deacon wrote on the advice of an Ingersoll librarian. From Mrs Ruttan he learned that McIntyre had been born in Scotland in 1827 across the street from Donald Smith, later of the Canadian Pacific Railway. At fourteen, McIntyre emigrated to southern Ontario. He hired out as a hand on different farms and later came to St Catharines as a furniture dealer. From there he moved to Ingersoll, where he started a furniture factory which, as was the custom, also manufactured coffins, beds, chairs, and pianos. He became known as a Liberal and was much involved in community life until his death in 1906. This information came as a response to the letter Deacon had written to Mrs Ruttan on 10 June 1927, in which he had enclosed a questionnaire. She added details about her 'daddy dear,' which revealed that the daughter had inherited a full portion of her father's originality: 'I have his scarf & buckskin apron in blue parallelograms & cardinal equilateral triangles. He (daddy) was Furniture Dealer, Piano Dealer, Undertaker – used to pay his debts – but he took in Wm Watterworth also Sam Crotty for partners. Then busted. Broke his heart & couldn't pay for a sitting hen.'[5]

Closely following the completed questionnaire was a request from Mrs Ruttan that Deacon try to have a collection of her poems printed and one or two published in *Saturday Night*. She explained that other copies had been printed at her expense by *The Orillia Times* and that 'I travelled 3 mos. last winter among my scholars of Auld Lang Syne a-selling same':

I wish you would make me an offer to publish another M or 500, you selling the books to Odd Fellow & Masonic Lodges & paying me for the privilege in cash. Of course they would have to be published under my own name Kate McIntyre Ruttan. I can not furnish any money to publish same but you give me the fame, & sell the same to your Masons & Odd Fellows. Do please make me an offer, & publish some of my poems in your Saturday Night especially my verses on my dear dead daddy. Here's one to Winnipeg Tribune who were always hauling him over the coals & he 21 yrs beneath the sod.

> *Kate McIntyre Ruttan in Her Daddy's Defence*
> Let him rest, a worthy Briton
> Why should you his poor corpse sit on
> Why should you discharge your wit on
> His true tetrameter
> He had the sparrrk o' nature's fire
> Whilk Scottish poets a' desire
> Poetic license ruled his lyre
> And heart's diameter.[6]

In the space of ten days, Mrs Ruttan wrote Deacon five times and sent him one telegram:

DO NOT PUBLISH YEAR OF BIRTH HE WAS UNIVERSALLY BELOVED DIED 1906 HIS FACTORYS FOUNDATION FELL FROM THAMES TORRENT COFFINS CASKETS CARD TABLES PIANOS PIANOLOS BEDS BUNKS ETC SAILED DOWN RIVER THAMES WILL WRITE TONIGHT AWAIT MY LETTER BURNED UP FLOODED DOWN KATE RUTTAN.[7]

She was an eccentric blend of humour, bravado, opportunism, and thoroughgoing likeability. Behind the fun of her letters lay the persistence of the pioneer spirit, the whole proud tradition of the village poet and, above all, her affection for her father and his work:

Dear Deacon,
We do not say Mister Shakespeare, Mister Byron, Mister Bobbie Burrrrrns, Mister Cow-per &c., so why do you allow a plebian patronymic in front of your noble name. You're the 3rd or 4th Ecclesiastic in the realm – 1. Pope 2.

Archbishop 3. Bishop 4th Deacon – Say there was once a clever 'Model' man in our Ingersoll School. 'Be' you this Model Master or be you or be-est thee a boy of he? Say, please don't publish date of Daddy's *birth*. It will hurt me very much. But you can say he died in 1906 (just 21 yrs ago). Say, don't be in a hurry. I can get a wonder acc. of his busy life inside a week. Also he was the bright & shining star of Ingersoll Literary Society, attended a Night School for Elocution, & taught (unofficially) the boys how to 'spout.' 'Spout' was his own word for 'declaiming or elocution or harangue.' One morn at six he heard the crack of doom & the crash of worlds. His 3-story steam furniture factory fell (note 3 f's.) 'Apt alliterations artful aid.' Foundation of furniture factory fell & sailed down to River Thames – Coffins, caskets, cupboards, card tables, chairs, pianos, pianolas, all commingled in confusion worse confounded. Also he was previously burned out. He wrote me his true townsmen collected Six Hundred Dollars for him that mournful morn. He was the loveliest man on earth.[8]

Mrs Ruttan sent Deacon a copy of her own collection of poems, *Rhymes, Right or Wrong, of Rainy River*, which had been published in 1926 by The Times Printing Company of Orillia. It is a collector's treasure, with poems ranging from 'Doctor McKenzie' – 'Oh Doc McKenzie was his name, / And sawing bones it was his game, / And when he found that getting fame, / Thought he, I'll run for Mayor' – to a sequence of three patriotic poems, 'Uncle Sam's Proposal,' 'Miss Canada's Reply,' and 'Miss Canada Reconsiders.' She also composed verses in praise of the British royal family:

The Prince of Wales
Thou art God's own Prince David, excelsia in gloria,
The peace-maker's mantle hath fallen on thee,
Thou art wise with the wisdom of good Queen Victoria,
To thee all Canadians bend lowly the knee.[9]

Her subjects were local events and people, famous literary figures like Burns, and famous historical personalities like Mary, Queen of Scots, Napoleon, and John A. Macdonald. But always, her chief boast was her 'daddy dear,' in whose memory she wrote several of her best poems:

TO JAS. MCINTYRE
An undertaker bold
Who can't be undersold,
Jas. McIntyre;

He has caskets rich and rare,
Fit for the young and fair,
   All you'd desire.

And incomplete our verses,
Did we forget his hearses
   All built of glass,
And draped with hangings golden,
Of barbaric splendor olden,
   None can surpass.

He can furnish out your parlor
And your kitchen and your larder
   In style complete;
His goods are quite artistic
For a man so Methodistic,
   They're hard to beat.

Cheer up, poor man that weepest,
For his goods are far the cheapest
   That you can buy;
Go furnish out your dwelling,
While he's so cheaply selling
   His wareroom's nigh.

His book he'll give you gratis,
Filled with divine afflatus
   And local news;
High on the wall of fame
He hath written out his name,
   Inscribed his muse.

We think it would be hard
To find a Scottish Bard
   Of genius greater;
He surpasses Walter Scott,
His equal we see not
   From pole to equator.[10]

Understandably, apart from his initial enquiry, Deacon's correspondence with Mrs Ruttan was one-sided. The spate of letters and telegrams over such a short period caught him at his busiest moments in the writing of *The Four Jameses* and there is no record of any mutual correspondence.

The quest for information about the other living James, James D. Gillis, was the most protracted of all and has all the elements of farcical drama including search, obstacles, and ultimate success, won through, and despite, quirks of personality and circumstance. Famous for his book on Angus MacAskill, the Cape Breton giant, and for his four-pole map of the world, Gillis proved a tantalizing and elusive quarry for Deacon. He had been born in 1870 on Cape Breton Island and was raised by an uncle, since his own father had died when Gillis was seven months old. He was both a bright and an eccentric student and began teaching school in 1888. His teaching was interrupted in 1907-8 when he attended Normal School in Truro, Nova Scotia, and in 1909, when, for three months, he was a student at Dalhousie University, an experience he did not enjoy. Gillis was in the army from 1914 to 1916, at which time he left for the Canadian west, where he spent six years primarily school-mastering. In 1922, he returned to Cape Breton, where he lived until his death in 1965. Colourful, with a flamboyant and unmistakable personality, the mention of Gillis in *Saturday Night* had prompted letters as early as 1923 from W.H. Bucknell of Antigonish, who supplied information and copies of Gillis's *Canadian Grammar* and *The Great Election* as well as anecdotes about Gillis's year in Normal School.

In his search for the historical Gillis, Deacon enlisted the help of his friend Evelyn Tufts of Wolfville. She contacted Thomas Allen of Halifax, Gillis's bookseller, and relayed Allen's description of him during the three months Gillis spent at Dalhousie:

He was most uncouth, & very abrupt. Invited to tea at Professor MacNeils, he ate everything in sight, & then seizing his cap remarked that he must be going, or he'd miss his 'good supper.' He said disdainfully that he learned more standing on a street corner in Boston in one hour than he did at Dalhousie in the whole three months he was there. – When he received a low mark on a geometry paper he complained to the prof. who told him it was because it was so full of errors. Gillis replied that he had noticed that Euclid was full of mistakes, but failed to see why he should be punished for it. – He had all the Highlander's suspicion about him – threatened to sue Allen's for 87 cents on one occasion, & when in their shop (or any shop), would always retire to a secluded corner to take out his purse.[11]

By mid-June, Gillis had been located in Scotsville, Inverness County, and it was there that Evelyn Tufts sent a letter of enquiry which was acknowledged but not in any sense answered by Gillis. She wrote him again, asking specific questions and even going so far as to enclose sheets of foolscap. At the end of the first week of July, no reply from Gillis had been received and Mrs Tufts swung into action. She immediately arranged for someone to take a questionnaire and secure a personal interview with Gillis. The interview was delayed for ten days while her emissary was being tried in court on an arson charge. Once acquitted, he set off on his errand and after much searching found Gillis, on the side of a hill in the late July twilight, playing 'Scots Wha' Hae' on his bagpipes. The poet was pleased by the interview and completed the questionnaire he had been brought, which was duly forwarded to Deacon.

With the receipt of the Gillis questionnaire from Evelyn Tufts, who later declined Deacon's wish to dedicate *The Four Jameses* to her, all biographical material was finally in hand and Deacon was free to devote the month of August to the completion of his book. Significantly, as he gathered together the necessary biographical data and acquired a more immediate and intimate knowledge of his subjects, particularly of MacRae and Gillis, Deacon's attitude towards them and his book underwent a change. He had thought he was going to have some fun at the expense of 'the worst poets of Canada,' but his enquiries, the responses to them, and his own enlarged comprehension fleshed out the four Jameses and humanized them, so that they were transformed from aberrant literary specimens, to proud, honest, and comic originals. When this distinction became basic to Deacon's understanding, his original satiric intention modulated into the mode that was his true métier as a comic writer – rounded, sympathetic irony.

To Charles J. Fish, a great-grandson of James Gay, Deacon wrote:

Your great grandfather was not a well educated man as we understand the term now, and it is consequently easy to make fun of his work. Some of it is undoubtedly absurd. But I have conceived an affection for James Gay and some other Canadian writers of his class, and I am writing in the spirit of the greatest kindliness. If my readers smile occasionally, it is because of what Gay says, not because of my comment. I am not being funny at the old man's expense, as others have. He was probably as well educated as my own great grandfather, who was also a Canadian pioneer; and I am sure Gay had more enlightened views than my own ancestor, for whom I have every respect – considering his opportunities and accomplishment.[12]

His letter to Fish was not meant solely as a palliative. Ten days later, he wrote his friend Charles Conroy in the same vein: 'I have been surprised as I went on with these gentry to find how fond I grew of them, and how sympathetic I became towards their literary efforts. I now take my book quite seriously, and while the quotations are generally absurd, I have grown very tender of my poets, and have worked out defences for them.'[13]

The Four Jameses was unique in being Deacon's first sustained work. *Pens and Pirates* and *Poteen* had been collections of miscellaneous essays, while *Peter McArthur* had required three separate approaches – biographical, editorial, and critical. Deacon's real success in the *Jameses* is in the skill with which he sustained the comic irony of the narrating voice to bring together the work of such disparate poets. The book is organized around its principal subjects and is framed by a preface, 'The Royal Line,' and by three final chapters. 'The Ladies: God Bless Them!' is a brief treatment of three female counterparts to the four men: Kate Ruttan; Anastasia Hogan, a Newfoundland poet who was writing at the turn of the century; and Lillian Forbes Gunter of Saskatchewan, whose *Loving Memories and Other Poems* was published at Regina in the twenties. 'Journalistic Prose in Newfoundland' highlights the unconsciously comic merits of the newspaper clippings sent to him by Charles Conroy. 'Poets of an Old Tradition' is his peroration, a powerful and moving defence of the Jameses as belonging to the ancient and honourable tradition of oral and popular poets. What he hit upon, in fact, was the same pseudo-serious critical voice that Paul Hiebert later used so successfully for *Sarah Binks*; indeed, one of his proudest tributes was Hiebert's acknowledgment of the influence of *The Four Jameses* on his own work.[14] With such a technique he could defend and display his Jameses and, at the same time, make sport of the pompous seriousness of any academic critic who might venture to train the batteries of his erudition on their work. Not the poets, but pedantry and critical pretentiousness are being ridiculed in *The Four Jameses*, as they are in *Sarah Binks*, an exercise that was highly congenial to Deacon's well-developed academic prejudices.

'The Royal Line' with which the book opens establishes diction, tone, and raison d'être; in a bantering way it links the Jameses to Thackeray and the writing of *The Four Georges*; most important, it introduces the author, who makes no pretence at conventional impersonality or omniscience. Rather, he centres himself squarely in the text by a liberal use of first-person pronouns and adjectives, which enhance the comedy, allowing the writer to move at will, sometimes to the side of the Jameses and sometimes to the side of the reader. The dual association thus created is congenial and sympathetic to the benign irony that holds the book together. The order in which the poets appear – Gay, McIntyre, Gillis, and MacRae – is loosely chronological, although MacRae is out of sequence because Deacon discovered him only in 1926. The life and work of each poet are discussed in turn, with the longest treatment devoted to James Gillis. There are liberal quotations from the work of each, linked by the pliable ease of the urbane narrative voice, which is as protean as its subject matter, by turns naïve, pedantic, incredulous, pragmatic and, always, endlessly entertained.

The James Gay section begins with reference to his assumption of the self-styled title of Canadian poet laureate. The eccentricities of his writing style are attributed to his lack of education and this, in turn, is construed as a fortunate circumstance: 'the freedom of his compositions from deformities resulting from the cramping rules of grammar were only possible to one who had escaped the severer forms of a classical education. Thus Providence saw to it that the poet's formative years should be unhampered by stale conventions...' (p 11) Deacon quotes from 'The Great Exhibition' with reference to Gay's showing the two-headed colt and selling copies of his poems at the same time:

> The greatest wonder for four days
> To be seen at the stall of the poet Gay's,
> His twoheaded Colt so tall and thin,
> The greatest sight that ever was seen.
>
> Come one, come all, as well you may,
> Ten cents will only be the pay,
> Gay's five-cent poems will all surprise,
> Both farmers and their loving wives.
>
> Then rally, strangers, from day to day,
> To hear the flute the poet play,
> Come forward, gents, both stout and tall,
> As fifteen cents will pay for all. (p 16)

In the section on Gay's poems, Deacon assumes a poker-faced mock-pedantic mask:

In considering the poems themselves, there is little use discussing their form. Either one accepts it, or one does not. Argument gets one nowhere: if a reader cannot feel the strength and beauty of these spontaneous utterances, he should stick to Milton and Pope and content himself outside the domain of modern art expression. I have no defence for Gay in his breach with tradition, beyond saying bluntly that he needs none. I fully realize that some people may not care for his poems: the loss is entirely theirs; and, further, I am bold enough to say that the very irregularities that Gay's detractors find annoying are the chief reason his poems are treasured by those who know how to appreciate them.

Having disposed thus of all questions of rhyme, rhythm, meter and tune pattern, we may enter at once upon the serious problems of intellectual content. (p 26)

Some poems are attributed to concerns particular to literary biography. The poet's view of scripture and his mastery of the rhymed verse form are elucidated through reference to his composition, 'A Few Remarks on Samson':

> It appears in his day he was both strong and fast, he killed thousands
> Of the Philistines with the jawbone of an ass. No such man, we are
> Well sure, ever lived on earth before. His wife betrayed him in a
> Cruel way, caused his death without delay. His strength returned
> Before too late; hundreds of his persecutors received their just fate.
> His faith was very great at the last; he killed more with himself than
> By the bone of the ass. Infidels say this is all a farce, Samson
> Never killed his enemies with the jawbone of the ass. All those
> Sayings spring by chance, just like Paris, the city of France. (p 29)

Deacon's technique is highly successful. He parodies the conventions of academic criticism and critical biography by references to Schopenhauer, Sappho, Milton, Pope, and Browning. These are capped by such statements as the observation that 'the gnomic quality of [Gay's] verses is certainly reminiscent of some of William Blake's.' (p 36) Other characteristics associated with literary biography, such as definitive critical statements – 'It ["The Elephant and the Flea"] stands – without predecessor or successor – unique and triumphant' (p 37) – and descriptions of the artist as the unconscious prophet of a new age, are lampooned, but without belittling Gay, who remains the source rather than the butt of the section's humour.

The second section on James McIntyre, 'The Cheese Poet,' is divided into three parts: 'Cows and Coffins,' 'The Song of Economic Salvation,' and 'The Wider Outlook.' The first is biographical and opens with a play on the biographical convention of portentous treatment of setting:

In the little village of Forres, Morayshire, Scotland, made forever famous by

Macbeth's slaying of King Duncan, which Shakespeare was later to immortalize in the most popular of his tragedies, two men were born in houses exactly opposite each other, in the early part of the nineteenth century. Both of them were to play significant parts in the upbuilding of the Dominion of Canada, that was not to come into federated existence for another forty years. (p 43)

The two men were Donald Smith and James McIntyre. Much of the first section deals with biographical detail and in it Deacon used some Kate Ruttan material. The second part centres on McIntyre's 'Ode on the Mammoth Cheese':

ODE ON THE MAMMOTH CHEESE

We have seen thee, queen of cheese,
Lying quietly at your ease,
Gently fanned by evening breeze,
Thy fair form no flies dare seize.

All gaily dressed soon you'll go
To the great Provincial show,
To be admired by many a beau
In the city of Toronto.

Cows numerous as a swarm of bees,
Or as the leaves upon the trees,
It did require to make thee please,
And stand unrivalled, queen of cheese.

May you not receive a scar as
We have heard that Mr Harris
Intends to send you off as far as
The great world's show at Paris.

Of the youth beware of these,
For some of them might rudely squeeze
And bite your cheek, then songs or glees
We could not sing, oh! queen of cheese.

We'rt thou suspended from balloon,
You'd cast a shade even at noon,
Folks would think it was the moon
About to fall and crush them soon. (p 60)

McIntyre's epigrammatic poems on Shelley and Whitman are quoted
to illustrate his 'sublime' lack of ornamentation: 'It has been obvious
throughout that he does not pad his poems, except for once in a long
time when he is at his wits' end for a rhyme.'

SHELLEY

> We have scarcely time to tell thee
> Of the strange and gifted Shelley,
> Kind hearted man but ill-fated,
> So youthful, drowned and cremated. (p 78)

The treatment of James D. Gillis is the most extensive in *The Four
Jameses*. Of all the Jameses, Gillis was to Deacon the most fascinating,
partly because he was elusive and partly because his fame gave him the
qualities of a living legend. He was also the James who continued to
give Deacon the greatest pleasure: 'Often I have laughed over Gillis till
the tears rolled down my cheeks, and at the same time I marvelled that
the human mind could possibly have thrown up the images and ideas,
which he presents so forcefully to the reader.'[15] Like Gay and
McIntyre, Gillis was eccentric in his person and his verse. He was, in
addition, a black Celt, at once the earnest and comic quintessence of the
Gaelic bards of old Scotland. Deacon divided his treatment of Gillis into
four parts: biography and minor works, a discussion of *The Cape Breton
Giant*, comments on Gillis's powers of natural description and treatment of his political and philosophic 'obiter dicta.' (p 139) The narrator
retains his mask of naïveté and understatement in his initial reference
to *The Cape Breton Giant*:

The New York Public Library is guarding one copy, and recently a friend of
mine met a man on a train who had had his bound in flexible leather that he
might carry it constantly as a pocket companion, from which to refresh himself
in moments otherwise idle, or at times of mental depression. Mr William T.
Allen said lately in an interview that the demand for it was 'perfectly
surprising.' An order from Detroit came in while the interview was taking
place, and Mr Allen mentioned having recently received orders from Alaska
and India. The author himself mentions correspondence from Honolulu and
other distant points. (pp 85-6)

Using details both from the biographical questionnaire Gillis had
completed for Deacon and from Gillis's poetry, Deacon reconstructs a
life that is marvelously eccentric and anecdotal. For all its understate-

ment, hyperbole, and radical contrasts between the assumed serious tone of the narrative and illustrative quotations from the works, the biographical sketch is warm and genuinely appreciative of an obviously amazing human being. The contrasts in Gillis's description of his pastimes – 'Playing the violin and bagpipe, mathematics and reading, visiting and conversation, climbing mountains, &c. I can fish, swim and walk on stilts' (p 98) – is matched by the narrator's remarks on his subject's *amours*: 'It was the great Scottish-German philosopher's [Kant's] rule to consider every matter fully before committing himself by word or act. Gillis had the advantage of Kant in being able to console himself in writing poems to those he loved and lost':

RUTH ANNIE

Attired in Eaton's latest
She's just a sight to view;
Her sprightly step is music,
And art attained by few
Her talk is light and free,
And healthful as the breeze
That roams the broad Atlantic, –
    She's life or death to me.

For years you've been my study, –
I labour but to earn
A moment with Ruth Annie
Among yon shaded ferns.
Then fairest maid my glee
Is perfect joy with thee, –
O there I see Ruth Annie, –
    She's life or death to me. (pp 102-3)

Discussion of *The Cape Breton Giant*, of Gillis's talents for natural description, and his obiter dicta consists almost entirely of extracts from the work linked by a loose narrative thread. The pretences of critical biography are still satirized through exaggeration and word-play:

Just as we read *The French Revolution* for the flavour of Carlyle, regardless of how interesting his facts may be in themselves, so we read *The Cape Breton Giant* for Gillis rather than MacAskill, and are richly repaid ... So I call Gillis artist first because his masterpiece contains a higher percentage of extraneous matter than any other book, and second because of his style – now Jamesian in its prolixity, now Stevensonian in its colloquial and conversational ease and gracefulness, but always essentially, and at its noblest, pure Gillisian and inimitable. (pp 115-6)

As always, Deacon's greatest delight is in quoting the master: 'It is of little interest to refer to that discovery of America by the Northmen. It was at best a slipshod affair, and resulted in songs which our ordinary people of this day could not understand.' (p 117)

Gillis's unconscious comedy is a source of mirth, not ridicule. Deacon quotes a long passage from 'MacAskill's Grave,' which highlights 'the author's specially apt choice of words.' (pp 133-4) The final paragraph of that passage is vintage Gillis: 'The breath of St Ann's cemetery is as fragrant and sweet as that of a flower garden. As one walks along he is apt to imagine that a costly deodorant has been sprinkled about a few minutes ago.' (p 134) The ingenuous tone of Deacon's narrative links, creates, and manipulates a skilful sense of timing and anticlimax in the contrast between Gillis's words and Deacon's comments:

Be it announced that Her Majesty Queen Victoria invited Angus MacAskill to Windsor Castle. He soon called upon her. She gave him a cordial reception. She chatted pleasantly with him for a few hours.

She was highly *interested* in his great size, and complimented him very warmly. She presented him with two rings of gold.

MacAskill regretted that there was no means of showing his power of lifting, but he thought of a plan to leave a token of his strength on the sly. He walked back and forth before the Queen, secretly pressing the carpet with his heels. When he left, the carpet, though thick and strong, was cut here and there in bread cutter fashion, by the heels of the giant.

The Queen said afterwards that he was the tallest, the stoutest and the strongest man that ever entered the palace. (p 130)

The narrator adds: 'What else the Queen said, when she discovered her ruined carpet, may be imagined most accurately by those who know how closely Victoria kept track of her personal possessions.' (p 131)

The appreciation of James MacRae continues in a similar way. Deacon reviews both MacRae's poems on Scots Canadians and *An Ideal Courtship*, a rural Canadian love story running to seven hundred lines, the work of his retirement years. Deacon remarks that when he first reviewed the book, 'I was under the impression that the author's principal aim was to write a moral tract in the palatable form of a story, embellished with the poet's art. Consequently I referred to the book as "an antidote to lascivious novels, treatises on birth control, and the evils of mixed marriages." I have since learned that his intention was not the implanting of ideals in the minds of young Canadians, but "to laud the Scotch".' (pp 154-5) Of all the Jameses, MacRae is treated with the least enthusiasm by Deacon. Although the interweaving of quotations and narrative links is skilful, there is a residual seriousness in Deacon's criticism which suggests an abiding antipathy to the doctrinaire, however harmless and amusing: 'But if MacRae did not consciously intend to preach, his mind, like Bernard Shaw's, runs to moral problems so much that his poem is as much a sermon as it is a story.' (p 156)

The following two chapters, 'The Ladies: God Bless Them!' and 'Journalistic Prose in Newfoundland,' are basically anthologies of poetry and prose and for the most part arose from the original 'Booby Prize' idea and from Deacon's correspondence in connection with the Jameses. In the concluding chapter, 'Poets of an Old Tradition,' Deacon relinquishes his comic mask in favour of an urgent and serious peroration in defence of the Jameses. In it Deacon reveals his compelling identification with these poets who represent in their best way what he espouses in his: the celebration of the native and the local in a distinctive, Canadian voice. The Jameses continue the great and ancient tradition of the minstrels who demonstrate

that poetry should be simple and grow out of the more memorable things in common experience; that any one with natural talent and a yearning to do so may make poetry; and that the poetry so made is primarily for home consumption, to be directly communicated to immediate associates and acquaintances – not printed in a far place, and picked up by curious strangers in the proportion of one to ten thousand or a hundred thousand of the population. (p 196)

Deacon was never more sincere or eloquent than in this final chapter. The Jameses he calls 'poets of an old tradition,' all of them except Gay of Scotch descent, owing much to the example of Robert Burns, and worthy in their own right to the honourable title of 'Caledonian Bards.' In their links with the past they are the voice of the pioneers:

As one recalls Loch Lomond and Melrose Abbey, and other names beyond count in British poetry, which stand for the love of a local scene, transmuted by the poet's art into an integral part of our racial heritage, he will not scoff at the power of the local to move the whole nation and even persons of other nationality; but will be anxious for the day when every Canadian plain and peak and lake wins immortal life in song or story. The local poets have a great work to do, even if their verses only teach the people of their communities to venerate the hills by which they are surrounded. (pp 200-1)

They are also heroes worthy of acclaim and, 'when the limitations of an old warrior like McIntyre are apparent, it is sanity and not sacrilege to smile at them; but it should be done kindlily, remembering always their inescapable disavantages, their valor and their chivalry.' (p 205) In his final plea for the Jameses, and charge to his readers, all the Methodist ministers in his background are very evident. Moved himself, his words are moving in a final description of his four subjects which is, in considerable measure, a portrait of every literary creator and certainly the final affirmation of his Jamesian comedy:

Their aspirations, their will to universal betterment, and their intuitive reach beyond the measure of their grasp is easily traceable through their writings, like the proverbial thread of gold. By these shall they be judged and not by flaws in the pattern. The more their work is pondered, the greater one's affection for them, the greater his admiration for their honest efforts to noble expression and the greater his tolerance for mistakes growing out of inevitable limitations of opportunity, and creating the human, personal touches that first attract readers to them. Who sees not this, has lost the better, sweeter half of their message, and is himself to blame. (p 206)

By the end of August, the manuscript was completed and Deacon was looking forward to early publication. Although Graphic Press was bedevilled by chronic problems of management and finance, by the end of November he was working on the page proofs and the book appeared on 20 December 1927. It was too late to take advantage of the 1927 Christmas book sales; even more aggravating, continuing problems at Graphic created maddening delays in distribution of review copies, promotional literature, and the books themselves. Sales were weak, and a few years later Deacon ruefully reflected on its fate: 'There is a constant trickle of demand for it; but its flavor is so distinct that it means nothing to the average reader; and so I do not know when a publisher will be tempted again.'[16] In the event, his pessimism was unjustified; Ryerson Press reprinted it in 1953 and Macmillan in 1974.

In spite of disappointing sales, Deacon had reason to be pleased by the positive critical response to *The Four Jameses*. He was especially delighted by the review in the 9 June 1928 number of *The Saturday Review of Literature*. In it William Rose Benét congratulated him on his mellow and sympathetic mood, and concluded that this book would have delighted Charles Lamb and Robert Southey: 'It turns up fresh furrows in a field too little tilled. One could wish that so ardent an appreciator as, for instance, Mr Louis Untermeyer, who has for years, as an avocation, collected the curious masterpieces of the humbler singers of the United States, would do a similar treatise upon them.' Deacon wrote to Burton Kurth, 'As this is the first foreign printed opinion on anything of mine, I feel very happy about it. Isn't Gillis a triumph of the Creator's skill?'[17]

In the Ryerson reprint of 1953 extra details were added from Gillis's correspondence concerning his trip to Palestine and his association with The Song Fishermen, a Nova Scotian writers' group. Then, in February 1963, Deacon was approached by Robert Weaver and gave his permission for an adaptation of *The Four Jameses* to be prepared by Tommy Tweed for CBC radio. He wrote Weaver: 'I was too subtle for the general public. I got letters denouncing me for publishing such trash. They had wasted $2 etc. On the other hand, one woman had hers rebound expensively in leather. My royalties were too small to be remembered. The book was caviar to the general.' His closing remarks showed, however, that he had lost none of his warmth of affection and respect for his four subjects: 'Of course Tommy will have to re-write *my* stuff. He would be stupid not to. But I hope to God he doesn't try to improve on Jimmy Gay or the Cheese Poet or any of those dear souls – all dead now. May they rest in peace, having made this earth brighter and funnier.'[18]

As a writer in the twenties Deacon had known marvellous years of discovery, emancipation, hard work, achievement, and reputation, which decisively transformed the apprentice into the professional. By 1928 he had established himself as Canada's premier literary reviewer. Pierce had flattered and promoted Deacon during his first months and years in Toronto, and out of that association had emerged two books which had made him a recognized literary figure. Graphic Press had given him the opportunity to become identified with Canada's first all-Canadian publishing venture and so to satisfy his militant literary nationalism. Whether arguing in *Poteen* against Canada's annexation to the United States, or against Arthur Stringer's egregious exploitation of Canadian subject matter, or writing a survey of Canadian literature, Deacon was articulating his mission in an arena he had claimed for his own. *The Four Jameses*, for and because of all its nonsense, was a celebration of local poets who were comically but no less importantly Canadian. By the beginning of 1928, Deacon could survey the previous eight years and be justifiably proud of his accomplishments. Doors had opened for him in ways that he had not imagined possible and his publishing achievements brought ever-rising expectations and energies to his career as writer and critic. With his unexpected departure from *Saturday Night* and the subsequent search for other work, his expectations were for the moment cruelly truncated, but in spite of that he had known, in the twenties, 'great days.'

CHAPTER SEVEN

The Survival Game:
Journalism in the Thirties

URING THE YEARS AT *Saturday Night,* Deacon had revelled in claiming for himself the distinction of being the first full-time literary journalist in Canada; for more than a decade after his dismissal in the spring of 1928 he was to experience all the hazards and insecurities of such a doubtful eminence. On the surface he assimilated the shock of dismissal with scarcely a tremor. He was buoyed up by Sally's unwavering faith in him, by his own untarnished sense of mission, and by his theosophist's conviction of personal destiny and inevitable upward progress. By mid-April he was working furiously to establish a syndicated book review service that, he hoped, would make his name familiar from coast to coast. Fortuitously, he met Laura Carten, 'Farmer Smith' of *The Halifax Herald* and his devoted correspondent, in Toronto two weeks after he left *Saturday Night.* She successfully undertook to secure the *Herald* for his new venture; he was on his way, he felt sure, to a brighter and broader journalistic future than *Saturday Night* alone could ever have provided.

The aggressive quest for advertising lineage that had taken so much time at *Saturday Night* now became the energetic pursuit of his own business. He wrote to newspapers in all parts of Canada and travelled throughout southern and eastern Ontario soliciting contracts for his work. Many friends and correspondents besides Laura Carten worked to further his plans – Emily Murphy, Ernest Harrold, John Murray Gibbon, M.W. Rossie of *The London Advertiser*, and Annie Charlotte Dalton were among those who used their influence and connections to add newspapers to his string.[1] He also sought out freelance projects, first considering the launching of a Canadian Book of the Month Club, and then planning 'Deacon's Book-News Service,' supplying 'editing, managership, illustrations, articles, advertising, and make-up – whatever is required – in any sort of periodical from a daily to an annual, and from a half column to a 32-page literary section.' Though neither of these ventures materialized, syndication gradually became a reality, although 'once I was down to 22¢ in the bank and less than $1 in my pocket.'² By the end of May he was syndicated in eight newspapers: *Halifax Herald, The Sentinel* of Woodstock, New Brunswick, *The Ottawa Citizen, Brockville Recorder, Port Hope Times, St Catharines Standard, London Free Press, Winnipeg Mirror.* In July he began publishing in *The Vancouver Province,* and by the end of the summer he had added *The Brantford Expositor* and the *The Border Cities' Star* of Windsor. Shortly thereafter he had acquired a total of thirteen papers in his syndicate.

Deacon's fee for large papers was '$5 per article, payable monthly' and subject to increase if newspaper circulation arose. For smaller papers like *The Port Hope Times,* he charged $1 per article. It was enough – just – to pay for groceries, but from the $65 a week he had just been making at *Saturday Night,* it was a tremendous financial drop for a man supporting a family of five .

He sold his wares to editors by stressing his own keen assessment of his potential audience: 'A thousand people want to know what is in the most-talked-of books for one who wants to buy them. I aim at a fresh, attractive newspaper story, not at criticism. By this method *The New York Times* built up its Book Review Section and made it the most read weekly feature of the paper.'³ To his friends, however, he confided his determination to educate his new and potentially far larger readership:

I am trying to be popular, and avoid the appearance of a book review. If I am left alone (I here impart a secret) I'll gradually attract and acclimatize my new group of readers; will write more and more freely; and by imperceptible degrees will change the thing from a feature article into a book review, or causerie ... I know, too, that some of the things my s.n. readers like are not in these newspaper articles; but I also know those things will come back as soon as I feel secure again...⁴

His syndicated feature articles, beginning in May 1928, were from 2,000 to 2,500 words long, designed to combine, in the persona of the reviewer, the qualities of the man of letters and the man in the street. Often they dealt with biographies, assuming the form of a highly personalized story, combining details of the book under consideration and of Deacon's own reactions to it. Always they were written with a keen awareness of the reviewer's tightrope walk between wooing his readers and compromising his principles:

The review must stand up as a piece of writing in competition with every news-story, feature article or short story and every novel ever written, or you will be addressing nobody who listens; and in this case you will soon cease to review at all. Never begin with the fallacy that people want to read you; they want to play cribbage or chat with a friend ... You have to woo an audience for yourself with all the devices that create liking and respect. Simplicity and forthrightness are the best means. No amount of cleverness can substitute for integrity. Readers will know when you are lying, even if you have argued yourself into believing what you are saying.[5]

By far the greatest stroke of good fortune to come Deacon's way in these early months of syndication was his appointment to Toronto's *Mail and Empire*. Fred Jacob, its literary editor, had died on 3 June 1928 and John Murray Gibbon immediately recommended Deacon to John Scott, the newspaper's managing editor. In September he was hired at $50 a week; within the year, with syndication, he was earning a weekly wage of $100.

With a circulation of 120,000 *The Mail and Empire* was some 20,000 copies ahead of *The Globe*, its morning competition. It had been acquired in 1927 by Isaac Walton Killam, the Montreal financier of Nova Scotian birth, and in Deacon's words it was 'traditionally capitalist and imperialist, the chief organ of the Conservative party and the leading morning paper of this Dominion.'[6] Within this apparently restrictive context, however, Deacon from the first found surprising freedom. As he confided to his friend, Donat LeBourdais, when endorsing the latter's candidacy for the CCF party in 1935, 'in return for the freedom the Mail accords me, I *voluntarily* avoid embarrassing them unduly by keeping their name out of my more radical activities.'[7] Although he had heavy responsibilities to his other syndicated papers, he was not slow to realize that *The Mail and Empire* was his flagship, relieving him of the worst of his tensions about his family's support and even enabling him to set himself up in a small office on Adelaide Street with the services of a part-time secretary, May Sharples, a fellow theosophist and former staunch assistant in producing *Saturday Night*'s literary supplements.

Originally entitled 'The Saturday Book Page Conducted by William Arthur Deacon,' the section was at times also called 'Saturday Book Reviews.' It was marked by a characteristic format which was to last throughout Deacon's subsequent career: a feature article on a book or a literary topic or event; usually four or five shorter reviews of other books; items and commentary on events and issues of literary interest; a briefly annotated list, often numbering from ten to twenty books or more, of recently published works of fiction, poetry, drama, criticism, history, politics. In his early period with *The Mail and Empire*, the book pages' items of literary interest bore the title 'News Notes on Current Books and the Men and Women Who Write Them,' successor to his popular 'Saved from the Waste-Basket' in *Saturday Night*. In addition, for the first six months, the book page included a 'John Wants to Know' section in question and answer style, which allowed Deacon to provide information about current literary techniques or to evaluate literary theories or tell amusing anecdotes. A recurring feature was the 'Books of the Month We Recommend' section. In the first months there were articles by Madge Macbeth, B.K. Sandwell, G. Frederick Clarke, and John L. Charlesworth. After January 1929, there were virtually no articles written by others except for Nina Jamieson's short familiar essays on a variety of non-literary topics, which she contributed over a period of several years.

Although Deacon's first columns with *The Mail and Empire* filled a complete page, his space was progressively cut down. He soon was sharing, and was for eight years to share, page space with practically every other department of the newspaper – 'Music and Drama Notes'; Bertha Green's 'Young Canadians' Section'; Thornton Burgess's 'Bedtime Stories'; 'Furniture, Antiques and Decoration'; radio listings; gardening and bridge notes; 'Realm of Religion'; church listings; 'Woman's Point of View'; 'Automotive Topics.'

In his first five years with *The Mail and Empire*, Deacon reviewed approximately 1,300 books. Of those, only a handful were reviewed by others like J.L. Charlesworth, Wilfred Reeves, and R.A. Farquharson. The schedule he established became his way of life for the next thirty years. He slept late in the morning, rose about noon for a mid-day meal, then went to his office on Adelaide Street in the afternoon for correspondence, business details, and meetings connected with those organizations to which he belonged in the thirties – the Writers' Club of Toronto, the Arts and Letters Club, the Canadian Authors' Association, the Association of Canadian Bookmen. After supper in town, he would return to his office to read for his Saturday page and write more letters, leave for home late in the evening and then read until two or three o'clock in the morning. When the increasing inroads of the Depression forced him to give up his rented office in October 1934, and to move home to work, he in no way relaxed his workload. Generally Sundays were given over to family and relaxation, but in the press of busy seasons they too were devoted to work.

By Friday afternoon the literary page was ready for typesetting or 'make-up,' which normally took two and a half to three hours. With his coffee in his hand, Deacon would go to the composing room and supervise the actual placing of the type, photos, and sketches in the page form. To do this, he would stand behind the compositor and tell him where to put various reviews. If the review was either too long or too short, it would have to be immediately revised in the composing room itself. Next, a proof-sheet would be printed and pulled, then checked and corrected by Deacon, after which appropriate changes and corrections would be made before the page would be 'put to bed' or locked up for printing. During the five or six busiest weeks of the year, in November and early December, the special two-page book week section and then the Christmas literary section could each take easily six to eight hours to make up. He thoroughly enjoyed Friday afternoons in the composing room, fraternizing with his colleagues and learning the ropes from 'Dandy' Faulkner, who made up the book page. He was most amazed at Matt Black who, while making up the editorial page, objected loudly and constantly to everything F.D.L. Smith, the editor-in-chief, had written: 'His lectures were highly informative. While delivering them, he would read the type of all my reviews – backward and upside down – and discuss the various books with me very intelligently.'[8]

Syndication, he soon found, required enormous tact and patience as well as working to a gruelling weekly schedule. Sometimes his papers did not print his articles and sometimes they didn't pay promptly or at all. There were many complaints about length and subject matter, but few, if any, favourable comments and virtually none of the 'audience participation' that he had enjoyed with his *Saturday Night* readers and that he was beginning to enjoy from his work on *The Mail and Empire*. Response to mail solicitations for further syndicate papers was disheartening – 'Out of 87 samples set out in typed ms. (fancy the work) I drew one (1) order from a $1 party for one (1) month's trial.'[9] Furthermore, as the Depression worsened, his papers dropped away alarmingly. A possibility of adding the Southam chain through the good offices of Ernest Harrold of *The Ottawa Citizen* came to nothing and when *The Montreal Herald* took him on, a great addition at the time, it was to drop him only a few months later. He had hoped to expand his syndicate to the point of hiring reviewers and leaving himself free to give his time to feature articles on chosen books, but along with millions of others he was inexorably pulled into the struggle of the hungry thirties, until early in 1931 he found even his *Mail and Empire* position seriously jeopardized.

In January, John Scott called Deacon into his office and issued an ultimatum: if Deacon could raise half his salary from book advertising revenues, then the Book Department, though drastically cut down, could continue. During the rest of the year his energies and experience were channelled into what amounted to a campaign of desperation to secure the required revenues. After private meetings with Macmillan, Musson, Thomas Nelson, Doubleday, and McClelland and Stewart, and then a joint meeting where he presented his case to all five, he was able to report a qualified success to Scott: 'They could not act as a body; but had sent each member a strong letter urging that I be favourably received when I came around to canvas them individually ... So I started around again, this time securing definite promises. Revenues from books should not be less than $3,000, and will likely not exceed $4,000 for the 12 months ending February 1st, 1932.'[10] By constantly soliciting advertising he was able to add other publishers to his first five, and in November 1931, he could report to Scott that he had raised the whole of his $2,500 salary in ten months. He had been so strikingly successful, in fact, that Thomas Colgate of the Advertising Department was appointed his assistant and together they continued to solicit the lineage they needed.

That particular disaster had been averted, but at enormous cost to Deacon's time and his nervous energy. He had, he wrote to Scott, a queer fear of a boss: 'Most of the men I have worked for have been gentlemen, and my good friends. But I never got over my fear; and that is why, sometimes, when you speak to me, I am so dumb and stupid. I just can't think at all ... Sometimes the sight of you coming along the hall just made me wilt instinctively.'[11]

The next blow was not for him alone: in 1932 *The Mail and Empire* reduced both pay and personnel. Deacon was one of the lucky ones; he was kept on, but at $40 a week instead of the $50 he had been getting. Money from his syndicate was reduced to a trickle and in 1933 he reached the nadir of his own particular Depression. Of his papers, only the *London Advertiser* was left; he was, he figured, $800 behind in taxes, mortgage interest, and office rent and he had to borrow $500 to keep going. To W.T. Allison he wrote:

How in the deuce I am to meet my ordinary debts and expenses I can't imagine.

However, it has been a long, hard fight of 12 years; and I really don't see anything for it but to struggle on in debt and poverty for as long as possible and sink with my colors at the peak when the pumps won't work and the ship won't float any longer.

One of the last things Janey [Emily Murphy] wrote me was 'What times to be living in; – or, can they be borne?' She's well out of it.[12]

Deacon's distress, as he well knew, was relative – he was still paid a weekly wage far beyond the reach of the vast majority of Canadians; some of his oldest and most prosperous friends were far less fortunate. Matt Hayes, for instance, lost his job, his home, his health, and his family. Deacon had Sally's unswerving strength and faith to support him, as well as her help in reviewing when the load became impossible; their children were healthy; and they even had a small but cheery addition to their reduced income – Sally bred and sold canaries. Besides, from 1931 to 1935 he added some $75 a year to his income as Canadian correspondent for *The Argus* of Melbourne, Australia. The Canadian Manufacturers' Association had chosen him from a group of twelve journalists and both the honour and the international exposure pleased him as much as the money. Furthermore, he was aided in these anxious years by the friendship and support of Robert Farquharson, who had come from *The Globe* to *The Mail and Empire* in 1927 and who, in 1934, became managing editor. Deacon's correspondence with Farquharson, whether about plans for the book page, advertising revenue, or salary, is characterized by a frankness and trust that rested upon mutual respect and sympathy. Another ally was J.V. McAree, whose daily column, 'The Fourth Column,' was a popular feature of *The Mail and Empire*. McAree would often write him a note praising an 'extraordinarily fine Saturday article,' and Deacon never ceased to be grateful for what he termed McAree's 'generous valor.'

Such precious associations in his own paper were immensely extended through his activities in the Toronto Writers' Club, founded in 1923 by Elton Jonson and Jack Charlesworth to take the place of the Toronto Men's Press Club, which had never lasted long in any of its incarnations.[13] Vice-president in 1930, Deacon became president in October 1931. Among the club's members were E.J. Pratt, Bertram Brooker, Merrill Denison, C.W. Jefferys, Wilson MacDonald, Gordon Sinclair, and Charles G.D. Roberts. Initially a business and social organization, the Club had also developed commercial ambitions. In the fall of 1930, its Marketing Committee prepared the 312-page *Canadian Writers' Market Survey*, an inventory of writing markets in the

English-speaking world, of Canadian periodicals, and of non-Canadian periodicals suitable to Canadian writers. In addition, it contained information about the specific requirements of various book publishers and the specific terms on which a selected group of authors' agents handled manuscripts. Deacon was part of the Marketing Committee and worked hard to prepare the *Survey*, which was published by Graphic Press in April 1931. It proved valuable to Canadian journalists and writers. More important than its marketing function, however, was the Club's role as a convivial social organization in bleak times: dinners and 'smokers,' with the presentation of plays and poetry readings, were occasions of general hilarity and relaxation, and the club's august publication, 'The Shovel,' was a compendium of irreverent nonsense designed to dispel the prevailing gloom. One such skit, a satire on a recent free speech controversy in Toronto, was interrupted by a fire on a cold January night in 1931. Club headquarters in the Brown Betty Tearooms were hastily vacated and 'we lost Judge Coatsworth's whiskers, Wilf Reeves' left overshoe, and all the Club's furniture. None of these was covered with insurance. We now carry insurance but so far have had no luck with it.'[14]

The Club's trademark was informality and its basic prohibitions covered both the membership of women, who had their own very active Press Club, and the reporting of proceedings or of members' conversations. In 1933, the tenth anniversary of its founding, Jack Charlesworth prepared a brief history for 'The Shovel' which captured the high spirits and lack of pretension that balanced the workaday professionalism of the Club's members. In the same issue Deacon summarized the Club's achievements: 'Of course, the Club's real distinction lies in having hung together through so many crises with a minimum of ill-feeling; and in having such a good time doing it.'[15]

The most important contributing factor to Deacon's morale and his developing skills as a journalist was the camaraderie he enjoyed with his fellow staffers at *The Mail and Empire* and the expansion there of his journalistic skills: 'I have never worked with such a splendid group of men. Decent fellows, far above the newspaper average in education and intelligence, always pleasant.'[16] Effectively in these years he became a generalist in his interests and his assignments, writing copy on current news every Thursday as well as doing art and theatre reviews. One of the latter, a panning of Shaw's *Too Good to Be True* in October 1932, sparked a controversy in *The Canadian Forum* that lasted until August 1933. In the midst of a flurry of articles and letters on the course of Canadian criticism, Deacon presented his case with blunt practicality:

The last thing I should be sensitive about is a theatre review. I do not profess to know the theatre, and hate being crowded for time. When I joined the Mail, the drama was no part of my job. Nowadays, I am so happy to hang on to a salary that I should be willing to write racing tips after a scrutiny of samples of the steeds' manure. The Mail only uses me where there is some literary flavour – Coward, Shaw, O'Neill ... I had to write a half-column article between the end of a late play and the make-up of our first edition. I had exactly 20 minutes. I write slowly at the best of times, and congratulated myself on being able to press down enough keys in the period.[17]

The range of his dispatches for the Melbourne *Argus* demonstrates the expansion of his journalistic interest and expertise. Roy L. Curthoys, its editor, asked for 1,500-word articles informing his readers about Canadian life and issues: 'I like discussion of those homely details which, while they are commonplaces to the inhabitants of the country from which the correspondent is writing, are of deep interest to Australian readers.'[18] Deacon's original dispatches, 'Canada, the Anomalous,' 'Canada's Hopes,' 'Is Canada Dry?,' 'A Land of Lakes,' were followed by articles on the Imperial Economic Conference held in Ottawa in July 1932, and then by a spate of articles on a range of timely topics, from the creation of the CCF to Canadian food and the federal Liberal victory of 1934. When he mounted a graphic attack on the Canadian penal system, 'Darkest Canada,' and a defence of pacifism, 'Canada and War,' Curthoys drew the line: the first was returned as 'too horrifying,' and the second because 'we do not want for reasons of public policy to present Canada as an unwilling partner in the Empire.'[19] Deacon continued his work for the *Argus* until 1935, relishing the chance to editorialize and also hoping, valiantly but vainly, to educate Curthoys, a conservative imperialist, to his views: 'As a writer, increasingly events have driven me from the "pure art" concerns of a critic to comment on affairs – economics, politics, international relations, social welfare, etc. – and the breakdown of capitalism and liberalism have shoved me out into the radical ranks. I am a pacifist, a socialist and a nationalist: these three run naturally together here.'[20]

At home, Deacon found the ideal focus for his broadened interests in the Couchiching Conferences of 1935 and 1936. A development of the YMCA, summer institutes on Lake Couchiching had been flourishing since 1905. In 1932 the Canadian National Council of the YMCA had initiated the annual 'Canadian Institute on Economics and Politics' at Geneva Park, Lake Couchiching, a response to 'the gradually increasing awareness of what were felt to be the prevailing injustices of the North American Depression economy.'[21]

The Institute was attended largely by Canadians and by some non-Canadians, by those interested in national and international affairs, and by a whole cross-section of Canadian society – businessmen, teachers at all levels, politicians, representatives from farms and trade unions, students, social and religious workers, representatives from various civic and community organizations. The ten-day conferences took the form of lectures presented by acknowledged authorities, questions, round-table discussions, and group meetings.

Deacon's discovery of the Couchiching Conference was quite fortuitous. He and Sally had given up their Bobcaygeon cabin and had begun holidaying at Wilson's Point, Orillia, some four miles from Geneva Park. In August 1935, he cancelled a planned canoe trip when he noticed that the Reverend C.E. Silcox, head of the Social Service Council for the United Church of Canada, was to speak at the Canadian Institute on Economics and Politics. Silcox wanted to discuss Deacon's recently published *My Vision of Canada*, which had appeared in 1933, and so he, with son Bill, paddled to the Conference. He not only met Silcox, but also heard several lectures and acted as chairman of one session. He was impressed by the speakers, by the chairmen, by the topic – Canadian foreign relations – and, naturally, by the fact that he even saw one participant carrying a copy of *My Vision of Canada*. He wrote to J.V. McAree: 'I hope that a bunch of us, writers and nationalists and such, can get together for 10 days at Lake Couchiching next summer to participate in the discussions of the Institute and also, in our own cottages and in free hours, stage our own little conference to discuss literature and destiny and so on.'[22] If Deacon found the mood and orientation of the Institute congenial, he also had come upon a non-literary institution characterized by a broadly representative attendance and a balance of instruction, discussion, informal personal contact, and intellectual challenge that was totally congenial to him.

The Institute itself was like a microcosm of the themes, demands, and expectations of his own professional career, and he also saw in the participants at the conference the embodiment of his ideal reading public. In August 1936, he returned to Couchiching in the double capacity of member of its committee and correspondent for *The Mail and Empire*. The subject of the 1936 conference was 'Canada's

Responsibility for World Peace' and Deacon attended forty-five sessions – lectures, round tables, discussions – in two weeks. There were 200 delegates and sixteen speakers, with Sir Robert Falconer as president. Deacon himself chaired five sessions, one of them featuring Professor Jean Bruchési of the University of Montreal, 'who came prepared to present the French-Canadian viewpoint against Orange hostilities and was left gasping at the welcome he got.' J.S. Woodsworth was present and made an impromptu fifteen-minute speech, 'the strongest and smoothest speech I ever heard him make.'[23] As well as enjoying the excitement, urgency, and confusion of sending his dispatches to *The Mail and Empire* by telegraph and telephone in competition with other reporters, Deacon was delighted by the calibre of the speakers and of the discussion and by the emergent nationalism of the conference. It was also on this occasion that his meeting with the historian, Arthur Lower, inaugurated a friendship that was to last for some twenty-five years.

Specific topics were of engrossing interest to him: Hugh Keenley-side gave two lectures on 'The Situation in the Far East.' Dr R.A. MacKay of Dalhousie University talked three times about 'Economic Considerations Affecting Canada's Foreign Policy,' and Lower addressed the delegates twice on 'The Canadian National Foreign Policy.' Raymond Buell spoke about the United States in three addresses – 'United States Neutrality,' 'The United States in the Pacific,' and 'United States Policy in Relation to Great Britain and Canada.' Colonel H. Crerar discussed 'Canada's Defence Policy' and A.A. McLeod gave a lecture on the topic 'Is Peace Possible under Capitalism?'

At the termination of the Institute, Deacon wrote a letter of thanks to George Sutton Patterson, metropolitan general secretary for the YMCA, to congratulate and thank him for the success of the conference. He described himself as 'elated over the results you have achieved,' suggested wider distribution of the Institute's annual report, more publicity in the form of newspaper advertising and wanted to put Patterson in touch with Frank McDonagh, his correspondent in the grass-roots nationalist group, the 'Native Sons of Canada.' He added, 'I should like to keep in close touch with you, and help to interest people, because there are at least 20 of my friends who ought to be active in the conferences and whatever groups are going.' His own conclusions were characteristically hopeful:

That last day I questioned each as I said good-bye and found a most optimistic mood universal. Educational work of this kind is legitimately within your province; the rising school of nationalists desire nothing better because we believe that the facts point to certain conclusions. I realize that when it gets to active politics you are out; but while giving all scope to all shades of opinion, you may be of inestimable service in providing a forum.[24]

'I would not have missed this show for the world,' he reported to Robert Farquharson, '[I] wish you could have attended, both for the pleasure you would have taken and that you might realize I am not exaggerating. It has been significant *very*... I crave the assignment for 1937.'[25]

While a temperamental insecurity had always threatened him and would continue to do so, Deacon had remarkably extended the range of his interests and his journalistic skills in these eight years with *The Mail and Empire*. A passionate nationalist he remained, but the field of his endeavours was, now, not so narrowly focused on literature. He highly valued his experience in writing for the *Melbourne Argus* and out of his syndicate *The London Advertiser* still remained; he was heavily involved with the Association of Canadian Bookmen and anticipated editing a magazine for them; he was active in all the affairs of the Toronto Writers' Club, the Toronto branch of PEN, the Canadian Authors' Association, the Arts and Letters Club, and he was constantly in demand as a speaker in Toronto and around the province. He did not, however, get another chance to cover the Couchiching Conference. By the time it took place in 1937 *The Mail and Empire* had changed hands and, in the realignment of staff, Deacon was strictly limited to literary reporting.

Meanwhile, by 1936 son Bill was 13, Deirdre, 11, and Mary, 10 – his family was speedily outgrowing his and Sally's first home on Dilworth Avenue. In a short-lived resurgence of confidence and security he bought a piece of land at Wilson's Point and a much larger home on Parkhurst Boulevard in Leaside, moving there in September, just two months before the eruption of the most terrifying crisis of the thirties for the Deacons. In the fall of 1936, George McCullagh, acting for mining magnate William Henry Wright, bought both *The Mail and Empire* and *The Globe* and in November merged the two into *The Globe and Mail*.

The last issue of *The Mail and Empire* appeared on Saturday, 21 November 1936 and in it was a notice from McCullagh that severance pay of four weeks instead of the obligatory one week would be paid to employees of *The Mail and Empire* who would not be working at *The*

Globe and Mail. Among them was Deacon, who in this last number placed his 'Swan Song' on his Saturday book review page:

To my host of loyal readers everywhere, this is good-bye. To close friends and to that greater number, whom I have never seen, my heartfelt thanks for consistent support and the wealth of warm, generous appreciation with which you have comforted and sustained me during our more than eight years together. God bless you all. With deep regret at the enforced parting and remembering fondly our long and happy association. William Arthur Deacon.

His dismissal at this time was an absolutely stunning blow, though experience had made him all too familiar with farewells. In turn he had left university, law, and *Saturday Night*. Each of these doors he had closed or had been closed on him and all of those partings had been final. Fortunately, as it speedily turned out, this last door was closing only long enough for another to open.

In the discharging and redeploying of staff on his new morning paper, George McCullagh had given the Saturday literary page – 'Life and Letters' – to Charles Jenkins, the old *Globe*'s literary man. Jenkins's tenure lasted exactly one week, for in discharging Deacon, McCullagh had not reckoned on the loyalty, interest, and confirmed reading habits of his subscribers, some of them well-known literary figures, but most of them simply readers interested in literature. They missed Deacon and clamoured to let McCullagh know. On the Monday following Jenkins's Saturday début in *The Globe and Mail*, telephone calls, telegrams, and letters swamped the office of the paper, and years later, Robert Farquharson reminisced: 'I joyfully remember fuss public raised when management of Globe and Mail thought it unnecessary to take Deacon over from Mail and Empire. Deacon was hired at increased salary within week.'[26]

Management response was indeed prompt. On Wednesday, 2 December 1936, the front page announced 'William Arthur Deacon appointed the *Globe and Mail* Literary Editor.' A short description of his career accompanied the announcement. His salary was increased from $50 to $75 per week – $50 for his book page work and $25 for what he would earn if he were being paid space rates for interviewing and reporting on literary personalities and events. In return, he agreed to relinquish all freelance work and write only for his own paper. In addition, he was made to understand that his responsibilities would not go beyond the book page and the reporting of literary events. The freedom of a generalist reporter that he had known at *The Mail and Empire* had gone, but with it a large part of the psychological and financial anxiety that he had known throughout the decade. Always a pragmatist, Deacon was the first to acknowledge his great good fortune; besides, it was highly gratifying to be acknowledged as literary editor. In 'Deacon's Annual' of 1937, a round-robin Christmas letter written just a year after he had been hired by *The Globe and Mail*, he commented : 'I forgot to say earlier that I still have a job, and am very proud of it and those new presses are about to turn, swift and powerful; and the stunning new building will soon be the home plate. Last year we mourned the dear departed; this season we look forward to the great metropolitan journal that is evolving.'[27]

He moved into his new job quickly and decisively. Of the weekly reviewing done on the book page, he carried virtually all the load, as he had with *The Mail and Empire*. Keeping detailed score, he also continued to solicit book advertising, which jumped between 1936 and 1937 from 11,000 lines to 40,000 and rose slowly but steadily thereafter. The book page reviewed an average of four to five books every week, with two and three pages of reviews, articles, book lists, and advertisements during Book Week and at Christmas. Even with an office at the *The Globe and Mail*, Deacon still did a great deal of reading and writing of columns and letters at home. He had promised McCullagh the 'best review medium in Canada' and he worked on all fronts to produce it, but he also kept up all his other literary associations:

In 1937, there were eight book fairs covering 31 days; one national convention of the authors, one poetry night; 14 committee meetings of the A.C.B. or book fairs committee, 6 meetings of the Poetry Magazine management, 8 public functions of the authors, 8 executive meetings ditto and 2 meetings of the national executive, besides half a dozen odd speeches, endless business correspondence, consultations by telephone and over the luncheon table. The only extension of this slavery is to make committee men occupy dormitories so they can confer further by talking in their sleep. During the year I have listened to at least 50 set speeches or literary papers or readings by authors, and very good they were, too; but I should also enjoy occasionally the quiet, free day that enables one to get a little writing done.[28]

In spite of the tangible success of his literary editorship, however, he had one final shock to suffer in this most troubled of decades. In June

1939, he received the following notice from E. George Smith of *The Globe and Mail*'s management: 'I beg to advise you that, effective from June 22nd, I have reappraised the Literary Editorship of *The Globe and Mail* at $50.00 per week. Please advise me if you wish to continue the work on that basis. I shall be glad, of course, to discuss this with you at any time.'[29] In spite of Deacon's shocked protest, Smith's decision stuck. He cut the book page from five to three columns and when war was declared two months later, wages were frozen for the duration.

CHAPTER EIGHT

A Community of Letters II: 1930-45

URING THE EARLY THIRTIES, when Deacon's own future was perilous and the Depression was a dreary reality for himself and everyone else, his avocation of letter-writing provided both relaxation and support for himself and his correspondents. Emily Murphy, his 'Mother in the Craft,' died in 1933; Raymond Knister, in Deacon's mind the most promising of young Canadian writers, was gone; but many other old friends and treasured correspondents remained – Billings, Hayes, Phelps, Allison, Pratt, Salverson, Duncan Campbell Scott, Tufts, Davidson, and Dalton among them. He added many others to his correspondents; sometimes they proffered mutual encouragement in a period of bleak hard times, and sometimes they diverted themselves and lightened their spirits by impassioned controversy.

Although he had corresponded with Duncan Campbell Scott since the early twenties, and had a special admiration for him as a fellow graduate of Stanstead College, it was the summer of 1931 before Deacon wrote and published in *The Mail and Empire* an appreciation of Scott's work. Though he was dissatisfied with what he had written and apologised to Scott for it – 'there are so many phases to your work – so many finenesses requiring extended consideration – that the length of any newspaper article is inadequate' – he printed it on Saturday, 1 August 1931: 'Far better, I believe, that I should say a few things, and badly, than say nothing. The inhibiting factor is that I have far too much to say, too many points to make.'[1] Scott was grateful:

Your 'introduction' gave me pleasure to read. It is one of the best things written about my poems. I have been so long out of the world of letters so far as current events are concerned that I feel you have re-discovered me, a lost island in this vast ocean. Many of your observations are acute and well stated and your chosen quotations are excellent and show that you really know what good verse ought to be. I am glad you dwell on my essential Canadianism. I think that is true and I hope to make a few more such poems when I am released from my fifty years' imprisonment with the Savages.[2]

Deacon's reply was hearteningly supportive for Scott's work, both past and future:

For I am convinced that, not only will the native note ensure enduring and growing appreciation of your poems, but they would be popular now if known. You have been presented as a highbrow, instead of as a man and a prophet. I have no difficulty kindling enthusiasm where I have a chance to read your work and talk about it. The pity is that those best capable of understanding it and you, and most open to and in need of the inspiration you provide, are too often the persons who tell me either that they have never heard of you at all, or that you are just a name to them and they have never read any of your verse.

Unfortunately, Canadians have such a low opinion of themselves that it is impossible for a Canadian critic to publish a volume of appreciative and expository essays and pay costs. But times are changing, even in that respect; and whether or not I can get my ideas about you out in book form, I will find other ways to do so. A quarter of a million people have had a chance to read this; and some of them have done so.[3]

He enthusiastically welcomed an attack on the CAA by Leslie MacFarlane, a young fiction writer living in Haileybury, Ontario, as the opening salvo in a lengthy correspondence which ranged with good-humoured gusto over all aspects of the writer's craft. 'I haven't time to waste on a long controversy on the obvious imbecility of the Canadian Authors' Association,' wrote MacFarlane. 'Perhaps it will be a novelty to encounter a writer who won't descend to the bootlicking you get from that gang of jitney geniuses.'[4] Deacon gleefully printed his entire contemptuous critique in *The Mail and Empire* as a yeasty, controversial entertainment for readers, and then went on privately to give MacFarlane large doses of advice and encouragement for his own writing over the many subsequent years of their friendship:

I think the novelist proper makes writing more of a true business and profession than the writer who is angling for momentary hits. Reprints are coming more and more into fashion, which is economically sound; and if I were a fictioneer I'd plug away at the real thing, gather your readers, get your reputation, come in for your share of lucky hits, and try to give the stuff permanent value. I don't say from an idealistic standpoint but a practical one. You can write, why build on sand? What the hell is the use of living in Hailey-bury if you are blind to the epic of your locality – the *great* Story of Northern Ontario that has never been written? Go back to the logging days, follow with the mining days, then on to the farm and the town and power. Not the adventure stuff, the epic. Get some real characters out of the old-timers. Begin just as Mackie and Booth are starting to drive back the fur-trade, and go on with the driving of the c.p.r. up the Ottawa Valley. Use up about three generations and 150,000 words, and have one old cuss still alive who went in as a chap of 25 in 1880. Take your country from the headwaters of the Montreal River to Mattawa, and show civilization harnessing nature in 50 years – and the sort of men bred by the country and the life. That story, conceived in a big way, painstakingly done, will go on being read – and earning royalties – while a detective story has a life of three months.[5]

Laura Goodman Salverson always felt stranded in Port Arthur, where she and her husband lived: 'I also know that everything I do is bad from the technical standpoint. It is one of my foolish dreams that one day I may land in a city where I could get someone like Mr. Allison to take me in hand for a little while.'[6] Deacon would not recognize any flagging of the spirit in her, however, nor would he indulge her in self-pity. Instead he wrote bracingly of her latest novel, *The Dove of El-Djezaire*: 'stick to your knitting, woman. Never try to imitate other novelists' matter or methods. If you do not get sales and recognition immediately, you will later. This is the real old stingo.'[7] In a letter to George Salverson, her husband, he extended his influence and advice.

This is a bad time for everybody but nobody is worse off than the writers of Canada. Publishing is in a knot here. Part of this is due to the whole base of the publishing industry in this country being fundamentally wrong. Anyhow, it's almost impossible to get into magazines or get a book out, or, out, to get it sold in reasonable quantities. That can't be fixed in a day. Meanwhile, there's damned little any of us can do but wait. What I'd like you to do is keep your wife cheered up and at work. She is at what may be her best creative period. Try to get her to write one short story and novel after the other, and store them away for later publication. There ought to be carbons, and one copy of each important ms placed apart, so that fire would not mean the work lost.

I can't say how long this state will continue. It may be two years, it may be five. Anyhow, the quiet coupled with productiveness ought to keep her busy, and find her with valuable stocks on hand when conditions change. For, always, after a bottled-up time like this, it goes the other way and there is more demand than good stuff available. She ought not to be writing then, but speaking, etc., etc. For her type of work there is nothing to fear about an ultimate market, final recognition and all the rest of it. But the work must be done now, and further, it ought to be big, ambitious stuff, with weight and dramatic power. Her poetry is not great; sometimes her short stories are thin, but the novels are *good*.[8]

After E.J. Pratt had read a part of 'The Titanic' to a meeting of the Writers' Club, Deacon wrote him of the enormous impression the poem had made: 'it cannot be on a lower plane than The Roosevelt and the Antinoe (which I still read with emotion, and involuntarily thrill to its power) and, from what fragments you read and your explanations, it is probably an advance on your previous peak – if that is possible ... I am looking [forward] to the completed product with immense confidence and joy.'[9] Pratt responded with ebullient appreciation and his own estimation of 'The Titanic' as well as its challenges to him.

It was so lovely and so characteristic of you to write that letter. Saturday night was such an event for us because I made my first tentative presentation of the poem. I had never read any portion of it before except with my own family, and it was such a joy to read it before 'the boys' at the 'Kit Kat' and receive such overwhelming responses. It was for me the perfect audience because I love the fellows like brothers and none more, believe me, then your own good self. You have been a grand critical stimulus to me over the years, only one other person having a like influence and that's naturally my colleague and chief, P.E. [Pelham Edgar]. I have to thank you for the very bumps I received in my raw and amateurish days ten years ago. I needed them as every 'youngster' does who is worth his beans. And through your excellent criticism there ran encouragement and confidence which has meant so much for me. And the appreciation is mutual, for I am honest when I say that I envy the prose style you have cultivated and attained over the years...

To revert to the Titanic, I read only a half of the stuff I had in the book which again is only a half of the total projected. I am simply swept away by the theme as I was in the Roosevelt only to a vaster extent. It is so much more complex, involves so many more philosophic, economic and artistic issues that I don't want to hurry it too much. I hope to get right at it as soon as exams are over, expecting to finish by September getting it out as a fall book...

The Roosevelt was a rescue of outright heroism simple in its texture. The Diapasons are all the time going in an event like that. But the alternations in the

Titanic, the Crescendos of cues and fears approaching panic, the terrible silences and innuendos, the tensions, the inward voiceless struggles that issued in decisions, the stark outline of the iceberg remaining immovable while the ship takes her plunge, grim, alone, and triumphant – well, the subject is unique and will test every resource for the treatment. That's the reason why I intend taking time off closeted and concentrated, so as not to botch the task...

Again Bill, my true-hearted friend, thanks. If the book should ever happen to 'take' on a big scale I'll pension all the Writers of the Club when they become superannuate. But it has to be done first.[10]

Perhaps Deacon's keenest continuing pleasure was his sudden recognition of new and unique talent among Canadian writers. His first of many literary friends among French-speaking writers was Georges Bugnet, a French immigrant to Rich Valley, Alberta, a writer and a journalist. When *Nipsya* (1924), his first novel, was translated by Constance Davies Woodrow in 1929, Deacon wrote a long and appreciative review in *The Mail and Empire*, thereby instituting a valuable correspondence with Bugnet, who was delighted to reply to his words:

Your article on my book 'Nipsya' just reached me. – (No, I do not live, and never lived, in Quebec, save for a few days.)

So far, you are the only one who gives me (in the first part of your study) some kind of explanation why Nipsya may be compared with Maria Chapdelaine.

Louis Hémon's masterpiece fell into my hands when I was writing the last part of Nipsya. Then, I had to murder poor Bonhomme La-Jeunesse. Why? Because, in Maria Chapdelaine, I found the long drawn illness of the old lady getting a little tiresome. It gave me the idea to try and do better. By the way, the *real* Bonhomme (81 years old) had really and recently died (pneumonia, too) and *he did walk* to his bed twenty minutes before his death. In my book, I did not insist on the twenty minutes. Life, in books, to be accepted as 'life as it is' must not be too accurately true to facts.

Outside of this plain case of murder, Hémon came too late to influence me. Of course, I noticed that, having chosen a somewhat similar phase in Canadian life, we accidently spoke of the same things, as many other authors meet. When I read *your* comparison I perceived the deeper analogies. Your judgment, I think, is fairly sound.

For all that, my opinion is that Maria Chapdelaine is far above Nipsya. It has the best mark of genius: greatness and simplicity.

Can critics be criticized? – My book a product of imagination because Mabigan had never seen such a display of *red* northern lights? – Well, I have lived in Mabigan's country since 1905. I happen to be one of the very few who saw such display (in November 1918 – may have been the signature of the armistice in the skies). Most Albertans have never seen one. But we have plenty of the usual and some of the unusual kind (see 'Nipsya' again).

Re the historic side, we Westerners would welcome a little more sympathy from our Eastern fellow-citizens. Western history has, so far, been written mostly by Easterners with prejudiced minds. An impartial historian will never use the words: Riel rebellion. – Riel was not a rebel. Was he an 'insurgent'? Even this is debatable. Our grandsons will call him a great patriot, a misunderstood genius.

As to the soundness of judgement on the part of the Métis, I wish an Easterner would come out and get stuck in a mudhole for half a day somewhere in central Alberta. Maybe he would understand why the Métis objected to have the land divided in squares with geometrical road allowances. We, who have to foot the bill, spending millions upon millions, we do catch the point.

In 'Nipsya' the purely historical part has only been pointed out because I fear that, by stressing it, it would crush the heroine.

But what I am after is that, again, life in books must not stick to facts. Had I painted in Vital a man of Riel's type, a Métis not only deeply but madly religious, with intellectual power and intensity of patriotism equal to Riel's, most readers (and critics) would have thought or said that the author was perfectly crazy. So I tried to draw a portrait of Vital from a milder but not very uncommon type. Moreover, I suppose I wrote the book with an unconscious feeling that most of my readers would be french catholic people...[11]

Deacon replied speedily:

you must forgive one of the English Protestant tradition, who was brought up in the province of Quebec, for weariness with the veneration with which the habitant has been treated in Canadian literature for the past ten years. We are faced with two to six volumes each season which pour unstinted adulation on the habitant. We English-Canadians, so far as we know the French-Canadian, like him and respect him. But we are not ourselves angels, and we suspect that the French-Canadian is not one either – a man with a little different cultural background (not so different, it is all European after all) a different language and a different religion (but both French and English are now more than racial languages; they are universal languages. And I understand that the two branches of Christianity both worship God in the person of his Son, Jesus). It seems to us that you French are a trifle over sensitive, ready to suspect us of holding you in contempt where no such idea is in our heads; and of any indications of a willingness to laugh at your own foibles, as we make fun of ourselves, we see not a trace...

It was not my intention to speak with disrespect of Riel. I used the word rebellion because we English always use that word. For myself, the rebel maybe either a good or bad man; he is just the man who is actively opposed to the government – say, an unofficial opposition. We English have magnificent rebels in our history of whom we are very proud. In Canada, we always speak of Rebellion of 1837 (here in Ontario) by William Lyon Mackenzie; yet we enshrine him among our great men, and always think of him with gratitude for having won us certain political liberties. Yet we still call him a rebel and believe he was one – a most praiseworthy rebel.

At this time it would be a splendid thing to get out a biography of Riel, about whom we English know very little. If you have done one in French, can it not be translated; and if you have not done one, will you not write his life to appear simultaneously in French and English? I can assure you considerable interest among us English.

Thank you for writing to me. Be assured that I admire your book very much, and still believe that from some viewpoints it is better than Maria Chapdelaine, from others not quite so good.[12]

Bugnet was obviously delighted to enter into further correspondence with one who so readily appreciated his work and the problems of the French in Canada:

My first letter must have been rather misleading. Of course, my English is not as clear as my French.

No, I never suspected you of accusing me of plagiarizing Hémon.

Re: French tradition of clarity – vs – Dickens' way of writing, this is a hard question to answer. Going to the bottom of it, I'm inclined to believe that there is a good deal of difference between the Anglo-saxon and the French minds. Taking the novel, an Englishman will prefer to see plenty of action, outward life, even down to its little peculiarities. French people prefer the inward analysis, and do not care much for many details. Regarding plays, same thing. Shakespeare is greatly admired in France, but Molière pleases us far more. Why? Because with much less action, outward action I mean, with practically no colours, he paints human character so powerfully that you recognize them everywhere and everyday around you. The Tartuffes, the Harpagons, etc., fill the world, in every nation.

I said 'he paints.' Yet, after all, I might make another comparison: between a novel (or a play) and another art: sculpture. I do believe that the greek canons of sculpture are the most perfect. And here again we find elimination of small details, idealized humanity.

The conclusion of these rambling considerations? Probably that your ideal in the novel would please everybody, myself included, – but who is going to write that perfect novel?...

No, I hold no brief for the French-Canadian habitant. I do not even know him (the Quebec kind, I mean). I am a Frenchman (from France) turned into a Canadian. A No. 1 hard Western Canadian. – I perfectly agree with you about the race and religious question. For five years I have been preaching – when editor of 'L'Union' – to all Albertan-French people, exactly the same ideas you preach me in your letter. (But I did like your preaching and am going to show it to a few friends – English protestants – as there is a good deal of belief, here, in Alberta, that Ontarioans are mostly fanatics.) Only, when I preached, myself, to my French flock (38,000 people) I placed the blame on themselves, because, I said, if our English-speaking fellow-citizens ignore you, this is due to your own silence, your own 'stand-aloofness,' (is that an English word?) your own lack of confidence in yourselves...

Re: Riel – it is this way. A *rebel*, in proper English, I believe, is a man who revolts against established authority, accepted government. In 1869 there was no established government in Manitoba or the Territories. Hence, the word 'rebellion' appears to me a quiproquo [sic], and rather misleading...

Yes, I would like to write Riel's history. But, to live, I have to farm, and my farm is miles away from any library and documents. I might have turned into a passable writer, if leisure had been granted me. Leisure, alas, is a rare fortune in my life...

Do believe, dear sir, that I appreciated your article, and your letter, very much. I have a proneness to discuss vehemently. Do not take me more seriously than I do myself. I am somewhat disdainful of human reason, my own included... [13]

A similar case, far more notorious as man and writer, was Grey Owl, whose meteoric popularity, in America and England, was a phenomenon of the troubled thirties. Grey Owl, his beautiful Indian wife Anahareo, their daughter, Dawn, his friends of the wilderness, particularly the Beaver, represented a combination of glamour and escape from harsh urban reality that throngs of people in the thirties found irresistible. Grey Owl, who in fact was Archibald Stansfeld Belaney, born in Hastings, England and brought up there, had a natural stage presence: his lean build, aquiline features, and long, braided hair were ideally suited to Indian garb and, as a public speaker, he was as brilliantly effective as were his books. [14] As he often did with writers he admired, Deacon sent Grey Owl a letter containing his review of *Pilgrims of the Wild* (1934) and, as usual, included a modicum of well-meant advice:

Permit me to say, as a critic, that I believe a reviewer has an important function in reporting and explaining books to the public; but I do not believe there is one chance in a thousand of a critic saying anything useful to the author. Go your own way; don't pay any attention to what any of us say in print about your work.

Privately, I will tell you that I enjoyed Pilgrims the more because it is a drama of the individual soul; I think men are most interested in actual struggles, inner and outer, of some particular man. It was also better because it does not bear the same evidence of conscious care and high polish that Men of the Last Frontier does. Historically, your first book is the more important; but for general interest and as literature, Pilgrims has the advantage.[15]

Grey Owl replied with an appreciation of Deacon's criticism that demonstrated a far more sophisticated and self-conscious writer at work than his admiring public liked to credit, though he tried to stress his own intuitive and untutored state:

When I went to Europe with the Canadian Expeditionary Force I thought, in my ignorance, that I was fighting for Canada. I thought Canada was an independent Nation. Under the yoke of Cockney Sgt Majors, who would have still, many of them, been cleaning spittoons in the Palmer House only for the war, (and whose attempts at vituperation by the way, I found very inept and unimaginative) – I found the difference.

I was born in the United States, which country I respect and admire (less the emasculate gigolo element we hear in the monkey band over the radio), but I have been in Canada since 1905, and am intensely loyal to this country. Aside from the fact that I have been made a Canadian citizen, my status as a native-born has been conceded by the Native Sons of Canada, who very courteously invited me to become a member. I am rather proud of my acceptance by them, and of my membership (Assembly 118).

But the formalities of my enrolment as a citizen affected me in a different way. I found I was to be a *subject*, first, and a citizen afterward. Now I read, in the folder you so opportunely send me, that the representatives of the Canadian people have refused to consider having a flag of their own. Our (pardon if I say 'our,' I feel that way about it), 'Maple Leaf,' or 'Oh! Canada' is submerged beneath the funeral strains of that servilely sycophantic Imperial Anthem. If the real Canadians took more interest in their country, and did not leave the handling of affairs to outsiders, such things could not be done. Hence

I look forward with pleasure to reading your book 'My Vision of Canada,' which I have sent for.

I must thank you for your very kind and discerning criticism of my own poor work. Knowing authors as you do, it is not much use me telling you I thought it poor, but it is customary to say that, apparently. I am no writer and have no intention of becoming one, professionally, realizing my limitations. But for a man who is trying his unskilled best to paint a few word-pictures of one phase of Canadian life that will soon be a thing of the past, opinions such as yours are a great encouragement, invaluable indeed.

I cannot agree that expert criticism by a reviewer is irrelevant from the author's point of view, not at least, in my own case. Your statement to the effect that Pilgrims is better written than the Vanishing Frontier book is a very valuable piece of information, to me. I had expected to be censured for having written too freely, supposedly with the carelessness of one who is just a little too sure of himself. The fact was, I made no attempt to dress the story in its Sunday best, but let it wear its own well-fitting, if simple attire. It is only by taking instant advantage of some such hints that I have been able to evolve some kind of a method; they are my only guide posts, as I am quite alone here and have to do the best I can.[16]

When, a few months later, Deacon abruptly challenged his alleged 'Indianness' – 'met an acquaintance of yours from the woods who says you are all Scotch without a drop of Indian blood in you; and suggests you assume the Red Brother for artistic effect. Do you want to deny the charge? What proofs of origin have you?'[17] Grey Owl replied with a detailed autobiographical sketch, assumed by H. Lovat Dickson, his biographer, to be his first written account of the story that was to become his own legend:[18]

Received your kind letter & the Australian review. Kind of reaching out eh? Have just sent away the M.S. of a book for children, 45,000 words, 18 sketches besides thumb-nail sketches for chapter headings. Lots of Wild Life; nearly every animal in the woods depicted. Believe my sketching technique is improving!

Now about my friend who suggests I have no Indian blood, but am all Scotch. Firstly, the only people who have known me real well since I came to Canada 30 years ago, are bush people and Indians of the type who do not go to Toronto, nor speak of 'artistic effect.' No one living in this country knows anything of my antecedents except what I have chosen to tell them.

If I have not analyzed my blood-mixture quite as minutely as some would wish, let me say here and now that here are the component parts. Mother – $\frac{1}{2}$

Scotch (American), ½ Indian. Father − Full White, American, *reputed* Scotch descent. Therefore I am a quarter Indian, a quarter Scotch and the rest reputed Scotch, though unproven.

Now there it is. You may know that all persons of ½ breed 'nationality,' also all persons having less divisions of Indian blood, are know as half-breeds. I never even stopped to figure the thing out. My friend whom you met, has only my word for it that I have a drop of Scotch blood. Some people, you must know, object to having a 'native' accomplish anything. As my whole life-training, my mentality, methods, and whole attitude is undeniably Indian, I have given credit for anything I may have accomplished to the people whom I look on as my own. Unfortunately most men of my type, in whom the Indian, at first glance, is not so strikingly apparent, spend much time denying their Indian blood, and claiming to be French or smoked Irish or something. This I refuse to do. Give all credit for my small success to the white people, (no offense intended) & leave the Indians, who taught me what I know, holding the bag? No sir. It is the admixture of Indian blood that I carry, with some pride, that has enabled me to penetrate so deeply into the heart of Nature; yet undoubtedly the white part has enabled me to express it adequately.

There are thousands of mixed blood like myself kicking around the North; some favour the Indian, some the White; those that favour the White deny their Indian which makes me mad as a wet hen. It is a strange anomaly that my wife who is nearly full-blood Indian could not, when she married me, speak 10 words in any Indian language, even her own, & knew no more about bush life than a young miss from the sidewalk on Yonge Street. I, who was 3 parts white, was the better Indian. Civilization plays strange tricks on us. Right now, so quickly she picked things up, Anahareo can shade many a practised woodsman, both in skill and courage. This last attribute is her most outstanding characteristic.

When I first commenced to write a few articles, the Editor asked who & what I was and I said I was a bushwhacker, a man of Indian blood. What I meant was, I was tarred with the brush, & felt I was admitting something. I expected he would at once turn me down. This has happened, socially, before, & often since. The artistic effect I never even thought of. I figured I would write a few articles till I got enough money to move the beaver to Ontario, & then quit, & follow my natural way. That the writing business would assume the proportions it since has, never even occurred to me. When the Government took me up, they used the word Indian in describing me, as they said 'breed' was derogatory, God knows why. I did not figure I should call myself a white man, because when it was found out, as it eventually might be that I had Indian blood, down I go with a wallop. I feel as an Indian, think as an Indian, all my ways are Indian, my heart is Indian. They, more than the whites, are to me, my people.

So my good friend was astray even in his knowledge of my Scotch ancestry. I can only claim of a certainty ¼ Scotch. His evidence is unreliable.

I do not intend to deny the 'charge' publicly. The Government is very strict on me avoiding any debate whatsoever. It is a queer paradoxical situation; the one thing that I was so particular to tell about, for fear it would be found out and so destroy me (apart from my sense of justice to these people), that same thing is now denied in the form of an accusation! Perhaps the gentleman is Scotch and would like to have me so also. I have never seen Scotland, cannot understand them when they are talking, & never thought very much about all these things one way or another until all this damnable publicity started ramming stuff down my throat. The wonderful reviews about my books, recognition for my work with the beaver, I welcome gladly. I never figured on all this racial stuff. I am a man, a kind of a one, who loves the woods, the waters, a good canoe, a good pair of snow shoes, my wife, my beaver, – and little children, I think, above them all. I am trying to do a little good in this old world of ours, so my life will not be entirely a reproach, & certainly don't want to get involved in any foolish racial quarrels with anybody. If I hadn't been part way successful, no one would care three hoots in hell what I was. Dogs will bark & snap at my heels, but I will, as you advised yourself, just keep on going, no matter who says what.

I wrote this Winter, what I feel is a beautiful little story of two Indian children & their beaver pets. I put my heart & soul right into it and used as characters a young Indian boy and girl I knew away back in 1906. I have never seen them since I left the village, & to me they have never grown up, neither they nor the beavers (Chilawee & Chikanee), & so I see them still as they were in those dear dead days of my youth, that are now far behind me. I hope by means of this book to become endeared to thousands of little children, while they learn, as they read, of the hopes & the fears, the struggles, the sorrows & the joys of others, both human & animal, who are not perhaps so well gifted as themselves; yet whose feelings are so very much like their own. This I consider to be much more important than bickering, or any attempts to establish who or what I am. Who the devil cares.

A man can call himself a China-man so long as he keeps on buying the drinks, but let him try to step out of the rut & do something, and see all the hands reaching to pull him back again. It would take very little, just a touch or two of discord and I will fold up my foolish pieces of paper and my piles of crazy notes & notions, and go back into the obscurity to which I belong, where I can at least be happy. Somehow all this public stuff has me buffaloed. Perhaps a fellow will get used to it. But the temptation comes very strongly at times to drop everything & hit for the North, where I don't have to wonder if some Smart-Alec hasn't twisted some of my statements to suit his fancy, & got me in wrong with somebody. It is only the beaver that hold me. I will be faithful to them, as long as either they or I shall live. My wife & daughter can follow me, but they cannot. And they are so utterly dependent on me for their safety. Always they *know* I am there; I am part of their lives. And they trust me. So I stick. Though I wouldn't give one acre of Northern Ontario for 5,000 square miles of this depressing Western Country. Homesickness has me down at times, & I sit for hours beside a fire, thinking of my few, but good friends at Bisco; they seem to be so far away & unattainable. You have heard the wind singing in the pine trees perhaps? There is no tree in this country can reproduce that sound. And then I hear that some one of my old acquaintances is taking what he considers, poor fellow, to be a rap at me. I wish some of them knew how I feel about *them*, counting the days till I see them again.

Though nothing has been decided, there is talk of me touring Great Britain on a lecture tour. If it materializes I intend to stop off in Toronto, & may call on you for a little advice. Pardon this very long & very dull letter. Blame it on nostalgia; it is a hobby of mine. I suppose a man of any strength of character would push it out of his life, but I can't; too firmly rooted in the pine-lands, & white water, & the smoky, balsam scented tents of the Ojibway Indians.[19]

Deacon's subsequent apology, 'I'm sorry to have upset you. Never mind. It's nothing. When a question of fact comes up, I like to go to headquarters to check,' went on with a lengthy and characteristically supportive letter concerning both Grey Owl's themes and his methods of writing:

Your children's book is the right move. It will do a lot of good as propaganda, and there is a steady market for juvenile books. It takes a wonderful adult book to be remembered five years but for a child's book there is a quick turn-over of readers, and it can keep going for 25 years. If it gets into the schools, as yours is apt to do, there is real money and steady money out of the royalties.

It ought to be a good book because you feel strongly about it. The way to move is to be in earnest yourself. Clever writers sometimes take apart other people's work to see what is in it; and then cook up something from the same recipe. Some measure of success can be got that way, which is the correspondence-school-method. But real writing, my friend, comes out of the heart and the soul, and its essence is not to be analysed and can't be copied. Very simple things can be powerful if genuine human will and emotion are behind them. Say what you want, what you feel. Don't ever hold off for fear you will be laughed at for being unconventional. Originality is a priceless quality in the popularity of books, and the genuine article only comes when heart speaks to heart and intuition is given full play. Be yourself always. Don't cramp yourself into moulds that appear fashionable. This is the thing in you that got a hearing from the editors. It is what is carrying your readers. If you get imitating, then Grey Owl is just another writer, not worth a damn because just like millions of others ... People are moved by emotion, not arguments. Therefore let the pure message of the heart come out of you in whatever verbal clothes strike you as most natural and easy-fitting.[20]

Grey Owl and Anahareo stayed with the Deacons in Toronto in 1937, a year before Grey Owl died, and though he was a notoriously difficult guest, always on the thin edge of revolt against social conventions, his subsequent apology for what he called his 'lapse from grace,' left them all the warmest of friends and with the warmest of memories:

Please give Mrs Deacon our very kindest regards, & ask her to please accept my apologies for my stupid remark at the studio that day. I was not myself, & a great deal of social stuff had been going on and I get sometimes pretty well confused even at my best. Ask her to please try to understand, to remember the vast gulf that exists between my normal life & the everyday life of a big city. I am sometimes rather at a loss.[21]

Morley Callaghan had been acquiring a reputation in the twenties, but Deacon had not known him; his understanding of Callaghan's work began with a review of *A Broken Journey* in 1932, for which Callaghan wrote and thanked him. Deacon was completely frank about his own limitations with regard to the work of young writers: 'I am of the last pre-war crop; you of the first post-war; and inevitably there is a gulf. On my part I am not willing to play only with the has-beens and it is much more important to me than to you that I should understand you. I am doing my damnedest and trust you will be patient in view of my limitations.'[22]

With the publication in 1934 of *Such Is My Beloved* Deacon's keenness for Callaghan's work came to an enthusiastic maturity. He was stimulated by the book, and also stimulated by the threat of censorship, which to him, was always a call to arms. He ended his *Mail and Empire* review of the work with an entirely laudatory and prophetic paragraph:

So, while Father Dowling's love is the core of the book, all other parts of this novel vibrate with life. Just as no Callaghan creation so far stirs the reader as does this good priest, so the mass-impact of this new novel is a new effect for Callaghan to have won. One is involuntarily stirred, moved; the emotions of a reader are roused, and he feels with the characters, as well as merely seeing them behave thus and so. Here is the element which was, in part, lacking before. While I believe 'Such Is My Beloved' to be the prelude to both greater and finer work, the book is more than a promise. It is, in itself, an achievement. For the first time, Callaghan wields authentic power. Reading him hereafter will be no less a duty, but considerably more of a pleasure, as insight and power increase to complete mastery. (*The Mail and Empire*, 24 February 1934)

He supplemented his review with a cheery letter to Callaghan, admonishing him to be strong against the attacks of would-be censors and closing with an added compliment to the strength of this novel: 'Your work has already become a genuine job for a critic and I foresee where it is going soon to be so engrossing I'll be unable to handle your books to my satisfaction in the maximum space editors think a mere novel is worth.'[23]

Callaghan's next novel, *They Shall Inherit the Earth*, impressed him even more and as soon as he finished writing a most favourable review, he once again added to that in a private letter to Callaghan:

Allow me, now that the last paragraph of my piece is finished, to congratulate you most enthusiastically on this novel. I am not only particularly pleased with it per se, but rejoice over the tremendous progress you have made over the past two years. You must be conscious of and heartened by this increase in your powers. In some ways I regret that I am not addressing a literary audience, because the nature of your book made it necessary for me to use much of my space for elementary instruction of unsophisticated readers. I want to anticipate objections to clear the ground for you; and I am not ashamed of doing pick-and-shovel work to let you get unimpeded into the consciousness of Ontario, because the capture of the home town is the hardest fight your popularity is ever going to have. And when you win Toronto the rest of Canada will follow like sheep.[24]

Deacon's correspondence with John Mitchell (Patrick Slater) began in 1930, when he wrote to Slater praising *The Kingdom of America* and Slater replied: 'I thank you for your kind note... I figure that anything that is simple, unaffected, and sincere, must be a work of art, however uncouth to the professional eye; and my little book does really set out in a homely way the point of view of great body of Canadians, who say little, perhaps, but who do a lot of thinking.'[25]

When Mitchell's *The Yellow Briar* came out in 1933, Deacon wrote to its author:

Now, between ourselves, your novel, considered coldly as a work of art, is weak on the end of plot, or structure or pattern. Your framework is sketchy, and on it you loosely hang description and anecdote in variety and profusion. By the rules your book is lame. That's the truth; and, thank God, it doesn't matter a damn.

Below structure, which is form, and may be artificial, there is something called LIFE, which is the essence of the whole matter. Its appearance always confounds the doctors. You have it; and, if Tommy [Thomas Allen, publisher] knows his onions, as I think he does with this sort of book, Paddy is going to steadily attain to popularity and will continue to sell for a very long time...

I am a man before I am a critic and a nationalist before I am an artist. A critic, looking only at art – that is, the form, the dress, the cut of the coat – can dispose of your book and mine in short order. But we bear witness to the truth; and we speak in a manner appropriate to the time and the need. Your book and mine will not ring down the ages; they will one day get quaint and be forgotten. But, right now, they are making better Canadians, some of whom can make better books for themselves in the future, when they reach it. We do our part now.

Of course your confidence will be respected, though I honestly think anonymity unwarranted in this case. (You ought to be proud of your book.) But I do publicly doubt the existence of the alleged narrator. Any experienced critic would see through your subterfuge quickly. If you had wanted any alert reader to believe in P.S. as a living person, it could only have been done by a preface by some well-known individual who would attest having known the author in the flesh. The 'manuscript among his papers' and the footnotes are an ancient dodge and too thin to carry conviction. However, even this is of a piece with the rest.

Your book is valuable historically as well as giving no end of pleasure. It evokes affection.[26]

Mitchell acquiesced to Deacon's request that he come out from behind the pseudonym of Patrick Slater and sent him his own idea of the piece that Deacon might write: 'You therefore have my consent to go ahead and print what you like. I shall be thankful, however, if you do not make me look like a dignified corpse or a pompous ass ... I enclose you herewith the sort of stuff that would meet with my approval':

The other day I met John Mitchell ambling up Bay street to the small law office he has somewhere up there. He is a stoutish bachelor on the wrong side of fifty.

I asked him how things were going. He told me he had seen a whiskey jack in the bush last Sunday and had noticed that his neighbor Simon Kearns, up in the Caledon hills was getting ready to tap the sugar maple trees. He thought there would be a fine run.

I accused him of having written The Yellow Briar.

He remarked that this last week or two he had noticed a pitying sorrowful look in the eyes of several of his friends; and he feared that, having flown across the continent in the company of Will Rogers, Thomas Allen, the publisher of The Yellow Briar, must have fallen into the habit of talking in his sleep.

'I'll be telling no lies,' he told me, 'because if I did the little folk might let me fall down and hurt myself.'

He expressed the opinion that the public are not in any wise concerned with the name or the qualifications of an author. It is the book itself that counts. He doubted that one person in a hundred can tell offhand the name of the author of the book of Genesis. Authors are like soldiers, he told me, who die in a ditch and have their names misspelled in the dispatches. He had given The Yellow Briar to Paddy Slater, in whose cheerful old heart glow the tolerance and loving kindness that came from the roaring hard wood fires that burned in the log cabins of Upper Canada. And the old man could have kept the book for all time so far as John Mitchell is concerned.

It may interest the public to know that the author of The Yellow Briar has all his great grandparents buried in Canadian soil. John Mitchell told me that it was the late Andrew J. Bell, of The Department of Classics in the University of Toronto who taught him anything he knows of the melody and sanctity of words.[27]

Mitchell termed *The Yellow Briar* 'built for easy reading,' and 'laid out on the lines of *Moll Flanders, Lorna Doone, Tom Sawyer,* not to mention some early medieval tales that occurred to anyone's mind.'

It was built to be 'a safe book,' adapted for Sunday School libraries – and if I could get it across the Alleghanies into the plains of the Ohio and Mississippi Rivers, I believe it would be a fair seller on the other side of the line.

I read the book myself last month, and in my opinion it is a regular frost – but there are others. I will say for old Paddy that he has written the most satisfying story of a dog that has ever been written.[28]

When John Mitchell was in the Don Jail in Toronto on charges of fraud, to which he himself had confessed and, indeed, for which he insisted on being tried, Deacon wrote to him offering sympathy and service in any way possible: 'it occurs to me that possibly you wished to entrust to me some of your literary affairs. Believe me, if I can serve you in this or any other way it will give me great pleasure to do so ...

With every good wish for a satisfactory solution to your present problems that have caused you such acute distress.'[29] Mitchell wrote back from the Don, sending Deacon a piece of 'gaol-made poetry,' 'The Buffalo Path,' and adding 'you have a big heart to bother writing me; but honestly, I am not the proper subject for kindly sympathy – that should be reserved for the honest folk who find themselves out their money. I have the crazy notion that somehow they may get it back from me after a while with something thrown in as a benefice.'[30]

In the thirties as in the *Saturday Night* years Deacon continued his general service to those interested in Canadian literature through the pages of *The Mail and Empire*. For instance, he received a letter from Gordon Pook, high school principal at Omemee, Ontario, asking him how to get photographs of the poets who were that year to be taught to the junior matriculation class: Roberts, MacDonald, Maclean, J.E.H. Macdonald, F.J.A. Morris, and Marjorie Pickthall. Deacon replied to him with a two-page letter, containing the most detailed of instructions and addresses. But he also frankly commented on the Department of Education's choice:

But what you tell me in this letter shocks and angers me. We have some able poets. From 12 to 20 of these are worth teaching in the schools. Of the six you name as on this year's course, only three are poets. The other half do not possess between them enough literary reputation to amount to a hill of beans.

Roberts, MacDonald (Wilson) and Pickthall are poets. Indeed they are.!

Despite my deep professional interest in Canadian literature I have never heard of H.J. Maclean, and cannot trace him in any of my reference books. I had never heard of F.J.A. Morris before receipt of your letter.

I know J.E.H. Macdonald personally. He is the most successful painter of the Group of Seven. He is no poet, but has written a few trifling lyrics, very slight, and these, or some of them, got published in The Canadian Forum because it was then in the hands of a small U. of T. coterie very friendly to Macdonald as a painter and personally.[31]

The most striking development in Deacon's correspondence in the thirties, as in his professional life, was its movement from the exclusively literary into the national and international political scene. Goaded by the anxieties of financial insecurity during the early depression years, stimulated by the writing of *My Vision of Canada*, and increasingly fearful of the international drift towards war, he set out to support through his writing any and every cause and movement which might serve Canada and, in the event of war, keep her at peace. His son

Bill's early memories of his father include a yearly Christmas ritual of family thanksgiving when Deacon would gather them all within the circle of his arms and rejoice in their safe passage through another year. 'My father, I think, carried a greater burden of anxiety than most men. He felt us to be in actual constant peril from hostile, outside forces.'[32]

The transition was easy and logical, a deliberate dispersal of his writing influence rather than any basic change in its stress. To his friend Carlton McNaught, who was at this time much involved in the newly formed CCF and the League for Social Reconstruction, he wrote of the function of Canadian literature as a cohesive force in the land:

What really holds a nation together is not laws, nor economics, nor a king nor a constitution, but adherence to those common experiences and common emotions loosely called its culture or tradition. Only the native can know in his bones what his own essence is and so express it that a fellow-native is able to recognize his own thoughts and feelings. Let me write a nation's songs, said the wise man, and I care not who writes its laws. That is the whole idea. With our problems of regionalism we particularly need the interchange of geographic backgrounds we can best get by having British Columbia books circulating in Nova Scotia and so on. In this manner we interweave the mental common denominator. Nobody makes the major decisions of his life *consciously* because Burns wrote To a Daisy; but, really, millions do, without ever knowing that 'country' means mostly the memory of books produced in that country and read in common by its inhabitants – phrases, which sum up philosophies, and pass current there as the coin of thought. We've *got* to have the literature. And there is quite a bit of it here now.[33]

McNaught, by profession an advertising man, a voluble nationalist, and busy with a multitude of Canadian affairs, not only enlisted Deacon's involvement with the party, but also his aid in a study commissioned by the Canadian Institute of International Affairs on 'How Canada Gets Its Foreign News.' McNaught was one of the strongest supporters of *My Vision of Canada*, writing several lengthy, favourable reviews in both the English- and French-language press, letters to prospective buyers, particularly to R.Y. Eaton and to C.L. Burton of Simpson's, urging them to promote and sell the book in their stores as a patriotic duty and, under the pen-name 'Libertas,' a strong letter to *The Mail and Empire* defending the book against an attack by Rabbi Eisendrath of Toronto.

In Deacon's opinion McNaught was more of an optimist than the times warranted. He was, for instance, deeply involved in work to save the reputation and effectiveness of the League of Nations, and wrote to Deacon of his reasons:

I had no idea of suggesting that Canada should become a European outpost. My only thought was that, the present need being for internationalism (not Imperialism) Canada might very well use whatever weight she has in that direction through the League, which by that means might conceivably be salvaged. If Canada made it clear she would not be dragged into the old game of alliances, which is now in full swing again, but on the other hand would co-operate fully in making the League a real agency for international co-operation, it might make Britain think – especially if it were made quite explicit that the alternative would be Canada's withdrawal from the League and the break-up of the 'Empire' ... I feel strongly that we should do our utmost to save the league, and desert it only when the last shred of hope that it can be made a medium of international peace-action [is] gone.[34]

On Deacon's side of their long and cordial correspondence there is often in these years of the thirties a note of hysteria and desperation – certainly he had no optimistic illusions about the progress of world affairs. First and foremost he wished Canada to break with Britain; then to isolate herself from world problems while building up her own strength; then to promote and enter into a Pan-American alliance extending to South America:

But I pride myself on being much more the realist than those who profess realism because they are doctrinaires, believers in formulae. I *know* that the world state is a long way off, because it is as yet impossible to elevate people's thoughts and feelings to the point where we care as much for the welfare of the Singalese [sic] as for that of our brother-in-law and his wife Mary and their children. The break-down of the tribal system was a terrific triumph; but it took a long time and is not altogether complete yet. It will take a long time to weld the nations into a unit...

Now your woolly-thinking altruists lack perspective. They think you can turn men into the complete god by currency reform, or electric refrigerators, or getting baptised a Christian, or any some other patent process. IT IS DELUSION. *There is no panacea...*

I am heartily with you as to the impossibility of peace without socialism. I regard myself as a socialist and welcome its approach. I work consciously for it all the time...

I am for socialism as a means, not an end. I am not in love with machines but products. I do not forget the *real objects*. That is where I diverge from *all* doctrinaires and panacea-hounds. I am for socialism, strongly, because it is the next step; but I know – all history tells me – that it will not solve all woes, it will eliminate evils and create new ones.[35]

Though his 'platform' remained the same, he was less urgent in his letters to J.S. Woodsworth, with whom he had first corresponded about a speech at the Toronto Writers' Club in 1930. Shortly after the provincial election in June 1934, in which the CCF had made encouraging advances in Ontario, he wrote to Woodsworth: 'A year ago, I celebrated Dominion Day by doing a preface for *My Vision of Canada*. This year I should like to mark the date by enlisting in your party, provided you are willing to take me on without committing myself to act blindly in party discipline.'[36]

In answer to his subsequent outlining of his own position, Woodsworth assured him of a welcome in the party and of his own considerable sympathy with many of Deacon's views:

With regard to your anti-imperialistic ideas – I think that you are not more anti-imperialistic than some of the rest of us. You fear a vague international socialism. May I suggest that all of us, capitalists and socialists alike, are being forced away from a vague internationalism into a very definite national planning. But I would point out that this does not necessarily mean an isolationist point of view. International relations are so close and complex in the modern world that I doubt if it is possible any longer for any one nation to live to itself. The older capitalist internationalism was built up on the export of surplus commodities. With the extension of the capitalist system into even less developed nations, this type of export is readily diminishing, and even the capitalist faces an entirely new situation. With this there is bound to be a revision of socialist tactics.

While we may recognize that capitalism is the same the world over, and that we cannot have a full measure of socialism until there is a socialized world, I think we must insist that our first job, as I tried to emphasize last year at Regina, is to set our own house in order, and that in doing so we must reckon with our distinctively Canadian situation and traditions. Here, of course, we come somewhat in conflict with the older socialists, most of whom have a European background. But our C.C.F. is distinctively Canadian...

... As you are aware up until recently there have been the two groups – Farmer and Labor, and these working almost in watertight compartments. The C.C.F. sets out to effect co-operation between these two, and also to bring in the third group of business and professional people whom I would in the phraseology characterize as proletariat, and who, if they can be won, will undoubtedly contribute very largely to the organization and policies of the new movement. In attempting to bring together these three groups we are undoubtedly up against a very great problem, but it is either a case of getting them together or heading right into chaos or fascism. The background and psychology of these groups have been very different. It will require a great deal of patience on the part of all, and further, a very steady effort to interpret the one class to the other. But I think that it may be done.

With regard to discipline – it is, of course, desirable that in so far as possible we may present a united front. No organization can tolerate those who are seeking to undermine it, as was the case with certain near-Communists in the Toronto affair. But, on the other hand, it seems to me that any party is in danger of becoming stereotyped, which does not permit of free discussion, and even considerable diversions of opinion...

Under these circumstances I see no reason why you should not be able to definitely join the c.c.f. Of course we are a democratic organization, and in joining you are apt to run up against some unreasonable individuals in certain local organizations. I am afraid that the wrangling that often goes on has sometimes disgusted those who would otherwise associate with us, but I fancy that you would be able to pick a group which you would find congenial. If this is impossible there is still the l.s.r., through which you could do definite propaganda work. But as the c.c.f. is a definitely political group, I would hope that you would find it possible to get right into the fray.[37]

Deacon replied, assuring Woodsworth that he was enrolling as 'a very private member in my own district.' He also declined to take an active part, feeling that his talent was for writing, not as a politician – 'while I wish to add what little weight I have to your party, both for its positive platform and as an anchor against revolution, I did not have any notion of taking what is called an active part – as by speaking, etc.'[38]

Always attracted to young people, Deacon had begun a correspondence with John Holmes, an undergraduate at the University of Western Ontario and editor of a short-lived literary journal, *The Hesperian*. He quickly recognized unusual capabilities in Holmes: 'May I assume a friendship that permits me to say bluntly that I was entirely pleased with you? Your considerable abilities are not narrow in focus, and your personality and naturalness of manner positively charming. I am sure your life is going to be very successful and useful...'[39] Holmes admirably fulfilled Deacon's prophecy in his long and distinguished career as diplomat and expert on Canada's foreign affairs. Shortly after their first meeting he wrote Deacon an account of the political ambiance of a summer YMCA college in Milwaukee at which he was working. At the same time he asked for Deacon's opinions on Canadian socialism:

The present Conference is decidedly Socialistic in tendency and the little red buttons, with 'vote for Norman Thomas' are very frequent. It is very interesting to me to see the changed attitude on the part of the University men in the U.S. in the last two years. Two years ago it was almost impossible to drag one of them into a serious discussion of social, or even literary questions, and if you succeeded, you got no more than an outburst of democratic and humanitarian cant, which for them had no more meaning than the preamble to the Declaration of Independence. At their conferences they did no more than spout formulas and proclaim the fellowship of all races, while they refused to sleep in the same tent with negroes. But the last two years seem to have sobered them, and made them more critical, and that is why they are turning to socialism, I think, for it implies a critical attitude to their dearest institutions.

Speaking of socialism, what do you think of the L.S.R.? I intended to ask you, when you were in London, if you considered the Forum a worthy Canadian journal. I always read it because I think its critical attitude is healthy even if it were misdirected, and I have become quite interested in Mr Underhill's League for Social Reconstruction. I am not yet a confirmed Socialist, but it is my distrust of my own ability to decide, rather than dislike of any of the implications of that term which keep me from being one. In the meanwhile I think that the very moderate Socialist Program of the L.S.R. and of Mr Woodsworth would mean a tremendous political and economic progress in Canada as compared with the dithering planlessness of our two great parties.[40]

Deacon's reply was decidedly sceptical:

Perhaps my opinion of the L.S.R., which you want, or did last June, is a bit prejudiced. I am fearfully skeptical over much good coming from anything so purely theoretical and academic. They are making an heroic gesture of intellectual independence where it is most needed (and will likely get their backsides tanned) but I've heard Frank Underhill empty his mind and, candidly, I wasn't impressed with the amount of horse sense he displayed. I know there is need of talk, debate, study, and that the universities ought to be taking a hand in public affairs. But, somehow, I've never found faith enough to join any of the numerous groups of amateur economists, who are paying rent to lecture each other in sundry halls in Toronto. It's not that I think I know any more than they do. For one thing, I'm getting awfully leary of the expert. It seems to me there are only two alternatives. Either organized business will comprehend the threat that hangs over it, and socialize itself; or there will be revolution. Reading the temper of the people, I don't think it will come to open, widespread rebellion, though that is always possible. Capitalist dictatorship is impossible. Reform, proceeding by steps and illogically, strikes me as the probable course – coming in time to nationally controlled production and international barter. The L.S.R. is purely Fabian in its tone and aims, and I think it's too late for that sort of thing.

Underhill told me the Fabians in 40 years had been able to elect a Labor Govt in England. I replied that the Labor Govt was not socialistic; and that I did not understand his desire to bring Canada, 40 years from now, to the same state of bankruptcy and want as England is in now. If 40 years of Fabian effort have produced, as he claims, the present political and economic state of Great Britain, then – ??

So far as I can see through the mess, which isn't far at all, we haven't produced a mind in this country capable of being trusted with the arrangement of the new order. That a new order must come, and soon, is beyond doubt in my mind. It would not surprise me at all if, when we are old, I should read in a history that the whole of 1931 and 1932 are treated as well within the sphere of the revolution : – Part I.

Now my time's up, worse luck; and I haven't said anything, except fail to discover precisely why I look at these budding economists with such indifference. But, before God, I think the Brook Farm experiment, crazy as it was, from a psychological standpoint, was somehow a better try at a solution than many many-worded friends of the L.S.R., who are still a long way from knowing themselves what they think and what they want to dó. Underhill's basic notion of fusing factory workers and farmers in one movement strikes me as obviously impossible.

Then, too, I want it proved to me that a farmer or a mechanic is any more intelligent, fairer, less prejudiced and less selfish than the professional classes. I don't want to see the poor oppressed and starved as they are today oppressed and starved. Neither am I particularly anxious to trust my destinies to their wisdom and benevolence. After all, there was something in Stephen Leacock's 'Unsolved Riddle of Social Justice,' though he is a miserable hireling of the capitalists.[41]

In Harold Innis, Deacon discovered a scholar and a writer whose intellect he respected enormously; one, moreover, who enjoyed a good discussion at the Writers' Club and who was remarkably free of the academic façade which so easily aroused all Deacon's defensiveness. Innis, for his part, was genuinely grateful for Deacon's understanding reviews of his work, not only of *Peter Pond*, the first of his reviews for which Innis wrote his thanks, but also for reviews of the more specialized and difficult *Select Documents* on the Canadian economy and its problems. Innis obviously enjoyed and admired Deacon's energy and nerve and a certain creative element in his thinking and writing, however idiosyncratic or downright cranky it sometimes became. He shared Deacon's dread of an inexorable drift into war and, as he said, when sending Deacon a paper on that theme that he had given to students, the two of them 'come out at the same point by different routes':

Among the few things I was able to do, during a holiday which involved illness, a trip to Philadelphia and the usual excitement, was to read your book. I can begin by congratulating you on the straightforward courageous fashion in which you have presented conclusions [in *My Vision of Canada*] which are held by large numbers who have not the courage to state them. You have done a magnificent service in this. I notice that you have had to endure some abuse but apparently it is still a minor crime to be Canadian.

My approach tends to be from a negative point of view rather than your positive point of view. It is partly explained in the attached paper prepared at short notice and read at a meeting of students arranged by our department to discuss Peace and War. I had hoped during the holidays to put it in shape for publication but illness has prevented. I would like it back in the not too distant future in case I should get time to work on it. I would agree in part with your optimism as to natural resources but in the main I think our natural resources have reached the stage which will not support any increase in population by immigration. We have been broken on the wheel with this immigration business and we shall probably be broken again. Moreover the problem of natural resources has reached the stage which involves a very material lowering of the standard of living on the part of those in Western Canada particularly. My chief concern is that we will fail to appreciate the amount of suffering and misery in Western Canada which is the exposed area and that unless a solution is found to the problem Canada will not achieve unity but will develop a series of festering sores with unfortunate results for all concerned. The only solution is an intense nationalism which will lead us to face our own problems. We come out at the same point by different routes. But I would like to talk over all these things which I hope we may do at not too late a date.[42]

In Arthur M. Lower, who in the thirties was teaching history at Wesley College in Winnipeg, Deacon found another activist for Canadian nationalism after his own heart. They met at the Couchiching Conference in 1935; both of them had toyed with the 'Native Sons of Canada' movement and found it well-meaning but insufficient for the gravity of the issues at stake; in January 1935 they got together over the possibility of forming a new organization:

I have one or two of the younger academics with me [wrote Lower], but there are few people who are really 'sold' on the question, few who see that the sole condition of our continuance as a political entity is the development of a genuine national life. How far that can be hastened I do not know, but I do know that I for one feel the heavy weight of the culture of other and older lands upon me and would like to have a life of my own, not an imitation of life, as in so many respects it is in the fate of a Canadian to have. For we cannot escape the fact that we are all colonials, more or less, simply because we are units in a colonial society. We need our own 'prophets,' our own movie stars, our own songs and all that sort of thing.

Is there any use talking in terms of an organization?[43]

In September 1936, Lower drafted a document designed to be charter and credo of a new group for which he suggested several names: Sons of Liberty, Committee of Canadian Correspondence, Nationalists, and Canadian Institute of Internal Affairs. In his autobiography, *My First Seventy Years*, Lower refers to the group as the 'Committee of Correspondence':

We hated Hitlerian terrorism as much as anybody, probably more than most, and we had no desire to escape our duty. When the showdown came, none among us of the English language would have wished to avoid throwing in his lot with his fellows. Nor were we unfriendly to Great Britain. We felt the same strong ancestral bonds as others, but we profoundly distrusted the British Governments of the 1930s, members of which we sensed were the people who should be accused of disloyalty – disloyalty to the liberal and democratic tradition and to the best interests of their country. But our feelings of devotion to our own country had come to outweigh traditional attachments. And so our aim throughout was limited, confined simply to staking out Canada's right to independent action. We must have had our effect, for when we went into the war, September 1939, it was on this stand, diluted by a typical piece of facing-both-ways on the part of Mackenzie King.[44]

In the document he sent Deacon, Lower first listed his general objectives: a new loyalty to Canada first, not to Britain; war on colonialism in every sphere; racial and religious toleration between the English and the French; an acceptance of a multiracial Canada; a strengthening of the federal government and diminution of the powers of the provinces; attempts to weaken provincial loyalties. These were followed by a matching list of particular objectives:

1. An enunciation of the principles governing our foreign policy which would preclude any possibility of taking it for granted that we would be in the next British war.
2. A campaign against further immigration, except of the most limited and self-propelling nature...
3. Some policy on the revision B.N.A. Act.
4. Termination of appeals to the Privy Council.
5. Limitation of the right of the defense forces to correspond with their opposite numbers in G.B.
6. A policy of national defence, without reference to our 'obligations' to the empire.
7. A cultural programme of an active nature.
Advocacy of agencies along the lines of Dominion Drama festival.
Consideration of a national theatre and national encouragement to the literary arts...
    Multiplication as energetically as possible of every device for heightening national consciousness and giving it an adequate content. Examples: national festivals, art galleries, museums, marking historic sites, etc...
8. An educational policy: The old drum and trumpet history should disappear from the schools and the history of the Canadian people take its place. Lamentable deficiencies of the average teacher of history to be attacked as also minor place of Canadian history in the curriculum.[45]

Lower wished copies of this document to be sent to a select group of possible leaders in the movement including Frank Underhill, Eugene Forsey, Frank McDonagh, the secretary of the Native Sons of Canada, and Professor E.K. Brown, of the University of Manitoba. He also wished to have a French Canadian nominated and Deacon immediately put forward the name of Jean Bruchési.

    Deacon was delighted with the possibility of the organization, professed himself willing to accept Lower's judgment on its platform, and nominated himself as its publicist. This flurry marked the beginning of the end of his active involvement in political and possibly controversial public affairs, however, since the next year he was hired by *The Globe and Mail* and charged by George McCullagh with strict neutrality about all political affairs. As Lower says, however, those yeasty years of the thirties saw a confused variety of good-hearted, well-meaning attempts by numbers of Canada's thinking men to move towards some solution of the economic problems besetting the country and of the international problems threatening its future.

Moving towards the same goal of an enhanced and militant Canadian nationalism, but in a line closer to his own vocation as a literary critic, was Deacon's suggestion to George M. Wrong, historian and head of the Department of History at the University of Toronto, that he write a one-volume, popular history of Canada for schools and for the general reader:

I suggest to you that a significant drama, rich in colour, has been enacted on this soil during four centuries. This has been for children and for specialists. Your 'average reader' of 30 to 50 years of age cannot get it without assembling a library of say, 200 volumes, the majority of which are not 'readable'. Your 'Rise and Fall of New France' is too long and too expensive for half the story.

My idea would be to assume the reader's mind to be a blank as to information. Then you would stand the chance of the book being used in foreign libraries and schools. It is pitiful watching departing visitors trying to find a book 'about Canada' to take home. There is a new reading class in this country, which is eager to get instruction – artisans and even business people in responsible positions, who learned little at school but now feel it vital to them to know what's what. You would have a polyglot audience; but in my estimation a very wide one, and your readers would be very grateful.[46]

Wrong replied immediately with great interest in the suggestion though, he added, 'I am not quite sure I have a touch light enough for the book and if I succeed it will be your kindly interest that brought my final resolution.'[47] Wrong's *The Canadians: The Story of a People* (1938) was the result. The two men were in touch from time to time throughout its writing, Deacon suggesting a chapter of supplementary readings, a kind of extension course outline in Canadian history, and Wrong accepting his suggestions with warm welcome:

Your idea about a list of books is admirable and I will try to carry it out. I have usually given lists of authorities for each chapter but the idea of a chapter in the same type as the rest of the book is new – and good. I will ponder carefully your own list...

Don't talk of presumption in suggesting to me or criticizing me. You know probably a great deal better than I do what is needed and I am humbled when I wonder whether I can meet the need. But it is a job to stimulate the best that is in me and I face it with mingled feelings of joy and dread.[48]

The finished book pleased them both: Wrong wrote with genial irony: 'That book of mine, of which you were the inspiration seems to be selling well. Macmillans in London sent it to the King and I had a letter from the King's secretary saying the King was reading it. If so, he is one of the very few Englishmen who have ever read anything on Canada!'[49] Ever after, Deacon referred with great pride to his part in Wrong's volume.

In the same arena, but international in its scope and intent, was Deacon's correspondence with B.H. Liddell Hart, the British strategist, military historian, and biographer. After reviewing his biography of T.E. Lawrence and receiving the author's thanks, Deacon began a series of letters urging Liddell Hart to write a 'broader dissertation with a greater proportion of your own ideas in it.'[50] Hart was intrigued and replied, asking him to develop his suggestions; Deacon, loving challenge, obliged:

I'm not particularly interested in war because I am looking to the future, and I regard war as an anachronistic survival, just as the duel long was. But I am satisfied that what you have to say, as a result of your war studies, is of vital importance to our generation. Perhaps in some ways that you do not foresee...

... I crave for the world in this crisis the light you alone can throw from that central truth within you, to which I see you turn every little while for reference, like a compass hidden under your coat.[51]

Liddell Hart took his suggestion seriously enough to jot down his '"thoughts" on various aspects of life as they come to me – not so much the military thoughts as the philosophical':

But how, or [by] what form, I could weave them together I still don't see. Perhaps you can here offer suggestions. Does anyone want to read a collection of thoughts? One might try to weave them into a novel – but would the novelistic part of any first essay in fiction be equal as a structure to what it had to bear? One might develop them into a book on practical everyday philosophy – but this would mean a considerable extension of my own study, to fill in gaps in my education on the scientific side.

I do not think you are correct in diagnosing my complaint as 'perfection-mania.' For I have always liked to get an idea out on paper as soon as it has taken form – although I do grow increasingly chary of writing half-baked stuff. Moreover my conclusions are constantly extending & developing, if not actually reversing themselves, except in minor details.

Do tell me more fully as to the words in 'Lawrence' that came as a help to you. It interests me.[52]

Deacon admired Hart as a writer and he spent a good deal of time and effort in the next few months trying to explain what his suggestions meant to him and what they could possibly mean to their recipient. He was convinced that Hart's writing genius was too great to be confined to books on war – 'war is incompatible with modern civilization and must go like the duel – quite soon, I think. Can't you contribute something broader and more lasting to human welfare? I'm sure you can. For one thing you have a nice glint of humor that bespeaks a sense of proportion and broad interests.'[53] Hart, on his side, confessed that he had been much struck, 'by the wider bearings, in all aspects of life, of my strategic theory of the Indirect Approach. Its philosophical implications seem to me of significance. Yet my personal difficulty is to reconcile it with my own growing inclination towards direct statement of the truth as one comes to perceive it.'[54]

The correspondence closes with Deacon's revelation of his own deep fears and anxieties about what increasingly seemed to him to be the inevitable coming of war. As for Liddell Hart, he was increasingly caught up in the coming war, and was shortly to become the adviser of the Minister of War, Sir Samuel Hore-Belisha. Liddell Hart wrote some thirty books, and it is impossible to trace the outcome of that correspondence, but it is true that for some time in the mid-thirties, he was thinking along the lines that Deacon had suggested. Whether or not he developed his theory of indirect approach from the military to the philosophical is impossible to ascertain.

The correspondence of the thirties is marked by an ever-deepening anxiety as Deacon and his friends battle with the public and private tribulations of the decade. By comparison, the concerns of the twenties seem like high-spirited children's games. To all of his correspondents, as of old, Deacon projected his sense of mission, the advice he loved to give and a considerable illusion of confidence that, often, he was far from feeling. He had extended his 'mission field' and, in return, he derived friendly stimulation and support from a widening circle of concerned, friendly, and grateful letter-writers.

CHAPTER NINE

Writings of the Thirties:
Open House, *My Vision of Canada*, and *The Literary Map of Canada*

I N THE THIRTIES, the foreboding awareness of the realities of the Depression and of international unrest was reflected in Deacon's books as well as in his correspondence: 'We face a world at its wit's end, with poverty rampant, and most of the nations anxiously consuming their forces making armaments from fear that some other nation will attack them.'[1] His first project, undertaken with Wilfred Reeves, an advertising man and a fellow member of the Writers' Club, was *Open House*. The overriding impetus behind their collection of essays was the cause of freedom of expression in Canada, in reaction to what the editors and their contributors regarded as 'the conservatism of the Canadian mind,' an intolerably inhibiting force, they believed, in Canada's growth as a nation.[2]

Contributors, all members of the Toronto Writers' Club, were given a free rein in terms of subject and viewpoint. Charles G.D. Roberts spoke on the strengths and weaknesses of modernism in literature and art, ending his article with praise for the work of Morley Callaghan and the Group of Seven. Wilson MacDonald attacked Canada's feelings of cultural inferiority. E.J. Pratt criticized the excessive modernist eccentricities of language, which elevated technique to the detriment of content. Deacon's article repudiated the contention that a young country cannot have a literature.

The essays on art addressed the censorship issue. John Herries McCulloch argued that movies, through their sexual explicitness, were coarsening the taste and artistic standards of Canada. By contrast, Bertram Brooker, in his essay, 'Nudes and Prudes,' decried censorship and argued that art is 'the inspiration to all kinds of positive conduct.' (p 103) To him, the nude human form as a subject of art symbolized the affirmation of man and the universe. Charles Comfort argued for the tolerance of impressionistic, as opposed to representational, art.

There were several essays on economics, appropriate to the Depression. Leslie Roberts submitted a satire on consumerism, entitled 'In Defence of Poverty.' H.M. Jackson, in a classic piece, championed the virtues of financial self-discipline. In 'The Importance of the Immaterial,' C.J. Eustace praised the spiritual superiority of traditional humanistic values over materialism. Austin Campbell outlined reforms for the stock market and John Armitage insisted on the need for Canada to concentrate on trade with China.

Canadian technical and engineering achievement was celebrated in W.A. Irwin's detailed description of the Welland Canal, 'Seven Steps to Supremacy.' Present and future achievement was the subject of Franklin Davy McDowell's essay on the emancipation of women – 'the next big leap' – although he balanced the securing of women's rights against the historical tendency for social structures to disintegrate in times of general emancipations.

The most controversial pieces in *Open House* touched on political issues. D.M. LeBourdais condemned Canada's barbarous penal system and recommended that 'criminal procedures be taken entirely out of the hands of the legal profession and turned over to specialists trained in the social science.' (p 77) He wanted to make Canada a pioneer in the rational and humane handling of criminals. Need for change in the three principal areas of divorce, political appointment of judges, and reformative treatment of criminals was the subject of 'Legal Facts and Fancies' by J.N.N. Herapath. Roy C. Greenaway described crime in Hamilton and Toronto and criticized Canadians' unjustified and complacent pride in their own policing and legal systems. R.A. Farquharson, in 'Debunking Imperialism,' described the long-standing inequities in Canada's imperial connections, arguing the need for a militant Canadian nationalism if a distinctly Canadian culture was to be created. He urged that 'there must be devised some means of safeguarding the Dominion from being automatically involved in Britain's wars.' (p 182) The most iconoclastic of all the essays in the collection was 'The Vice of Victory' by Edward Turquand Chesley, who died before *Open House* appeared. Ostensibly about returned soldiers' rights, the article is an enraged and bitter indictment of the total futility of the Great War and of the indifference of society to those who returned handicapped physically and psychologically: 'Write down in what way the country is better for the incalculable pain and loss of the war years! I see suffering and want, abject poverty and deadened spirit, all shivering under the dark cloud of hypocrisy, false witness and baseness of spirit. Wealth and greed, bolstered up by political power, ride rough-shod over the land.' (p 38)

Although most of the essays are serious in tone, some are characterised by the informality and humour of the familiar essay. Leslie Roberts's 'In Defence of Poverty' is pointed and witty. Merrill Denison's 'Thoughts on Radio' debates the issue of private versus public ownership of the air waves. He concludes comically with hope for a renaissance of theatre, when the radio, having first usurped the newspaper, has itself become exhausted as a source of entertainment. John Charlesworth contributed 'The Unknown Goddess,' a satirical essay about Listrina, the goddess of social acceptability.

Deacon and Reeves had hoped for pieces that would be 'candid and intelligent and contain at least one idea – not mere pleasant writing,'[3] but *Open House* was by no means radical in content. Deacon was aware of and somewhat disappointed by the relatively conservative tone of the book: 'Some of the articles are reactionary; some just pleasant essays; some are liberal. Not one is the sort of thing a pamphleteer goes to jail for ... I hope the boys will be a little more courageous and original in the next book. For Canada, and for a start, this one is alright. We shall be able to beat it next time.'[4]

Graphic Press published the collection on 20 September 1931, and critical reception was, on the whole, disappointing. John Garvin, in a lengthy review, described *Open House* as 'valuable,' and stated that most of its contributors 'are seeking to bring about changes and reforms for the betterment of the community.'[5] *The Canadian Magazine*, however, found fault with the collection for an overstated introduction which raised expectations about daring the limits of free speech that were in no way satisfied by the various articles. In fact there was nothing in *Open House* that 'might be tabu in even the sedatest journal.'[6] Writing in the autumn literary supplement of *Saturday Night*, Frank Underhill wondered at the lack of any sign of economic radicalism in the book and 'so little discussion of the "red" economic ideas in which all the world except the Toronto Writers Club seems to be chiefly interested nowadays.' He spoke favourably of essays by Chesley, LeBourdais, Denison, Brooker, and Deacon, but his conclusion, however much it accorded in spirit with Deacon's own disappointment in the conservatism of the book, was marked by a condescension which Deacon heartily detested and which prejudiced him against Underhill for the rest of his life:

But for his [Deacon's] faith that we are on the eve of producing a great literature in Canada this collection of essays supplies little evidence. There is no zest or passion here. I am afraid that 'Open House' is one more proof that the trouble with Canada is not, as most of these authors seem to assume, that our young men are repressed and prevented from pouring forth the ideas that are surging up within them. The sad fact about our country is that when our young men do burst into print they have nothing much to say.[7]

Despite constant problems with Graphic about promotion and advertising, and consequent sales that were almost as discouraging as Underhill's review, Deacon and Reeves were undaunted. They immediately planned a sequel, *Open Minds*, to which *Open House* would be seen to be to have been simply a series of warming-up exercises. The next volume, they determined, would replace 'pleasant essays, discussions of art and literature,' with hard-hitting articles on economics and practical affairs, and they immediately began to canvass the contributors they desired. Though they successfully enlisted writers such as Salem Bland, Carlton McNaught, and Father Athol Murray of Notre Dame, the experimental college in Wilcox, Saskatchewan, they could not find a publisher who would commit himself in advance to their sequel. Their second volume rests as a partially completed manuscript in the Deacon Collection.

Meanwhile, Deacon was hard at work on his first '*big* book': 'It is to be called "My Vision of Canada," and it will be a sermon – deadly serious – on the land that ought to be, and will be if we all live according to the best that is in us, *for* the people who will come after us to inherit the great nation we have made. It is the *last* stage of pioneering.'[8] He had begun the book in 1927, when his position at *Saturday Night* still seemed secure, but the shock of his dismissal and subsequent anxieties had delayed and discouraged him; when he did, finally, write a first draft over a six-month period between Christmas 1930 and late July 1931, his own experience and the inroads of the Depression gave his work an edge and urgency that his original plans had not included.

Graphic Press had agreed to publish *My Vision of Canada* and had announced the book in its catalogue of 1931, but Graphic's financial problems and subsequent failure in the spring of 1932 precluded publication. Deacon left the manuscript for a year, making further corrections and revisions and in mid-June of 1933 he took it to S.B. Gundy, a Toronto literary agent and publisher. Gundy was enthusiastic about the manuscript and worked swiftly to come to an agreement with Wilbur Best, owner of the Ontario Publishing Company, whereby Best would publish the book and Gundy would advertise and sell it. The first copies were ready in August 1933, manufactured and out in only thirty-four days.

Utopian in intention, didactic in tone, and romantic in structure, *My Vision of Canada* begins with a dream and concludes with a prophecy of 'a golden age that is to be.' It might well have been a dreary dissertation, but in Deacon's hands it became an impassioned drama, challenging Canadians to a destiny of quest, struggle, conflict, and victory. It was, as he said, his 'version of the national romance – one of the most enthralling romances of all time ... I must paint, and swiftly, the promised land we shall live to inhabit.' (p 3) In 'Explanation,' the foreword, Deacon gave his own version of Franklin Roosevelt's first inaugural address of a few months earlier: 'there will be no more fear once Canadians open their eyes to the realities of their own situation, and apply reasonable intelligence in dealing with their own assets for the comprehensive good and well being of the people of Canada.'

He adapted the ideas of many writers to his own theme, but the three men whose work probably influenced him the most were John S. Ewart, Hugh Keenleyside, and John Mitchell. John Ewart's *The Kingdom of Canada* (1908) had advocated full political autonomy for Canada: 'Nationhood; self-control; political equality with the United Kingdom, instead of subordination and subserviency to the Colonial Office; The Kingdom of Canada, instead of many "Dominions beyond the seas".'[9] Ewart's tone was militant, far different from the dispassionate, analytical approach of Hugh Keenleyside in *Canada and the United States* (1929). In 1928 Keenleyside had gone from being a professor at the University of British Columbia to the Department of External Affairs in Ottawa; his book examined Canadian-American relations in terms of the various historic conflicts between the two nations, arguing for peaceful co-existence and an enlightened nationalism to preserve Canada's independence.[10] John Mitchell's *The Kingdom of America* (1930) had a dual thesis: first, that 'Canada is a daughter of The British Empire; but the child has no present title to family estates'; second, that 'the Canadian people have felt for a century the constant, aggressive pressure of a great over-shadowing republic.'[11] Mitchell (Patrick Slater, author of *The Yellow Briar*), argued that because of such pressure the native-born are intensely, if often latently, nationalistic. He traced the evolution of Canada from adolescence to adulthood as her people realized more and more that only they could serve the country's best interests in terms of boundaries and tariffs, and he urged the preservation of the pioneer virtues of indomitable patience and courage, to be passed on to the next generation.

Permeating a text that incorporated these influences into Deacon's own passionate convictions were the inspiration and energy of theosophy. As that movement had played its part in the intense nationalism of the Irish literary renaissance of the 1890s, so now it lent its powerful stimulus to the work of Deacon and other Canadian nationalists. Fred Housser, a tireless proselytizer for the theosophical movement, published 'Some Thoughts on National Consciousness' in the 15 July 1927 issue of *The Canadian Theosophist*: 'The background of American peoples, and especially of Canadians is replete with potentialities for the creation of an idealistic national consciousness which is creative and which will inspire contributions of literature, art, philosophy and science to the world at large and which will draw other nations of the world to us instead of, as in the past, our being drawn to them for inspiration.'[12]

Theosophy enabled Deacon to reconcile the divergent but equally impelling qualities of his temperament: his sense of mission, his nationalism, the utopian impulses underlying his Methodist heritage, the pacifism inherent in his concept of universal brotherhood. He based *My Vision of Canada* on a conviction of Canada's destiny that was part of the doctrine of the Canadian branch of the society. Athens, they thought, had marked the beginning of a cycle which would culminate and terminate in Canada, 'the final resting point and ultimate glory of European impulse and spirit.' Canada was destined to 'endow all humanity with the only thing of lasting worth, an example. That example shall be the fairness and beauty of educated intelligence, lit by spiritual aspiration, bound by justice and softened by compassion.' (p 304)

A modern reading of *My Vision of Canada* must be situated in the context of Deacon's theosophical beliefs – once these are accepted and, in their broad outlines, understood, the general romance structure of the book can be seen to complement the idealism of those beliefs. The book's twelve chapters can be seen to be a balanced pattern of cause and effect in which the first six explore the reasons for Canada's unrecognized potential and the last six describe the momentous consequences of that potential. The pattern itself reinforces Deacon's theosophical belief in inexorable destiny, the web of individual, racial, and national destinies converging in the theosophical notion of 'dharma,' complemented by the moral balance that was essential to their concept of 'karma.'

My Vision of Canada cannot usefully be looked at as history or political and social commentary. Seen as a romance, however, as a dream vision and an exercise in fantasy wish-fulfilment, it is immediately comprehensible. Its first part is concerned with dream, quest, and treasure and its last anticipates conflict or war, transformation, and final victory. Its first chapters, 'A Dream Comes True,' 'They Came Seeking Homes,' 'More Than Ye Can Ask,' 'The Unwanted Child,' 'Our Neighbor,' 'A Race Evolves,' cumulatively describe a Canada poised on the threshold of greatness: 'Despised, rejected, ignored, this slow, irresistible force has captured and knit half a continent over such natural obstacles as have never been placed before on anything like the same expanse of territory. The dynamic or driving power of that force is yet to be released.' (p 1) The last six chapters, 'War,' 'China, by Westward Passage,' 'The Reign of Justice,' 'Imperialism,' 'Uplands of Destiny,' and 'In Serene Splendor,' detail and discuss the trials and tests of the past, the present, and, fearfully, of the future. In particular Deacon saw the eruption of another war as imminent: 'It remains to Canada to be the first great Pacific power of the modern world ... From her origin, the ideals we see at work in her practical, everyday life, it is reasonable to believe that no other country is quite so fitted to lead the world out of the barbarity of war into enlightened ways.' (p 145) Economic boycott or self-defence from invasion were the only acceptable forms of activism to Deacon and it was, in his view, incumbent upon Canadians to fight the militarists and imperialists who were anxious to exploit Canada's educational wisdom for their own bellicose purposes. Deacon had not forgotten 'the catastrophe of 1914-1918' and he urged: 'we have the option of following the Europe that has not yet learned down into the worst degradation of history in the next and worst war; or we may walk past the pit safely – preserving our sons and our daughters – and leading on a new road which all must soon follow for the reason that the only alternative has become humanly impossible.' (p 162)

Economic strength as a means to national power was of the utmost importance to Deacon and he was keen to advocate Canada's need to become a manufacturing nation and to forge primary trading links with China as a destination of raw and manufactured goods from Canada. Because she had suffered at the hands of Europe, China should be encouraged to trade with Canada on a clear-cut, businesslike basis, and Canadians should be aggressive in competing for Chinese markets – 'China should be the pivot of Canada's foreign policy.' (p 178) A transformation in foreign policy should be accompanied by a change in domestic policy.

'The Reign of Justice,' he thought, would take place under socialism, which implies 'the paternalism of the democratic state, undertaking to further the well-being of the individual in every possible direction, and consequently demanding the obedience of the citizen to state decrees, and the state's regulation of personal matters, to an extent never before demanded.' (p 179) Against the gains of socialism, Deacon readily admitted, and accepted, that for 'the individualist, the coming cycle of socialism will mean distinct sacrifices by the invasion of his personality through state interference with his habits.' (p 189)

'Uplands of Destiny,' the second to last chapter of *My Vision of Canada*, is a prophetic description of Canada's development between the time of writing and 2000 AD, and the final chapter, 'In Serene Splendor,' sets forth Deacon's vision of Canada in the year 2000. Dominating the world in commerce and culture, Canada will have attained 'undisputed intellectual leadership' (p 279) and will fill the role of international mediator. This material and cultural primacy will be evident in the beauty of Canadian cities, in the growth of the population, and the success of the country as a socialized super state along with other nations such as Germany and China. The absence of war, the administration of peace treaties by international courts, and close co-operation between Canada and the United States and between Canada and China will place the Canada of 2000 AD in a position of security incomparably beyond the dubious position she occupied under supposed British protection in 1900. Using Vilhjalmur Stefansson's *The Northward Course of Empire* to show that 'power, as applied to nations, has moved steadily to the colder regions of the north from the birth of civilization in the equatorial belt of the Upper Nile' (p 285), Deacon provides a prophetic description of the development of the Canadian North. He then predicts the prodigious growth of Canadian cities and the annexation of Newfoundland in 1975. Citing the accuracy of George Grant's prophecies about the Canadian prairies in from *Ocean to Ocean*, he restates his belief in personal destiny – 'man has a queer faculty, not at all understood, of making come true what he wants to see come about' – and, as a logical extension of that, in national destiny as well:

The nation I have been picturing as the Canada of 2000 A.D. may seem fantastic to those who live in the moment; but it is no more than a logical extension of the nation we inhabit today. The advances claimed herein for the next 70 years are no greater, relatively, than those which took place during the 70 years immediately past. Of course there will be acceleration in speed of growth, and attainment of power, due to momentum already acquired. Force, in a rising nation, is cumulative. (pp 301-2)

The last two chapters of *My Vision* are replete with fulsome metaphors of utopian wish-fulfilment and hope which are the quintessence of romance. Deacon's excesses of language, however, were not accidental but deliberate. Writing to Burton Kurth, he conceded: 'I know you will laugh at the piety and grave moral tone of the homilies. I laughed myself. Many passages were so like my dear old Welsh Methodist grandfather. But, when I had been amused, I let 'em stand. For, oddly, I mean just that.'[13] He wished to symbolize, however imperfectly, a future which he could only intimate: 'It is a gesture, pointing towards a new Canada and a new world.'[14] He was aware of his limitations and wrote to Henry Weekes, a young Canadian student at Harvard:

Where I stumbled in My Vision was in the last two chapters on the future. The terms, norms, values, etc., are going to be different from anything we have known. There are as yet no names for them; but my trouble in transmission was deeper: I don't know that country. I know the direction and can point towards it, but no more. You young fellows will have to go into it; and plan a new life by dealing familiarly with factors quite beyond me.

He was, however, certain of the spiritual strength inherent in his unwieldy metaphors and he addressed Weekes as the representative of the new generation: 'I have a word of advice for you, however; and that is to think highly of faith. Not only to keep faith, but to realise the sterility of cynicism, and the fertility of belief, which is positive. Don't mind if they laugh at you for being serious. You have work to do that you mustn't jumble ... Don't be negative; don't be afraid; and don't be restricted.'[15]

My Vision of Canada, inspired by the hopes of the twenties and written in the midst of the stringencies and disappointments of the early thirties, was certainly, above all, Deacon's act of faith in Canada and Canadians. Its details are often eccentric, its rhetoric becomes hectic, its theosophical discussion of racial developments is unacceptable to a post-Nazi world. There is a terrifying combination of prescriptive idealism and naïveté in Deacon's description of the socialist state to come:

With regulated work and leisure for all, two forces will make predominantly for happiness. Those without much initiative will respond with contentment to the creature comforts of their environment. Propaganda, which will have become a science, will foster a general acceptance of the system, including those trifling but frequent invasions of personal liberty, which would otherwise annoy many trained under the individualistic system, out of which we have already begun to move. Of the other type, the restless ones, who yearn for exploration and adventure – the scientist, the inventor, the philosopher and the poet – they will have opportunities, now often denied them, for the working out of their ideas. Art no less than industry will be nationalized. Men will paint and model for love of it and for honor; the hunger of the garret will go, and with it the great material rewards for the lucky hit. (p 207)

Deacon realized that he was taking a considerable chance with the powers-that-be at *The Mail and Empire* in writing a book so anti-imperialist, pacifist and socialist in nature, but he was prepared to stake both reputation and career on it. He was all the more relieved and pleased, therefore, when *My Vision* was warmly accepted by his own colleagues, and he was astounded by the responsive chords it struck in many other readers across the country. By the first week of December 1933, 'something like 85 reviews have come to me so far, many running 1, 2, and even more columns each.'[16] By Christmas 1,400 copies of a first edition of 2,600 were sold. The book was the subject of several church sermons and a national radio broadcast at Thanksgiving, and by the end of the year Deacon was looking forward to the need for a second edition.

As might be expected, the poles of critical opinion were centred in Toronto. J.V. McAree in *The Mail and Empire*, Salem Bland in *The Toronto Daily Star*, and Carlton McNaught in *The University of Toronto Monthly* understood, commended, and shared Deacon's nationalism. McAree defended the book against the anticipated attacks of imperialists, anti-socialists, and continentalists; Bland contended that *My Vision* had done for English Canada what *Maria Chapdelaine* had done for French Canada – defined its spirit and anticipated its destiny; McNaught, a member of the League for Social Reconstruction, saw Canadian nationalism as Deacon saw it – fundamental independence in an interdependent world:

It is, in short, a very positive kind of nationalism that Mr Deacon preaches. But it is a nationalism very different from that of a Hitler or a Mussolini. There is no threat of arms, no swashbuckling; there are no cries of 'Security first.' Mr Deacon lives in a modern world – a world in which we have a League of Nations, and the beginnings of a community of action between peoples of diverse race to resolve their differences peaceably and amicably and work together, each according to his own genius, for the common good of a planet that is 'growing up.'[17]

McNaught also saw to it that *My Vision of Canada* was included in the official recommended reading list for the League for Social Reconstruction.[18]

The mixed and negative reviews were also not slow in coming: W. Stewart Wallace, who reviewed it in *The Mail and Empire* while Deacon was on holiday, found it so selective in its interpretation of Canadian history as to border on the fantastic, though he termed it 'brilliantly written'; Rabbi Eisendrath of Toronto, who had favourably reviewed *Open House*, was seriously concerned about its racist implications; and, once again, Frank Underhill administered the coup de grâce in *The Canadian Forum.* Under the title 'The Importance of Being Earnest,' Underhill described the book 'as a sort of national tonic, very much as the *Mail* brings out its Sunshine Editions from time to time as the depression deepens.' He did, however, acknowledge the presence in *My Vision* of views sympathetic to his own political beliefs:

It is only fair to add that mixed in with all this is a good deal of sound sense. Mr Deacon is a strong anti-imperialist and says things about Canadian business that will awake the shudders of anybody on King Street. In fact, the editor of the *Mail and Empire*, who has recently been growing alarmed about 'Young Turks' in Hart House and who shows signs of starting with his colleague of the *Globe* on another professor hunt, might do well to nose around the literary department of his own paper before he invades the University campus.[19]

One of the immediate results of *My Vision*'s publication was Deacon's temporary close liaison with the Native Sons of Canada. Founded in Victoria, BC, in 1921, the Native Sons had been granted a federal charter the following year. Pro-Canadian and anti-imperialist in sentiment, predominantly Anglo-Saxon, middle-class, and protestant in composition, by 1928 they comprised over 100 assemblies across Canada with about 30,000 members, increasingly concentrated in Ontario and Quebec. By 1930, the circulation of the organization's magazine, *Beaver Canada First*, was 34,000, with over half of the subscribers in Ontario. The society's aims were political:

1. To provide a non-partisan, non-sectarian influence in the administration of the affairs of the Dominion of Canada;

2. To create and foster a distinctively national spirit, and develop Canadian institutions, literature, art and music;
3. Generally to promote the interests of the Dominion of Canada and Canadians.[20]

Deacon had been first invited to speak to the Riverdale assembly of the Native Sons of Canada in December 1931. Over the next four years, he spoke to different assemblies in Toronto and Hamilton. In the fall of 1933, he prepared a reading list of Canadian books for the Hamilton branch and in March and June 1934, he authored two fifteen-minute radio scripts for broadcast by the Native Sons over Hamilton radio.

In February 1934, Deacon was approached by Clarence and Lloyd Smith of Hamilton, both disaffected members of the new Co-operative Commonwealth Federation party, who wanted to establish 'a small local organization for study and propaganda on trade and money problems only.' They had come to Deacon for counsel and he, for the moment, saw far more significant possibilities. He urged something broader and argued that the organization should become more active and visible as a political force in publicly addressing and debating a wide range of issues – 'possible political and war crises, also general education of Canadians (including us), constitutional problems, revision of the B.N.A. Act, etc.' Although others were quick to deny the formation of a national party as an objective of the Native Sons, this was a development that seemed inevitable to Deacon, who wrote that 'what we organize will not be called a party. We are just public-spirited private citizens, until the right day.'[21] He hoped for a union between the Smith brothers, Frank McDonagh, who was the national secretary of the Native Sons of Canada, and John Atkins of the Canadian Newspaper and Periodicals Association, 'who has done wonderful work along (roughly) N.R.A. lines in cleaning up printing industry.'[22]

Deacon's 'First Epistle to the Canadians,' sent to nationalist friends and colleagues such as R.A. Farquharson, Carlton McNaught, Leslie MacFarlane, Harold Innis, and Eustace Ross, urged that 'homeless nationalists' should move strongly into the Native Sons, bringing a new energy and activism to the group. Quite quickly, however, he lost his impetus: 'the unattached nationalists particularly, who would have had to supply initiative, drive and plans, are too individualistic for harness.' He reverted to the role he found most congenial: as with the CCF, so with the Native Sons, he believed essentially that every man working in his own place would best further the general purpose: 'no label, no slogan, none of the usual machinery.'[23] He was temperamentally, and cannily, a lone operator.

In the fall of 1936 Deacon's *Literary Map of Canada* was published by Macmillan, a graphic celebration of the nationalism he had articulated in *My Vision of Canada*. The idea had been with him since 1928, when Douglas MacKay of the Parliamentary Press Bureau had suggested it to him as a possible supplement to *Saturday Night*'s literary section. In the summer of 1936, however, hoping to make some extra money for the down payment on the Parkhurst Drive house, he mentioned the project to Hugh Eayrs, who responded with enthusiasm. By September he had engaged William Cutts, an artist living in Port Perry, Ontario, as illustrator, and was working at full speed, the goal being to get the map out in time for the Association of Canadian Bookmen's November Book Fair.

He sent letters to different Canadian writers – among them Frederick Philip Grove, Charles Gordon, Grey Owl, Katherine Hale (Mrs John Garvin), Marshall Saunders, Robert Stead, Arthur Stringer, Adjutor Rivard, Robert Choquette, Jean Bruchési – asking them to pinpoint the settings of their different novels and poems. Among the replies were two maps drawn by Grove – the first locating precisely the settings of *Over Prairie Trails*, *Settlers of the Marsh*, and *The Yoke of Life*, relative to each other; the second, a map of North America roughly tracing Phil Branden's wanderings with Grove's admission that 'my *own* trek across America was vastly more complicated – and longer.'[24] Deacon sent his enquiries about the inclusions of Francophone works to Robert Choquette, Jean Bruchési, and Camille Roy, who was ill and who deputized l'abbé Emile Bégin, professor of Canadian literature at Laval. All three replied with lists.

By the middle of October, the map was being prepared at Rous and Mann, a quality printing firm in Toronto; William Cutts was no longer part of the project, and Stanley Turner, the artist whose name is on the map with Deacon's, was in charge of graphics. The map was ready by the end of October. Now a collector's item, it was – and is – a thing of beauty. Measuring 34″ × 20″, it is a striking blend of four principal colours – gold for Canada and the title block; blue for lakes, rivers and oceans; green for miniatures of forests and muskeg; white for the United States and for the tiny figures illustrative of different titles, such as a tent for Duncan Campbell Scott's 'The Height of Land,' a cart and oxen for *Maria Chapdelaine*, a prospector panning for gold for Tom MacInnes's 'The Lonesome Bar,' sled-dogs and sled for Arthur Heming's *The Drama of the Forests*. Places and events of interest are identified by orange banners and in the territory or vicinity of each province is reproduced its coat of arms. The map also includes two inserts which permit more literary detail. The largest – in the top, right-hand corner – is entitled 'Some Books of the St Lawrence Basin' and consists of an enlargement of the Windsor-Rivière du Loup corridor with appropriate notation and illustration. In the bottom, right-hand corner, a smaller insert, 'The Land of Evangeline,' is an enlargement of the area covered by southern New Brunswick and central Nova Scotia.

The whole is extremely handsome and delightful to the eye in its use of colour, in its uncluttered printing in black ink of abundant detail, and in its successful compression of so much information. Entries range from the popular – Mazo de la Roche's *Jalna*, Grey Owl's *Tales of an Empty Cabin*, and Louis Hémon's *Maria Chapdelaine* – to little-known Francophone works – Antoine Gérin-Lajoie's *Jean Rivard*, Nérée Beauchemin's *Patrie Intime*, and l'Abbé Casgrain's *La Jongleuse*. *The Literary Map of Canada* was priced at $2.50 a copy and advertisements were placed in leading Canadian newspapers and magazines, but it was subject to 'dribbling sales, [and] Macmillans got sick of mailing out single copies and dumped the lot on me to do as I liked with.'[25]

Neither *My Vision of Canada* nor *The Literary Map of Canada* had added an appreciable amount to Deacon's income in the thirties, and he often said later that he had 'died as an author' with the publication of *My Vision*. In the writing of that book he felt, with justification, that he had put all of his own physical and nervous resources, and his family's security, at risk. In 1934 its total sales stood at 1,800 and a second edition never materialised. The course of future events caused him to radically re-evaluate the opinions he expressed in it, renouncing his pacifism and isolationism: '[my own views] have been changed by the rise of Hitler concurrently with the publication of the book in 1933,'[26] but to the end of his life he retained his visionary faith in Canada. Writing in 1954 to Bruce Hutchison to congratulate him on the essay, 'The National Character,' which had appeared in Malcolm Ross's anthology, *Our Sense of Identity*, Deacon still stood firm in his faith in Canada's glorious destiny: 'all that really concerns me is the *future*; and it's GOOD. By God, we'll justify our existence yet; though the full flowering – far hence. I'm grooming my four grandsons for it. They are of the sixth Canadian generation. They will see it –maybe. Anyway, it's there – out there.'[27]

He was reiterating for his grandchildren the confidence that he had expressed in a dedication to *My Vision of Canada* written for his own family and addressed to 'Billy and Deirdre and Mary, my dear children':

I leave you the land. Of all, that by any turn of fortune I shall be enabled to bequeath to you, it is incomparably the richest portion of your inheritance. No matter how poor I may be otherwise, this gift will still pass to you. Moreover your estate is more strictly entailed than is allowed by law in the case of any other form of property ownership. That is you cannot sell it, but must leave it in your turn to those who shall come after you ... Above all, do not be afraid. Truly I think you will all be too busy to be afraid. What I should have said is: do not be over-anxious. I have utmost confidence in you, and your fellows. Over the land of my vision is a star – the star of a great and sacred destiny – and it is very bright. Whatever you do will be right. God bless you, and give you in full measure the vitality and wisdom you will soon need in the youthfully exhilarating period into which you have happily been born. Signed: Your father.[28]

CHAPTER TEN

The Canadian Authors' Association

ON 28 JUNE 1946, AT A BANQUET in the Royal York, William Arthur Deacon became national president of the Canadian Authors' Association. The occasion was a splendid one, celebrating the Association's twenty-fifth anniversary. The new governor-general, Lord Alexander of Tunis, an immensely respected war-time leader, presented the Governor-General's Awards and a galaxy of the most distinguished authors in the land, Mazo de la Roche, Hugh MacLennan, E.J. Pratt, Earle Birney, W.G. Hardy, and Thomas Raddall, mingled with the hundred-odd members who were present. This was the high point of Deacon's public career, a recognition of his own quarter-century of involvement in the cause of Canadian literature in general, as well as his equal length of service in the affairs of the Canadian Authors' Association. For the two years of his term in office his letterhead carried three titles of which he was very proud: National President of the Canadian Authors' Association, Chairman of the Governor-General's Awards Board, and Chairman of the Leacock Award.

A charter member of the Winnipeg branch of the CAA in 1921, he had served as a member of the banquet committee and then as local treasurer, feeling like 'the smallest of the small fry' among such notables as John Dafoe, Hopkins Moorehouse, the Reverend Charles Gordon (Ralph Connor), and professors W.T. Allison and Arthur Phelps.[1] In 1921 he published 'The Affability of Peter McArthur' and 'Six Canadian Anthologies' in *The Canadian Bookman*, at that time the official organ of the CAA, and he wrote to Mackenzie King, as did many others, arguing in support of the private member's bill which called for the repeal of the licensing clauses in the Copyright Act.[2] As soon as he came to Toronto he joined the Toronto branch and became active locally, throwing all his resources in *Saturday Night* into enthusiastic support for the Association's National Book Week project, often making his 'Saved from the Waste-Basket' a forum for members' views and assiduously recruiting reviewers for his literary sections from among the national membership. Though he was unable to afford either the time or money to attend national conventions, even though John Murray Gibbon, on at least one occasion, offered him a free pass to Banff on the CNR, at the 1926 convention in Vancouver a paper on literary criticism was given for him in absentia. Understandably, because 1928 and 1929 were years of acute financial and professional anxiety for Deacon, his membership lapsed. However, in 1930 he appeared as a 'new member' on the Association's list, and during the thirties the influence of his personality spread beyond the Toronto branch to affect the policies of the national organization and, eventually, to point him towards the national presidency.

His work for the CAA in the thirties was based on the goal of 'craft solidarity' for Canadian writers, from which he never wavered: 'self-help, mutually, is our justification as an organization. There is no other.'[3] Basic to the realization of this goal was the need for a writer to feel self-respect by shaking off what to Deacon was a groundless sense of inferiority and impotence. His approach was eminently pragmatic. He was, for instance, constantly concerned about markets, the importance of sales to a writer's self-respect. As one of the instigators of *The Canadian Writer's Market Survey* (1930), the product of a year's work on the part of fourteen contributors from the Writers' Club, he immediately saw and acted upon both the book's usefulness to members of the CAA and the financial benefits to the Writers' Club of good sales. He wrote and obtained from Howard A. Kennedy, the national secretary of the CAA, the Association's mailing list for solicitation. In turn, he prodded members of the Writers' Club to join the CAA.

This first communication with Kennedy in 1930 signalled his renewed involvement with the CAA. In 1932, impelled by the failure of Graphic Press the previous April and his own and others' subsequent problems with their royalties and their books, he attended the national convention in Ottawa and delivered a paper on 'The Practice of a Critic,' decrying the deplorable state of editing and publishing in Canada. At no time did he deign to recognize the deadening effect of the Depression as the potent factor it actually was in the precarious situation of both writers and publishers: 'What we need is a publisher.

With all Graphic's many defects, 100 good books got out, nearly all at the publisher's risk; and the existence of this firm made far easier than it has ever been before or since for a meritorious Canadian book to find a Toronto publisher on a proper commercial basis. Just as soon as Graphic failed, the Toronto houses closed their doors.'[4]

In a radio broadcast during the November 1934 Book Week, he continued his campaign for recognition, self-respect, and markets for writers:

In the spiritual realm which finds expression through the arts, and especially literature, we have not yet shown the courage and enterprise of pioneer farmers, of the railroad builders, of our army in Flanders. Accomplishment has been splendid; but the old attitude lingers – that Canadian books are in some mysterious way inferior, because they are Canadian. And the worst of that attitude is that the creative writers become afraid to tackle the most ambitious sorts of work.[5]

He continued: 'There is only one way to help practically; and that is by buying, not renting, as many Canadian books as you can afford ... I do not apologize for pleading for support for home industry; certainly not where the purpose is wider than money-making.' In fact, three developments within the CAA in 1934 and 1935 answered Deacon's call for further enterprise and achievement: the establishment of *The Canadian Poetry Magazine*, the formation of the Association of the Canadian Bookmen, and the founding of the Governor-General's Awards.

The first development originated with the Montreal branch of the CAA, which had published a *Poetry Year Book* since 1925. In it had appeared poems by Leo Cox, Robert Choquette, Hector de Saint-Denys-Garneau, Ralph Gustafson, Dorothy Livesay, Leo Kennedy, Charles Bruce, Anne Marriott, W.D. Lighthall, and Audrey Alexandra Brown. Poems were both contributed and entered for competition with the result that the *Poetry Year Book*'s reputation grew and it became extremely popular. In 1934, there were 1,200 entries vying for publication. A special committee was consequently appointed by the Montreal branch to consider the possibility of a Canadian magazine for poetry. Although the committee's report was generally favourable, subsequent study revealed financial risks which the branch was unwilling to undertake. Nevertheless, J.M. Gibbon remained deeply interested in the proposal and secured the co-operation of Albert Robson, president of the Toronto branch, who agreed to assume the position of chairman of the magazine's management board. Robson (1882-1939), managing director of Rous and Mann, seemed a splendid choice. In addition to his publishing experience, he was a painter, writer, and the author of *Canadian Landscape Painters* (1932). He had been a founding member of the Arts and Letters Club, art editor of *Grip*, the Toronto satirical magazine, one of the original governors of the Dominion Drama Festival (1933), and had worked hard to help the Group of Seven, especially Tom Thomson, sell their works.

The national scope of a Canadian magazine for poetry and the consequent increase in prestige and memberships for the CAA, should it sponsor the magazine, were potent arguments in favour of its support. The 1935 convention in Montreal approved the magazine, provided that it could be edited and financed within the means of the Association. The venture was blessed by Pelham Edgar, national president, and by the governor-general, Lord Tweedsmuir, best known as the writer, John Buchan. Two years later, on 24 November 1937, Tweedsmuir supported the venture publicly by speaking at a poetry night celebration held in support of *The Canadian Poetry Magazine*, at Convocation Hall, University of Toronto. Meanwhile the first number of *The Canadian Poetry Magazine* had appeared as a quarterly in January 1936, under the general editorship of E.J. Pratt, who worked with four other editors: Katherine Hale, Sir Andrew MacPhail, Sir Charles G.D. Roberts, and Duncan Campbell Scott. Production was of extremely high quality, with expensive paper and printing. The editor was salaried and a commercial firm was hired to handle the business part of the magazine, even though this was ostensibly Robson's job. In spite of the enthusiastic début, expensive production and lack of practical journalistic experience on the part of both editors and management nearly led to disaster by the third number, which appeared in July 1936. Subscriptions and circulation stood at 600, considerably short of the 1,000 that had been anticipated. Losses came close to $1,800 and could not be met by the CAA. As a result the fourth issue was postponed and payment to contributors and prize winners were suspended. There was talk of killing the magazine, but at this point a new business manager was found in Dr Jacob Markowitz, a young Toronto physician interested in poetry. His practical business sense and generous, regular financial support helped get the magazine on its feet again and the fourth number appeared in March 1937.[6]

The year 1935 marked another innovation in the work of the CAA. Response to Book Week, while generally enthusiastic in the first years of the Association, had begun to wane seriously in the thirties, even though, since 1925, media coverage in the larger centres had grown to encompass radio. Lack of interest was the continuing problem and prompted the CAA, on the initiative of its National Executive Committee, to meet with publishers, book-sellers, and librarians. As a result, the Association of Canadian Bookmen, an alliance of authors, publishers, critics, book-sellers, and librarians, was formed in November 1935, in order that writers and all those involved in the literary world might work together rather than separately and often at cross purposes in the writing, publishing, promotion, and marketing of Canadian books.

Fears that the ACB would be too independent of the CAA were initially allayed by the number of CAA members serving as executive members of the new Association. Pelham Edgar was president. Hugh Eayrs was honorary treasurer and Deacon was honorary secretary. Officers of the ACB included J.M. Gibbon, B.K. Sandwell, and A.H. Robson. Other prominent members were book-sellers William Tyrrell and Roy Britnell and publishers Thomas Allen and John McClelland. For a $2 membership fee, the ACB provided a free book chosen from a list of thirty-five, comprehensive book lists and literary news bulletins, gift certificates, free admission to ACB book fairs and written lectures, and reading courses for literary clubs and groups. The inaugural meeting of the Association was held on 22 February 1936, in the Concert Hall of the Royal York Hotel, where Lord Tweedsmuir gave his first address as honorary president of the CAA and patron of the ACB.

The immediate tangible result of the formation of the Association of Canadian Bookmen was the first National Book Fair held at the King Edward Hotel in Toronto 9-14 November 1936, in conjunction with that year's Book Week. It was a total success. Nearly 15,000 attended the fair and ACB membership reached 2,500. Speeches and letters were given by 'Grey Owl,' 'Ralph Connor,' Wilson MacDonald, E.J. Pratt, Marius Barbeau, John Gunther, Carl van Doren, and others: the attendance on opening night was over 1,700, and when Grey Owl spoke some 500 had to be turned away.[7]

The book displays – nineteen exhibits, mounted by the Toronto Public Library and individual publishers – drew large crowds who bought $1,000 worth of books and who were also examining the displays four and five hours before speakers were scheduled to appear. The CAA was given, free of charge, the largest and most visible display case in which were exhibited hundreds of Canadian books and rare editions and 'a young pyramid covered with portraits of Canadian authors.' The fair was described by Hugh Eayrs as a 'brilliant success' and 'proof to bookmen, wholesale and retail, that there is a much larger public in 1936 interested in books than they had supposed.'[8] At the same time he urged that subsequent annual book fairs be held to boost the languishing Canadian book trade.

Enthusiasm had already produced results in the book fairs held in the same year in smaller centres in Ontario, like Whitby's spring exhibition and the fall festivals of Pickering, Barrie, St Catharines, and Guelph. The second Book Fair was held the next year in Toronto 4-13 November and in Montreal 18-27 November. The 1937 Toronto fair was organized much as it had been the previous year, with the addition of display contributions by Canadian artists like C.W. Jefferys and of motion pictures on literary topics. The Toronto branch gave a dinner followed by a 'Canadian Night' entertainment featuring as speakers, novelists Arthur Stringer and Kathleen Strange, and Louis Blake Duff, a journalist and patron of Canadian letters. The fair was then dismantled, transported to Montreal by rail, and re-erected on the top floor of the Mount Royal Hotel where, to the CAA's and the ACB's intense disappointment, it was much less successful than it had been in Toronto.

The first serious chink in the aggressive new armour of the ACB appeared in Leslie Gordon Barnard's presidential address at the CAA convention in Ottawa in 1938. Barnard was cautious about the future of activities like the book fair, though Pelham Edgar, the president for 1937, had been one of its enthusiastic instigators. By 1938, however, the Bookmen had begun to cool towards participation by the CAA in the annual Book Fair and by 1939, Edgar had reversed his earlier position, requesting Barnard to withdraw the CAA from the ACB. By this time president of the Toronto branch, Deacon seconded his request, convinced that publishers were determined to use the CAA's membership and its financial resources for purely commercial ends, and equally convinced that the publishers had no intention of giving the Association any future power in the ACB in return for their financial support: 'Confidentially, my Friend, we have been played for suckers and have been suckers.'[9] Barnard acted immediately on Edgar's and Deacon's advice; with the withdrawal of the CAA, the Bookmen's Association, claiming financial hardship through the loss of sustaining members, formally disbanded in May 1939.

The liaison had achieved one gloriously successful book fair, but it had brought to the surface the always latent distrust of writers for publishers, the ever-present 'we-they' syndrome of the writers' craft. What Deacon had learned from his experience with the ACB confirmed his complete dedication to non-commercial, literary, and democratic principles within the Authors' Association.

The national literary achievement of which Deacon was always proudest and in which he had played a primary role, was the establishment of the Governor-General's Awards for Literature. Canadian writers had captured several important American literary prizes in the 1920s. Martha Ostenso's *Wild Geese* (1926) won the $13,500 Dodd Mead prize and Mazo de la Roche's *Jalna* (1927) won the *Atlantic Monthly*'s $10,000 award. Earlier, other writers like Marshall Saunders, Ralph Connor, and Lucy Maud Montgomery had received international recognition through the highly successful sale of their works. In 1922, the province of Quebec had instituted the Prix David, named in honour of Laurent Olivier David (1840-1926), journalist, biographer, and senator. This award, for literary and scientific endeavour, carried with it cash prizes worth a total of $5,000. The CAA had been lobbying for literary prizes to match the Prix David since 1922, but in 1935 Canada still had no national prizes apart from the Montreal branch poetry prizes, established in 1925, whose total annual value was $150.

The appointment of John Buchan as the next governor-general of Canada had been announced early in the year and was extremely popular with the leading figures in the Authors' Association, who hoped that he would do for Canadian literature what his predecessor, the Earl of Bessborough, had done in establishing the Dominion Drama Awards. Buchan was a literary celebrity, his adventure novels and biographies were best-sellers, and early in his career, he had worked for the publishing firm of Thomas Nelson. The Association felt a further affinity with him, since he had been an early and enthusiastic supporter of their trip to England and Scotland in July 1933, and had formed part of the committee of welcome which met the group in London. Raised to the peerage as Baron Tweedsmuir of Elsfield just prior to his departure for Canada, Buchan agreed during the summer of 1935 to become first honorary president of the Canadian Authors' Association.

In retrospect, literary developments in Canada during the summer and fall of 1935 are like similar but separate paths towards the common goal – public recognition of Canadian literary achievement. In August, Howard A. Kennedy, national secretary of the Association, had sent a letter to all members of the executive committee announcing the intention of the Dodge Publishing Company of New York, working through its Canadian agent, George G. McLeod Limited of Toronto, to sponsor a Canadian book contest with two $1,000 prizes for the best work of fiction and the best work of non-fiction. The Dodge Company's proposal was submitted to the CAA, who agreed to endorse the contest after certain amendments to conditions and terms had been made. Although the terms appeared generous, their basis was strictly commercial, with winners bound to give Dodge first option on their next two books. The $1,000 prize was designated as advance on royalties. The contest was publicly announced in newspapers and magazines in September 1935 with a closing date of 1 June 1936. In lending its support the Association had requested and been given permission to name one of the three judges, and Pelham Edgar was thus appointed. The other two were S. Morgan-Powell, literary editor of the *Montreal Star*, and Charles R. Sanderson, deputy chief librarian of the Toronto Public Library. When the contest closed, 170 manuscripts had been submitted of which fifty were kept for evaluation. Kathleen Redman Strange of Winnipeg won the non-fiction award for her autobiography, *With the West in Her Eyes*, the story of an English girl's experience of Canadian farm life. No work of fiction was recommended for an award. The CAA's endorsement of the contest had been lukewarm, at best, and Howard A. Kennedy subsequently rejected out of hand the Dodge Company's request that Lord Tweedsmuir be asked to act as honorary chairman of future competitions, adding that the CAA intended shortly to present him with other suggestions more likely to meet his approval.

Another suggestion for the governor-general's consideration had, in fact, already been discussed. Shortly before Albert Robson had begun his duty as Toronto branch president in May 1935, he had queried Deacon about what measures could be taken to recognize and help Canadian writers. Deacon suggested, as a first step, the establishment of a system of literary awards: 'On the request of Robson I wrote a memo before he took office outlining these desirable honors. That was the genesis of the medals ... Edgar made the arrangements with Lord Tweedsmuir in a general way, leaving me to fix details, which I did in Doctor Pratt's library.'[10] In the December 1935 issue of *The Canadian Author*, Pelham Edgar duly reported having met with Tweedsmuir, who approved the institution of 'a special award of merit for literary work in the Dominion' and who had 'offered the Association the use of the name of his office in perpetuity, provided that the Association take full responsibility for finances, judging and everything else.'[11] Watson Kirkconnell tells another story, of Edgar being roundly snubbed by Tweedsmuir when he asked for money to finance the awards.[12] In any case, the official name was secured and the subsequent series of meetings of the CAA executive established the categories, judges, and nature of the awards which were to be made for two sections, English and French, in the divisions of fiction, non-fiction, and poetry.

Works in these categories had to have been published by Canadian citizens in 1936. Each category of each section was to be adjudicated by three judges of the appropriate language group appointed in the following manner: one from the CAA, one from the Royal Society of Canada, one from the Association of Canadian Bookmen. They were to be named in May 1936, and to have reached their verdict by the end of May 1937. The award itself was to be a parchment signed by the governor-general. The administration of the awards rested in the hands of the Authors' Association. The French section, however, did not materialize, because the recently formed Société des Ecrivains Canadiens, founded in March 1936, had discovered a new independence and sense of creative solidarity which complemented the long-established tradition of the Prix David. In the opinion of Francophone writers, the newly proposed Governor-General's Awards scheme was simply attempting to establish in English Canada a similar recognition of achievement and, in its renewed sense of itself as an independent literary culture, French Canada was not ready to take part.[13]

The presentation of the first awards took place at a carefully chosen moment, 24 November 1937, 'Poetry Magazine Night' at Convocation Hall, University of Toronto. Organized by E.J. Pratt, the editor of *The Canadian Poetry Magazine* and his associates, the gathering was an effort to raise support for the quarterly from subscriptions, donations, and endowments. It was a rousing success: some 2,000 people attended the rally and heard speeches from Lord Tweedsmuir and Pelham Edgar, poems from Sir Charles G.D. Roberts, Wilson MacDonald, and E.J. Pratt, and other Canadian works sung to music by Healey Willan. Shortly after the second part of the program began, the 1936 literary awards – not parchments, but bronze medallions, designed and commissioned from Birks by Deacon – were presented by Tweedsmuir. Bertram Brooker, illustrater and abstract painter, received a fiction award for his novel, *Think of the Earth*; George Roberton received posthumously for his father, T.B. Roberton of *The Manitoba Free Press*, the non-fiction medal for the essay collection, *T.B.R. Newspaper Pieces*. There was no poetry award since the judges felt that no important volume of new poetry had appeared in 1936. Lord Tweedsmuir had, however, in the March 1937 issue of *The Canadian Poetry Magazine*, promised a special award 'for the outstanding poem appearing in this magazine,' and by coincidence, Margaret Howard, a past president of the Toronto branch, had just instituted the Seranus Memorial Prize of $25 for the best poem in the first four numbers of *The Canadian Poetry Magazine*. The prize, in memory of the Canadian novelist and poet, Susan Frances Harrison, who wrote under the pen name of 'Seranus,' was annexed to the Tweedsmuir award, since each award recognized the best poem in the four-issue volume. This prize was presented by Tweedsmuir to Professor George H. Clarke of Queen's University for his poem, 'Hymn to the Spirit Eternal.'[14]

The 1936 and 1937 awards were chosen in consultation with the Royal Society of Canada. Initially, the winners were selected through consensus arranged by Howard Kennedy, whose son Roderick took over duties as acting national secretary upon the sudden death of his father in February 1938. The judges specified their individual choices to H.A. Kennedy and then to his son who, in turn, communicated with the others until a winner had been chosen. The announcement date was a bone of contention. In the first two years, the winners had been announced in November primarily to coincide with Book Week. In subsequent years, it was felt that the announcement should come earlier, in late March or early April, when chances for the sale of award winning books would be considerably improved. A motion was passed to this effect at a national executive meeting in 1938.

Criteria for the awards constituted another consideration. Each section to be judged – fiction, poetry, general literature – had a chairman appointed by the CAA national executive and each chairman appointed his two co-judges. After 1938, in order to expedite the evaluation process by placing it entirely within the administration of the Authors' Association, the Royal Society was not asked to take on the adjudication process. As chairman of the general literature (non-fiction) section for the 1938 awards, Deacon worked with V.B. Rhodenizer of Acadia University and E.J. Pratt. In a letter addressed to his co-judges entitled 'What Every Young Judge Ought to Know,' he outlined procedure. Rhodenizer and Pratt were each to send him a list of the top five books in order of importance and Deacon would then send a report of the three judges' findings to the national secretary. Evaluation was not to be idiosyncratic: 'It is felt that this year we ought to pick a substantial work, and not a slight thing like Roberton's bits of essays ... The National Executive defined the qualification as "literary merit," but declined to define this term, but it means more than mere style. It means a good, readable book.'[15] The Board had considerable difficulty in choosing between John Murray Gibbon's *Canadian Mosaic* and George Wrong's *The Canadians*, but finally, after much hectic correspondence with Eric Gaskell, at this time the national secretary of the Association, and with Leslie Gordon Barnard and Pelham Edgar, the president and past president, Gibbon was chosen the winner.

The competition continued and over the succeeding five years,

1939-44, issues were gradually clarified. Nationality, not residence, was the basis upon which citizenship was to be decided; an author could enter the competition as often as he or she had published a book in the appropriate year; a translation into English of any book by a Canadian author originally published in another language might be considered in its proper class in the year of publication of the English translation; *all* judges should be appointed by the awards committee of the national executive, 'granting the Chairman of each division authority to complete his complement of three should any judge so named decline to act or otherwise default'; judges' names were to be made public after the announcement of the award winners; the original three divisions became four – poetry, fiction, creative non-fiction, academic non-fiction.[16]

Then, in the spring of 1944, a crisis occurred which led to the complete overhaul of adjudication procedures. In that year, three awards divisions had made their decisions by 1 March as requested. The fourth – creative non-fiction – had not yet reported. Contacted by several telegrams, the chairman of the division wired on 13 March to Charles Clay, the national secretary, that two of three judges had chosen Merrill Denison's *Klondike Mike* and were waiting for the third vote. Deacon quickly telegraphed Clay that Denison was an American citizen and the two judges were asked to reconsider. One judge wired back quickly, the second did not reply until 31 March, saying that the third judge had still not made a decision and asking the executive committee to arrange for an arbitration committee which would decide between two other works on the list. Simultaneous announcement of the four award categories was customary and the Authors' Association was frantic to conclude its already much-delayed deliberations. A quickly constituted arbitration committee chose John D. Robins's *The Incomplete Anglers*. On 8 April, the chairman of creative non-fiction committee wired Clay that two of three judges had now picked, as first and second choices, two books other than *The Incomplete Anglers*. Roderick Kennedy, national president, replied that the arbitration committee had made its decision, and that it could not be withdrawn. Predictably, heated protest from the creative non-fiction judges followed.

Deacon acted with his characteristic speed and decisiveness and within a few days had placed before the national executive a motion designed to stabilize and institutionalize the regulation of the Governor-General's Awards, whose prestige and survival demanded revisions in procedure to counteract the recent disarray. His motion included the following provisions: the establishment of a board of five members, appointed for a three-year term, responsible for the administration of the awards, the formulation of a set of rules and regulations for submission and evaluation of entries, the proving of eligibility of all titles, the nomination of panels of judges, the tabulation of judges' results, and the announcement of winners. In addition, the board was to be the final authority in all problems connected with the awards. His resolution, together with nominations to the awards board, was passed by the national convention in Hamilton in September 1944 and he was made first chairman of the awards board. The other members were Fred Landon, librarian, University of Western Ontario; S. Morgan-Powell, editor-in-chief, *The Montreal Star*; Professor V.B. Rhodenizer, Department of English, Acadia University; Charles Sanderson, librarian, Toronto Public Library. Deacon held the post of chairman until 1949.

In the thirties he had seen *The Canadian Poetry Magazine*, the Association of Canadian Bookmen, and the Governor-General's Awards as essential to the revitalization of creative morale, which had been failing at both the branch and national levels of the CAA. His visible involvement in these institutions which sprang out of the CAA had led him inevitably back into its executive structure and in April 1937, he was elected president of the Toronto branch, a position he held for two years. He had several objectives for the reconstruction of the branch which was then, he thought, part of a 'pretty dead organization': the settlement of arrears; the consolidation and increase of membership, particularly of young writers; the creation of a new sense of purpose and direction; the establishment of permanent headquarters; more representation of branch interests at the national executive level; the location of the 1939 national convention in Toronto. His leadership was, as always, dynamic and, in the pursuit of these goals, it was strikingly effective. He worked obsessively, spending the equivalent of two days a week on branch business. The Toronto membership grew from 156 to 218, much of the increase coming from the 'New Writers Group' under the leadership of Leo Kennedy. These young writers felt the need of their own organization to discuss the aesthetic and commercial aspects of their craft. Deacon encouraged them to form a junior affiliate of the Toronto branch in 1938. He clearly saw this young group as the essential inheritors of his own vision of the Association, which, he felt, was not nearly sympathetic enough to the pressing needs of young writers, who were hard up against the wearing economic and psychological stringencies of the Depression decade.

To him growth was indicative of health, and as his term continued he was more and more apprehensive of the inhibiting effect of what he called the Old Guard – Pelham Edgar, W.G. Hardy, B.K. Sandwell – on the Association's ability to change and adapt. He moved aggressively towards strengthening the Toronto branch and, at the 1938 convention, he was successful in proposing and having accepted an amendment providing for a national council of fifty members elected, not at the annual convention, but by the branches in March or April of each year, 'the number of such councillors being based on the proportion which the number of the paid-up members in each bears to the total number of paid-up members of the Association.'[17] The national executive remained as constituted. Deacon's conviction that the national effectiveness of the Association depended on the vitality of its branches was thus activated. In the process he secured his ambitions for the national influence of the Toronto branch, which comprised, at the end of his term as president, almost thirty per cent of the total membership of the CAA. He also won for the branch the right to collect fees. Previously, dues had been sent by individual members to the national executive, who in turn gave to each branch a stipulated percentage for capitation fee. Since the national executive was constantly pressed for money, capitation grants were often late in coming to the branches. By collecting fees at the local level, Deacon was able to establish a kind of financial independence which was important in paying off Toronto's outstanding debt, in re-establishing its solvency, and in providing sure control of branch strength within the national organization. The innovation was successful, and by 1939 the branch was restored to solid financial health. Close fee surveillance had effectively reduced, for the first time, the number of non-paying members whose names had previously appeared on the rolls. At the same time, there had been an impressive increase in the number of new, paid-up members.

Deacon also understood that a sense of community and continuity was important to corporate life, and he actively sought the establishment of permanent headquarters. Up to this point branch meetings had been held at the Arts and Letters Club, the Heliconian Club, and various members' homes. In October 1938 quarters were secured in the Women's Art Association on Prince Arthur Avenue, where the Toronto branch met for the next eight months. In the spring of 1939 an arrangement was struck between the Toronto Writers' Club and the Toronto branch about sharing headquarters at 99 Yonge Street, where they were shortly joined by the Women's Press Club. Their housewarming, on 12 June 1939, just after Deacon relinquished his presidency to E.J. Pratt, marked a tremendous achievement for the branch:

Guests, numbering about sixty, were welcomed by Sir Charles G.D. Roberts, Honorary National President; Doctor E.J. Pratt, Toronto Branch President, and Mrs Pratt, Mr William Arthur Deacon, past President and Mrs Deacon. That is – 'officially.' Actually, they wandered in, hailed a friend or a group of friends in the spacious rooms, chatted a while, openly and enthusiastically admired the new linen slip covers of King's blue with red bindings, criticized the arrangement of bouquets – of which there was a large assortment on the piano, over the fireplaces, and around on the tables. They strolled into the freshly painted and newly equipped kitchen with the dietitian, who was preparing delicious coffee and had huge piles of sandwiches in readiness. They compared notes regarding the cups and saucers, one of which each guest had brought as a 'shower' gift to the housewarming.

In fact they made themselves perfectly at home in the new quarters, which are designed to be, not only a literary centre for staid meetings, but a social rendezvous, where all the year round members may drop in and avail themselves of club privileges with services of the dietitian and kitchen.[18]

Deacon loved leadership and the feeling of power to influence events; he also loved to be seen to be leading. He had every reason to call, as he did, for three rousing cheers at the end of his term of office, but he was less than discerning about the likely effect of his success on many members of the national executive. They did not agree with him that 'reasonable autonomy is a safeguard to the national interest, not a threat against it.'[19] The weakening of interest in the CAA's western branches, the growing lethargy in Montreal, and the subsequent depletion of the Association's finances provided sharp contrast to the activity, growth, and solvency of the Toronto branch. In January 1939, Deacon had, at the request of the national executive, addressed the Montreal branch, giving them plain-spoken advice about the need for reorganization and a new commitment at the branch level of the CAA. He therefore considered that the reprimand on the subject of branch autonomy given him a few months later at the spring national executive meeting was an insult, added to the earlier injury of having Toronto rejected as the site of the 1939 convention. His conflict with the national executive came to a head when it refused his request that the Governor-General's Award for fiction, won by Gwethalyn Graham for *Swiss Sonata*, be presented at the annual Toronto branch banquet in May, instead of at the Halifax convention in July. Deacon was disappointed and furious: 'if we have made any progress here [Toronto], it is not because of the national authority, but in spite of it ... As long as the c.a.a. continues to travel on old, conventional lines, as it is still doing essentially, nothing much can be done.'[20]

He was more than a little mollified, however, when a group of members, their spokesman Sir Charles G.D. Roberts, suggested that he stand for national president. Unfortunately he had pledged his support to Madge Macbeth, novelist and successful president of the Ottawa branch, who had already been offered the national presidency by John Murray Gibbon and Eric Gaskell. In the six weeks or so before the convention, he was thoroughly embroiled in what was shortly known as the 'Madge Muddle,' a political tempest in a teapot in which no credit is due to either of the candidates or to their supporters. Macbeth carried the field; in fact she was president for three terms, in 1939, 1940, and 1941, thereby setting a double record in the Association – as its first woman president and as its only three-term president. Deacon retired from the conflict, ostensibly with relief, but in fact with both reluctance and resentment, though he continued his work for the various concerns of the Association as one of the national vice-presidents and as honorary president of the Toronto branch.

In November 1942 he was seconded from *The Globe and Mail* to the Wartime Prices and Trade Board, where he was in charge of the rationing of paper until January 1946. During these years he was somewhat distanced from the executive structure of the CAA. He did, however, in 1944 revise and codify the criteria and procedures associated with the Governor-General's Awards, and, speaking strongly for literature, he also helped establish and procure government support for the Canadian Arts Council, composed of the different national societies of the creative arts, among them the CAA, La Société des Ecrivains Canadiens, the Royal Canadian Academy of Arts, the Dominion Drama Festival, the Federation of Canadian Artists, the Sculptors' Society of Canada, the Royal Architectural Institute, and the Canadian Society of Landscape Artists and Town Planners.[21]

The war inevitably undermined the activities of the CAA both on the national and the branch levels. Membership fell off radically. By 1942 the treasured club rooms at 99 Yonge Street were in irreversible financial trouble, and by 1945 many of those who had provided energy and enthusiasm in earlier years were gone: Robson had died in 1939, Hugh Eayrs in 1940, and Jacob Markowitz, who had done so much administratively and financially for *The Canadian Poetry Magazine*, had become a prisoner-of-war of the Japanese in Singapore and Malaya.

Branch activities – readings, lectures, Book Week, participation in the Canadian Writers' War Committee – continued, but contact with young writers, vital to the continuing life of the branches, had not been sustained.

The first heartening signal of post-war rejuvenation came in September 1945, with the publication of a slashing criticism of the Association by Keith Edgar, a returned serviceman who had proposed the formation of a new society, the 'Authors League of Canada,' to his young friends and had met with an astoundingly favourable response. His complaints against cliquish parochialism in the CAA were weighted with irony for old-timers like Deacon who recalled the combination of professional and craft idealism behind the establishment of the Association in 1921 and, indeed, had never relinquished their original goals:

But [wrote Edgar] – does anyone mention *writing*? Does anyone mention current problems of authors? Does anyone touch upon the need for revision of our copyright laws? Or the income tax laws to meet the peculiar needs of authors who spend several years writing a book and have to pay the resulting proceeds back to the government as one year's income?

Does anyone discuss fundamental practical manners relating to authors? Horrors, no! How dare we suggest such a thing at a CAA meeting![22]

As honorary president of the Toronto branch, Deacon met with Edgar and supported, not the formation of a new Association, but the founding of a Forest Hill branch. He announced its formation in the 13 October 1945 edition of *The Globe and Mail*, a branch intended only for professional or semi-professiona l writers, 'to make the c.a.a. a militant organization of some benefit to writers and to take definite action toward this end.' The branch began with ten members and a waiting list of twenty-five.

The prospect of new, renewed, and militant branches was guaranteed to stir up Deacon's fiery energy once again, and though he had not even responded to a suggestion that he stand for national president in 1944, he was very open to a plea from Roderick Kennedy to members of the Toronto branch that 'people of our age and kind keep going until younger folk in the new professional class can man the post.'[23] This time there was no complication to his nomination; in March 1946 he was unanimously chosen by the national executive as the incoming president, as were three of the vice-presidents he had suggested: Will Bird, Gwethalyn Graham, and Philip Child. In addition, three other members of the Toronto branch were nominated for positions – Jacob Markowitz for national secretary, A.H. O'Brien for counsel, and Elsie Pomeroy for treasurer.[24]

With all his old obsessive energy, Deacon immediately swung into a series of preparations to make the convention, the anniversary of the CAA's quarter-century, the most glittering occasion in its history. With enormous wear and tear on his own nerves and on those of Kennedy, the out-going president, he succeeded. Publicity was arranged on an unprecedented scale – radio, the National Film Board, the Canadian Press, and Toronto newspapers. Deacon himself asked for and got extra coverage from *The Globe and Mail*. He bombarded his writer friends with letters urging their presence and more often than not he persuaded them. Even Morley Callaghan, who had never joined the Association, agreed to lead a round-table discussion on the short story. Inevitably, however, some of his schemes went awry: although he negotiated with Watson Kirkconnell about the presentation at the convention of the honorary doctorate that Frederick Philip Grove had received that spring from the University of Manitoba, but had been too ill to travel to accept, Grove was still unable to come to Toronto; he proposed to J.G. Althouse, chief director of education for Ontario, a provincial literary award system with cash prizes totalling $5000, but although his proposal was received with favour and he confidently anticipated announcing the coup at the banquet on 28 June, the department's enthusiasm evaporated before that happy day. However, he did successfully generate enormous excitement for a great occasion and though he was next door to nervous exhaustion by the time he made his presidential address, he rose above fatigue to voice once again his old faith and conviction:

Let me put the issue to you *boldly*: either Canadian literature triumphs, overcoming all the unique handicaps and obstacles confronting the Canadian writer – and in the result Canada becomes a great nation, realizing her potential; or we fail to manufacture the cement of a strong native literature, and Canada ceases to enjoy a separate existence, becoming merely a northerly extension of the economy of the United States.

That is what is in the balance.

Nothing so puny as individual incomes or doing the kind of work we like; but the *fate* of our *country*.[25]

The peak enthusiasm and energy from which Deacon sailed into his two-year presidency were matched by two important achievements of the CAA's standing committees. In 1945 the Standard Book Contract Committee had been struck under the chairmanship of Gwethalyn Graham, and the Income Tax Committee under the direction of Rod Kennedy. By the end of 1946, both committees had successfully completed their work. An income tax brief was submitted to J.L. Ilsley, Minister of Finance, in time for its recommendation to be implemented in the June 1946 federal budget. The CAA thereby won for its members the right to spread income tax declarations springing from the sale of a single book over a three-year period.[26] The Standard Book Contract Committee had its model contract ready for CAA members in December 1946. To Deacon it was the 'most valuable thing we have done yet.'[27]

For Deacon the Association was at a critical stage of transformation from an amateur society into a true craft guild. His first priority was reconstruction. In May 1946, Kennedy had found the national office in Ottawa in a chaotic state; accordingly, it was moved to Toronto and housed in a garage on Forest Hill Road belonging to Jacob Markowitz. Files were reorganized, accounts revised, unpaid fees collected, or members struck from the rolls. An additional $3,000 was required to keep the Association alive. To meet this need, a designation of 'sustaining membership' was established, by which members were encouraged to contribute from $25 to $100 above their regular annual fees. In this way, $2,000 of the necessary $3,000 was raised in 1946, and the campaign was continued for the 1947-8 year. Book Week was entrusted to May Pashley Harris of the Windsor branch and membership to Maida Parlow French of Toronto. Paul Kuhring of Montreal was in charge of the freelance project, which was to provide interested members with information about markets and writing for periodicals. In addition, regional vice-presidents were directed to take an active interest in the branches under their charge. Deacon urged Earle Birney to take over editorship of *The Canadian Poetry Magazine* after Watson Kirkconnell's resignation and, in the spring 1947 issue of *The Canadian Bookman*, defended him after his editorial standards and practices had angered some of the members of the Association. Deacon's practical contributions to the Association were fundamental in establishing morale, and membership grew as radio and textbook writers began to join.

In November 1947, he received a letter from Philip Child, who was both CAA vice-president for Ontario and member of the Canadian Arts Council. At the request of the Department of External Affairs, the Arts Council had undertaken to set up the 'Canadian UNESCO Literary Project Committee,' whose job it was to prepare a list of pre-1900

Canadian literary 'classics' in English and a second list of English-Canadian works worthy of translation. Deacon and Lorne Pierce were the Authors' Association members who were to work along with B.K. Sandwell and Philip Child from the Royal Society, Watson Kirkconnell and E.K. Brown from the Humanities Research Council of Canada, and W.S. Wallace and F.C. Jennings from the Canadian Library Association.[28] A list of 100 books was prepared and later integrated into the brief from the Canadian Authors' Association to the Royal Commission on National Development in the Arts, Letters and Science (the Massey Commission), submitted on 31 October 1949.

The brief as a whole was written by Deacon, Philip Child, and Cecil Lingard. Its preamble was characteristically idealistic: 'A national literature is only an encyclopaedia for the information of persons inside and outside the country; it is also the coherent expression of a people's traditions and aspirations...' It was also pragmatic and its recommendations were specific: a $2,500 cash award for each Governor-General's winner and an honorarium of $100 for each judge; cash prizes for winners of the Leacock Medal for Humour and for the juvenile category; eight annual scholarships of $1,500 to $ 2,500 to writers who had published one book, five awards to be distributed to each of the geographic regions of Canada and the remaining three prizes to be awarded regardless of region. The Authors' Association also strongly urged the adjudication of these scholarships by working writers and by members of the CAA.

The Association thrived in other ways. The December 1947 and March 1948 issues of *The Canadian Author and Bookman* were sold out and with the June number, paid circulation reached an all-time high of 4,500. Total membership over the two years of Deacon's presidency increased from 924 to 1,001, and at the June 1948 convention he announced that annual fees had been raised to $10 as the result of a ballot mailed to members. In April 1948, *First Serial Rights*, a quarterly newsletter for CAA members only, made its first appearance. It was designed as a forum for Association business not felt relevant to the content of the mass-distributed *Canadian Author and Bookman*.[29]

During this time, Deacon had, of course, carried on his work for *The Globe and Mail* and he had continued to chair the Governor-General's Awards Board. The enormous demands on his time were more than balanced by achievements involving the new sense of strength and purpose in the Association. His feeling for the national relevance of the Association was also reflected in his desire to get to know Francophone writers better and to enjoy a closer relationship with La Société des

Ecrivains Canadiens. One of the first letters he wrote after becoming president went to Jean Bruchési, whom Deacon addressed in his dual capacity as president of the CAA and chairman of the Governor-General's Awards Board: 'We feel strongly that there should not be two groups of writers in this country which are as separated as French and English have been during recent years. While for many purposes it is reasonable that we operate in the different organizations, we think there should be much closer liaison between us.'[30] By the end of Deacon's term in 1948, the CAA was able to count among its members three very successful French-Canadian writers – Gabrielle Roy, Germaine Guèvremont, and Roger Lemelin – and Deacon could say of the Association, with complete conviction and assurance, 'we face an enviable future.'

After his retirement as president in 1948, Deacon served as past president until June 1950 and then as an executive committee member until June 1951. The convention in Montreal in 1950 was a special high point for him, with one entire afternoon devoted to addresses by Francophone writers – Germaine Guèvremont, Roger Duhamel, Roger Lemelin, Louvigny de Montigny, and Jean Bruchési. For him, it was 'the most impressive gathering so far,' and he was particularly anxious to retain and strengthen the bond with the Société des Ecrivains Canadiens, which he saw as a steadying influence during the transition from the old guard of long-standing members to the new post-war group.

It was also a convention that proposed to do something specific about what Deacon perceived to be a top priority problem with the Association – the need to enlist the sympathy and support of young Canadian writers. Thirty-two-year-old Scott Young, writer and journalist, had been elected as a vice-president, and Deacon wrote a letter to him that was, effectively, his own valedictory to the Canadian Authors' Association:

Your participation in this convention and election to the executive was the high point of last week for me. Of course I think you did exactly the right thing in the interest of your age group and of professional writing in Canada. I hope you will take hold, bit by bit, in co-operation with Henry Kreisel and other young men. 'To you with failing hands we throw the torch' etc. Personally, I think I have contributed everything I have of value to give and want to ease out free to get back to my own writing.

He advised Young about the future of the CAA: 'What you have to see to in your active years is that new, strong people are gathered in and understand that it is their show from here out ... Success lies in the acquiring of dynamic, talented younger writers,' and added: 'You are an answer to prayer. During the past five years the officers have worried a lot about how they were going to get the abler young men to take over and run the machine that has been built slowly since 1921.' He concluded:

For your comfort in this move, I want to close by saying that I have been an officer of some sort for 15 years. I want to get out now, having contributed all I can. But the effort was worth while. However little we have been able to do compared with the much which should be done, there exists a working body of working writers; and I firmly believe in the fruitfulness of co-operation in the interest of common ends, material and idealistic. Craft solidarity is the main point of my philosophy. You and your contemporaries should, and will make a better job of it than we did. Men like [Will] Bird and I are just waiting to step aside in favor of our juniors and betters.

All luck to you and thanks for taking hold.[31]

The myth of the Canadian Authors' Association as an absurd group of ineffectual people has been perpetuated to our own day, largely because of the repeated anthologizing of Frank Scott's 'The Canadian Authors Meet.' Even Mary Vipond, the only scholar who has written of the Association, was affected in her approach and her conclusions, by that witty, superficial poem.[32] In fact, though 'craft solidarity,' Deacon's most cherished goal for the Association, forever resists measurement, it is certain that the CAA's practical achievements for the writers of Canada were many and major. In four decades of activity, Deacon was involved with all of those achievements and was a dynamic force behind many of them.

CHAPTER ELEVEN

The Globe and Mail Years

EXCEPT FOR 1942-5, when he was seconded to the Wartime Prices and Trade Board to manage the rationing of paper, Deacon remained literary editor of *The Globe and Mail* from 1936 until his retirement in 1960. During the optimistic years of the twenties he had established his reviewing style, but the subsequent period of struggle and insecurity had, perforce, not only broadened his journalistic competence, but had also markedly widened the range of his interests and concerns. The experience of those years had changed his writing style. He now spoke with authority, as always, but far less often with the tone of brash defensiveness that had sometimes sounded in his *Saturday Night* reviews. The critical perspective of his later years he referred to as 'reasoned admiration' for all potential talent; his reviews lost some of their earlier impassioned advocacy or dismissal, but they gained in range and balance.

There were factors besides experience and maturity which contributed to such a change of style and tone. His work in *Saturday Night* had been directed towards a smaller and, in general, more privileged readership, one which combined genuine interest in literary matters with the social and cultural ambitions, and the purchasing power, of comfortably-off Canadians of their day. *The Globe and Mail*'s Saturday book page, on the other hand, was addressed to a wider audience, of which only a small segment were book-buyers and an even smaller fraction claimed literary interests. His years of syndication had taught Deacon to discuss different kinds of books for a wide variety of audiences; during those years he had also developed the elasticity and the range of technique necessary to a good journalist. First and foremost he knew that the public's interest was alarmingly fickle and that the prime job of a journalist on a large daily paper was to catch that interest and hold it.

At *Saturday Night* his 'Saved from the Waste-Basket' column had been his most consistently popular feature, drawing literary news and gossip from correspondents all over the country. Accordingly, in January 1937 he began a column called 'The Hell-Box': 'Discarded type goes into the Hell-box for melting and recasting. Good paragraphs may reach there without seeing print; so many an odd item in a critic's life misses his readers without a confessional for fragments ...' (*GM*, 16 January 1937) Three weeks later the column was renamed 'The Fly Leaf' in deference to the tender sensibilities of *The Globe and Mail*'s 'league of decency' readers and, as such, it became Deacon's signature. Chatty, newsy, full of information and literary gossip, it once again invited Canadian writers, readers, publishers, and booksellers to a community of common interests as 'Saved from the Waste-Basket' had done so successfully in the twenties. He printed in it notices of literary events and often used the column to precede or follow up a book review with praise and publicity for an author. For the writers he especially admired he fulfilled a press agent's role, keeping their names before the public and supplementing his reviews with personal notes or figures on sales or, in the case of Gabrielle Roy, for instance, on translation negotiations. Occasionally he would have a colleague or a writer take over the column for a feature article, as when Jessie L. Beattie wrote 'A School Girl's Memoirs of Bliss Carman.' (*GM*, 27 July 1957) Once again, his formula proved infallible and Deacon and 'The Fly Leaf' became synonymous in the minds of readers.

For Deacon the rules of reviewing applied to all genres and began in one immutable dictum:

there is no such thing as a good or bad book. There can only be the favorable or unfavorable reaction of the individual reader. For the moment, you, the reviewer, are that reader ... it is not matters of fact that are going to confuse you in judgment but the author's success in creating art ... You will use the words good and bad for the sake of convenience, a kind of shorthand, but it is important for you to realize they don't mean that. You only state your opinion.[1]

Within that frame of reference his reviewing always managed to convey a sense of sheer reading enjoyment combined with a marked ability to summarize, to pick the brief, illustrative quotation, and to present himself as the prototypical reader with likes, dislikes, a sense of humour, and a judicious common sense. His reviews combined, in the persona of the reviewer, the qualities of the man of letters and the man in the street.

His own preoccupations in the thirties had intensified his interest in cultural history. Van Wyck Brooks had long been one of his own models; in the *Life of Emerson* and particularly in *The Flowering of New England*, he saw a culture undergoing the same kind of transition as the Canada of his own day. For Deacon, Brooks was 'fulfilling the highest function of a critic in interpretive writing' and was without peer in the English-speaking world: 'I ask Canadian writers to note the emphasis on the natural inspiration of one's own place ... It has long seemed to me that Canada is going through now the same sort of evolution that the United States experienced from 1815 to 1865 ... When reading Brooks, please note the sturdy nationalism that produced the worthies of whom he writes so entertainingly.' (*ME*, 14 November 14, 1936) He praised Gerald Heard's psychological studies of Western culture and history – *The Emergence of Man*, *These Hurrying Years*, *The Source of Civilization*, and *The Third Morality*. Biography as a focus for cultural history remained a prime favourite as he appraised the works of Stefan Zweig and Emil Ludwig. Increasingly through the thirties and early forties, he reviewed numbers of books on contemporary politics and history, among them Harold J. Laski's *Democracy and Crisis*, Edgar Snow's *Red Star over China*, the *Inside* series by John Gunther, Liddell Hart's *The Defense of Britain*, William Shirer's *Berlin Diary*, and John F. Kennedy's *Why England Slept*.

Canadian works, of course, gave him intense satisfaction: the League for Social Reconstruction's *Social Planning for Canada* was a landmark in the economic life of the nation, he thought, and F.R. Scott's *Canada and the United States*, by reason of its clear thinking and simple, compact writing was worthy of the title 'Canadian Primer.' Bruce Hutchison's *The Unknown Country* was 'the best book ever written to explain Canada' and a rallying cry for Canadians. In style, theme, and prophetic stance, Hutchison's book appealed immediately to Deacon: 'He chats about our history, economic problems, our folkways and our future in a manner to win the heart and instruct the mind at the same operation.' (*GM*, 21 February 1942)

His criticism of fiction moved markedly towards an appreciation of 'sharp high realism' wherever he found it, but especially in the work of Canadian novelists. He had always believed that W.H. Blake's translation of *Maria Chapdelaine* marked the end of Canadian literature's early apprenticeship and heralded a new movement towards maturity. In the twenties its romance form had seemed to him the proper model for

Canadian fiction and he had rejected realism, arguing, for instance, that de la Roche more successfully captured the Canadian essence than Grove. In *My Vision of Canada*, in fact, he had written his own prose romance of English Canada and among its reviewers Salem Bland, at least, had demonstrated its parallels to *Maria Chapdelaine*. By the late thirties, however, as the pressure of events had broadened his experience and his skills, so fifteen years of reviewing had trained his critical understanding.

Having roundly condemned the brutality of Hemingway's *To Have and Have Not*, he now praised *For Whom the Bell Tolls* for its 'plan [which] is perfectly conventional' and for the fact that it was 'a supremely good action and character story, tender without mawkishness and strong without brutality. It moves like a play, with interpretation implied, not stated, with a cause demonstrated, not argued.' He considered it by far the best book to come out of the Spanish Civil War, 'the most illuminating, however fragmentary it may be as history.' (*GM*, 30 November 1940) He admired John Steinbeck's *The Grapes of Wrath*, 'a vicious novel in the new photographic manner. It has little plot, but it is a mute protest against despair, a revelation of suffering.' (*GM*, 22 April 1939) About Thomas Wolfe's *The Web and the Rock*, Deacon wrote, 'of Wolfe's sheer power, there can be no doubt. His prose is like his vast, troubled, bulky self, without discipline or poise.' (*GM*, 29 July 1939) Faulkner's *Sanctuary* (1932) he thought had 'touched the limits of the coarse and disgusting,' but *The Unvanquished* (1938) he considered affirmative in tone and conservative in style and subject matter, 'outstanding for its verve and originality.' (*GM*, 28 May 1928)

More often than not Deacon's receptivity to a novel's technical complexity was directly linked to its extra-literary content. Thus he was more willing to accept 'the new photographic manner' in Steinbeck and in Dos Passos' *Adventures of a Young Man* (*GM*, 12 August 12, 1939) than Faulkner's technical experiments in *Absalom! Absalom!* (*GM*, 20 February 20, 1937) because he was more sympathetic to the social criticism of the first two than to Faulkner's tragic sense of life. He accepted departures from the descriptive techniques of traditional realism and the narrative logic of traditional romance only to the extent that the novelist was writing *littérature engagée* and furthering his purpose by his experiments. Of course, in this as in other matters, Deacon was always the first to admit that he remained at heart a Methodist with a strong leaning towards, almost an insistence on, the didactic in literature.

When he recognized artistry and truth in the work of Canadian writers his tone soared in satisfaction. Ringuet's *Thirty Acres*, 'competent in form and simply terrific in social significance,' presented an entirely new picture of rural French Canada. 'A very sad story, but also a marvellously brave one,' *Thirty Acres*, like *Madame Bovary*, 'has classic strength and proportions; and readers of imagination cannot fail to be profoundly moved by its personal tragedy that symbolises the tragedy of a race.' For Deacon, Ringuet's novel was 'the quintessence of the genre form. Do not let its quiet, casual tone deceive you; this is a great book.' (*GM*, 16 November 1940) He found Sinclair Ross's *As For Me and My House* distinguished by its 'mature character interpretation,' its frank depiction of the Bentleys' life and by 'its uncompromisingly sincere craftsmanship.' Deacon commended the novel's sustained sober tone, its 'pitiful photographic accuracy,' Ross's 'tender, intuitive perception of the human heart' and his remarkably consistent depiction of Mrs Bentley. In the realism of his approach and the soberness of his tone, Ross, according to Deacon, 'is distinctly the sort of young novelist who should be encouraged. I shall await his future books with keen anticipation. He is interpreting contemporary Canadian life earnestly and skilfully, and in so doing is performing the most useful function of a writer.' (*GM*, 26 April 1941)

There was no satisfaction in Deacon's whole career to match his joy at the emergence of these novelists as well as the four whom he considered the front-runners in the rapidly maturing field of Canadian fiction: Hugh MacLennan, Gabrielle Roy, Gwethalyn Graham, and Roger Lemelin. He could be, and was, a severe critic of MacLennan's work, particularly in the privacy of their correspondence, but of MacLennan's developing talent he had no doubt. For Gabrielle Roy's work he had an awed regard, as he had for her herself when he came to know her. Her great gift to Canadian literature was, to him, a 'firm, sharp realism of observation, that is the antithesis of the customary romantic atmosphere of our fiction in both English and French.' (*GM*, 27 April 1946) In the forties and fifties her kind of realism became his highest criterion of fictional success.

The autobiographies of two Canadian writers were also revelations to him. Charles Gordon's *Postscript to Adventure: The Autobiography of Ralph Connor* was one. Deacon had consistently derided Connor's work along with that of L.M. Montgomery, but reading Gordon's autobiography revealed him as 'a man whom I should have loved could I have known him as he reveals himself in his final volume, the only one about himself.' (*GM*, 2 July 1938) He confessed that he 'came to literary awareness when that sort of thing [the muscular Christianity of *Black*

Rock and *The Sky Pilot*] was scorned by bright young persons who had not learned how hard it is to write any kind of book, let alone a fairly good one.' Deacon was impressed by the fullness of Gordon's life, his enthusiasm, his affirmation, his ongoing apprenticeship to the craft of writing in his later works, and his importance as a Canadian national figure; he also recognized in Gordon's autobiography the embodiment of much of the romance of his own vision of Canada.

He had known Laura Goodman Salverson for fifteen years when her *Confessions of an Immigrant's Daughter* was published in 1939. Though what he termed her 'self-conscious defiance' was totally familiar to him, he valued her stubborn recording of the truth as she saw it, her 'fierce desire for accuracy,' and her success in writing an autobiography that reads 'like a novel' and that is 'a first-rate piece of implied social criticism ... brave and refreshing and honest.' (*GM*, 6 January 1940)

Not surprisingly, considering his predilection for narrative, E.J. Pratt was the poet for whom his praise was constant. In his *Saturday Night* days he had roused the ire of A.J.M. Smith and then of the entire *Forum* group by his cavalier dismissal of modernist poetry. About the work of Pratt, however, he had no reservations; all through the thirties each succeeding poem fulfilled his expectation of what poetry should be and finally, in *Brébeuf and His Brethren*, he found a poet 'at the peak of power,' the story 'so superbly reverent as well as heroic that the critic does not want to pull it apart, even to point out merits.' (*GM*, 27 July 1940)

Writing to Earle Birney in 1947, he admitted his own sense of inadequacy as a critic of poetry, as well as explaining the practical reasons for his infrequent reviews:

I can do an A.1. novel in a third of a column (it is a unit) but need more than half a column for a 50-page booklet of verse. Consequently, you, Pratt, and half a dozen others are the only poets we ever review, and no non-Canadians at all ... I am unfit to pass judgment on the new poetry as I do not understand it. I have a good knowledge of poetry from Chaucer to, say 1930, but I lack the brains to comprehend many of the newer poets.[2]

Though he always remained somewhat baffled by the work of the modernist poets and more than a little defensive about all poets and critics he felt to be of the academic world, his reviews of A.J.M. Smith's *Book of Canadian Poetry* (1943) and of Ralph Gustafson's anthology *Canadian Poetry* (1942) were generous, if somewhat backhandedly complimentary to Canada's younger poets: 'Nothing could have been healthier for poetic literature in Canada than to telescope the senior poets slightly together to make room on equal terms for these juniors who have been, as a group, as disdainful of the public as the public has been ignorant of them.' (*GM*, 6 June 1942) His introductory remarks about Smith's anthology were even more acid: 'an attempt to popularize a group of highly mannered writers, who make a cult of obscurity to the point that they have been unable as individuals to make any impression at all upon the reading public.' He did, however, deliver a detailed and judicious criticism of the work, praising Smith's attempt to explain the merits of the McGill Group in his prefatory essay and finally applauding the collection's intent:

What the book presages is the teaching of Canadian poetry in schools and universities, a thing greatly to be desired. If the youngsters do not enjoy the dull poems of the early nineteenth century, they will certainly revel in such modern items as Pratt's The Cachalot and Amber Lands by Tom MacInnes. Finally, Prof. Smith has exhibited in his selections a taste, if at times severe, yet always sound. Far more popular collections could have been made, but Canadian poetry emerges from this test extraordinarily well. The labors of Prof. Smith have given Canadians something of which they can be genuinely, if soberly, proud. (*GM*, 30 October 30, 1943)

He recognized that Desmond Pacey's *Creative Writing in Canada* (1952) was also designed for a slowly growing market in schools and universities and gave the book a long review, but by captioning it 'An Attempted Appraisal of Canadian Literature' he damned it with faint praise. Predictably, he challenged Pacey's emphasis on the modernist poets at the expense, he thought, of adequate coverage for Canadian fiction and of total exclusion of French Canadian writing. (*GM*, 17 April 1952) His summary, 'a very useful book,' was tantamount to total dismissal from Deacon, the Canadian literature enthusiast, and was certainly somewhat coloured by his old anti-academic prejudice – indeed, he and Hugh MacLennan, in their private correspondence, joined in utter disregard for Pacey's work.

In Northrop Frye, however, Deacon was quick to recognize and publicize a major critical voice. His review of *Fearful Symmetry* was at once an article on Blake and an appreciation of Frye's book: 'It is one of the finest pieces of interpretative criticism in the language. All lovers of poetry will rejoice that Blake can now be understood easily by the many, who have always believed these prophecies must contain noble ideas artistically expressed in cryptic form, but who never themselves sought the keys to those supposed enigmas.' (*GM*, 17 May 1947) Subsequently he was often to prophesy that Canada would first gain international literary recognition in the field of criticism.

A normal book page contained a feature review article of 1,200 to 2,000 words, four or five shorter reviews, 'The Fly Leaf,' and an annotated list of recently published books. The burden of work increased tremendously during the heaviest reviewing months, November and December. The first week of November was Canadian Book Week, when Deacon prepared his annual special edition of the book page to mark the occasion. On at least one full page and sometimes two, there were special articles on literary items of the past year and on events or authors of interest. Often the Book Week pages were liberally filled with photos of writers. In November 1938, there were photographs of Robert Borden, Virna Sheard, Stephen Leacock, E.J. Pratt, Laura Goodman Salverson, and Jessie Beattie, as well as a reproduction of Clarence Gagnon's painting, 'Spring Thaw.' The feature review on Robert Borden's memoirs was followed by 'Canadian Headliners,' a list of the best books of 1938: de la Roche's *Growth of a Man*, Gwethalyn Graham's *Swiss Sonata*, George Wrong's *The Canadians*, Ralph Connor's *Postscript to Adventure*, Edwin Guillet's *Lives and Times of the Patriots*. The Governor-General's Awards for 1937, presented to coincide with Book Week in 1938, had been won by E.J. Pratt for *The Fable of the Goats*, Laura Goodman Salverson for *The Dark Weaver*, and Stephen Leacock for *My Discovery of the West*, and Deacon included a section on them. Throughout the year there would from time to time appear a small 'Books for Children' feature on the regular Saturday page, in which current books would be reviewed, often by children, among them his daughter, Deirdre. Sometime in November or December, an entire book page would be devoted to children's books with ten to twenty reviews and a 'Just Off the Press' section devoted to books for youngsters. This annual review was designed to coincide either with Children's Book Week, which took place at the same time as the general Book Week celebrations in early November, or with the Christmas season.

The most onerous reviewing burden came with the 'Christmas Review of Books,' which filled two or three pages on the first or second Saturday in December and sometimes was supplemented by a mid-week page. In the meantime, of course, the regular Saturday book page continued to appear every week. Deacon did the bulk of the Christmas reviewing by himself, thanks to four or five weeks of twenty-hour days. There would be two or three long feature articles, anywhere from ten to fifteen reviews of new books, and a section on books recommended for gifts, most of which had been reviewed earlier in the year. A one- to two-sentence synopsis followed each title and the list could number as many as seventy-five books. Frequently included was a small section entitled 'Children's Books.' Publishers, anxious to advertise in the Christmas edition, were often ready to pay a bonus for a specific place on the page, and advertising usually took up one-third to one-half of the Christmas section.

When, in 1951, Robert Farquharson left *The Globe and Mail* to become editor of *Saturday Night* and then director of information at the NATO headquarters in Paris, he was succeeded by Thomas Munns, who, like Farquharson, was a good friend to Deacon. In 1953 Munns lightened Deacon's work-load, ordering him to cut down his own reviewing by a quarter and to get more help from outside reviewers. He was given a budget for this purpose as well, and it was at this time that he began seriously to seek out and train a team of reviewers. This was an assignment entirely congenial to him. Sally, of course, had never stopped reviewing under her maiden name, Sally Townsend. Deirdre had reviewed as well; from children's books she gradually worked into adult literature. Now, from among his old friends, like Carlton McNaught, Isabel LeBourdais, and Viola Pratt, and more recent writer-correspondents, like Dorothy Dumbrille, Joan Walker, and Kathleen Graham, he recruited and, as he proudly stated, personally trained ('individual coaching for at least one year') about twenty-five reviewers. His aim was to make them specialists in the various fields of literature that his columns covered.

With his out-of-town trainees he was in his element, assuming the teacher-prophet role that he loved, writing and exhorting them with all his missionary zeal in play and, at the same time, giving them sound advice and instruction in the craft of book reviewing. To one of his team, shocked by the explicit sex in a book he sent her, he replied tactfully, but with uncompromising common sense:

mine is a literary department, not a school of morals. From earliest time the love story has been the main stock of the novelists (among early Romans, Renaissance Italians, etc.) and the stock device to complicate man-woman relations has always been adultery. That is all right because it is a good old human custom of which you may read in the Bible and in the earliest pagan literature. Right or wrong, men have always gone to bed with other women and women with other men. You will recall Helen of Troy and the latest scandal in your own village ... If it [the book in question] is an addition to your library, by all means keep it. But if it is an embarrassment, send it back as we can get rid of it without incendiarism and I have never burned a book yet.[3]

Old friends like McNaught and Isabel and Donat LeBourdais needed no such handling; they were fully as sophisticated readers as Deacon himself. Yet he knew that he needed reviewers for all his variety of readers and he cultivated them patiently.

Joan Walker, an Englishwoman trained in journalism who had emigrated to Kirkland Lake, and who won the Leacock Award for Humour in 1953 with *Pardon My Parka*, had a sense of humour very like Deacon's own. Anticipating her special usefulness on his team, he took particular interest in her training, to their considerable mutual enjoyment. When she reviewed a ponderous novel for him and suggested the heading 'Literature's Longest Yawn' for it, his reply was both technical and theoretical:

There is no reason why you should not write your own heads. But the worry about them is mechanical. I'm fussy about two lines of equal length, whether single or double column – with an air-space at each end. These look attractive...

...Literature's Longest Yawn is a single line double; and clever; but ... that wording shows atrociously bad judgment ... Your phrase is le mot juste, I grant. But NEVER put on a head which will keep readers from reading your article. The chief function of man may be to glorify God; but the chief function and aim of a writer is to get himself read. Put on a head which will entice your reader, rouse his curiosity, tempt him to plunge into the text below. Don't drive him away by proclaiming that the whole thing is a bore. You break that gently to him later.[4]

With, finally, some thirty reviewers ready to contribute to the book page, Deacon could and did choose to write the reviews and to feature the works which satisfied him most. Aside from the works of the few novelists he considered the best in Canada, he reviewed little fiction in the last decade of his career; instead, he consistently found his greatest satisfaction in the achievements of Canadian non-fiction writers: Bruce Hutchison's *The Incredible Canadian* (1952) and *Canada: Tomorrow's Giant* (1957); Donald Creighton's *John A. Macdonald* (1952, 1955) and *Harold Adams Innis: Portrait of a Scholar* (1957); William Kilbourn's *The Firebrand* (1956); and W.L. Morton's *Manitoba: A History* (1957). Pre-eminent among these, in his opinion, was Malcolm Ross's *Our Sense of Identity* (1954). This anthology of forty-four pieces by forty-two writers, including Deacon's own 'What a Canadian has Done for

Canada,' the parody of Stringer's *Empty Hands* that he had written long ago, fulfilled the promise that Deacon had always seen in Canada and that he had been preaching and prophesying for thirty years:

[Ross] has treated the prose non-fiction writers as the voices of the Canadian people and has composed a major work of interpretation, as a musical conductor would use instruments in the hands of many players to create intelligible harmony ... The concept of the bewildered, imitative Canadian with no mind of his own disappears. These writers use the most diverse inflections, talk about utterly different things; yet none apologizes for his or her country's existence. The exciting task of the reader is to decide, each for himself, the several common denominators that, somehow, make sense of putting Susanna Moodie, W.H. Blake, Emily Carr and J.S. Woodsworth between the same covers. (*GM*, 30 January 1954)

During all the years at *The Globe and Mail* Deacon, as always, made time for numbers of causes and concerns. In the mid- and late-forties the sense of new beginnings and boundless opportunity that fueled his energies as president of the CAA carried over into all his other activities as well. During his years with the Wartime Prices and Trade Board, Sally had proved herself an admirably efficient deputy literary editor. He had always been on hand to direct her work and to do some of the important reviewing, and he had continued to see to the lay-out of the book pages usually going to *The Globe and Mail* after his office work at the WPTB was finished. But she had proven herself an entirely competent journalist and for the rest of his career she was the first in his team of reviewers, besides being, as always, a general support staff of one, of inestimable value to his morale. From 1942 to 1945 she had been paid $2,500 a year by *The Globe and Mail* and Deacon $4,500 by the WPTB – 'the years we were rich,' the children called them. Bill, Deirdre, and Mary were approaching adulthood; both the Parkhurst home and the summer place on Wilson's Point had ceased to be draining financial burdens; and for both Deacon and Sally there was a new, still strictly limited, but real sense of freedom and security.

The Writers' Club, which in the thirties had been such a source of craft solidarity and therapeutic tomfoolery, broke up in 1943 for lack of funds to maintain premises, but Deacon carried on his associations with the old members. He also once more became active in the International PEN Club, as secretary-treasurer, though he did not manage, as he hoped to do, to attend its 1946 conference in Stockholm. He did, however, thoroughly enjoy all the opportunities for travelling that his CAA work offered him, and his and Sally's trip to the Vancouver convention in 1947 was the holiday climax of their years together. His acceptance of the Governor-General's Award on behalf of Frederick Philip Grove for *In Search of Myself* was one highlight of that convention; his officiating at the unveiling of the Pauline Johnson Memorial in Stanley Park was the other. In 1948 he was asked to speak at Stanstead College at a ceremony commemorating Duncan Campbell Scott, perhaps the College's most distinguished graduate. He was flattered by the invitation and excited by the prospect of a trip back to the Eastern Townships, which he had not visited since boyhood. This time he and Sally went by car – with Sally driving, since they had long since agreed that Deacon was both too jittery and too absolutely non-mechanical to be entrusted with the family's safety. In his mind the trip became an epic journey to times past, and none of the actual details disappointed him. He delivered a graceful tribute to Scott, at the same time taking the opportunity of giving the college a large share of credit for his own literary career, and he basked in the pleasure of being an honoured guest for the occasion.[5]

He had never had any confidence in himself as a speaker; certainly, to the end of his life he insisted that he was *not* a speaker, 'the writer without quick wit. A DULL CLOD.'[6] In these post-war years, however, he had so much experience with the CAA alone that he largely forgot his inhibitions, accepting all kinds of speaking engagements to Canadian Clubs, universities, public library groups and radio broadcasts. The most extended effort in public speaking of his lifetime was the series of lectures he gave for the Ryerson Institute of Technology in Toronto in 1951-2. On the invitation of William McMaster of the Ryerson faculty, he agreed to take on an evening course on Canadian literature between 1 October 1951 and 1 March 1952. The series of twenty lectures was called 'Contemporary Canadian Literature,' but in fact it became a survey of the history of Canadian literature, very broadly based, including history and biography, French as well as English Canadian writers, arranged, not chronologically, but in Deacon's own order of importance. The object of the course was, he said, 'to supply an introduction to Canadian literature that you may form some idea of its scope, variety and present vigor; and to prevent you, if possible, from reaching hasty, erroneous conclusions based on knowledge of a handful of books by a few writers of a particular group.'[7] Implicit in that statement, and in the entire course, was a declaration against any academic canon of Canadian literature and, especially, against the supremacy of the Montreal group of poets. As always, barring the works of Roberts, Lampman, Campbell, Scott, MacInnes, MacDonald, and Pratt, Deacon's own preferences veered strongly away from poetry and in his approach to his course he was, as in all else, sharply idiosyncratic.

The manuscript is 189 pages long, with a missing segment of thirteen pages in the section on histories and historians, from the *Jesuit Relations* to the work of Brown, Lower, McInnis and Creighton. His introductory lecture placed Canadians squarely in a continuing colonial situation: 'We stand in the earliest pioneer days of Canadian literature. We are still importing at least three-quarters of our reading matter. Thirty years ago it was 98%; and no educational institution in my youth would consider teaching anything except imported literature. Hence the controlling minds [of today] were formed by colonial influence and the principles on which a literature is based have not been properly understood.'[8]

The overall theme of the course was Deacon's once-and-always text, the need, desirability, and inevitability of a national, Canadian literature:

A national literature comes into being in response to the deeply felt need of every society to understand itself...

And the ideas, the themes? They are in the air, a part of that familiar environment, which is the raw material of every creative writer. There is originality in the inter-play of these factors; but the material is the field of common experience, and while the urge appears to a writer to be the vanity of self-expression, the real dynamic is a society which must know the significance of its special destiny.

It is only when a people feels itself united, free and strong that there exists the equation which demands its own literature for its inspiration and guidance, because a people not in control of its own fate feels no need to be self-regarding...

Canada's course seems to me to prove neatly the theory that any national literature of importance is a necessary psychological part of the historic process – not a frill, not a mere amusement, not a flower to be cultivated because we can now afford such a luxury.[9]

From this thesis his secondary theme emerged logically – the need for *writers*, trained, encouraged and, above all, paid a living wage for their work.

Deacon spoke with the same conviction and the same rhetoric with which he had begun his literary career. He did not claim a world-forefront place for Canadian literature – yet; but he did recognize progress, in that, over the past thirty years, fewer and fewer writers had found it necessary to leave the country for advancement. So far, however, he thought that Canada had produced only one world-class book, Richard Albert Wilson's *The Miraculous Birth of Language*: 'An elderly professor at Saskatoon took 20 years to develop a theory so simple that it takes only about 100 pages, so adequate that it has not been challenged in its 14 years of life.'[10]

From this establishment of the thesis of the course the lectures proceeded to discuss a series of individual writers: MacLennan, Roberts, Grove; four French-Canadian novelists (Roy, Guèvremont, Ringuet, Lemelin); Raddall. Then Deacon considered groups: the Confederation Poets (Carman, Lampman, Scott, Campbell, Johnson, MacInnes); writers of country life (Peter McArthur and Kenneth McNeill Wells); biography, autobiography, history, historical fiction, humour, and romance. Every lecture was written from the perspective of his thesis and all material was governed and directed by Deacon's own years of experience and his own strong beliefs and prejudices. Hence, there was a great deal of practical information about the craft of writing and even more anecdotal material about the writers, the majority of whom were, of course, his friends and correspondents. Critical evaluations were always subjective and often shrewdly perceptive:

there are grave structural errors in *Two Solitudes*. The first and more serious is the death of Tallard at the halfway mark; and the story died with him because the problem could only be resolved in the person of the French senator, who saw and sympathised with both contending parties. The latter half of the novel deals with the younger generation and there is no power in it. When I asked the author why he killed Tallard, he replied: 'when I was writing the book I did not realise the strength of that character.' It was an honest but fearful admission.[11]

One of his best efforts was on the four French-Canadian novelists, Roy, Guèvremont, Panneton (Ringuet), and Lemelin, all of whom he knew well and whose work he deeply admired. His section on *Thirty Acres* ends this way:

The tragedy is that Euchariste could never understand why he had failed, why he couldn't live an 18th century life in the 20th century. When I interviewed Dr Panneton at his club, I asked: 'Do I interpret *Thirty Acres* correctly when I say that it is a demonstration that the dream of Laurentia – an independent French

Republic on the banks of the St Lawrence – is a mirage, and that the destiny of your people is to be assimilated into the English-Canadian majority?' He replied: 'Of course that is what I meant; but please do not say so in print as it would be bad for my medical practice.'[12]

In every lecture his students were treated to his own knowledge of the writers as individuals, as well as to his own readings of their texts and his convinced, often unconventional, ranking of their works – he was sure, for instance, that *The Precipice* was Hugh MacLennan's best work to that date, and that, though Grove's *The Master of the Mill* was his 'most ambitious piece of fiction and by far the best,' his *In Search of Myself* was truly his master-work: 'for an example of the sheer impact of the written work, when handled by a performer of genius, I recommend this autobiography as a tour-de-force.'[13]

This whole series was an enormous amount of work and for it all, by the time he paid his taxi fares, he netted $80. He had typed out the complete script for every lecture and he was very particular in his dealings with Ryerson to retain copyright on his material. He began with twenty students, but after Christmas attendance dropped off, partly because of the weather, partly because of a Toronto Transit Commission strike which made getting about in Toronto very difficult. For the only time in all their years together, Sally was away for an extended visit with their daughter, Mary, a nurse in California. Deacon felt utterly helpless – and domestically he *was* helpless – without her. Furthermore he was used to speaking at special gatherings and gala occasions, with an audience responding enthusiastically to his presence and his message. The typing out of every lecture was a wearisome job on top of all his other responsibilities, and the final lectures, information-saturated though they are, show his weariness. They sometimes become compendiums of book summaries, interspersed with flashes of anecdote and his old rhetoric, but they lack the confidence and driving energy of the earlier ones.

He had had no experience of teaching and though he reported to his son Bill that he was getting along better than he expected, he later wrote more frankly to Lorne Pierce: 'I have no idea how to teach. When Mr McMaster made the suggestion a year ago, I accepted because this was a means of forcing myself to bring order into a subject I have been dealing with in bits and pieces for exactly half my lifetime. Nothing like complete order emerged. A start was made – no more ... Those Monday night lectures were torture. I cannot face it again.'[14] However, he did derive considerable satisfaction from the experience: there was the possibility of a book evolving from his lectures, and 'the main point is that the Institute is still experimental and I rather feel that I have put Canadian literature on the permanent course of what will soon be a degree-granting educational institution.'[15]

Lorne Pierce was very interested in his manuscript. He did not consider it publishable as it stood, and neither did Deacon: 'It was a relief to me that you could not find any logical pattern for what I want to say, anymore than I can find it.'[16] Pierce, however, gave a good deal of encouragement and editorial consideration to the work. His editorial suggestions to Deacon were well-meant, but they are supremely ironic because, of course, he could not see the future of Canadian literary studies. What he tried to persuade Deacon to do was to remove his nationalistic theme, to produce an objective, factual study of the progress of Canadian literature. Having structured his whole series on the basis of that theme, Deacon could not transform his work in the way Pierce wished. In fact he did not wish to do so; though he said he had no 'logical pattern,' and that was quite true, his most strongly held emotional convictions were both source and pattern for his work. Since 1967 and the spiralling of national consciousness, Deacon's thesis would have been completely acceptable as a basis for his work; in the fifties, to Pierce, it was not.

In fact, Pierce was eager for Deacon to do two books, one, the history of Canadian literature and the other, a series of literary memoirs. Deacon responded warmly to the stimulus of his encouragement, but as time for writing had always been a problem, so now energy was becoming one as well. To Bill he confessed that he was tired and slow and extremely forgetful. For a short time he worked sporadically on a revision of his manuscript, but he had to put it aside in favour of the other commitments always swarming around him. Besides, he still clung optimistically to his early dream of reverting to a full-time writing career after his retirement.

During the forties and fifties he was constantly at the call of various publishers as an editorial consultant. He and Frank Appleton of Collins were personal friends, as were he and Theodore Pike of Longmans. When Appleton retired in 1947, Deacon was organizer-in-chief of a gala dinner in his honour. For Appleton he often acted as a reader (for a fee of $25) and he advised for or against publication, backing up his opinion with a detailed report. He had been instrumental in the publication of Grace Campbell's *Thorn-Apple Tree* (1942) and was particularly pleased with that book's wartime success. Appleton also often asked him for biographical sketches of authors for book jacket purposes and, of course, he was often also the recipient of Deacon's unsolicited advice about writers and their publishers. With Pike of Longmans, his role was that of a writer's agent. He had obviously been invited to scout for likely manuscripts and because he was so accessible to writers, he was often in a position to suggest Longmans' interest to them. A $25 honorarium for directing Ralph Allen's *Home Made Banners* to Pike was typical of this kind of transaction. Sometimes he also read manuscripts for Pike.

George Nelson of Doubleday consulted him from time to time, particularly about the publication of possibly controversial works and, of course, was given massive doses of Deacon's anti-censorship, anti-puritan convictions. Both McGraw-Hill and McClelland and Stewart explored the possibilities of his editing anthologies for them. McGraw-Hill he turned down on the grounds that the royalty payments he would have to make to authors, by the terms of their suggested contract, would far outstrip any possible financial benefit to himself. The McClelland and Stewart project, an anthology called, tentatively, 'Ontario: A Portrait,' sounded far more promising; however it, too, failed to develop beyond the discussion stage.

In 1951, Marilyn Robb, fine arts editor of *The American People's Encyclopaedia*, wrote requesting him to do a five-hundred-word survey of Canadian literature for their annual supplement, 'because you have your finger on the pulse of Canadian literature.' Deacon accepted and continued the yearly chore until 1961, moving up to 750 words (for a fee of $30), and insisting repeatedly on the inclusion of significant Quebec literature.

In 1951 the executive of the Women's Canadian Club consulted Deacon about an annual literary contest which the club planned to initiate. They were searching for talented young writers, particularly poets, and they proposed to offer annually the Canadian Club Prize of $200. No more in his sixties than in his twenties could Deacon refuse a request for literary help and advice; besides he had a special affection for the Women's Canadian Club, having begun to speak to their various groups and, on occasion, to suggest speakers to them, in his early days at *Saturday Night*. He responded with enthusiasm though he urged them to consider fiction writers as well as poets; thereafter, until 1961 he prepared a short list each year for their judges. Every year he was delighted to publicize their contest in 'The Fly Leaf.' The link was a happy one; the small honorarium they sent him annually was always accompanied by a warm letter of thanks and just as warmly received. In 1961, working at home on his own writing, and without his former access to review copies of new books as they were published, he terminated his friendly association with the Club, congratulating its award committee once again on the encouragement they were offering to young writers: 'Nobody except the professional writer can understand how lonely his life is. His life is spent alone in a silent room.'[17]

Perhaps the most consistently pleasurable of all the post-war literary causes in which Deacon was involved was the establishing of the Leacock Medal for Humour. In 1944 Stephen Leacock had died and a group of Orillia friends and admirers formed a memorial committee to set up a Leacock collection in the Orillia Library; to commission a bronze portrait bust of Leacock by Elizabeth Wyn Wood, a sculptor who had come from Orillia; and to establish a Leacock Memorial Medal to be awarded annually for the best book of humour written by a Canadian. C.H. Hale, editor of *The Orillia Packet and Times*, and two old friends of Leacock, Maude Ardagh, librarian, and Paul Copeland, an Orillia lawyer, were the prime movers in the project. Because of Deacon's focal position in Canadian letters, especially his chairmanship of the Governor-General's Awards Board, and because he was a summer resident of Wilson's Point, on the outskirts of Orillia, he was consulted on every detail from the very beginning. Predictably, he was enormously enthusiastic, drumming up support with a flurry of letters and arranging with the CAA that the judging of the Leacock Medal be added to the annual duties of the Awards Board. In 1947 the first winner was announced – Harry Symons, who had written *Ojibway Melody*, a humorous and deeply affectionate account of cottage life on Georgian Bay. At a dinner in June, Deacon presented Symons with a bronze medal, designed, cast, and donated by the sculptor Emmanuel Hahn, the husband of Elizabeth Wyn Wood.

From the first the annual dinner was a festive occasion. At this inaugural dinner B.K. Sandwell, at his witty best, was the chief speaker, Deacon presented the award, and the program included a competition for the best and funniest six-minute speech, the prize a copy of *Sunshine Sketches of a Little Town*. Yousuf Karsh, Emmanuel Hahn, John Robins, Franklin Davey McDowell, Deacon, and Symons himself were contestants. Each year, weeks of planning made the dinner a memorable affair and Deacon presented the award annually until 1962.

1951, 1955, and 1958 were especially vintage years, the first because Leacock's bust was unveiled in the library, and the memorial committee became the Steven Leacock Associates, their goal the acquiring of the Leacock home on Old Brewery Bay. Eric Nicol was presented with the Award for *The Roving I*, C. Harold Hale, for sixty-four years the editor of *The Orillia Packet and Times*, was an honoured guest, and Louis Blake Duff, journalist and writer, was the guest speaker. Duff's and Deacon's subsequent exchange of letters was brimful of mutual congratulations finally climaxed by Deacon's report on the satisfaction of the organizers of the affair:

If you and I as outsiders were thrilled, happiness among the townspeople was ecstatic. We got a good show; they got their heart's desire, reached the goal of months of hard work. Just as one instance (again confidential): Miss Ardagh, Miss Tudhope and Mrs Copeland, after saying goodbye to the last guest at 2 a.m., got into a car and toured the adjacent landscape till morning, dropping in for coffee here and there over 30 miles radius – and talking and congratulating themselves over success. The ladies returned home for breakfast; but when Sally and I called on them in mid-afternoon, none of the trio had been to bed yet. And I've never seen Miss Ardagh look so happy. Proprietor of the hardware store was discussing the speeches with me on the following Monday. Orillia will talk about this all winter.[18]

Another highlight year was 1955: Robertson Davies was presented with the award for his *Leaven of Malice*, his acceptance speech was televised nation-wide, and as Deacon officiated at the dinner for the ninth time he obviously felt that the awards project had come to full fruition: 'My satisfaction ... is infinitely increased by the fact that Mr Davies is a humorist, since humor is always the ally of sanity, the foe of absurdity. The Award is therefore a unique contribution to the development of Canadian literature as a whole.'

In 1958 the town of Orillia acquired the Leacock home from L.M. Ruby of Toronto, and the Historic Sites and Monuments Board of the federal government donated $15,000 towards its restoration and upkeep. Coinciding with the award dinner for Eric Nichol's *Girdle Me a Globe*, the Leacock Memorial Home was first opened to the public. Ruby had donated Leacock's library and personal papers to the town and Dr Ralph Curry, author of *Steven Leacock: Humorist and Humanist*, was engaged as curator. In 1959 the Associates took over the responsibility of judging the award from the Governor-General's Awards Board. Deacon continued to officiate at the award ceremony until 1962, when he stepped down so that his old friend, Arthur Phelps, should be the one, upon Deacon's recommendation, to present the medal to W.O. Mitchell for *Jake and the Kid*.

During the 1950s Deacon was closely involved with the work of the Canadian Writers' Foundation, an institution for the relief of needy writers that he had helped to found in the thirties. Raymond Knister's and Charles G.D. Roberts's financial difficulties and Lorne Pierce's fund-raising campaign to raise $25,000 for a memorial to Bliss Carman *after* his death had all triggered his awareness of the pressing need for funds to help living writers. After a series of ten letters to and from the office of Prime Minister Bennett, a meeting at the Arts and Letters Club was chaired by Pelham Edgar and the Canadian Authors' Foundation was formed. The permanent Board of Governors included the presidents of the Royal Society, the CAA, the National Council of Women, and the Association of Canadian Clubs, with Edgar as the permanent Secretary. Both Bennett and Mackenzie King, leader of the opposition, supported the Foundation and Parliament granted it a small annual appropriation. In 1946 Theresa Thompson, wife of Don Thompson, a prominent Ottawa journalist and national CAA officer, was appointed executive secretary-treasurer. Until 1966 she administered the Foundation with unswerving enthusiasm and success, finally achieving an assured annual income of $20,000, double the amount first suggested as a goal by Deacon in his original letter to Bennett. Scores of writers were assisted by the Foundation, some of them on a regular basis. Deacon, of course, was a prime source of information about needy authors and constantly in correspondence with 'Terry' Thompson about the Foundation's business. In a *Globe and Mail* column he called her 'the Florence Nightingale of Canadian letters'; on her part, and her husband's, Deacon was the 'grand old man of letters,' and as such, and as a faithful annual donor, rated a special yearly report on the Foundation's progress.[19]

From the public and professional perspectives, the late forties and fifties were triumphant years of harvest and recognition for Deacon; from a private perspective, however, the mid-fifties were his years of greatest anxiety. Since meeting Sally he had never been emotionally insecure and now, with the children grown up, they should have enjoyed a freedom they had never known before. Particularly in the summers at the built-by-hand complex of cottage, cabins, and boathouse on Wilson's Point, they rejoiced in a release from daily pressures and deadlines: 'Every day starts with a swim in invigorating water, and ends in a most comfortable bed up against two big open windows where I can see the stars and my trees. This room, aired and lighted by eight casement windows – 48 panes 12″ by 14″ plus a screen door – is good enough for me. And here are a pair of King birds, looking in.'[20] But the years of his assertive front of optimism and energy brought their reaction: every vicissitude of the children's maturing and every threatened insecurity brought agonizing worry with it, voiced in numbers of letters to friends and family. When, for instance, *The Globe and Mail* was unionized in 1955 he foresaw penury in retirement under the new pension scheme, instead of the secure old age that he and Sally had anticipated under the old system; he worried about his failing memory and about the longevity of his father's family, foreseeing for himself a long decline into helpless old age.

From time to time he also felt that some of the goals of his career were forever unreachable: the CAA had not received the transfusion of new, young blood that he had hoped for. Instead he watched with considerable, and often vocal, dismay when Frank Stiling, a professor of English at the University of Western Ontario, became chairman of the Governor General's Awards Board in 1952, national president of the CAA in 1954, and negotiated the removal of the Governor General's Awards from the jurisdiction of the CAA. Stiling was not, as Deacon indignantly reiterated, a writer . He saw Stiling's presidency as a move from the academic world to capture and hold power in the realm of the arts in Canada.[21] He was even more distressed by the outcome of the Massey Commission, to which he had so enthusiastically presented a brief on behalf of the CAA. The policies of the Canada Council, founded in 1957, were, in his opinion, a betrayal of the arts in Canada, and its name in French, Le Conseil des Arts du Canada, a bitter irony: 'The arts have benefited by, say, anywhere from 1% to 10% of the money. Real beneficiaries are the universities, who get millions yearly ... There are 75 annual grants for people who hold B.A.'s and want to be M.A.'s; 135 grants a year for M.A.'s who want to become PH.D.'s. For writers, provided they are doing research work, 15 grants. That is a ratio of 210 to 15.'[22]

His family, the demands of his job, or the consideration of old friends could always rally his spirits, however; in December 1956 Lorne Pierce, facing his own imminent retirement, wrote him a warm letter of thanks: 'I want to tell you this morning, as I have so often wanted to say, how magnificent your service to letters in Canada, and to Canadian letters, has been this long generation ... If you can think of something you would like as an old colleague will you not be candid and let me know?'[23] Deacon drafted three long letters to Pierce before he sent his answer in January. He finally expressed to his own satisfaction the integrity of his career as he saw it and the satisfactions it had brought him:

Never get the idea that I'm a frustrated poet or envious of successful novelists.

What I do takes all the skill I have. Don't imagine some great genius has been wasted. Reviewing demands all my powers; and I am grateful to have found my right place, doubly grateful that men like you think my product good enough for the time and place.

Don't imagine I suffer from lack of appreciation. From time to time I am surprised to receive compliments. Happily, I don't get a swelled head because I can't take much time out to gloat because xxx has made flattering remarks. I have had all the evidence of approval it is healthy for a fellow to receive – more than I deserve by a ton.

I am a proud man, hence grateful to the gods that I have only worked for top papers. (Nobody else would have me for a gift.) But it is a deep satisfaction that, when I approach a stranger with: 'I'm Deacon of the Globe,' I get instant, respectful attention, not a snarl. Even among the French of Montreal, I hear them say: 'That's a Globe and Mail man'; and it evidently means something.

What man could be happier in his home and family life?...

That eliminates everything except the honors business and I'm too old to get any satisfaction out of mere vanity. You spoke once of trying to wangle me into the Royal Society. Please desist. I am now getting out of all organizations and embroilments. I don't need it for prestige; its only function would be an extra line in the obit.

So, my dear and thoughtful friend, we reach the conclusion that there isn't anything in particular that you can do for me.

There hasn't been much time for social life; but friendships have been rich and valued – by no means least valued yours.[24]

The next year, at the CAA National Convention in Windsor, he gave the valedictory address of his professional career. In a talk called 'The Reviewer,' he presented a rationale for the reviewer/critic dichotomy that had always plagued him. Once again he also celebrated his choice:

In our time there has grown up a sharp distinction between the reviewer and the critic. The reviewer is a newspaper hack. The critic is an exalted person, generally a university professor, whose own style may be dull, who may use long hard words, and who generally, but not always, is concerned with the work of long-dead authors.

Unfortunately for the validity of this distinction, the greatest critic who ever lived was a reviewer. Sainte-Beuve was educated as a doctor. As a hospital intern of 20 he wrote his first articles. Three years later he proclaimed the merits of Victor Hugo, forsook medicine for reviewing and, during the following 42 years, he won the title of Father of Modern Criticism.

It is said of him: 'he was creative rather than dogmatic.' For the last 20 years of his life his articles appeared every Monday morning in Paris newspapers...

Sainte-Beuve was followed 40 years later by William Hazlitt in England – a hack who wrote on space rate; and I am far from alone in regarding him as the greatest of English critics. I mention him here for two reasons. He preferred to be a commentator rather than a creative writer. He said: 'I would rather be a man of lesser genius, free and able to appreciate truth and beauty wherever found, rather than a man of more original and commanding genius, bound up forever in that small protion of it (truth and beauty) which I had been able to create.'

Hazlitt led what the ordinary person would call a miserable life. He was poverty-stricken. Being an opinionated, quarrelsome fellow, he lost many friends. His unhappy marriage terminated in divorce. His remaining friends, full of pity, stood beside the bed on which he lay dying at 52. Hazlitt looked up brightly and astounded them by saying: 'Well, anyway, I've had a happy life.'

The happy life of the reviewer...

The creative writer, who may produce 12 to 30 books in a working lifetime, is not only dependent materially on the commercial success of each of them, but he must have such a degree of concentration on his theme – on a particular aspect of life at a given moment in time – that he must tend to draw a distinction between 'I' and 'the world.'

When so many vital things are happening around the globe, in so many different spheres of existence, the reviewer is forever conscious of the teeming life of the human race, in all its aspects. The reviewer is daily conscious that he is a part of all happenings in a dramatic age; that he, personally, is constantly enriched by the ideas that bubble around him like champagne.

The reviewer, while he must stand apart momentarily while judging a particular book, can never stand outside the human drama. The unity of mankind is the greatest discovery of our time. That is the vital, fundamental truth of life. The reviewer is in the best position to grasp it. The reviewer is a specially privileged spectator and should be happy. I think most of us are.[25]

CHAPTER TWELVE

A Community of Letters III: 1946-60

ROM HIS RETURN TO *The Globe and Mail* in 1945 until his retirement in 1960, Deacon's avocation of letter-writing continued unabated. In these years he almost certainly had his greatest satisfactions as a letter-writer. In the thirties his extra-journalist energies had been dispersed and diffused by his anxious espousal of various extra-literary causes; now, except for letters to family and old friends, and a necessarily voluminous business correspondence during his presidency of the CAA, he wrote predominantly to writers about the craft that he loved, and he found both enormous satisfaction and vindication of his life's work in the activity. He also gathered abundant material for 'The Fly Leaf' from his letters, for he made it quite clear to his correspondents that his weekly column was a combination of writer's gossip, a notice board of literary events, and free and valuable publicity for themselves and their works. He encouraged writers like Roy, Raddall, MacLennan, Guèvremont, and Lemelin to keep him abreast of their work-in-progress; sometimes their acquiescence resulted in lengthy exchanges about theories and the technique of writing; in all cases their replies drew forth his strong support and understanding of their endeavours.

From the beginning of his career, and because one of his strongest articles of faith was his belief in *Maria Chapdelaine* as a watershed in Canadian literature, its translation heralding the achievements of writers of the twenties, he had been especially keen to cultivate Francophone writers. Germaine Guèvremont became a grateful friend because of his support of *Le Survenant*, both before its translation as *The Outlander* (1950) and after. She was on the executive of La Société des Ecrivains Canadiens, the sister association to the CAA, and as a courtesy gesture she attended the 1946 convention when he took over as president. Edith Ardagh of Macmillan had reviewed *Le Survenant* in 1946 and Deacon had mentioned the book with approval in 'The Fly Leaf,' making Madame Guèvremont his devoted reader:

I am greatly interested in your book page. Every Monday I now go to the library just to read it. However, Ringuet was slightly mistaken when he said 'We have exhausted rural areas' – what he meant to say was 'Rural areas have exhausted me.' I feel that matters having to do with the land, novels about the land, are like the land itself – eternal – even if I were to write a novel in which the action takes place in a city, I would still feel that way.[1]

After the book was translated Deacon's enthusiastic review gave her support and impetus for a continued writing career: 'Often, during dark hours, I have wondered if writing was worth while. Now, I know it is. But as you say so well, with this book we shall "take the pulse" of the reader in Canada.'[2] She had 'tasted the poison, the dope of writing for radio,' and added, 'Radio is a golden spider. Once in its web, it is hard to get out.'[3] Deacon replied with his customary practicality: 'My advice is to earn the money now it is there. The book in your mind will not disappear. But later, when there is time, you must sit down and write 8 hours per day – no housekeeping. Just the book, day after day.'[4]

He consulted her when he needed information about Quebec writers and she informed him of the current work of Roger Lemelin, André Langevin, and Robert Rumilly, whose *Bourassa* (1953) she reported as 'the most important book of the year published in French Canada.'[5] On one occasion she described with delight a fishing trip she and her husband had taken with Claude-Henri Grignon, author of *Un Homme et Son Péché*, whose main character, the miser Séraphin, later became the subject of an immensely popular television series.

Deacon's friendship with Roger Lemelin began with Lemelin's gratitude for his favourable review of the translation of the *The Plouffe Family* in 1950. When Lemelin went to Paris in that year, he sent back a lively account of his impressions in his inimitable style to his English-language publishers, McClelland and Stewart, for circulation among his friends in Toronto. It is not only an entertaining letter, but an important one, for in it Lemelin comes to an understanding of his own essential 'Canadianness' and to a statement of his faith in Canada:

I must point out that on Blvd Montparnasse one day after leaving Montreal, I felt more at home than in Montreal, a city which I have never liked because it has no real character, but an hybrid one. Difficult to explain: with these Frenchmen, I felt like them and at the same time, very different. Our reactions, our language, our humor was the same, but they seem to lack the optimistic wisdom and youth I felt in myself when comparing it to them. I was more logical. About my French accent: they thought at first I was from Switzerland, and were very surprised to hear I was from Canada. They had the same prejudice about our French as the people of Toronto: we, French Canadian are supposed to talk 'patois.' I was so shocked that I corrected them on five or six of their expressions like: 'J'ai réalisé qu'il avait raison.' They should have said 'Je me suis rendu compte qu'ils avaient raison.' 'J'ai réalisé' is a translation from 'I realised.' The same thing for: 'Frigidaire' instead of 'réfrigérateur.'

They told me I was more boring than ever and decided to bring me to a little bar called 'Chez Adrien,' where I would see what was the French légereté and fun. The bar was packed with Paris girls, tourists, and Americans from the left bank. In a corner there was a pianist, and the girl accompanying me, who would have liked to give herself to anybody and had told me she was at nighttime a student for opera, started to sing 'Chiribiribi.' She was not extraordinary, but she had forgotten four or five notes. She told me to shut up, that I was boring; an iceberg does not know nothing about music. There was much applause. She sang again and the audience repeated in chorus. I felt very serious and started calmly to drink champagne. Suddenly, after two bottles of Champagne, electricity went through my body, and to the bewilderment of my companions who accused me of being a Canadian iceberg, I jumped on the piano, and started to sing with my loud baritone voice, and with an entrain I have never had, Italian, French and English light operetta songs. I was having a tremendous success. A Swedish consul there wanted me to marry his daughter. And the most surprising: there were there American and Canadian journalists and students; they had heard me talk French and thought I was from Paris; when they learnt I was from Quebec, the Canadians from Toronto surrounded me; I was a Canadian, I was their own; I was the Canadian who talked French; they were no more lost among these French there; I was the trait-d'union. If all the English Canadians who have prejudices against the French Canadians would go to Paris with all the French-Canadians there would be no more prejudices. And the same for the French-Canadians towards the English Canadians. I felt more akin to the English Canadian students and journalists there than with the Frenchmen and it was very funny to see me talk French with the French character and talk English with the English character. I understood everybody. When I started to sing French Canadian folklore chorus song, the English Canadians awoke. Everybody was so excited that the slightest incident would have started a fight. Canadians were at home in Paris. The agents cleared the place at 5 o'clock in the morning. When we went out in the morning, I was full of pep, but my companions, who accused me of boring them, were dead with fatigue and whispered: 'Ah, these Canadians, what extraordinary men they are!' They became real friends to me and the boy who had joined the charming girl on the next chair at Café de la Coupole, told me all about his sorrows and ambitions. He tipped me on many aspects of Paris life and warned me against certain types of girls and boys. Had I told him I was a novelist he would not have trusted me, but I did not. He was a salesman in silk hand-designed handkerchiefs. I spent two days with him on Les Boulevards and sold handkerchiefs with him.

One afternoon, I was in a taxi on Place de l'Etoile, when there was a jam in the traffic. I paid the taxi driver and went out on my left. The door touched the footstep of another car and I started walking. But a kind of giant of seventy years old, with long mustache gauloises starts to cry after me: 'Effronté, vous avez brisé mon auto. Vous allez payer. Je vais appeler les agents.' I faced him very calmly and told him: 'But, monsieur, I hardly touched it with the door, and moreover, it is a very old car you have there. It is worth nothing.' He cried louder. 'Comment osez-vous me parler ainsi, malappris.' People were gathering and watched us. 'Shut up, old fool. " I told him. With indignation, his fist on his chest like Tarzan, he howled, 'Comment, me parler ainsi. Mais je suis général de 1914, moi, je suis un général!' Imagine, saying that to a French Canadian who was against conscription, a general. I smiled and replied: 'Do not be so excited, old boy, I am an admiral, nous sommes quittes.' Everybody laughed and the old man was so surprised that he did not say a word and I had time to quit.

In Paris, I had dinner with intellectuals and writers like François Mauriac, Jean Paulhan, Georges Duhamel, Charles Morgan, Jules Romains and many others. They talked only of themselves and did not ask me any questions about my books. Canada, for them, was very far. That was all. I went to theater and saw many premières of Claudel, Montherland and Giraudoux. When 'Au Pied de la Pente Douce' was officially published, Flammarion, my publishers, organized a big party where the French Intelligentzia was invited. I was not impressed and while drinking champagne with André Maurois, I was thinking to my wife and boys, to the trout fishing I would make in Canada when coming back. The final impression I gathered from all this country is the following: Many centuries of culture have produced treasures of art and the young generations growing up has been born with a kind of maturity that stops them from having illusions and hopes to do better. These treasures are so dear to them, that they do not even have the courage to try and imitate them. Like Descartes said: 'Il faut faire table rase de tout ce que nous avons connu et admiré.' They cannot. This has led them to intellectualism, an intellectualism which leads them to despise the qualities of the heart. Too much place for intelligence, not enough for sentiments. We Canadians, have not their culture, their refinement. We are eighteen years old and have the illusions and enthusiasm of our age. We have the blind faith that transporte les montagnes. And a great litterature, and masterpieces have been built with faith and illusions.

We are what the geography of our country has made us. That is the main difference between ethnical groups. That is why, in a sense, we are nearer to English Canadians than to Frenchmen. After a month in Paris, which I loved with all my heart, I just the same got very lonesome for our trees, and the sight of the Laurentides and the horizon of Quebec. I felt lonesome for the Canadian sky so vast and so grandiose. In Paris, you have pieces of sky. To resume, I felt like this in Paris. Suppose you would have been a magician and would have placed on the Plains of Abraham, one shiny Sunday afternoon a Museum containing the treasures of the earth and of the universal culture. I would get in at one o'clock. At two o'clock it would have still seemed wonderful. So at three. A little less at four, and at five, I would have liked to go out for some fresh air. I came back to Canada; it was Fresh air. The Laurentides were still there. What a country we have. St-Laurent, George Drew, with their defects, what good men, honest. My visit to Paris has permitted to feel what I never had before: patriotism. What a country we have! And you feel it when the vessel gets in the St-Laurent estuary.

I would have preferred to write you this letter in French... I know this English is bastard, but you will understand it.[6]

In February 1951, Lemelin came to Toronto and spoke to the CAA. Among the notes that Deacon took of that speech is the author's 'secret of success' for writers – sincerity, blindness, and flame. Lemelin pictured himself as sitting before the typewriter for two hours daily, whether he thought he had anything to say or not, and he told the story of the publication of his first novel which, as he said, was 'a little confused. I lent it to a notary who had come to see my father about a mortgage.' He later 'heard from a publisher who gave him a contract providing 75% royalties to the publisher if it was translated into English; 8% royalty to author on French copies and a printing bill against him for [publisher's] changes.' Since he had used his own name for the main character and had to change it throughout to Denis, he was charged $250. When the book was published, 'the book-seller advised buying a copy today as it would be banned by the church tomorrow.' When Lemelin took his place in the choir the next Sunday, 'the curate said that the parish had produced 99 priests, but one of their young men had gone bad and had become a commercial traveller of hell. But the book was not banned.'7

A comparable statement of commitment to Canada was written by Malcolm Lowry, as he negotiated for the Canadian distribution of *Under the Volcano* with Macmillan in 1947:

But perhaps this is worth saying: the book, though the groundwork for it was done in Mexico, was written – in fact written three times – here in Canada, in a shack on Indian Arm, where my wife and I lived winter and summer, and I had liked to daydream of the book as being some kind of humble contribution to Canadian literature, should it turn out any good, that was.

In answer to your other questions; yes, my intention is, if possible, health permitting, to make Canada my permanent home. In fact our shack *is* home to me, and always will be. It's the only one we have.

I am passionately fond of the place where we live and devoted to our few friends, mostly fishermen, who also live permanently along the beach and I think it would take death itself to pry me loose from here, though I am British and slightly uncertain of my status at the moment. Nonetheless I am certainly as Canadian as Louis Hémon ever was.

This is the second shack we have had. The other burned to the ground, taking a thousand pages of work with it, and our friends unselfishly helped us to rebuild it. This is one of the few places and few communities in the world where I have ever encountered friendship and charity in the true sense. It would seem that among such people as our British Columbian neighbours genuine unselfishness is a matter of course.

Yes, I certainly would like to write a story with a B.C. setting and in fact have already planned out a short novel laid here. I would not in any case have to move very far for my material for I do not know anyone here who would not make the hero of an epic.8

After the war Deacon made haste to look up writers, Sinclair Ross, for instance, with whom he was out of touch: 'Where in hell are you? Your friends and admirers want to know, and that includes me. Please come clean. Are you going back to the bank or what? Have you written another Canadian novel, if so, is it placed yet?'9 He had previously written to the Department of National Defence in Ottawa, trying to track Ross, and had been told that Ross had been discharged from the army in March. Ross answered:

No, I didn't get married. Afraid I'm destined to be a grumpy, solitary old bachelor. The ones I want don't want me – though I will say I don't work very hard on it.

No, I wasn't wounded or – at least to my knowledge – incapacitated. Stayed in England – London, most of the time – experienced nothing more dramatic than the flying bombs. Enjoyed London thoroughly.

No, I haven't a novel completed, but am hard at work on one. A long one – perhaps too long. I find myself with abundance of material, and am going straight ahead with it. About 100,000 words done – first draft – and at least that many more to go. I will do some whittling and tightening, of course, when I get to the revision.

Yes, so far as I know now I am going back to the Bank, but not until about July 1 – I am taking as much time off as I may and working on the novel. I write slowly, though, and won't have the first draft done in that time, but should have its back pretty well broken.

I don't look forward to going back, but I don't see how I can better myself. I think I would take the plunge if I were alone, but my mother is 70, nearly blind and dependent upon me. We live comfortably now, and naturally I don't want to expose her to the hazards of a free-lance's income. Besides, being practical about it, I'm not at all sure that my commercial possibilities as a writer amount to much. I hope this novel will give me an answer.[10]

When W.O. Mitchell wrote to him in thanks for his review of *Who Has Seen the Wind*, and, incidentally, asking him for income tax advice, Deacon replied with both advice and praise in full measure:

Talking about expenses, you have created some for me. I'm buying four copies of Who Has Seen The Wind to give to my friends. Gave one to my managing editor ... Look at it this way. I take the N.Y. papers. I saw the lousy seven inches of patronizing comment the Times printed. What were you worth to the Globe and Mail (in the middle of a newsprint shortage, too)? - 26 inches of type, 5½ of picture (even a poor picture). Who Has Seen The Wind will sell in Canada, slower at the start than Two Solitudes but a darn sight longer. This will just go on and on, like Sunshine Sketches of a Little Town.[11]

Among the many young writers who wrote hopefully to him was Margaret Coulby, an unemployed graduate of the University of Toronto and an aspiring journalist and writer, who asked, 'What do women do in this writing game?':

I now realize why my devoted father suggested, even urged that I embark on a career in Biochemistry rather than writing or English (especially since I absolutely refuse to ever teach!), why he used to mutter in his beard when I remarked loudly and cheerfully that I wanted to be a writer 'Writing is no field for a woman. It's a *tough* sport!' At the time I youthfully and egotistically thought that he just didn't acknowledge my talents. I could, of course, accept my family's kind offer to loaf at home this summer at the cottage and then return to University in the fall for an M.A. in English but where in heavens would an M.A. get me if a B.A. isn't doing any good? I'd be two years older and still trying to start from scratch. I absolutely refuse to accept the inevitable. I am still going to be a successful writer in ten years, even if I do have to discard my well-heeled but resentful family (who are all reared in the traditions of science!) and live on one meal a day. That undoubtedly would cure the evils of my rather over-plump, but none the less attractive, figure and I might then be enabled to make a much lusher living with a lot less work, having sacrificed my too-idealistic philosophy of life.

I would be truly grateful for any advice or suggestions you could offer me, barring only the one, 'Go home to the family and science.' Are there any openings for women on your paper?[12]

Deacon replied with a letter of advice that was good for Miss Coulby (now Dr Margaret Whitridge, both scholar *and* writer) and still holds for an aspiring young writer of any day and age:

All you tell me about yourself is encouraging. Of course you can be a professional writer, if you care enough about it to undergo a long, hard apprenticeship – teaching yourself how to write, getting experience – living. You must accept the fact that nobody at 22 has anything of great value to give the world. The B.A. is fine, but you start from there, as a child. By 32 you are still young enough to take the first real steps in a writing career. Meanwhile, keep your eye on the ball, write, write, write, publish as and when you can, getting as much for your stuff as you can coax out of editors.

With graduation, start to read. That is your real literary education. The B.A. is just an entrance exam. If you can get going at 32, you can arrive at 45, will have 15 years on top of the world and thereafter coast on your reputation.

... More writers fail because they have nothing to say than because they can't write. We all use words, many with ease and effect, but as it says in Hamlet, 'but the matter, my lord?' You are still an ignorant girl. Time, willpower and practice will cure that. Meanwhile, learn something definite to write about. Master a specialty. You have to fill the tank before you can pump it out ...

The times were never more favorable for young folks like you to take the initial steps. Writing becomes more profitable every day. But you have everything to learn and unless you are patient you will not learn; unless you are conscious of your present ignorance, you cannot learn. With all the help everybody can give you it is hard enough so that you need to be a strong and courageous person or you will not last.[13]

Almost certainly Deacon derived his most sustained literary enjoyment in these years from his lengthy exchanges with Hugh MacLennan and his wife, Dorothy Duncan, with Thomas Raddall, and with Gabrielle Roy. His correspondence with the MacLennans began, as his letter-friendships so often did, with MacLennan's thanks for his 'grand review' of *Two Solitudes* in April 1945. Deacon had had strong reservations about *Barometer Rising*; he thought that the Halifax explosion, though brilliantly described by MacLennan, had usurped the fictional shape and impact of the book. *Two Solitudes*, coming as it did in the last months of the war, and the first fictional statement of faith in a joining of English and French Canada, he considered to be a novel of unique importance to Canadian literature. However, he frankly voiced his reservations about the final section of the novel, and MacLennan admitted their validity: 'And I certainly did a colossal amount of re-writing – used about 7000 typewriter pages in all. In retrospect, the trouble seems to me to have been mainly this: I had not realized the full weight of Athanase Tallard, and the effect his death would have on the subsequent chapters.'[14]

As MacLennan said more than once during their long correspondence, Deacon was the one 'who more than any other individual made me realize that I must ground all my best work in this peculiar country of ours.'[15] So now he confided in Deacon his own compulsion to write *Two Solitudes*:

From my standpoint, I had to write that book to orientate myself toward any future work I might do. It is my complete conviction that no writer can function in a vacuum. As his point of view, his method of regarding phenomena, derives from his childhood environment, he can't help writing out of the society in which he was produced. It gradually dawned on me – very gradually, I'm afraid – that so far as I was concerned my own society was obscure, not clearcut, a queer congeries of various subtle inner and outer relationships which in my own time were gradually coming into focus. Unless it were possible for me somehow to effect something of a fusion of this Canadian dichotomy, I felt myself stymied. TWO SOLITUDES was the result of that, and now that it is finished, I feel greatly released. Whatever the book may have done for others, for me it has put something like solid ground under my feet.[16]

Their correspondence quickly ripened into a three-way relationship of mutual affection and respect, for Deacon was as quick to support

Dorothy Duncan in her periods of writing discouragement as he was MacLennan. In 1944 she had won the Governor-General's Award for non-fiction with *Partner in Three Worlds*, the biography of a Czechoslovakian, Roger Ritter (Jan Rieger in the book), who served on the German side in World War I, came to the United States as a businessman between the wars, and served with the Canadian Army in World War II. Because of ill health, Dorothy Duncan was never able to work as consistently as she would have liked, and in the last years of her life, before her death in 1957, she moved from writing to painting as her medium of expression. After the first massive dose of Deacon's dynamic optimism for her future as a writer, she acknowledged his effectiveness: 'It did end my discouragement. That's the great trouble with being a writer; we're lonely people. Only a few understand our shop-talk and problems. So your letter, from one who knows both sides of the business of writing, was good to have.'[17] She was as gifted and enthusiastic a letter-writer as Deacon himself, and their correspondence ranged over a wide spectrum of interests, from gardening to their mutual friends and acquaintances in the CAA.

With MacLennan himself, Deacon wrote more exclusively of literary shop-talk and writers' problems, particularly with publishers. 'I crave further enlightenment about your principles re art of fiction,' he wrote, thereby sparking a passionate rejoinder from MacLennan on the sorry state of academic criticism and the teaching of Canadian literature:

I can truly say that I know the academic grove in my sleep, and on the humanities' side, in all its aspects. The dankest corner of it all is labelled 'English literature.' English literature should never be studied in a separate compartment. Personally, I had two courses in it only, and both were compulsory. The result of such academicism is the production, not of a man who can appreciate books, not of a man who has learned either philosophy or history, much less economics and science, but a specialist operating in a vacuum. Their complaint about affairs in Canada is so naive it is pitiful. They feel a grievance we have no writers who can produce sufficiently abstruse books to warrant endless academic articles written by them!

E.K. Brown seemed to be a little better than most, but he said nothing right that you hadn't said twenty years ago, and he said a good deal wrong you never said at all. The truth is that professors, for all their boasts to independent thought, are conventional through and through. The political type of professor is as conventional, seemingly, as an Ontario old maid. The rebellious one is conventional in reverse; i.e., they are automatically against anything which happens to be popular. I know that nineteen books out of twenty that are excessively popular are tripe. Any newspaper man knows far more about the gadgetry that makes a popular best-seller than they do. But ever since Q R. [Q.D.] Leavis, back in 1932, wrote THE NOVEL AND THE READING PUBLIC, they have automatically assumed that if a novel sells more than 10,000 copies it is *ipso facto* bad. I think Canadian literature has been done harm by the indiscriminate praise bestowed in the past on costume novels and third rate stuff. That is beside the point. The whole issue, to my mind, rests now on whether it will be possible for us to join the mainstream of world literature or whether we are doomed to be considered regional. This is highly complex, and requires a knowledge these professors not only lack, but don't want to obtain.[18]

Travelling across the United States in 1947, for the first time since the war, MacLennan was confirmed in his belief in Canada as a place of superior opportunity for novelists:

After travelling across the United States this time – the last time was before the war – I've been more than ever struck by the potential richness of Canadian society for a novelist as compared to the scene here. Superficially the United States offers a much easier environment, but this apparent ease is deceptive. More than ever before, Americans seem to be growing outward rather than inward. What they do is infinitely more important than what they think, feel or are; and what they do which is interesting is more conditioned by scientific and engineering techniques than by the characters of the doers. Also I feel that they are much more committed to history than we are. Their course has been to a large extent determined. This seems the reason why their non-fiction at present and for the past half dozen years, is both more interesting and more important than their fiction. I don't believe any serious American writer today can feel the same kinship with the public, or get the same response from the public, that a writer can experience in Canada. As you yourself said, in one of your recent lectures, the growth of writing in Canada has to a great extent been determined by the kind of response Canadians have given their writers.[19]

MacLennan wrote slowly and rewrote laboriously; he was both comforted and encouraged by Deacon's reiterated and cautionary counsel, citing Balzac, who 'wrote himself to death':

Anyway, I think each one of us has just so much to say and it is a question of personal choice whether it is concentrated in a few years, like Cervantes, or in a few important books gathered over a lifetime, or spread thin by constant poor writing. Unless one anticipates early death, there is no need to hurry. It gets riper with reflection.

Because of this and because of market considerations, I think a serious novelist should publish not oftener than once in two years; once in three years is better; but there should be a book at least once in four years.[20]

MacLennan was not a writer who talked about his problems with work-in-progress or gave out any details about his current novel. Late in 1947, however, he reported that, having worked for two years on *The Precipice*, 'with six months of pondering before that,' he felt 'like an empty pail.'[21] He was more than glad to engage in letter-chat about writers of the past, however, setting forth his own theories and problems in the process:

Since I finished my book, I've been rereading Balzac and Dickens – or, I should say, reading them for the first time, for it's years since I touched either. What can one make of them? Certainly that they are vastly over-rated. It isn't good enough to assert blandly – and with deliberate and calculated self-interest – as Maugham does, that the two best novelists the world has ever seen were both bad writers. They were neither of them near the two best novelists the world has ever seen. Fundamentally, Dickens wrote for maids, and if that's a snobbish statement, I'm sorry for it. He has no understanding of women or respect for them. He is incapable of putting his mind into anyone who ever lived except a child – at which he is supremely wonderful. He has no knowledge of the poor – he writes of them either sentimentally, as the Victorian middle-classes did, or regards them as criminals. And yet he is a titanic genius, as Balzac was too. But what is a genius? The Victorians thought genius was everything, and did not know its nature. Surely it is nothing but a peculiar combination of will-power, tenacity and the ability to make one's subconscious work for one. It follows therefore that a man can be a genius without being an artist, though the converse cannot follow. Art is, was and ever shall be a process of selection and balance. Yes, you were right about Balzac, though I do think it doubtful if he would have written so much had he not been driven by such an insane compulsion to make money and by an equally insane one to spend it before he had it. But, if possible, a writer should wait. Without contemplation he can't grow. I learned in my last book that the hardest thing a writer has to learn is to wait – not for inspiration (that is meaningless), but for understanding, which can seldom come quickly unless one is a Shakespeare. And one should never forget that Shakespeare was, in a sense, as much of a playdoctor as a playwright and so could work more quickly, was untroubled with the tedious business of framing his plots and settings.[22]

Having joyfully saluted MacLennan's talent and potential as a novelist in his review of *Two Solitudes*, Deacon found his hopes confirmed when he read *The Precipice*. This third novel, which switches in its setting from an Ontario small town to the United States and is MacLennan's vehicle for a cultural and economic comparison between Canada and the US, he had hoped would make his name in the latter and confirm and consolidate his position in Canada. Noncommittal on the first point, Deacon had no doubts about the second:

This is your crucial book. You win. Formerly you were the most brilliant Canadian novelist, the man from whom everybody hoped most. But you were also unpredictable. Here you have shown the fruits of the discipline that has turned you into a sound writer. I doubt whether that means a darn thing in terms of immediate popularity. It means that you will not fail – ever. Your life is justified. Twenty years from now people will be reading better MacLennan novels. Somewhere along the road you will strike oil – nobody can guess when or where or how, but it will happen without special planning. One day it will turn out that the new book catches public interest on the date of publication and appetite for it will be insatiable. Otherwise, before and after the big bulge, you make a living in a self-respecting fashion and must be content to live the life you desire and get by in reasonable comfort, not luxury.

The Precipice is a more native book than you may realize. That is why there may be relatively small excitement over it at first. It is also the reason why it will last. 'My God, how Canadian' ...

For me, the best thing about it is that my doubts and slight worries about you are ended. Like other Canadians, I watched you with admiration tinged with a vague question: Had you the capacity for the awful drudgery of fitting 100,000 words together for maximum effect, to say what you really meant without depending on extraneous excitement. I am now satisfied. I can read you now with calm enjoyment.[23]

In the course of their discursive and mutually satisfying correspondence during these years, two further letters are outstanding, illuminating the lives and works of two of the most intensely nationalistic Canadians of their time. MacLennan wrote for Deacon his beliefs about the teaching of literature:

I have never formally taught English and have never formally studied Anglo-Saxon. However, I speak German (or used to) fluently, and have a fair speaking and reading knowledge of French. My work as a writer has acquainted me with a wide perspective of English literature, though I must say, quite frankly, and in fairness, that it has also given me a different attitude to English literature from what I received when I myself studied it at college. I believe literature should be viewed in a wide cultural perspective, with close relationship to social, economic and religious pressures of the times which produced it. I believe it should be taught in two ways: first, as a source of pleasure to the student; secondly, as a concomitant to the understanding of the history of a culture. It is wrong, in my opinion, to consider it in a separate compartment. One never so considers the literature of Greece and Rome. Finally if the course has time, I think it would remove confusion if teachers were honest when they approached the classics, and if they understood that many passages which have produced doctors' dissertations in Germanic universities could have been explained on technical grounds, by practical technicians like George Kaufman and Moss Hart, who never darkened the door of a graduate school, but have at least enough practical experience to understand that Lysistrata is good theatre now and will be good a thousand years from now while Beowulf is a chore now and always will be.[24]

For MacLennan, Deacon wrote a prophetic statement of faith in his abilities and his future that has certainly been confirmed in its broad outlines, if not yet in all of its details:

My theory has always been that the man who proves his ability by 40 is exactly on the beam. Your best 25 years as a writer are immediately ahead of you. In them, you will do increasingly good work; and Canada has reached the point at which a top flight novelist can be assured of a living. After 65, you'll be an institution – acceptance is automatic, no matter how lousy your performance. By 80, you'll be the Grand Old Man with whatever honors go with it. When you get absolutely punk at 90, the young lads will be writing biographies of you, and the nation will celebrate your birthday with a special issue postage stamp. Don't imagine that the literary Canada of the end of this century will be a small thing to be king of. You were just in luck to grow up between the wars and, if you work *hard* and maintain your artistic integrity, the remainder of your life will be smooth.

Now I have to repeat for your private comfort what I have proclaimed publicly and more generally. There is no particular causal relation between literary merit and the popularity, which means, finally, money.

Popularity is a matter of sheer chance – luck if you like. Popularity means that, at the moment of publication the writer just happens to catch the public ear because it chimes with public mood at that minute. Public mood is a resultant of forces too complicated to guess at 2, 3, 4 years previously when the book is being written. Irene Baird's *John* was a best seller. Her *Waste Heritage* flopped as a war casualty. In the fall of 1939 nobody wanted to read about the late depression – any youth could have a job in uniform. Reasons in her case are easy to deduce. In other cases, God Himself does not know why the public suddenly reaches for a particular type of book or, just as often, suddenly ceases to read a once-popular author. Look over 10-year old magazines at any date ... and you will be amazed to find 90% of the surefire writers of a decade past have vanished from the table of contents ...

I feel that it is a writer's business to write as well as he can, to publish to the best advantage, and then go on to the next job. No Canadian novelist of your ability in the middle of this century need fear the future. I think a writer handicaps himself if he expects to get rich. The world owes him a living; and you will get it – varied with the occasional flop commercially and jack pots from time to time. It will average up a damn sight better than the fellows who suddenly make a killing and then fade right out. The steadiness of Canadian character involves steady patronage for writers they respect. We're not as volatile as the Yanks – crown you one year and forget you the next...

The Canadians will stand by you, Hugh, just as long as they feel in your work seriousness and sincerity. Their patronage is a growing factor; it will grow all your lifetime. Meanwhile, of course, more and more of your books will go out into other countries. That's the whole trend of the Canadian literary movement...

You are in the peculiar position that this public (home public is always the most important) first loved you for your faults, just as we love our friends for their human failings, not often for their virtues. The explosion was magnificent reporting, but, structurally, it blew up your story as well as the city. You lugged in the adultery of Mme Tallard, which got you a lot of readers – and lost you a lot, too. But now, by God, you have given a demonstration of fiction so honest, so able, so effective; and it is on the surface less spectacular. Discerning readers will thrill to your sheer power; they will admire your restraints – no crude sex for one thing. Nothing crude or pyrotechnic at all. Just the goods. It was a hellish hard book to write to keep emphasis true at all points and you never slipped once...

You are very fortunate in your dates. Grove, Salverson and company in the 1920's were pioneers. Canadian public had been too well taught to expect its good stuff from outside. Not even Jalna (1927) broke that down – her Canadian sales were never proportionately as good as in U.S. But you come along when there is far greater internal interest, when Canadians realize their writers are standing up to foreign competition. And you are one of the leaders; you will ride the crest of this wave, which is going to augment as long as we both shall live.[25]

Deacon's letter friendship with Hugh and Dorothy MacLennan was satisfying to all three of them in every way. Their belief in Canada and their tastes in literature were totally compatible; Deacon's support of their work, voiced in public and in private, was received with gratitude; his decades of experience with publishers and publishing were always at their disposal – and MacLennan was a writer constantly anxious about the details of publishing and marketing his books. Above all, their temperaments were complementary: MacLennan's ingrained, Calvinistic pessimism was countered and temporarily held at bay by Deacon's invincible optimism. Deacon could and did lose his patience: 'For God's sake, man, stop worrying and get on with your life, with your writing. Enough of the world is yours to satisfy anybody except a hog ... The Precipice is now "my last book." Please don't burn energy pointlessly by stewing about its fate which is out of your control. Steady your mind with some tennis and an article or two and start "my next book".'[26] MacLennan, for his part, could and did accept such a homily with grace and gratitude:

No writer can ever have received advice or comfort more helpful. If I seemed worried about THE PRECIPICE at first, I think it was mainly a fear that the book would flop so badly that I would have to go back to teaching to earn a living, and I have so much more work, and I hope better work, I want to do. Every word of advice you so clearly give me I accept thankfully. It is utterly right, and your analysis of the literary public of Canada is so good I hope you print it some time ... I feel now that my period of 'definition-making' is over; I feel finally released to delve directly into story and human nature.[27]

Like MacLennan's, Thomas Raddall's correspondence with Deacon began with the author's response to a review, in this case, of *Roger Sudden* (1944): 'A word of thanks for your ripsnorting review of my "Roger Sudden" in last Saturday's issue. I have a rosy picture of all the sixteen-year olds in Toronto rushing to buy the book and – who knows – I may become the Frank Sinatra of Canadian literature despite the news-photo at the head of your page, which makes me as bald as any victim of Roger's scalping knife.'[28]

Raddall checked Deacon sharply, however, for calling the novel 'frankly escapist': 'My dear sir, it is an historical tract written in what I hope is a palatable coating of fiction. I have long wanted to do a story showing what really happened in the first ten years of English settlement in Canada. A multitude of escapists from the truth, beginning with Longfellow, have so obscured the period that no historian would recognize it.'[29]

His further details provide an admirable gloss on the historical/
fictional elements of the novel:

This is not to claim infallibility for myself. But at least I have kept my eye on the
documents. 'Roger Sudden' is a fictitious character, of course; but his
adventures and business methods are well in accord with certain affairs
recorded by the historians. Actually it was Joshua Mauger who sold the
Acadian cattle to His Majesty's navy, and he engaged in other practices which I
have described. Eventually he retired to England, where he died in 1770,
leaving a fortune of £300,000 – which makes Roger's haul seem very small
indeed. I have drawn 'Roger' to a considerable extent also from the career of
Michael Francklin, a young English gentleman who came to Halifax in the
early days with his pride (and little else) in his pocket, amassed a fortune and
eventually became lieutenant-governor of the province.

Le Loutre, Gautier, Father Maillard, Gorham, Jean Baptiste Koap are actual
historical characters, faithfully described. Madame Ducudrai really did keep a
cabaret at Louisbourg, and her husband really was the chief French spy at New
York. Captain James Johnstone, the Scottish Jacobite exiled at Louisbourg, was
a real person, and all the details of his extraordinary career were taken from his
own memoirs – there is a translation of them (they were published in Paris) in
the museum library at Louisbourg. I provided him with a beautiful sister; I'm
sure his shade won't quarrel with me for that ...

But your mention of coincidence reminds me of an interesting point in the
construction of my plot. Wolfe commanded the 20th Foot in the Highlands.
His predecessor in the command was none other than Cornwallis! And since
Wolfe was a 'man of Kent' himself there is no valid reason why he and
Cornwallis could not have been travelling on leave together in the Rochester
coach when Roger robbed it. Certainly Cornwallis was in the vicinity of London
at that time. As you can see, this opened all sorts of possibilities for my plot. But
after consideration I rejected it and made the Colonel of the 20th Foot a purely
fictitious 'Colonel Belcher.' Truth may be stranger than fiction but a fiction
writer must be tender of his plausibilities.[30]

Deacon was never happier than when he could feel himself in some
way responsible for a book that he admired: he had suggested the
writing of *The Canadians: The Story of a People* to George Wrong, and
The Champlain Road to Franklin Davey McDowell. Now, to his intense
satisfaction, he found himself credited by McClelland and Stewart with
having suggested to Thomas Raddall the writing of *The Nymph and the
Lamp*. Raddall confirmed Deacon's part in the book in a letter describ-

ing, step by step, the genesis and progress of his work. Of all Deacon's correspondents, Raddall was perhaps most consistently the story-teller; he made an engrossing narrative out of every letter:

It is just four years to the day since I left home for that busy speaking tour in Ontario and Quebec, and I've been refreshing my memory from the brief entries in my logbook. Foster is right in his recollection that you mentioned at the Carlton Club a notion that I should not devote my work entirely to the historical, and that I should make use of my observations and experiences in the coastal radio service. I can't recall that you mentioned Sable Island specifically, although you must have known (from the jacket blurb of TAMBOUR) that I had been there. What impressed me there, and again at the meeting with the Toronto branch, CAA, was that in conversations aside you urged upon me the same point – that I should not let the success of PRIDE'S FANCY blind me to the strong human value of tales of my own time, using material of the kind that I had revealed in the short story 'Tambour.' You kept referring to 'Tambour' then, and later on, in the hasty notes and scattered conversations we have had since. This chimed with my own feeling, despite the well-meant efforts of publishers and many friends to convince me that the historical novel was my forte and that I should forget everything else. Therefore, as soon as *Halifax* was published, and despite the misgivings of the publishers (especially the U.S. publishers) I began to write THE NYMPH AND THE LAMP. I had broken with Doubleday, and my agent's efforts to secure a contract and cash advance from other publishers in the U.S. failed. They all said the same thing – I had built up a reputation in the costume novel field that was highly promising, and a contemporary novel now would be a wild gamble. The result was that I had to finance myself during the whole eighteen months I was writing it – a very considerable mental burden added to the strain of so long and careful a piece of work.

At the end of February, '49, when I had been working on the book for four months, and was still feeling my way doggedly along the thread of my story in a most profound darkness, I got a wire from Stanley Salmen [of Little, Brown] saying that he was catching a Furness Liner at Halifax on his way to England, and would like a chat. I went up and had dinner with him and his wife, and afterwards a long talk in their cabin aboard the ship. I told them, so far as I was able, what I was trying to accomplish. They looked very grave, and said that a novel about a man of 46 and a woman of 30 would be a very difficult thing to bring off. The worst of it was that I couldn't describe the story with any clarity because of course at that stage I couldn't see it clearly myself. However I talked about the life on 'Marina,' the oddly romantic nature of the work itself in such a place. I'm not much of a hand at talking, but a couple of drinks loosened my tongue, and I went on about it for quite a bit – parrying the keen criticisms that Salmen and his wife had to make from time to time. I suppose I came completely out of my shell. At any rate I must have revealed my own passionate faith in what I was doing, for when I stopped there was a little silence, and Mrs Salmen exclaimed, 'I believe you can do it!' Salmen was non-committal but he got me to promise that he should see the completed manuscript before anybody else.

So I went home and went on with it. When I met you in Halifax in the summer of '49 I mentioned briefly what I was doing, and you were enthusiastic, mentioning again the impact that 'Tambour' had made upon you. That Fall, when I had been working on the book roughly a year, the eternal groping paid off, for suddenly the whole shape of the thing became apparent. It still had to be worked out, chapter by chapter, even paragraph by paragraph, to say exactly what I wanted to say. I knew that I had a great theme, and the difficult thing was to tell it with the proper restraint. The path to Hell may be paved with good intentions but what takes a writer there is emotion on the loose. What might have been magnificent then becomes the merely maudlin and the simple humanity of the characters becomes drowned in a slobber of words.

The Nymph may or may not become a classic of its kind, but of this I am sure – it is a piece of life, of authentic Canadian life and earth and sea, in which every word has meaning, and no one could have written it but I, myself. It is as much a part of me as my hand, fiction or no fiction. For as you may have guessed, the tale is not entirely fiction, and in the happy-go-lucky 'Sargent' you have in all his cocky glory a Portrait Of The Author As A Young Man, not quite the fool he seemed, even to himself in those days, but very eager for the taste of life and noting every detail of it.[31]

When the book came out Deacon was delighted: 'It is in the top rank of Canadian novels, of course; but I'll not know till I've cooled off, weeks hence, whether it is slightly above or below A, B, or C. Things like this need time to digest; but I'm a disciple of POWER, and this is strong.'[32] Raddall reciprocated with a letter that communicated both the effort and the faith required for the writing of that, or any other, novel:

I'm not writing to thank you for that heart-warming review, for that would be impertinent, but I do want to tell you it did just that – it warmed my heart. I've just been looking at my diary. Typical entry, last Feb. 14th. – 'Working 8 to 10 hours a day on my novel but it still goes slowly, every sentence literally wrenched from my mind, & then mulled over carefully.' Again, four days later,

'Working on the novel 9 hours, and thinking about the next chapter as I took my afternoon walk to Milton. I am seldom to bed before midnight, sometimes at it till 1.30.'

Finally, on April 1st (an odd day to finish so long & serious a labor) there is this: -

'Saturday. I worked all day and towards five in the afternoon wrote the last word of my novel, which I began in November '48. Think I shall call it 'Castaways' or 'One Fair Spirit.' It will take about a month to type clean copy for the publishers & do the last-minute polishing. There won't be much of the latter, for my work is all edited and much re-written at the close of each day. Now that the novel is finished the plot seems simple, even trite, & the characters in no way distinguished, yet it is the product of the longest & most arduous labor I have yet performed – deliberately refusing to 'dash off' so much as a paragraph, & spending an hour sometimes over a single phrase. It is a romance of course but I think I have sketched faithfully life in an isolated wireless station as I knew it 30 years ago, & a glimpse of Halifax & the Annapolis Valley in the hectic post-war days of '20 & '21.'

There you see my state of mind at the finish – exhausted and despondent but clinging to my faith in the tale as something worth doing well. And perhaps you will see what such a review as yours can mean when the last step has been taken & the book is irrevocably out. Notice that I later changed my mind about the title. 'Castaways' sounded too much like an adventure tale for juveniles. 'One Fair Spirit' is of course taken from the lines of 'Solitude' that Carney recites on P. 159. But the practice of lifting titles from lines of verse – often by the crudest of Caesarian operations & dismally contrived – has become so banal that nowadays I'm suspicious of any book bearing such a label, so I chucked it out. When after much thought I hit upon The Nymph & The Lamp, which said everything & was fresh & clean, I wrote it down & knew at once that nothing else would do.[33]

Among all of Deacon's correspondents over the decades, Raddall was the most articulate about the background and genesis of his novels, and probably the most realistic about their chances of success. About *Tidefall* (1953), the story of Sax Nolan, who made a fortune out of rum-running in Nova Scotia in the 1920s, he wrote:

I think Tidefall may not have the popular appeal of The Nymph, because women buy most of the books nowadays, and Tidefall is more of a man's book; moreover it's the story of a most unpleasant character, whereas the people in The Nymph were all fundamentally decent. However, we shall see. Popular or not it is a book I wanted to write. The character of 'Sax' (who really lived) has been in my mind for a long time, together with the problem of a woman who finds herself married to such a man, and the bleak scene in which the tale is set has haunted me ever since I first saw it years ago. Apart from all that I wanted to set forth something of the era of the rum-runners, in many ways the most fantastic chapter in Canadian nautical history. It was a chapter that belonged to the freebooting 16th and 17th centuries, and yet it was schemed, worked and fought out of Canadian ports in the 20th, a private war against the United States conducted by a class of men to whom the Elizabethans would look pale. Many of them I knew, and here in the 20's I had a unique opportunity to study them and to see what was going on. Looking back, many of their adventures seem incredible; and yet at the time, the hard times of the 20's here on the coast, they were as natural as codfish and ten times as profitable – more.

Tidefall was a more difficult book to write than The Nymph (which cost me sweat and blood enough) and took much longer, I suppose because it is easier to write about people one can admire. But then I have never found writing easy, it is always toil, always a struggle with frustration and despair, and perfection is always dancing just ahead like the carrot before the burdened donkey, something he never gets but which leads him over the road with his burden anyhow.[34]

As their friendship developed and mellowed, Raddall too wrote to Deacon for counsel about publishers. He had his reservations about 'Old John' of McClelland and Stewart; 'my impression was that he'd never had much contact with authors and thought they all wore horns and a tail.'[35] Deacon reassured him, however, about 'Young Jack': 'Off-hand, I'd guess Young Jack is shrewder than his father, better equipped to be a publisher; and I shouldn't wonder that he will pull things together nicely ... There is at least this – whereas Old John is reputed never to have read a book in his life, Jack does. He is reading mss and has ideas about them – right or wrong, he's trying to be a publisher. He is, further, a believer in Canadian books. What kind of internal nonsense he's up against I don't know.'[36]

Though Raddall (b. 1903) was thirteen years younger than Deacon, they considered each other contemporaries and peers. Raddall described the basic impulse of his own work: 'I have always looked upon my writing bent, not merely from the viewpoint of the sea, but from a deep and sincere interest in the *genus homo*, male and female, afloat or ashore, past or present.'[37] All Deacon's work, certainly all his correspondence, stemmed from the same abiding interest. In correspondence with MacLennan (b. 1907), though he was only four years younger than Raddall, Deacon was always conscious of himself as belonging to an older generation. Their mutual respect was grounded on the recognition of the older man for the younger's promise, and of the younger man for the older's experience. To Gabrielle Roy (b. 1909), two years younger again than MacLennan, Deacon wrote with paternalistic pride, a 'Father in the Craft' to her as, long ago, Emily Murphy had been his own 'Mother in the Craft.' After *Bonheur d'Occasion* his regard for her talent bordered on awe; Gabrielle Roy, in spite of her shyness and the ingrained reserve of her nature, responded gratefully to the warmth of Deacon's regard, not only for her work, but for herself. He had first had a report on the novel from MacLennan – 'Beyond any shade of doubt, it's the best novel of any large city ever done by a Canadian ... This book is every bit as good and valid as Dickens at his best, written with terrific verve and the command of the Saint-Henri dialect which is literally magnificent.'[38] That testimony was enough for Deacon: though he could not easily read the French original, he went into action on the book page and in 'The Fly Leaf,' earning a follow-up acknowledgment from MacLennan: 'I thought the page on Gabrielle Roy splendid, and believe me a grand thing for inter-provincial relations. She is becoming, in a mild way, adored in Quebec ... She is a first class human being, and probably the best natural novelist this country has ever had.'[39]

Deacon took the initiative in writing to Gabrielle Roy: 'I believe it is time we tried to know each other across the language barrier.'[40] Soon, because of his obvious sincerity of intention and the mutual warmth of their personalities, they were addressing each other as 'dear friend.' 'Have you considered writing a Manitoba novel,' he enquired, and followed with another suggestion: 'I have often thought it might be an interesting experiment for a Canadian of French blood to live a year or two in Ontario in some very English section of the province – perhaps even Toronto – and to write a novel about our life but from your viewpoint – writing in French for subsequent translation. This might do a lot of good on both sides of the barrier.'[41]

He wrote her a brief story of his life and asked her to reciprocate, so that 'the more profitable will be our hours together when we do meet.' She responded in English with a long letter:

I too was born in Manitoba, in the very catholic little French town of St Boniface. I went to convent there, and learned that although English and protestant people might go to heaven by some indirect route, it wasn't right for us to mix with them. I was a good little girl, very studious, the youngest of a family of eight. I went to Normal School in Winnipeg, and following in my sisters' tracks, I became a school teacher. My mother thought that it was a profession noble, lady-like and highly respectable. I taught school in a small village the first year and then in St Boniface. Throughout those dreary empty years I found escape in theatricals playing with amateur groups such as Le Cercle Molière who won the French trophy twice in the drama festival and also with the Winnipeg Little Theatre. I had some success as a small town actress and I fancied myself gifted with great histrionic possibilities. I saved as much as I could of my small salary and eventually I had enough to start on a trip to Europe. I studied dramatics in London, but I found myself attracted to writing so much more than to the stage. Before leaving Canada, I had had a few stories published in English and a few in French. A trip to France, a brief stay in Paris finally convinced me that the French language was my proper medium. I used up the last bit of my money, by the way, on a walking tour of the south of France with a girl friend. After nearly two years in Europe, I returned to Canada six months before the war and settled in Montreal as a free-lance writer. It was tremendously difficult and tremendously exhilarating. I sometimes think those were the most wonderful years of my life. I wrote short stories, reportages, feature articles for several French-Canadian periodicals. I laid aside two or three months each year to write my novel. It seems that it is quite a success and this surprises me greatly for I wrote a simple story about people and a way of living evident to all.

I am now in California trying to forget that I ever wrote *Bonheur d'Occasion*. As you must have experienced yourself many times, joy springs not from what is done but from what is to be done. I really came here to find solitude, a condition which I have dreaded all my life and which I have found impossible to elude. For more than a month now I have lived in a cottage by the sea. The only people I know around here are some distant relatives whom I haven't seen since I was a child. To say the truth, in spite of the sea and abundant sunshine, I am very lonesome.

I too love Canada dearly. My folks, originally from Quebec, led a pioneer life in Manitoba, and I felt as they must have the thrill of adventuring along fresh trails. No, I don't think that I would care to live in any other country although, of course, I should be glad to visit France again some day.

I don't know if these details will help you much. Our life cannot be told in facts, don't you think, but in inner strivings and conflicts, very difficult to record.

I cannot tell you what my next book will be for it isn't clear in my mind yet. Perhaps it is that I do not choose a subject matter, but that a certain subject chooses me. I know this is poorly expressed; I haven't written in English for a long time and I'm full of misgivings concerning the prepositions.[42]

In this letter relationship, Deacon's best qualities of warmth, under-standing, and adaptability were released. He was neither defensive about his own work nor did he overwhelm her with unsolicited advice about hers. He supported, encouraged, and rejoiced in her talent with a delicacy of feeling and expression that she welcomed with complete trust: 'Don't read my books when you come home,' he wrote, 'they are all long out of print; and I have grown beyond them. I am ashamed now to have been once so young, so naive.'[43] 'Certainly , you must write in French,' he continued, 'they told me in St Henri that a reader of your novel could *smell* St Henri ... But you are a writer for the world, not just Quebec; and it is most important of all that your novels shall be known and read in English Canada. The translation route is correct.'[44]

When she came to Toronto in the spring of 1946, she stayed with the Deacons, extending the warmth of her friendship to Sally and the children, and to Margot Syme Christie, a daughter of Sally's first marriage, with whom, years back, she had acted in the Winnipeg Little Theatre. Subsequent to this visit her photograph occupied a place of honour beside Sally's on Deacon's study wall.

The Tin Flute, the translation of *Bonheur d'Occasion*, was published in Canada by McClelland and Stewart in April 1947. Deacon's letter on this occasion was both a celebration of Gabrielle Roy's particular talent and success and a celebration of his own deepest personal and professional satisfactions:

As my life is devoted to Canadian literature, and as The Tin Flute is the finest specimen of it in the 26 years of my labors, there is simply nothing I can say to express my satisfaction adequately. I'm prouder of you all, you writers, than of anything I do myself; and when your book is really the best, artistically, as well as a success, my feelings are beyond words. I know words – not tongue-tied a bit. But I don't know how to tell you the great exaltation I feel because a Canadian has written as wonderfully as Flaubert. I'm very excited. Just as a writer, you mean more to me than I can say.

Then, on top of all that, you are a fellow Manitoban, and let me be your personal friend. So I am all lit up like a Christmas tree, inside; probably it shines out through the skin also ... May the honours and money roll into you in ever increasing streams. But right now you have brought me great happiness.[45]

Their letters continued through the years, on personal matters (her marriage to Marcel Carbotte, her precarious health; his and Sally's hopes of a literary retirement and his children's careers), on business advice which she sometimes asked for, and on her experience of Paris with Marcel in 1949. 'Small children, cats, flowers, lovely Sally, her merriment, your books, rime poetry, optimism: what wealth is yours

Bill and how wise you are to know that it is so,' she wrote from France.[46] In a later letter, after their return, she sketched the reasons for her own delight in Paris:

We have been wonderfully happy together in France. Yes, dear Sally, our hearts ache for Paris. You ask me how is it that Paris captivates people so. I suppose it is through many qualities sweet in themselves, but mostly by their perfect blend, just as perfect, aged wine. Life in France is incredibly sweet and free and thoroughly humane. One breathes freedom in the very air. There is respect for love, for man and for whatever comes to his mind. There, I think, lies the charm of Paris and of France. Beauty too, of course. There is beauty for the eye, satisfaction in almost every street in Paris – La Place de la Concorde has perfect dimensions. It is really vast. And how wonderful to come across large, open spaces in a city of men! To see so many trees, water, statues, lovely vases! In other words, so much that is unnecessary, gratuitous. We reproach their impractical nature to the French, but in a way that is how they created beauty. Their motive is seldom practical; it tends to please the eye, the mind. And even nowadays, buildings and homes go up slowly compared to our standard, but what houses compared to our own! In the first month of our stay in Paris, I witnessed, for example, a curious thing. There were entire cities to reconstruct, bridges, ports, roads to rebuild; yet, along le boulevard Raspail where we lived, I saw a whole gang of men at work, derricks, a truck, all employed in planting a full-grown tree to match the others along the boulevard. There was work far more urgent. Yet who knows! Perhaps this tree is just as important as an office building. For weeks, I watched it, afraid to see it die. Men came to water it everyday, and finally, in the Spring, I saw it come out into buds, as large, as beautiful as the other trees in the street. In the midst of strikes, of uneasiness and devastation, we also saw expert workers setting up the stained windows of Chartres, the reconstruction of Rouen's cathedral and of Orleans, of Lisieux, of Caen – Dear Saint-Malo, however, I'm afraid, is beyond repairs...[47]

As her books appeared and were translated during the fifties, she looked to Deacon for understanding when other critics, she felt, failed her:

The first write-ups about Alexandre have come out in the French press and it is just as I expected: they understand nothing. My dear Bill, I begin to see that this chord I'm always trying to touch – this theme of human love regardless of nationality, of religion, of tongue, this essential truth doesn't mean much to my people and although I know the necessity of patience, I'm a little sick at heart, sometimes. How can people be so blind to the one truth we should learn as we live, the one truth that matters![48]

As always, he was ready with an appropriate, sincerely-felt and totally supportive reply:

> My dear girl, realize once and for all that this deep quality in you of human understanding and grasp of human relationships makes you a world writer. It doesn't matter what any particular group anywhere thinks of a particular book. You are writing for human beings, wherever they are; and you are sufficiently an artist so that your novel will be appreciated – never fear.
>
> You and I, as Manitobans, really don't belong to any special region. I've always been so glad I was born in Ontario (Pembroke) was brought up in Quebec (Stanstead) lived my 12 formative years, 21-32, in Manitoba (Dauphin and Winnipeg), and lived a few months in New York.
>
> Remember, too, that sometimes there is local jealousy. In one way, French-speaking Canadians are proud of you; but some of them may not be happy because we English-speakers regard you as ours, too; and you have a world audience. You have outgrown the nest. The time will come when EVERY CANADIAN will be proud of you. Don't feel badly if some local people resent the fact you have outgrown them.[49]

When in 1955 *La Petite Poule d'Eau* was accepted as a textbook by Ontario's Department of Education, she credited Deacon with this 'lovely triumph! I think that, in the beginning, you labored and worked towards this achievement.' And when, in the same year, *Alexandre Chenevert* was translated as *The Cashier*, she prized his review, 'although I can't see how I remind you so much of Flaubert who was a very determined novelist leading his characters by the hand and just where he wished them to go – whereas I like to follow them wherever they decide to go and try to wait for them to reveal themselves to me':

> I specially thank you for this sentence ... 'which finally shows the reader that Chenevert invariably did the best he could in his cruelly limiting circumstances.'
>
> If we understood others fully, completely, we would seldom judge or condemn, would we not? Such is the vocation of the novelist, it seems to me; to plead for better and better understanding. In any case you have well understood the strange little man. And about myself you write lovely things which I would like to deserve, indeed.[50]

Deacon's understanding of the tragedy and meaning of Alexandre Chenevert's life confirmed once again their longstanding trust and prompted Deacon to a recapitulation of his own faith and commitment, his credo for himself and all writers:

You know, Gabrielle (speaking as a fellow Manitoban) we have finally to leave things to Higher Powers. My life has spanned the great stretch from 1890, when agriculture was the main industry, into the industrial age. I am not fitted to deal with problems ahead. So I am not of any use to the rising writers. Thank God I have not received any favors from the rising generation. But I am happy in having looked with favor on younger people of merit.

Remember one thing. Nobody demanded that we be writers. My Winnipeg friends did their utmost to prevent me leaving the lucrative profession of law. They called me 'a damned fool'; and I guess I was. But I have done what I wanted and that is all that matters to me now. I turned writer and critic from inner compulsion.

Nobody owes me anything (I have had a happy life) and, thank God, nobody owes me anything. I've had fun. God bless you both.[51]

The Retirement Years

IN NOVEMBER 1960 DEACON was notified by the *Globe*'s management that he would be retired at Christmas time and that William French, who had been on the staff since 1948, would replace him as literary editor. Though for years he had talked of retirement as the time when, finally, he would be able to devote all his time to his own writing, when that time came he was profoundly shocked and personally affronted: 'At first, I felt as if I'd suffered dishonourable death.'[1] He had nothing against French, whom he called 'a good young man,' and he, himself, was seventy, five years beyond the official retirement age, but he felt that he was being unfairly discarded – even more crucially he was afraid of his own and Sally's future, feeling that his pension would be entirely inadequate for their needs. Though he had gone through a period of intense financial anxiety about the future before *The Globe and Mail* became unionized in 1955, he had persuaded himself that his case would be an exception to the new rules and that he would go on and on, in the time-honoured tradition of old newspapermen – S. Morgan Powell of *The Montreal Star*, for instance, who had retired in 1954 at the age of eighty-seven.[2] *The Globe and Mail* dealt fairly with him; his pension was supplemented to an adequate monthly income and he was also invited to continue writing 'The Fly Leaf' for as long as he cared to do so. All the same he resented his forced retirement with an outspoken bitterness that he had never allowed himself to show under his earlier professional vicissitudes, such as his dismissal from *Saturday Night*.

His friends rallied round to give him what support they could muster, and under the direction of Hugh Kane, then managing editor of McClelland and Stewart, they organized a farewell dinner in his honour, to be held at the King Edward Hotel on 11 January 1961. The success of the event delighted the organizers and astounded Deacon: the demand for tickets necessitated booking the ballroom, the largest room in the hotel; letters and telegrams flooded in from all over Canada from those who wished to honour him but could not be present; and on the night some 350 guests gathered, not so much to say good-bye as to celebrate Deacon's – and Sally's – forty years in the service of Canadian literature, and to present them with a sizable purse of money. The souvenir menu, its cover a clever mock-up of 'The Fly Leaf' with a cartoon of Deacon in the centre, lists 'Sundry Speakers in Praise of William Arthur Deacon,' among whom were John Gray and Jack McClelland; Dr E.J. (Ned) Pratt on 'Redressing the Balance'; and Marjorie Wilkins Campbell 'In Praise of Sally Townsend.' By 11 January Deacon had had time to adjust somewhat to his retirement; moreover, he was truly astonished by the manifestations of affection and good-will that had been showered on him in the previous weeks and had climaxed in this gala event. When, finally, his turn came to speak, he called himself the corpse at the funeral, but in jest, not bitterness. On this occasion, the last public speech of his career, he paid his own public tribute to Sally : 'two people are retiring tonight ... I have been specially blessed in having an active partner of kindred tastes, who often substituted for me. We consulted constantly; and often the words I wrote expressed her ideas. Few men have the good fortune of there being no separation between their domestic and professional lives.'[3] He recapitulated his career and reiterated the basic motivating force behind all of it:

I should like to attack the Deacon Myth that I always sacrificed myself for others, whereas the truth is that I have lived a perfectly selfish life.

Something really has to be accounted for. I have long been troubled by the cordiality of your attitudes towards me. Surely the capable and honest critic would not be tendered a banquet. He would be hated and reviled – possibly stoned. Wherein have I failed?

I've tried to rationalize the equation by telling myself that I am basically a patriot, who realized that what Canada needs most in this century is a strong native literature as a cohesive force. That argument doesn't do much good in the light of Samuel Johnson's definition of patriotism as 'the last refuge of a scoundrel' ...

I believe in the significance of Canada in world history. Whether or not this is a rationalization, this faith has been a dynamic force in my life – probably my most basic impulse.[4]

There was no time for a cruel, post-retirement letdown: he had 'The Fly Leaf,' which he continued until 1963; he had to decide among the four publishers, Macmillan, McClelland and Stewart, Ryerson, and Doubleday, who approached him to write a history of Canadian literature and his memoirs; he had to sort and bring into workable order the mass of letters and books that had grown voluminously over the years; and, first priority, he wished to answer all his retirement correspondence, a chore that took him some three months even at his prodigious rate of letter-writing. There was time now, however, for a more leisurely enjoyment of daily pleasures than he and Sally had ever known: for reading without deadlines, for the cribbage and bridge they both loved, and for uninterrupted summers at Wilson's Point, when children and grandchildren would move in and out of the cabin and the boathouse, and he and Sally would remain in the cottage, the fixed centre of a seasonal Deacon community.

His interest in letter-writing never flagged and, as always, he derived his greatest pleasure from promising young writers, Peter Newman, for instance, whose *Renegade in Power: The Diefenbaker Years* (1963) stirred in Deacon all of his old spirit:

Thanks for your book on Dief, which I'm enjoying. But I'm only part-way through because (a) I'm old and tired, (b) I'm writing a book myself and it goes terribly slowly because it involves much research...

I'm a poor judge of such a book because I've never been intimately involved in politics – just the average voter. I thought Eugene Forsey dealt well with 'Renegade' in the swell CBC-t.v. presentation last night. Diefenbaker was at times rash ... but my impression [was that] ... he was not a son-of-a-bitch like Mackenzie King, who would disembowel his brother to retain office. At the time of the Customs scandal, over which the Liberals should have been ejected, King walked into the middle aisle, wept, and told the Commons that when he was a boy sometimes his mother didn't have enough to eat. In the first place I don't believe it; and in the second what did a hungry mother have to do with flagrant graft in the Customs Dept 50 years later?

Best P.M. we ever had was John A., chief architect of the B.N.A. Act. He took Canada out of colonial status and made it a 'self-governing colony' – which is a contradiction in terms. The further he went the less inclined he was to make decisions; and was called 'Old Tomorrow.' Once in the Commons, when the opposition leader referred, rather crudely, to his drunkenness, most members were very sorry for him. Macdonald rose to reply, the picture of contrition, head hanging, shoulders stooped and in. He started to speak in a low voice, barely audible: 'I am aware of my weakness and am very sorry for it.' Gradually he straightened up, the famous smile spread across his face, his voice strengthened and finally rang out: 'But I would rather be old Sir John drunk than George Brown sober.' The house got as near a cheer as the rules permitted...

But I want to say this to you in general: What I think you should always remember is that Canada is a miracle. It can be and has been plausibly argued that (a) Canada is an anachronism; a self-governing colony is a contradiction in terms, (b) it is a miracle that we were not swallowed by the u.s.a. long ago. It happened because two other powers held misconceptions. The Americans thought that Britain would fight for us, which they would not have done. The British thought (mistakenly) that we were taking the first step towards severing all ties with 'the mother country.'

To supply some kind of rationale to our inconsistencies, we invented the Commonwealth. It's a pretty good club. The English-speaking peoples include the land of Gandhi, Nehru & Co. We are practical and pragmatic, not logical like the Latin countries. You often see General Vanier, commander of the Van Doos, Canada's banner regiment, going in and out of Rideau Hall, where he is substitute monarch in this kingdom – an inspired appointment. You and I as Canadians can't be kept out of Britain because we are subjects of Elizabeth. When she comes here we cheer. Theoretically she rules us, whatever that may mean after the parliament in London is, at the request of the parliament at Ottawa, now revoking the b.n.a. Act because they no longer want to keep on amending it *at our request*. Now we must amend it ourselves. We are an autonomous part of the Commonwealth. It is to laugh? No. To be grateful. In a beautifully British way we have 'muddled through.' We eat our cake and have it too.[5]

Only the years and worsening health were the enemies: 'Sally and I are now entering the last phase cheerfully but recognizing [that] the years are numbered, and only so much strength remains.'[6] Even in the 1950s he had been disturbed by his failing memory. After retirement he steadily lost confidence in his ability to concentrate on his work: in general, 'Old age is an experience for which nobody is really prepared.'[7] Nevertheless he worked valiantly at the history of Canadian literature for which he had signed a contract with George Nelson of Doubleday, concurrently compiling notes for the volume of memoirs which was to follow it. Nelson was constantly supportive and encouraging: sometimes their correspondence shows Deacon at the top of his old form, charged with energy and optimism about his work; but sometimes, and, over the years, more frequently, Deacon's letters communicate an intense anxiety about his ability to finish the work.[8]

In 1967 Sally's illness was diagnosed as Parkinson's Disease. As long as she could be home, Deacon nursed her; when she had to be moved to Riverdale Hospital he went every day to give her her dinner and just to be near her if she needed him: 'I should not be shocked but am. After living with one woman for about half a century, it comes as a shock that such a satisfactory union should ever come to an end ... we have both been pretty busy. And partners. And lovers.'9

After the crisis of Sally's illness that year he was able to do almost no writing at all. As her health had failed, he had already withdrawn an application for a centennial grant to finish his work. After her death in 1969 he did no more serious work and, effectively, he entered a long twilight, increasingly incapacitated by a series of small strokes, ending with his death in August 1977. His family did not often find him unhappy in those long, last years – in fact he suffered less from the constant pressure of anxiety than he had at any other time of his life. For a long time his son, Bill, and Deirdre, his daughter, kept up the kindly fiction of helping him with his work-in-progress; many of his days were spent writing letters as he had always done, even though these letters were never sent.

His unfinished manuscript of some 300 pages is a draft history of Canadian literature from Confederation to the present, arranged chronologically and by author. It is not markedly different in content from his Ryerson lectures of the fifties, but it is less interesting in its dictionary format than was his earlier grouping of authors and topics for lecture purposes. In fact, and with hindsight, the time for the useful publication of Deacon's history of literature certainly was the early fifties, when the book would have been unique, informative, quirkily entertaining, and extremely valuable to the infant field of Canadian literary studies. Ironically, by the mid-sixties he was swimming desperately against the tide: the academics he had so volubly distrusted for so long had moved ahead in strength and Klinck's *Literary History of Canada*, Conron and Sylvestre's *Canadian Writers/Ecrivains Canadiens*, and Pacey's *Creative Writing in Canada* among them covered the field.

No one, throughout his life, assessed and reiterated his goals and ideals more often than did William Arthur Deacon, and no one, to the limit of his energies, kept faith in them more stubbornly and devotedly. Mercifully, before the darkness closed in on him he was able to see and rejoice in the exuberant nationalism of the late sixties. One of the last coherent letters that he wrote, to his son-in-law, Lloyd Haines, celebrates and vindicates once again his entire life's work: 'I contributed to a rising literary movement in Canada – a nation without a strong literary life is no shakes as a nation. I staked my life on it and I believe I won.'[10]

In that statement, the optimism and the dedication are as untarnished as they are in the statement of mission he had written to his mother forty-five years before. Deacon was extraordinarily single-minded in the goal he set for himself and held, and he was fortunate that neither age nor illness dimmed his satisfaction in the signs he saw around him of his dream realized. Yet circumstances had forced great modifications upon him: he came to *Saturday Night* as an iconoclast and a self-designated prophet; Whitman was his model, the development and democratization of Canadian literature his goal. He saw himself as a literary journalist, but also as a writer, a Canadian front-runner in the tradition Whitman ascribed to Thoreau: 'his lawlessness – his dissent – his going down his own absolute road, let hell blaze as it please.' During the years at *Saturday Night* and, concurrently, his enthusiastic sponsoring by Lorne Pierce and the publication of his first four books, the path to the realization of his ambition seemed a smooth, broad highway. Then the exigencies of growing family responsibility combined with the times themselves to frustrate and inhibit his grandiose plans. His dismissal from *Saturday Night*, the onset of the Depression, the struggle to establish and maintain a freelance circuit of literary reporting, the precious, not-to-be jeopardized financial security of *The Mail and Empire*, and finally his traumatic, narrowly aborted dismissal from *The Globe and Mail*, radically modified his sense of his own potential.

As he had written to Burton Kurth in the twenties, his and Sally's three children were miraculous to him because they had come relatively late in his life, from a love that they both unceasingly felt was specially ordained and correspondingly deep. In no way would he put his family at risk. *My Vision of Canada*, planned in the ebullient days of the twenties, required an enormous effort of will and courage to finish and publish in the thirties. He really believed that the book's radicalism, particularly its heated strictures against Canada's continuing colonialism, might well cost him his job and when he weathered its publication safely he knew that he would never take another such chance: 'That book marked my death as a writer.' In personal growth, however, there were more compensations during the decade from 1928 to 1938 than he realized: his brash confidence had been forever eroded, but events had pushed him into far broader and deeper fields of interest and professional competence that Deacon, the literary tyro of the twenties, had recognized.

His career spanned the decades in which literature was being institutionalized in the universities both in the United States and Canada. When he came to Toronto from Winnipeg, having already written essays and reviews for a number of American publications as well as the essays *In Fame's Antechamber*, he was as much influenced by the freshness of approach he discerned in the writing of Carl Sandburg and Edgar Lee Masters and the criticism of Henry Seidel Canby, Christopher Morley and the Englishman, John Cowper Powys, as he was repelled by the old-style academic élitism and the adherence to Victorian literary values he had deplored in his classes at Victoria and particularly in the social and pedagogical attitudes of Pelham Edgar. Then, like Arthur Phelps, his Winnipeg friend and patron, he considered himself among the avant-garde. As Leslie Fiedler has recently written in 'Literature as an Institution' (1981), 'in the years just before and after World War I the taste of the disreputable dissenters triumphed in the larger literary world, and it seemed only a matter of time before their taste would carry the day inside the university. Its spokesmen had redeemed the reputations of Herman Melville and Walt Whitman and upped the value of the hitherto depressed stock of John Donne and Gerard Manley Hopkins, while they down-graded the value of Milton and Shelley, Longfellow and Tennyson...'[11] The young dissenters in Canada and the States were proponents of modernism, early Canadian 'New Critics' like A.J.M. Smith and others of the Montreal and the *Forum* groups. To Deacon's vision of himself as an iconoclast, however, was linked his deep ambition to be a Man of Letters in the style of the great essayists of the past, and he was never as radical in his literary opinions as he thought himself to be. He did not understand or approve a commitment to modernism, and the establishment of a new critical élitism to displace the old, Victorian-based élitism was anathema to him, for above all he believed in Canada and the development and democratization of its literature as he understood that process from his own fervent patriotism and theosophical faith.

As he grew older he gave as much credit to his Methodist background as to theosophy for his unremitting sense of mission, but whatever the balance of its roots, he never diverged from its path. His enthusiasms demanded some strange compromises and one of them was his advocacy of Wilson MacDonald, a far cry from Whitman, whom Deacon persuaded himself was the genius among Canadian poets of the twenties. The modernists could never have understood that or forgiven him for it – and yet, in the service of a national literary movement MacDonald, along with Roberts and Carman, the only poets touring and reading in the schools at that time, gave thousands of young people, absolutely ignorant of their own literature, a first memorable experience of poetry and the poet.[12]

Compromises aside, Deacon's successes were milestones in the history of Canadian literary culture: working in tandem with the burgeoning CAA in the twenties, he did establish a community of Canadian writers and scholars – we have never since achieved in any one publication anything like the coast-to-coast fraternity he assembled for reviewing in *Saturday Night*'s Literary Supplements. Writers were his constant, primary concern and the causes he instigated and tirelessly supported all had to do with encouraging, supporting, and publicizing them: from the early twenties he lobbied for the setting up of the national literary prizes that were eventually established as the Governor-General's Awards; he wrote the first half-dozen letters badgering Prime Minister Bennett to establish the fund for indigent writers that became the Canadian Writers' Foundation; he was the publicist and the executive organizer of the Leacock Awards; and his terms as Toronto Branch President and then National President of the CAA were successfully marked by his own high enthusiasm. Most constant and perhaps most effective of all, for over forty years, were his letter-friendships with Canadian writers. The best of his own writing skills went into his letters – energy, generosity, optimism, wit, and enthusiasm – and his correspondents replied in kind. They knew him as a writer's critic, knowledgeable about their concerns, endlessly ready to respond with encouragement, friendship, and advice, and above all free of the academic establishment that most writers have always regarded as warily and defensively as did Deacon himself.

During the writing of this biography we have searched out and written to scores of writers and their heirs for permission to publish their correspondence with Deacon. No one has refused us permission. The letters in reply to our request constitute yet another new correspondence, a memorial of gratitude and warm remembrance, which is characterized by the following tribute from Gabrielle Roy:

Je me hâte de vous féliciter de préparer une biographie de cet excellent ami des écrivains canadiens, de langue française et de langue anglaise, qui fut William Arthur Deacon. C'est lui qui prit l'initiative de m'écrire peu après la parution de Bonheur d'Occasion. J'étais à l'époque, très timide, très apeurie – je le suis peut-être encore – et il me semble qu'il s'appliqua à me donner confiance en moi-même. C'était un homme d'une exquise générosité. Il me semble qu'il avait donné un petit party pour moi qui devais m'arrêter chez lui à Toronto, de retour de Californie, et une photo de moi fut prise chez lui à cette occasion. J'ai mille souvenirs heureux de cet homme bon, perspicace et grand ami des Lettres.[13]

Selected Writings of
William Arthur Deacon

'What a Canadian Has Done for Canada,' first published in *The Literary Review* of *The New York Evening Post*, 19 July 1924, is a parody-review of Arthur Stringer's novel, *Empty Hands*.

ANADA IS A CONVENIENT, far-off place of which the English novelist sometimes avails himself, possibly to the satisfaction of his English patrons, but frequently to the amusement of his Canadian readers. This Dominion affords refuge for criminals fleeing from justice; a place where sudden death may overtake the villain of the story at a fit distance from the scene of the hero's triumph and happiness; a remote spot to which a jilted suitor may be packed off, and whence he can return presently with a fortune. Up till recently the vagueness of the allusions to such incidents protected the English novelist: we smiled at the transparency of the conventional device of 'a legendary place,' but were unable to object pointedly because almost anything may happen almost anywhere provided 'corroborative detail intended to give artistic verisimilitude' be carefully avoided.

Lately the list toward realism has upset the balance somewhat, and English novelists are starting to describe scenes and events which betray their ignorance of localities and conditions and to supply Canadian reviewers with material for many a jest. About four years ago, for instance, an English writer of standing put his hero on a horse at Montreal in the morning, and had him riding into Edmonton the same night. It was stated that the horse was very tired – a conservative enough estimate of its condition considering that it had covered a distance which a fast train travels in about four days. Last year May

Wynne, in *The Ambitions of Gill,* wound up her book with a chapter entitled 'In Far Muskoka,' where the hero was represented as living the life of a prospector completely isolated from other human beings. Actually, Muskoka is the most populous of Canadian summer resorts and yields no minerals except the minted coins that tourists spend with commendable freedom. The heroine, seeking her beloved, walks miles to his cabin through the wilderness, which in the description resembles an English park more than the reality. In that country covered with evergreens, whose largest branches grow close to the ground, it would be impossible to see 'at some distance a herd of deer feeding quietly beneath the trees.' And the final touch is added when she comes upon 'some wild boars looking for truffles,' as there are neither wild boars nor truffles anywhere in North America.

As an aid to checking this tendency by showing how the Canadian scene should not be used, we may consider *Empty Hands* by Arthur Stringer, a native author and until recently a resident in Canada, but now a naturalized citizen of the United States. His book caps the climax for absurdities about Canadian woods life. On one score, however, I am very pleased with him. The literary world has long been in dire need of a second Munchausen; and though Stringer owes something to *Robinson Crusoe, Swiss Family Robinson,* and *The Admirable Crichton,* his narrative partakes far more of the bold, sweeping mendacities of the great Baron. Certainly Oscar Wilde would never have written his lament on *The Decay of Lying* if he had foreseen the mighty renaissance of that ancient and delightful art that was to come in 1924. Because a fairy story loses half its charm when it is accepted as fact; and because Stringer, being a Canadian by birth, may be mistaken for a realist by readers in other countries, I hasten to correct any such erroneous impression, and to proclaim him for the rightful monarch he is – the Prince of the 'Canada Fakers' he once denounced in an article under that title in the New York *Herald.*

Like all fairy stories, the scene is laid in a place hard to locate on any mundane map, no one point in Canada fulfilling all the conditions. From seven scattered paragraphs I gather that the author means northern Manitoba. 'North of the Pas,' 'the Land of Little Sticks' and 'on the fringe of the Barren Grounds' seem to indicate this; yet on page 53 Hudson's Bay is spoken of as 'hundreds of miles away ... to the north,' which is true of Toronto but not of the barrens far north of the Pas. Yet the mistiness of the location serves as useful cover enabling the author to bring together the strangest collection of northern and southern fauna and flora ever seen outside a zoo or a museum.

In the timber-lands at the fringe of the Barrens, then, is a mining camp; and it is the purpose of the author to turn naked into the wilds a young Canadian engineer of 30 and a wealthy and useless, though somewhat ornamental, New York society girl of 19, as hero and heroine who shall create civilization with its many inventions out of the raw material afforded by Nature. The launching is accomplished by the girl getting caught in the rapids leading out of Barrier Lake while she is fishing in her canoe before breakfast. Grimshaw, the camp-boss, still in his pyjamas, sees her go and rushes to her aid by rowing a York-boat. Now a small York-boat is 30 feet long, carries four tons of freight and a crew of eight to twelve men. Why he did not take one of the other canoes is one of the myriad entrancing mysteries in the book. But single-handed he propels the York-boat down the lake at break-neck speed, and the two of them shoot the seven miles of rapids. The hero is evidently an acrobat too, for his boat springing a leak, he, standing, tossed by the furious waves, removes both parts of his pyjamas to mend the leak. He also 'steers' the drifting boat by means of a sweep, though this is physically impossible. The girl's bathing suit rips and comes off, though such garments usually stand contact with water. Both craft are lost, so the people reach shore at the lower end of the rapids naked and without baggage.

Though they started shortly after dawn, and were hurled down at lightning speed, they reach the bottom of the rapids late in the afternoon. I, having shot a seven-mile rapid in about half an hour, deplore this dilatoriness; but am forced to admire the efficiency and speed of the hero once he is on land. Between, say, 4:30 P.M. and dark he manages to cut and weave clothes for them both out of willow branches; erects a substantial log house and puts a roof on; makes beds out of 'armful after armful of cat-tails'; makes a barricade for the door; catches two fish with his hands – one a five pound maskalonge, not native to that section of the country; makes a bone knife, bark platter and drinking cup; cleans the fish; goes out and inspects timber, climbing uplands to do so; notes bear and moose indications; digs cedar roots, though no cedars grow that far north; collects punk and bird feathers.

The author is careful to tell us that the seven miles of land separating the twain from the camp (where Mr Endicott, Claire's father and Grimshaw's employer, is at the moment) is impassable on account of rock faces and muskeg. As a matter of fact, a long, precipitous rapid could not flow through a muskeg. The walls of the river were high and rocky, and any rock can be scaled or walked around. But the story must go on; hence this mythical screen cutting the castaways off from their kind. And in the book it is three months before an aeroplane can reach them.

Miracles now happen thick and fast. The accomplishment of the first evening is a mere nothing to this superwoodsman, who makes errors in woodlore discreditable to a boy scout. After supper on the first full day in camp, Grimshaw attacks a bull moose of 1,000 pounds weight and actually succeeds in drawing blood by striking it on the neck with his deer-rib knife. The bull is infuriated, as it has every right to be, strikes the man with its 'fore-paws,' knocks him down and jumps on him. An ordinary moose with hard, sharp hoofs would certainly have killed him; but this one, doubtless because equipped by the author with 'paws,' only succeeds in giving him 'a bruise or two' which cause him no trouble. Claire, witnessing the first part of this unequal combat, leaps on the animal's back and 'paralyzes' it by thrusting her wooden, stone-tipped spear through its spine, a moose's spine being about as soft as reinforced concrete sewerpipe. The beast was possibly paralyzed with astonishment, went into hysteria and suffered a nervous breakdown. Anyway, Grimshaw kills it – with the deer-rib. There were two bull moose when Grimshaw came up, but the author makes a concession to realism by telling us that 'the other one got away.' Hardly less wonderful is the episode of a later day when Grimshaw kills a caribou by sticking a spear into her rump.

Of all the necessities, conveniences and sheer luxuries manufactured by the marvellous Grimshaw, it must be remembered that most of them were the products of the first six days' toil. He worked very hard. On the second full day in camp, for instance, he got breakfast of berries and bannocks made of parched bulrush bulbs pounded between stones into flour, and broiled moose meat; rewashed the heavy-haired skin, and laid it out for scraping; split the moosehead and saved the brains; washed and stretched the intestines for fish lines; dug out the precious white sinew along the spine; found the prow of his boat with some iron on it; made wooden, stone-tipped tongs to handle hot metal; made a stone hammer; made a kiln; made charcoal in the kiln; made a forge of stone, chinked with clay; made a bellows for the forge out of moose-hide; made a leg-bone into a draft conductor; got two slabs of tamarack; charred the slabs; resmoked the moose hide over the fire, dressing it with a mixture of fish-fat and brains; drilled holes through the slabs; fixed leg-bone to slat; fitted and sewed discs of moose-hide; finished bellows and forge; made another kiln of charcoal; from the iron he made a chisel, a knife, an axehead, two sewing-awls and a spearhead. Then he called it a day, and laid off!

About two weeks after landing they had plenty of time to build a fine, large log-house, whitewashed and decorated, divided into rooms, having windows, a planed floor, furniture, a brick chimney and bake-oven, and a fireplace of glazed tiles. They possessed two iron table knives, forks and spoons of bone, a razor made from a single 'medium-sized' nail (presumably a wire nail), cups, saucers and plates of glazed earthenware ornamented with colored designs, storage crocks, pails and tubs, wash basins, candles, curtains and rugs, willow chairs, tooth brushes, scented toilet soap, scissors, and the following articles all of solid gold: a comb, hair pins, buttons, a ring and a frying pan the last of which is made out to be a *useful* cooking implement. In the third month preparations for winter were so complete that time hung heavily upon their hands, and one wonders why they did not make a Mah Jongg set, or construct a radio and get the news from home, or even send a message to Dad, seven miles away, telling him where they were.

'In all this world I don't suppose a man and a woman have ever been thrown together as we've been thrown together in this wilderness,' remarks Claire, and I cannot help agreeing with her that the author did throw his characters together somewhat heedlessly. He calls their life 'a splendid crudity,' and spoke more truly than he knew. For within nine days the girl, who had probably never even dressed herself, had become an expert cook, dressmaker, archer, hunter and woodsman. Her first attempt at sewing resulted in the satisfactory cutting-out and making of garments. She eats birch-buds in the fall, though they grow only in spring. She put a fish in a jack-pine to protect it from mink, marten and wolverine, whereas all of them can climb and the marten *lives* in trees. But she was a greenhorn and can be excused for her author's faults.

With Grimshaw the case is different. 'By instinct and training a woodsman ... he preferred to remember only his woodcraft.' The trouble is that he remembers it wrongly so much of the time! Thus, Stringer gravely assures us that he found and used swamp-elm, box-elder, Canada-balsam, wild plums, wild rice, elk, maskalonge, ironwood and cedar, none of which are to be found in that part of Canada – the last three being beyond the margin of possibility by several hundred miles. For the author has fixed his latitude by the introduction of a vast herd of 10,000 to 15,000 caribou, and these are only to be found in these numbers on the Barrens and in the forest at their southern extremity. If Stringer had limited his caribou herd to ten or twelve animals we might suppose they were woodland caribou, which go father south, but even then most of these items would be beyond the geographical limits. Furthermore, he speaks of 'partridge *and* Canada grouse,' evidently ignorant of the fact that the two names are synonymous. His famous woodsman loses his companion in a swamp, notes her steps going in, and goes home thinking she is dead – *without circling the swamp to pick up any out trail,* which any second-rate woodsman would have done. Of course she did emerge on the other side of the swamp. Ignorant of woodlore as he was, Grimshaw might have been sure that Stringer could not afford to spoil the story by letting her die.

After that revelation I am almost ashamed to mention other lapses, such as Claire's coming on a 'slashing' in the primeval forest, where no man had been to cut it. A slain bear is disembowelled first, though the custom is to skin the animal first so that the hide will be kept clean. He does not seem to know that spruce grows in swamps. He refers to a 'tanned' jacket as 'rawhide.' He calls the same beast an elk and a caribou alternately, and knotted tamarack poles turn into hemlock by the same carelessness of pen. And the author's reiterated contention that salt and green vegetables are essential to life is groundless.

'Stretching it' used to be a synonym for the kind of fiction this author has fabricated, and a literal case of it occurs in what the castaways made out of the original moose-hide. It is an elastic substance, but could hardly be 'stretched' to cover more than half of the articles made, which include a 'knee-length,' two-piece suit for Claire, a two-piece suit for Grimshaw 'with trousers that reached almost to his moccasin tops,' moccasins for both with double-ply soles, thongs for rabbit snares, withes and binding-strings for tying clothing, strings for forge tongs, the whole bellows-cover, strings for two bows and sundry fish lines. The same tendency to stretch is found in Grimshaw's hair which, a month after landing, has grown 'half-way to his shoulders.' This feat will enable him to earn his living henceforth with the Seven Sutherland Sisters, for since the appearance of Stringer's book he will have to give up his old profession. In spite of his miracles, no one would hire him as assistant guide after reading of his ignorance of elementary woodlore. His gormandizing in itself is disgusting, for we learn that four days after getting 'several hundred pounds' of meat from the moose, he and Claire are eating the last of it.

Yet, I have a tender spot for him. I see him on that third day clad only in willow sticks – the leaves must all have withered and blown away by that time – standing before his hot forge while the summer sun blistered his skin. The black-flies and mosquitoes would be all over his body having a regular Christmas dinner. The author does not tell us so, but I know the North. The sparks were flying out from the forge and burning him dreadfully. Oh! Why did not the author 'stretch' the moose-skin far enough to make a blacksmith's apron for him? I see him dancing around bare-footed on the hot rocks, burned and blistered all over; and the girl blowing the bellows, and forcing more heat at him. And I am very sorry for poor, ignorant, wonder-working Grimshaw.

But, while they cannot have any respect for the hero, Canadians owe a boundless debt to Mr Stringer. They have writhed for years under the misrepresentations of English and American authors, who have written absurd tales purporting to depict life in the Canadian woods. There was only one way to stop it: to tell such a 'whopper' as to elevate the myth to a place among the great imaginative classics of the world. Stringer has done that. He has 'stretched' credence till it burst asunder and his imagination soared to the heights of the divinely unbelievable. It is a matter for national pride that one of our native authors has made two people 'disappear' down a rapid as Lewis Carroll took Alice down the rabbit-hole, has made his hero slay a moose with the rib of a deer as an earlier fighter slew a thousand Philistines with the jaw-bone of an ass – has, in short, achieved a *tour de force* in that superlative kind of untruth we love under the name of fairy-story, and, at the same time, has erected a monument of unconscious humor. I hereby tender the country's thanks to Arthur Stringingus.

'The Bogey of Annexation,' commissioned by H.L. Mencken, was published in *The American Mercury* in November 1925.

ANY STATEMENT OF the national sentiment at a particular time about any specific question is valueless without knowledge of that nation's history and an understanding of the character of its people. Germany was taken by surprise when England declared war in 1914 because German statesmen had underestimated certain factors. Military unpreparedness, suffragette disturbances, Irish troubles and a dozen indications of domestic and imperial strife pointed to the conclusion, proved utterly false in the event, that Britain would not, and could not, fight. In much the same way the American business man of to-day reads a few snatches from Canadian newspapers, glances at trade and population statistics, takes a squint at the map of North America, and sits back confident that in five or ten years at the most Canada will be applying humbly for admission to the

Union. What he seems slow to realize is Canada's position in the Empire, and real attitude toward it; and the nationalistic sentiments and aspirations of Canadians, which have their roots far back in the 162 years of the country's history as British territory.

After the Seven Years' War, during which Quebec fell to Wolfe in 1759, England was by no means proud of her new possession; instead she was keen to own the little island of Guadeloupe for sugar was just beginning to be an important commodity. France being equally anxious to retain the island – in preference to Canada – a deadlock in the peace negotiations lasted until Benjamin Franklin, who later became Canada's first postmaster-general, pointed out that, while Canada was worthless in itself, it might be dangerous from a military standpoint to have a foreign power situated so near the New England colonies. So Canada became British. The American Revolution hastened the granting to Canada in 1791 of representative government and extensive control of her internal affairs; but George Canning, British foreign minister, was sure that it was only a matter of a few years until Canada would join the revolted colonies, and therefore all attention to Canadian affairs by the British Parliament was a waste of time. This opinion has been held by many Englishmen until quite recent years. When Sir John A. Macdonald and his Canadian associates went to England in 1866 to obtain ratification of their plan for federating the provinces, which included complete autonomy as to internal affairs, their business was treated as of negligible importance. Macdonald compared the progress of the bill granting Canada a national constitution to 'a private bill uniting two or three English parishes.' Sir A.T. Galt, one of the Canadian delegates, said that England was possessed of 'a servile fear of the United States' and would prefer to abandon Canada rather than defend it against that country. Among the English statesmen engaged, Bright and Gladstone were indifferent, while Sir Frederic Rogers merely looked on the federation 'as a decent preparation for divorce.' During the latter part of the 19th century, Toronto was the home of Goldwin Smith, an eminent English essayist and writer on political matters, who had been private tutor to King Edward VII; and no stronger advocate of annexation has ever lived. All of which facts are intended to indicate that the British connection has been maintained by the will of the Canadian people in spite of the apathy, and often gross ignorance, of the English people and their statesmen. Since the late war, Canada has become a land of promise in the minds of the English masses, and Canadian opinion is taken into consideration by the framers of imperial policies at

Westminster; the secession of Canada from the Empire would now be considered a grave matter by the inhabitants of Great Britain; but no one believes that force would be used to prevent Canada leaving if she stated her intention of doing so.

Neither British nor Americans have ever been able to see exactly why Canada has wished to maintain her transmarine connections. Consequently, at her slightest move, her representatives are always having to deny the rumor of her incipient apostasy, which the English have always expected, and latterly feared, and which many Americans have long awaited with the complacent expectancy of a spider watching a fly in the vicinity of its web. That they have both been waiting for over a century does not seem to convince either of them that the event is not imminent, any more than a millennial dawner loses faith in his theory because all previous predictions of the date of the world's end have proved false. When W.L. Mackenzie King, the then premier and a grandson of William Lyon Mackenzie, the leader of the 1837 rebellion, was in London recently, he was kept busy denying the assertions of the London newspapers that Canada was about to withdraw. Sir Robert Falconer, President of the University of Toronto, speaking to the Pilgrim's Club, London, on May 11, 1925 said: 'At one time there was talk [in England] about annexation *because Canada was dragging Britain into North American questions.* Such talk is never heard now, except sometimes among ourselves [Canadians], when people get depressed.' He had gone to England to deliver a course of lectures upon 'The United States as a Neighbour,' so that his remarks were not the idle utterances of a casual after-dinner speaker.

British fears are based upon a misconception of Canadian nationalistic aims and aspirations, American hopes upon ignorance of the historical experiences that over several generations have left upon the Canadian mind a deep impress, which cannot be ignored in a discussion of the likelihood of Canada's union with the United States, since it colors, and at times dominates, the Canadian's political outlook. The history of Canada's constitutional development is a series of steps toward completer autonomy than any part of any previous empire has known. For the last 60 years Canada has been in control of her internal affairs with representative and responsible government and a constitution similar to that of Great Britain, the Governor-General (an English appointee) taking the place of the King as titular head of the Government, and the premier, here as there, being the actual head of both legislative and executive branches. Once or twice Governors-General did not quite understand, and tried to govern; but the last instance of that was a long time ago. At first international relations were theoretically and actually in the hands of Great Britain, but gradually Canada began negotiating directly with the United States and other powers: if a treaty of magnitude resulted, Great Britain signed on behalf of Canada; but a hundred little deals and arrangements have been made without the intervention of Great Britain at all. Need being felt for a Canadian diplomatic representative in Washington, a plan has been devised for such an official, who is to be an appointee of the Canadian government, authorized to substitute for the British Ambassador when Canadian business is forward. It was the United States, however, and not Great Britain, that required this representative to be, nominally, a plenipotentiary of Great Britain.

Canadian nationalism did not begin with the late war: that merely helped to crystallize and reveal it to the world. Canada entered the war hastily, and without stipulations: she took care that in quitting it she did so with due recognition that she had fought as a free nation. She signed the Peace of Versailles and was accorded membership in the League of Nations. Ever since, she has guarded jealously her national status, as her ratification of the Turkish Peace shows. When England had negotiated that peace, a cablegram reached Ottawa demanding Canada's consent to the terms, which were unknown to the Canadian ministers, and in spite of the fact that Parliament was not sitting. To shorten a long and rather humorous story, the Canadian Government, in the face of Great Britain's desire for haste, only ratified peace with Turkey several months later, after debate in the Canadian House of Commons. This whole episode was a significant gesture only. Canada's relations with Turkey are not such that she was vitally interested in the terms; but Canadian statesmen of both parties have long made it plain that Canada will not consider herself bound to assist in the enforcing of treaties in whose making she took no hand. Declarations to this effect were made repeatedly in the House of Commons by Sir Wilfrid Laurier, Liberal Premier, by his successor Sir Robert Borden, Conservative Premier, by Mr Meighen, the Unionist Premier, and by Mr King, Liberal Premier. Thus the last four premiers are agreed upon the principle that Canada can only be bound by her own acts and covenants.

When Sir John A. Macdonald succeeded in federating the provinces, he wished the country called 'The Kingdom of Canada'; and this was only vetoed by British statesmen for fear it would offend American susceptibilies. Had this name been used instead of 'Dominion,' Englishmen would have been quicker to recognize Canada as a sister nation of freemen, entitled to all political liberties and advantages in like measure. Since Canada has never encountered any serious difficulties from England in the attainment of her ambitions, it is altogether likely that the dream of an independent and sovereign state in closest alliance with Great Britain will be realized eventually as the logical conclusion of Canada's steady progress through the various stages of autonomy; and, if so, Great Britain will ultimately find that the bogey of secession was only an imaginary terror, and that she is much better off with a strong, self-reliant ally than she could ever be with a colony, no matter how 'loyal.' But it must never be forgotten that the British connection has been maintained primarily by the will of the Canadian people; and that in speculating as to his country's destiny no Canadian is withheld from advocating independence or annexation out of fear that Great Britain might use military measures to force Canada to remain a part of the Empire.

Goldwin Smith predicted and advocated the annexation of Canada to the United States on the grounds that the natural lines of trade on this continent lay north and south, and that the countries were not divided by language, or by racial origin or creed except in the case of Quebec. In order to have a nation at all it was necessary to build transcontinental railways at great expense, and many of the difficulties which Goldwin Smith foresaw have materialized; but his prophecy remains unfulfilled because sentiment plays a larger part in national affairs than he, and others, were willing to believe. And here we touch the very basis of present popular misconceptions in the United States. For the mention of sentiment will doubtless convey to an American reader a sentimental attitude on the part of the Canadian for the land where his father, or his great-great-grandfather, was born. In reality, this sentiment is far less of a romantic love for the British Isles than the outcome of Canada's relations with the United States.

At the time of the American Revolution, Canada was essentially a French colony England had acquired almost unwillingly: the first important wave of immigration came from the United States, and was made up of people who had been driven from their homes because they were opposed to the Revolution. In the United States they were known as royalists: in Canada they were called Loyalists; and they established a tradition, and founded a national sentiment, which has affected the whole trend of Canadian thought and of which the present Canadian nationalistic movement is a natural outgrowth. They had been assured protection in the revolting colonies; but Alexander Hamilton, yielding to popular demand, confiscated their property: so they came to their new homes with a grudge and a grievance, believing they had been hardly and dishonorably used. About 100,000 of them came in all, settling in the Maritime Provinces, in Quebec and in Ontario. A great proportion represented the old colonial aristocracy, and were persons of wealth and education. Into Nova Scotia alone in the first migration went no less than 200 graduates of Harvard and 200 graduates of other colleges, including the Chief Justice and three out of the four puisne judges of the Superior Court of Massachusetts. They were used to North American life and while they went as exiles, sorrowing for their old homes, they were imbued with a love for free institutions, and early determined to build up in the north the kind of country they had desired to make of the American colonies.

Judge Thomas Chandler Haliburton ('Sam Slick') was the Nova Scotia born son of one of these Loyalists. In a recent biography of him Dr J.D. Logan says: 'The Loyalist *emigrés* of Nova Scotia, even past Haliburton's earlier days, continued to regard the revolutionists of the United States as renegades so inferior to themselves in birth and culture that eventually the vulgar democracy of the United States would of necessity become self-cancered, and the people politically enfeebled. Meanwhile the descendants of the exiled Tory aristocrats would grow into a mighty people in British North America, and this new, strong nation in due season would win over the enfeebled Republic to join with them.'

Since Canada has only one neighbor, all her difficulties have been with the United States in disputes over boundaries, fisheries and other matters. Arbitrations have always given the Republic what Canadians consider the best end of the deal; and they attribute this long list of disappointments not so much to the shrewdness of the American negotiators as to the general willingness of Great Britain's representatives to conciliate the United States without due regard to Canadian interests. Though, happily, there has been no war of aggression against Canada by the United States for 112 years, the Fenian raids during the middle of the last century were looked upon as an unofficial attempt at invasion, and it may be that the numerical superiority of the Americans, and their evident desire for expanded boundaries, caused a mild apprehension as to their ultimate intention respecting Canada.

If any one doubts the power of anti-American sentiment to rouse the Canadian people to precipitate action, he need only review the history of the 'reciprocity' negotiations of 1911 to find proof. The Liberal Government of the day had arranged a tariff deal with the United States so far-reaching that a general election was held to give the

Government its mandate for ratifying the treaty. Most sound financial critics agreed that the terms were fair and promised solid benefits to Canada; but comparatively little fiscal argument was used by Conservative orators, who had only to wave the flag, to hint that this was the thin edge of the wedge in the 'commercial conquest of Canada,' in order to win their audiences. The election resulted in an unprecedented Conservative landslide. Whether Canadian fears were justified is outside the scope of this enquiry, the case being cited merely to show how little economic advantage will weigh with the Canadian voter if he is asked to endorse an annexation policy.

If this phase of the question appears to be overstressed here, it is only because Americans do not seem to understand the situation, and are all too ready to accept at their face value the compliments they are tendered at formal banquets. They see the enormous consumption of American goods, the circulation of American books, magazines and movie films, and calculate hastily that 'the Americanization of Canada' is in its last stage, whereas, if they saw beneath the surface, they would discover a deep, steady resentment of all such 'influences,' which often have precisely the reverse effect of that presumed by Americans. The movie is supposed to be the subtlest, most penetrating, of these influences. In the year following the armistice, the chauvinistic tendency of the Hollywood producers, with their exclusive glorification of the United States soldier, led to such a feeling of revulsion on the part of Canadian 'fans' that Peter McArthur, a prominent Canadian author and journalist, felt impelled to write a book called *The Affable Stranger*, whose avowed purpose was to allay Canadian hatred of the United States. The press has no more staple editorial pabulum than deploring American influence; and more than one serious attempt has been made to secure legislation that would tend to curtail the circulation of American periodicals in Canada.

To obviate misunderstanding, it should be added that the Canadian dislike is for 'Americanism,' and not Americans, who, as *individuals*, are found exceptionally congenial by the average Canadian, who generally finds them more like himself, and therefore easier to understand and get on with than the average Englishman. Large numbers of Canadians and descendants of Canadians are living in American cities, and usually retain their connections with Canada and their sense of Canadian nationality, in contrast to the American settler in Canada who soon loses his identity with the United States; and these expatriate Canadians contribute to the general friendliness that undoubtedly exists between people on both sides of the international boundary.

Canadians also are immensely proud of their 4,000 mile unarmed frontier, and the international goodwill that makes it possible. It is only the aggressive, flag-flapping citizen of the Republic, loudly disdainful of all he sees outside his own country, who fails to find Canadians friendly to him. But it is not this type of American visitor that causes the Canadian to shy instinctively from union. It is the idea of absorption that is repugnant, and not a dislike of ill-bred specimens, and much less of the better class of American citizens, who usually penetrate into this country as tourists or on business. Canada and the United States can be the best neighbor nations the world has ever seen; but they will be more friendly as separate political units, and it is only political fusion that would breed bitterness.

Lately American readers of our journals, and American travellers in Canada, have been unduly impressed by talk of secession of the Maritime Provinces and of the Western Provinces. In the Toronto *Star* of February 21, 1925, more than a page was devoted to a sensational article entitled 'Will Maritime Provinces Quit Canada?' which outlined the grievances of eastern Canadians. Even in the House of Commons some such threat was made, though it was generally interpreted as a bluff to draw attention to the needs of the people along the Atlantic. Picking up a book like *The Canadian Provinces* by John Nelson, the foreign reader would certainly get the impression that the Dominion was divided into sections so alien from each other in aims that unity is non-existent except on paper, and that each section is in somewhat of an impasse, at its wits' end, and taking it for granted that it need not look for help, nor even understanding, to any other section. It is true that the Canadian desires to prosper; it is also true that the distances and the sparsity of population tend to regional rather than national thinking; and it is equally true that all the rumors of provincial secession from the Dominion arise from sectional discontent in money matters. But, as the question is being threshed out, it is asked repeatedly: What have political affiliations to do with it, and in what way could the situation be improved by the secession of any province from the Dominion, or the secession of the Dominion from the Empire, or the affiliation of the Dominion with the United States?

The Canadian pays less in taxes than the resident of Great Britain, but more than the American citizen. The national debt of $3,000,000,000 is accounted for largely by the war, to which has been added very heavy expenditures laid out for the acquiring and maintaining of the Canadian National Railways. Like all tax-payers, everywhere, the Canadian grumbles that he is paying too much. But separation from England certainly would not relieve him of his obligations, and no one in his right mind supposes that the 48 states of the Union would pay his debts – even for the pleasure of his company.

Besides high taxes, which cripple trade to some extent, and certainly cause wide-spread discontent, there has been a business depression following war-time high prices, and intimately connected with the tariff policies of the United States. Nearly a century ago Sam Slick, in satirizing the Nova Scotians, said: 'They buy more nor they sell, and eat more nor they raise.' So far has this condition been left behind that to-day Canada, with a population of 9,000,000, in sheer bulk of imports and exports, stands fourth among the nations of the world and absolutely first on a per capita basis. She has a favorable trade balance, amounting to $264,000,000 for the year ending March, 1925, and she is the only country whose currency has been quoted in New York at a premium over the American dollar since the late war. What, then, is wrong? Canada is dependent upon foreign trade to a surprising degree: she is the greatest raiser of wheat for export of any country on earth, and has the second largest wheat production, having grown 417,000,000 bushels in 1925; and unless she can sell almost all of it abroad there is nothing to do with it. In lesser degree, cattle, forest products, minerals, fish and furs must similarly find foreign markets or go to waste.

Until recent years, the United States bought the bulk of Canada's raw products and sold, in return, the bulk of the manufactured articles that the Dominion imported. In 1921 a prohibitive import tariff on cattle knocked the bottom out of Canada's livestock market in a day, and many cattle-raisers, particularly in the West where winter feeding was too expensive, were ruined overnight. Since then, this industry has recovered, and is said to be on a sounder footing than ever as stock men have learned to find markets elsewhere. The Fordney tariff, with its rate of 42¢ a bushel on Canadian wheat, caused momentary consternation in the Canadian West, but as the American millers had to have the harder northern grain for mixing with the softer American wheat to make high grade flour, and as the millers arranged for a rebate of the duty if the Canadian grain was exported from the United States as American flour, the shipping south of wheat continued, and prices in the winter of 1924-25 were higher in Winnipeg than in Chicago. (In 1925-26 Winnipeg prices were below Chicago's.) But the warning had been taken and Canadian grain dealers have sought and are finding satisfactory markets elsewhere. The tax of 3¢ a pound on Canadian fish is too recent to yield much data. Whether a perishable commodity, like fish, can be shipped satisfactorily to far lands is doubtful.

It all looks to the Canadian as though the United States were trying to slam the door in his face. Already Canada's trade statistics show the effect of the changed American attitude. Canada remains the United States' second-best customer, but the United States is no longer Canada's best customer since her exports to the rest of the Empire for the year ending March, 1925, amounted to $466,000,000 as against $416,000,000 to the United States. Should Canada place an embargo on the export of her pulpwood, it would make a still greater difference. During the year ending March 31, 1925, Canada's exports to Great Britain increased by $35,000,000, and imports decreased by $2,000,000. In the same period Canada's exports to the United States decreased by $13,000,000 and imports decreased $90,000,000. In so far as trade is concerned as a factor in the hypothesis of annexation, Canada and the United States instead of drawing nearer together seem to be getting farther apart; and many thoughtful Canadians welcome this – despite temporary inconveniences – as a sign that their nation's prosperity does not depend to so great an extent upon conditions in any one foreign country; though these figures must be taken with reserve because they are partly the result of the prosperity of branch factories located in Canada by American firms, financed by American capital and established to take advantage of the lower tariff on Canadian goods in European countries. Some of these branch factories are huge affairs; and it is obvious that the interests of the parent firms require Canada to remain a separate country that they may continue to enjoy advantages as exporters over the parent factories in the United States.

Here the question arises of the United States opposition to the annexation of Canada. Were the latter country taken into the Union it would not be possible to maintain tariff walls against its products. The same producer of grain, cattle, fish and what-not, who now fears Canadian competition, and is powerful enough to persuade Congress to pass Fordney tariffs, will undoubtedly have something to say if he is told that Canada is to be annexed and the Canadian producer placed on a parity with himself. To be specific, the New England fisherman will not relish Nova Scotia fish flooding the American cities. Arable lands in the prairie states are worth several times what equally fertile lands are selling for across the boundary. If that boundary is abolished there is going to be a levelling: Canadian land is going up, and American land is going down. There is no doubt that annexation would make Canadians wealthy who are now only potentially rich; but that profit would be at the immediate expense of American citizens. Then American tourists, and boot-leggers and their customers, who now appreciate their opportunity for getting liquor in Canada, would be as opposed to annexation as any province would be to find itself automatically under the Volstead Law [American Prohibition Legislation 1919].

Returning now to the discontent in the east and west of Canada, it may be doubted whether any section of the Dominion could make a better trade deal for itself than the Dominion as a whole, with all its resources, has been able to make. A prominent New Brunswicker recently told me that his neighbors' troubles were being laid to Confederation whereas they really are due to geographical situation and other natural causes. The Atlantic Provinces, being largely settled by Loyalists, would be more inclined to seek to re-unite with their kinsmen in case of a breach with the Dominion than the West would, despite the ancient and deep-rooted prejudice of the Bluenose against the Yankee. In the West, the secession talk is quieter but more serious. These newer provinces have always felt that they did not receive sufficient consideration from Ottawa for their sectional needs, but as they grow more populous their representation increases and they obtain more and more legislative power, and thus outgrow their suspicion that 'the East,' as they call the central provinces of Ontario and Quebec, is making a mere convenience of them. That there is secession talk in the West is true, but practically none of annexation: the complaint of the westerner is against the moderate tariff schedules Canada now maintains, and if joined to the United States he would find himself under much higher tariffs, which would raise greatly the cost to him of English and other foreign goods. Annexation talk anywhere in Canada can only be safely interpreted in the light of history: it is heard whenever there is a period of hard times, and dies down as soon as confidence is restored. Those who remember the serious annexation agitations of 1891-92 simply laugh at the rumors of the past year or so. The 1925 edition of *Chambers's Encyclopaedia* does not exaggerate when it states: 'The question of annexation is dead, and few Canadians expect ever to see it revived.'

Americans settled in Canada are seldom annexationists. Many of them are successful farmers in the West, and many have risen to prominence in business in the central provinces; but having become used to Canadian laws and customs, they are usually well satisfied with their adopted country and seldom express a desire for the merging of the two countries. The Canadianized American of the central provinces in his private as well as his public life is apt to be more emphatic than the native-born in his repudiation of annexation. The type who is most apt to favor it is the English-born Canadian.

Despite adverse tariffs and high taxes, sectionalism and other ills, nationalistic feeling never ran so high as at present. Everywhere organizations of all kinds are springing up with the aim of establishing and maintaining better relations between the different parts of the country. The English and French are paying each other visits and compliments: everyone is determined that there shall be a better understanding between Canadians of all classes and localities, and that the unity of which the British North America Act was but an adumbration shall become immediately a firmer reality. That awakening of the national spirit is the outstanding fact about Canadian life to-day; and in the face of it talk about annexation is the idlest gossip to the majority of citizens, and those who do talk secession will be silent as soon as they feel that their interests as individuals or communities are not being sacrificed to the benefit of others.

Quebec is strongly national in sentiment. Under the constitution the French-Canadian is guaranteed his language, his religion, and his hereditary civil law – the Code Napoleon is in force. Who dreams that the Constitution of the United States would be amended to give special sanction to the Roman Catholic Church and the French language in an area as large as several goodsized states? Would the habitant care to come under the rule of the Invisible Empire? The unpopularity of the French-Canadians in the New England states, where they have penetrated in great numbers, is due to their habit of working in American factories until they have secured a competence, and then retiring to their ancestral acres. Thousands of French girls go south to earn their trousseaux, and return home to be married. With the negro problem, and all the other problems on its hands, Congress will be as slow to undertake a French-Canadian problem as the habitants would be to part with one tittle of their ancient rights.

Canadians may be 'slow,' but they have been impressed by the number of murders in Chicago, and the number of lynchings in the South, and the goings on of the Ku Klux Klan; and they show a marked partiality for their own system of the administration of justice, with its speedier, simplified court procedure, under judges appointed (not elected) for life, and so independent of political influences and affiliations. They seem perfectly content to go a little slower if their way can be more serene than what they see of American life – and it should not be forgotten that Canadians have visited the States in greater proportion than Americans have visited Canada, and through a hundred media are more conversant with American life and history and institutions, than Americans are with Canadian.

'Canada first' is the cry of the hour, and that may lead in time to theoretical independence in addition to the de facto independence that is already here. Except at Canada's request, Westminster would no more think of legislating for Canada than Washington would. The British connection, moreover, has been valuable financially, and in a military way, and in connection with immigration, which is Canada's greatest present need. It has been wholly beneficial, and is therefore clung to, because it has enabled the younger country to grow and find its feet without undue parental restraint. And for these benefits Canada was grateful enough to leave 52,000 dead on the battlefields of France out of half a million who served overseas. But it may happen that at the councils of Empire Canadian interests will be found to conflict with those of Great Britain, and if no compromise can be found, it might be expedient for Canada quietly to withdraw. It would be no 'throwing off of the yoke' but a friendly dissolution of partnership leaving each merely the freer.

Mr John S. Ewart, a celebrated lawyer and political writer of Ottawa, used to publish the 'Kingdom Papers' discussing Canada's national status, and reminiscent of Sir John A. Macdonald's old wish that Canada's true position in the Empire – mutual allegiance to one sovereign with Great Britain – be indicated by the name the Kingdom of Canada. It is significant that Mr Ewart has re-commenced publication for the first time since the war, and has re-christened his pamphlets 'The Independence Papers,' feeling now that trouble will be avoided if the remaining political link is severed before any difficulty arises.

My own feeling is that annexation could only be a live topic after Canada had become in every respect independent. Canadian susceptibilities are often wounded by the failure of the United States to recognize Canada as a separate political entity – as at the Pacific Conference at Washington, which had its origin in a debate in the Canadian House of Commons, and to which Canada, though vitally interested, was not invited by the United States, and in whose deliberations Canada only participated through the courtesy of Great Britain, whose interests were not, in all respects, identical with those of Canada and the United States. As an important part of the British Empire, Canada will never consider becoming a subservient part of the United States. Should events lead to Canadian independence, some understanding with her one neighbor would naturally be a necessity, though organic union would hardly be desirable to either nation.

It is interesting to quote Haliburton again to show how little

Canadian views have changed in a century, for he believed independence preferable for the Canadian provinces to annexation. Recently *The Listening Post*, a magazine published at Montreal, printed an article favoring annexation and purporting to be written by an American. The editor attached a note disclaiming the views of his contributor. His next issue contained the editor's apology, and three out of the many vigorous protests he had received in reply – all condemning the annexationist's platform. So far as I can learn no other paper even mentioned the controversy. That significant ignoring of *The Listening Post*'s challenge indicates how little Canadians think of the idea of annexation.

'Literature in Canada – in Its Centenary Year' was written for Bertram Brooker's *Yearbook of the Arts in Canada* (Toronto: Macmillan 1929).

WHILE CANADA WAS MOURNING for Bliss Carman, her best loved poet, who died at his home in New Canaan, Connecticut, June 8, 1929, and critics in Winnipeg and Toronto, surrounded by unprecedented literary activity from coast to coast, were duelling with each other over whether or not there is a Canadian literature – the gong struck. The first century was over. For, in Halifax, one hundred years ago, Joseph Howe published the first book of Thomas Chandler Haliburton, *An Historical and Statistical Account of Nova Scotia*. By an accepted definition, a work or author that survives for a hundred years may fittingly be styled 'immortal.' Several recent editions of Haliburton's works – not only *Sam Slick*, but *The Mail Bag*, and other writings also – attest his continued popularity. And since our first 'immortal' has proved up the full century, we may say that Canada's literature has a century of history.

The death during the year of Dr J.D. Logan, author of *Highways of Canadian Literature*, the first comprehensive survey thereof, prevents that vehement and much missed critic from arguing, as he surely would have done if alive, that the beginning was made in 1828, with Howe's publication of his own book of descriptive essays, *Western Rambles*, which Dr Logan called 'the foundation of an independent prose literature in Canada.' If so, Canadian literature is 101 years old. But Howe's essays are, regrettably, out of print. Besides, his greater title to fame is as statesman, while Haliburton, though an able judge, is remembered almost exclusively as a man of letters. Hence the more conservative, and therefore more Canadian, view would indicate 1929 as the centenary year of Canadian literature.

Nor is Ontario as far behind as some historians have implied, since this year is also the hundredth birthday of its oldest publishing house, the Ryerson Press. In 1829 Egerton Ryerson, in his fight with the Family Compact over education, decided it was needful to print independent textbooks. He got twenty members of his party to promise $100 each for the purpose. Of these, seventeen paid up. With the $1,700 in his pocket, Ryerson mounted his horse and set off for New York. There he bought a printing press, which he brought to Toronto on the backs of horses, and set it up and commenced business. No memorable works of native authorship were printed there in its early years; but with the impetus felt during the latter half of the nineteenth century and the first decade of the twentieth, the majority of Canadian books of merit were issued under its imprint.

Last year Vilhjalmur Stefansson, Canadian explorer and humorist, published *The Standardization of Error*, in which he said: 'The philosophers of the Middle Ages demonstrated both that the earth did not exist and also that it was flat. To-day they are still arguing about whether the world exists, but they no longer dispute about whether it is flat.' Just so, Mr J.M. Elson of Toronto, author of the novel, *The Scarlet Sash*, and Mr Thomas B. Roberton, literary editor of the *Manitoba Free Press* and author of the pungent book of historical essays, *The Fighting Bishop*, may go on quarrelling as long and as noisily as they please over whether or not there is such a thing as Canadian literature; but neither of them, nor any one else, can deny that it is now a hundred years old.

Looking down that long avenue of time, one sees Major John Richardson, our first native-born novelist, after making a reputation in London and Paris, returning to Canada, here trying futilely to make a living by writing; and then going to New York in 1852, selling his beloved dog to buy his last meal, and lying down to die of starvation because he was too proud to beg. One sees Anna Jameson and Susanna Moodie, pioneer settlers and pioneer writers. One notes James de Mille and Sara Jeannette Duncan opening the way for Peter McArthur and Stephen Leacock. Till finally, in 1877, William Kirby's *The Golden Dog* revealed the richness of the treasure-house of material the native writer has in the romantic history of our country.

But shortly before publication of *The Golden Dog*, an equally significant voice had whispered. Charles Mair, in 1868, had put out a slim book called *Dreamland and Other Poems*. Mair, whose memory will always be associated with the early days of the settlement of the

Canadian Northwest, was a poet of ability, who was peculiarly dedicated to the ideal of nationalism. He praised the native flowers; he wrote a poetic drama around the Indian warrior Tecumseh. He was almost the first really to see the landscape that met his eyes; and he loved it. He held also in his heart a clear image of the united nation that was to be. Therefore he became the forerunner of the most portentous aggregation of genius of the first century. When the vibrant, prophetic tones of the twenty-year-old Charles G.D. Roberts rang out in 1880, proclaiming:

> O Child of Nations, giant limbed,
>   Who stand'st among the nations now
> Unheeded, unadorned, unhymned,
>   With unanointed brow –

letters became, as they must always remain, a decisive formative factor in the life of Canada.

To that noble group, which included Bliss Carman, Archibald Lampman, Charles G.D. Roberts and Duncan Campbell Scott, we owe not only the homage their writings demand, but also that the profession of letters is held in whatever small degree of honour it actually is held in this country. They and their associates are called the Group of '61 because they were all born between 1860 and 1862, both years inclusive. They were all poets; and in a manner analogous to Tennyson's overshadowing of English literary life in the nineteenth century, the Group dominated Canadian letters for forty-five years, until, by 1925, the up-push of vigorous young talent attracted the public's interest, though it did not alienate the public's affection from its old idols. The present accomplishment of literary genius to-day in Canada, and the greater promise of a fine flowering to-morrow, are from seeds planted by Howe and Haliburton a century ago, and watered and cultivated from the past half century by the Group of '61.

Of that group, Bliss Carman was the best known and most popular, as well as the supreme lyric voice, and most picturesque figure. His death on the hundredth birthday of Canadian literature creates the most dramatic moment in our literary history. Born of United Empire Loyalist stock at Fredericton, N.B., in 1861, he traced descent from Ralph Waldo Emerson. Graduating with a gold medal from the University of New Brunswick in 1881, he took post-graduate courses at Edinburgh and Harvard. For a time he taught under Dr (later Sir) George Parkin; but in 1890 went to New York to take up his literary career. For some years he was connected with leading magazines – notably the *Outlook*, as assistant editor under Dr. Lyman Abbott – and was a prolific contributor of verse to all sorts of periodicals. After a time, he was able to devote himself exclusively to creative work. Many honours came to him from many quarters – from, for example, the universities of California, McGill and Oxford. In 1927 the Royal Society of Canada awarded him the Lorne Pierce Gold Medal for distinguished service to Canadian literature; and in 1928 appeared *The Oxford Book of American Verse*, which he had been commissioned to compile as a representative American poet. Though he lived in the United States for the last forty years of his life, his lanky figure, genial smile and uniquely wide felt hat became familiar on the streets of Canadian cities during his last decade, as he went about filling recital engagements.

Beginning with *Low Tide on Grand Pré*, which came out in 1893, the list of his published volumes is exceptionally long. His production continued unabated to the end, *Wild Garden* being issued only a few weeks before his death. As a melodist he ranks with the best of his contemporaries using the English language. Quite naturally, the intellectual content of his work seldom equalled its lyric grace. He published four volumes of essays to explain his philosophy; but as he was essentially a mystic, and as his utterances were therefore emotional and intuitive, rather than the result of reason, they do not rank with his poetry, which was his logical vehicle. In so far as his attitude towards the universe may be styled a philosophy, it was a simple pantheism, made harmonically lovely. From first to last he never wearied of expressing his central perception of the unity existing between God, man and nature, which we find, decked with characteristic artistry, in *Vestigia*:

> I took a day to search for God,
> And found Him not. But as I trod
> By rocky ledge, through woods untamed,
> Just where one scarlet lily flamed,
> I saw his footprint in the sod.

Carman has left to the country of his birth a bountiful legacy of beautiful lyric poetry. He won a place in the literature of the Anglo-Saxon peoples. His death in the centenary year suggests forcibly that the time has come to drop the old and empty controversy as to whether there is a Canadian literature. There has been much pettiness on both sides of this idle dispute. Common sense demands that the books, now issued in quantities, by novelists, poets, essayists, playwrights, historians and humorists from all parts of the Dominion, be designated literature. Since many of them reflect the spirit of the country, or some section of it or class in it, no other definition is available except Canadian literature. No literature worthy of preservation has anything to fear from criticism, no matter how misdirected; and only an unhealthy sense of inferiority would prompt a reply to the wholesale condemnation, which has been often heard in recent years.

For example, in defence of Canadian literature's right to exist (surely an inalienable right!) Mr Robert J.C. Stead some five years ago said, in the course of his inaugural address as President of the Canadian Authors Association, that a Canadian book was like a Ford car, lowly, yet meeting a certain demand. Such humility deserves a reward to itself among the beatitudes; but the analogy fails because the purchaser of the Ford is restrained by lack of cash from getting anything better, while poor books and good ones cost exactly the same price. From arguments on this level let us free ourselves.

What is of profit to discuss is just how good or how bad contemporary Canadian literature is, the causes of defects and shortcomings, and the probabilities for improvement. And it must be admitted that the productions of the past year contain altogether too many specimens that justify the simile of the Ford car, though of course not Mr Stead's reasoning based thereon. He might have gone further and compared a large proportion of Canadian books to second-hand Fords, not in best state of repair. But that is more or less true of any contemporary literature; and the only disquieting feature is the relative lack of compensating Packards at the other end of the scale. We could stand countless failures and misfits if only we might see materializing about us the masterpieces a young, vigorous country has a right to expect about this distance from its historical beginnings.

No masterpiece, in the most exalted sense of that term, was produced in the year 1928-29. Of the twenty-six books sufficiently well done, or of enough importance, to merit consideration in an annual survey, only four seem, at this writing, to possess quality and significance in such a degree as to make them outstanding works beyond any cavil. Professor George M. Wrong, after a lifetime of study on a period that is peculiarly well documented, and which dozens of historians have explored, published *The Rise and Fall of New France*, which combines literary charm with historic accuracy. The factor, however, which chiefly gives this book both its interest and its value is the originality of the approach, since the author views the settlement of

French Canada always in the light of contemporary European events, and as the complex result of world happenings. In a similar but smaller way, since he was dealing with a single individual, Professor W.T. Waugh's *James Wolfe, Man and Soldier* is a delightfully graphic biography, written to the novel thesis that Wolfe's limitations and defects as a human being in early life evolved, with the advancement of his career, into his most conspicuous professional virtues, and brought him to a final, rich fulfilment, the instrument having accomplished the purpose for which it was forged. In both cases, the authors' powers have been interpretative rather than creative.

In the novel, Miss Mazo de la Roche's *Whiteoaks of Jalna*, which is an enlargement and refinement of her earlier book rather than a sequel to it, establishes her as the ranking Canadian novelist. Her skill in character delineation, which is the essence of the true comic genius, has made of her family chronicle a robust patch of imaginary life, beside which Frederick Philip Grove's *Our Daily Bread* seems to remind us that its author's arid view of a western family comes as much from the Scandinavian tradition as from the prairie life he is observing. Factually, Mr Grove's realism can no more be challenged than Miss de la Roche's romance should be. Disregarding her wider range emotionally, and greater variety of types, the difference between them is that one picture is made up of hard lines in severe black and white, the other is coloured. The one has strength, the other vitality. Both have real art; but Miss de la Roche's alone has, naturally, a resilience that marks it as the genuine native product. After ten years of almost steady progress, Miss de la Roche occupies a unique place in Canadian literature as a creative artist.

Morley Callaghan's perfection in his own technique of direct, objective narration is at least a portent. His emergence as a novelist and short story writer is an event. His absorption in the hitherto almost neglected drab and sordid side of Canadian life may have wider consequences than the development of his individual career as an author, which will certainly not be commensurate with his gifts unless he learns to see life with a more penetrating eye than that of a police reporter. While the critic exceeds his function in dictating subject matter to the creative writer, criticism would be renegade to its responsibilities towards this brilliant debutant if it did not point out that Mr Callaghan has neither in *Strange Fugitive* nor in *A Native Argosy* said anything much that justifies the skill with which he says it. The effectiveness with which he uses words is an object lesson. May he get an idea to match his craftsmanship.

Of the remaining twenty-two, each has something commendable

about it, and some are very good; but each has some lack or limitation – perhaps self-imposed – which precludes it from being placed unreservedly among the first rate. Possibly the material was excellent but the writing was lacking in finish or distinction, as in Henry John Moberly's *When Fur was King* and Katherine Hughes' *Father Lacombe*, both of which are historically valuable and intrinsically interesting. Norman Gregor Guthrie's poems, *Flake and Petal*, however, show this chromatic lyrist at the peak of his form; he has a fine, controlled poetic style; but there is nothing in his book that is big with the spaciousness of Duncan Campbell Scott's *On the Height of Land*, nor yet any reflection of experience emotionally profound with the moving quality of Scott's *Spring on the Mattagami*. So we might go on.

It is not good enough. As the record of the centenary year, it is not nearly good enough. The absence of impressive books, on large themes adequately treated, and striking in their power or beauty, is the most notable and most regrettable fact about the present state of Canadian literature. The deprecatory critics of the school of Mr T.B. Roberton and the late Mr Fred Jacob are justified in their generous use of the word 'mediocre' as to scarcity of monumental works, of those peak performances by which a national literature is always hastily judged. What such critics have uniformly omitted to credit is the relatively high average of merit in Canadian writing. We are totally free of anything to correspond to the servant girl brand of fiction emanating in quantities from England, and almost as free from the cheap, machine-made crime, love and adventure stories of the lower-grade, commercialized United States literature. What we have struck is a comfortable, dignified, midway course between the best and worst, with a few deviations upwards or downwards, descending to literary atrocities as seldom as we climb to world-commanding eminences. But in all the arts the second rate is doubtful merchandise, and the fourth rate cannot be tolerated.

Condemnation should not descend upon the authors who, if they are not doing their artistic best, are expressing in a negative way the limitations of perception and sympathy imposed on them by the society in which they live. Canadians have been called 'a debt-paying people'; and the phrase is shrewd in pithy appraisal. Canadians are a conventional people; their innate conservatism is their outstanding trait. Till recent years, they called it 'remaining British,' and shunned the new-fangled outlook and ways of those vulgar Americans. But since the war it has become disturbingly evident that Britain is now the more liberal in theory and practice, and the English example is repudiated. A socialistic government is a fact in Westminster, but no more possible at

Ottawa than at Washington. Free speech of the most inflammatory kind is permitted in London, but public meetings of communists are suppressed as ruthlessly in Canada as the United States custom is to stamp out minority opinion. When London entertains the congress of the World League for Sexual Reform, Canadians can only shake their heads.

Such conservatism makes for solidity; the danger is stolidity. Art was ever at war with the conventions. The ambition, originality and daring that Canadian literature chiefly lacks must be attributed primarily to a distrust of the novel and spectacular instilled into the native author from birth by his environment. Painter and musician can experiment, and if the public protests, they can, and do, say that this is art, which they know all about and the common man knows nothing about; and, faced with a mystery, the common man subsides pathetically until the innovation is established, or has been dropped as a worthless fad. Because literature, through use of words, is more closely united to work-a-day life than the other arts, the author cannot take refuge behind a mystery. He may not say that his audience must not be expected to comprehend his work, since its essence is the conveyance of ideas by intelligible words – the more lucid the better.

Should the creative impulse or the lure of ideas tempt the native author to infringe the national taboos, his work is received coldly, and he is admonished in the name of literary criticism. Under the somewhat meaningless title of *The Gleaming Archway* Mr A.M. Stephen of Vancouver put out a sound, realistic-romantic novel of labour troubles on the Pacific Coast, uniting a love interest with scenes from the underworld of the water-front. It was a creditable book. Having had the temerity to introduce a police spy, of the type which are used as stool-pigeons by all police forces everywhere, he was rebuked in a printed review by Mr John W. Garvin: 'No, No! Our Government and the Mounties are too wise to employ such a degenerate, and they should not be libelled even in fiction.' Consequently the novel was summed up as 'unreal' and 'unconvincing.' This innocent, if puerile, faith in the purity of governments and the saintliness of policemen is a typical expression of the reactionary spirit of Canada. That it should come from Mr Garvin, who has the interests of Canadian literature at heart, is shocking; and proves the insidious nature of this taint. Instead of speaking for literature, for art, and for its freedom to report, and within limits to invent, this literary man of some standing must voice mob prejudice under the guise of criticism.

On its appearance, *Whiteoaks of Jalna*, the outstanding imaginative work of the year, was greeted thus by the Toronto *Globe*: 'Here is a sequel to Jalna, the novel which won the $10,000 *Atlantic Monthly* prize in 1927. The victory brought many congratulations, modified by regret that sordid happenings had been included in the plot. Were the Whiteoaks typical inhabitants of rural Ontario? Did Canada wish to be judged by such characters? There was a widespread opinion that Canada did not ... The story (*Whiteoaks of Jalna*) closes in sordid depression, Finch, the unworthy, in possession of the fortune ... The pages are marked with many bits of fine writing, but it is fortunate that the characters described are not typical of Ontario.' This pious self-congratulation is positively Biblical in its unction, reminding one of the parable of the prayer of the Pharisee, who raised his eyes to heaven and prayed aloud: 'I thank thee that I am not as other men, unjust, extortioners, or even as this poor publican.' The only inference the author can draw is that the morality of her characters and the patriotism of her aim – the representation of her countrymen as sinless – is of more importance than any and every artistic consideration.

Even on that basis, poor Finch was in no sense 'unworthy.' To the normal awkwardness of a half-grown boy was added the ineptitude of a budding genius. He was a musician in the making – sensitive and impressionable. Naturally, he lacked the bourgeois virtues of self-assurance, tightfistedness and commercial astuteness; and, equally naturally, he was despised by his brothers. For a 'critic' also to misunderstand, despise and abuse him is not natural; for one of the distinctions of a real critic is that, by instinct and experience, he understands the artistic nature better than others can, and consequently has more sympathy with it. It is barely conceivable that Miss de la Roche might be censured for being unduly romantic in the act of poetic justice of giving the legacy to Finch, who needed it most, and whose life was going to be of more importance to the world than that of all his brothers put together. It is not conceivable that any one having the faintest glimmer of comprehension of art could think of Finch as 'unworthy.' Such stupid, irrelevant comment must be having a very bad effect upon Canadian writers, since instances of similar lack of intelligent sympathy toward artistic literary endeavour could be multiplied indefinitely from the printed opinions on Canadian books, made by those in Canada who have assumed the powers and privileges of critics, while alien to the spirit that animates true criticism.

Greatest of the national taboos is that against sexual irregularity. In all countries and eras, the story-teller has found in love his most frequent theme, and in adultery the readiest and most natural device for complicating his plot. In this, the great story-tellers from Homer to Hardy are more at one than on any other point except that there must be a story to tell. But the Canadian author does not find favour at home by following the practice. Canadians read such books in about the same proportions as inhabitants of other countries; but the tolerance extends only to importation, sale and consumption, not to manufacture. Hypocrisy is no more implied than in American consumption of Canadian whisky under prohibition. That nation does not wish to give sovereign sanction to alcohol, and legislates against it, while permitting the illegal purchase and use by individuals. Canada, as a society, fervently hopes that no native writer will so far forget himself as to compose anything like *Jude the Obscure*, *The Scarlet Letter*, or *Tom Jones*, while allowing the free sale of the works of Mr Arnold Bennett, Miss Ellen Glasgow, Miss Mary Webb and Mr Theodore Dreiser.

Hence Mr Louis Arthur Cunningham horrified his own city of St John, New Brunswick with his well-written tale of a St John prostitute, entitled *This Thing Called Love*. Regardless of artistry – and this novel, incidentally, shows a great advance from his previous *Yvon Tremblay* – Mr Cunningham is storming the triple-barred gate of a national prejudice. Had his drama been as good as Shakespeare's *Antony and Cleopatra*, or as Shaw's *Caesar and Cleopatra*, it would have met the same fate at home – of pained silence. In this respect Mr Barney Allen's *They Have Bodies* entirely failed as a radical gesture, since he had, in his passion-ridden Canadian business man, a real story, which can be faintly discerned beneath the gibberish of his 'stream of consciousness' technique, the limitations of which he illustrated with unconscious humour, instead of delivering his story.

Effectively barred by social disapproval from the serious, faithful treatment of love, especially in its carnal aspect, or from social or political studies of a liberal nature, the Canadian novelist is thrown back upon the historic novel of the French regime, which has now become a mere costume novel, with dummy actors and stock trappings, since Sir Gilbert Parker started by imitating Kirby and continued by imitating himself; and later practitioners in a more and more diluted way imitate Parker. Religion – another vital matter – is likewise barred, except in such a state of antiquated orthodoxy as to be too dull to attract readers. Canadians do very well in animal and nature fiction; and Miss L.M. Montgomery and Mrs Ethel Hume Patterson succeed admirably in stories for 'teen age girls. Mr John Herries McCulloch, in *The Splendid Renegade*, with Scotch canniness avoided all the obstacles and pitfalls, and retold the life of John Paul Jones freshly and competently. Mr C.H.J. Snider and Professor Archibald MacMechan, from the safe harbour of nautical archives, issued collections of narratives of marine adventure off Nova Scotia in the earlies[sic]. *Under the Red Jack* told stories of the 1812 privateers with gusto; *There Go the Ships* was more varied in subject matter, and was pervaded with the charm of an accomplished essayist.

It is of some interest that Mr Maurice Constantin-Weyer's *A Man Scans his Past* won the Goncourt Prize for 1929, since the scene is the Canadian West, of which the author, who is a Frenchman, was a resident for twelve years prior to 1914. His drama, stripped to essentials, moves in sharp relief against impressively spacious backgrounds, like men walking across trackless snow. His method is in one of the best French traditions; and his novel might be useful as a model in Canada, except that his plot concerns one of the subjects practically forbidden to the Canadian author.

A few new things have been attempted during the year, which are in varying degrees encouraging. Hon. Martin Burrell's *Betwixt Heaven and Charing Cross* was the first collection of book reviews by a Canadian critic to be printed; and it is abundantly apparent that a strong native criticism is obviously required. For the first time in Canada that modern mood in verse, which blends flippancy and cynicism with poignancy and wistfulness, was expressed with wit and fine feeling by Joseph Easton McDougall in *If You Know What I Mean*. Professor Watson Kirkconnell was also an innovator with his elegiac exercise, *European Elegies*, wherein one hundred poems on death and bereavement were translated metrically from fifty languages. Mr J.W.L. Forster's autobiographical *Under the Studio Light* is the first record of its kind by a Canadian painter. Mr Raymond Knister deserves credit for his compilation of *Canadian Short Stories*. Some of his own have been highly artistic. His novel, however, *White Narcissus*, is tame in tone and unambitious in scope, after the manner of most Canadian fiction, for reasons assigned above. His debut, nevertheless, should be noted. He has it in him.

The issue of Mr Arthur Stringer's volume of poems *A Woman at Dusk*, which was quite the best thing of the year in verse, brings up a sad reminder of his defection, which borders on the tragic. If there is one thing this generation of Canadian writers needs besides freedom in choice and treatment of subject, and criticism directed to artistic merit, it is leadership. The best Canadian writers of the moment are nearly all young, scattered, and without a single senior and established, yet practising man of letters to perform the indefinable function, subtle yet pregnant, that results from the existence of a commanding figure. Mr Stringer's early work proved his ability; his presence and personality precisely fitted him for this high office in our generation. His turning his back on Canada to write pot-boiling fiction in New York may have been his privilege; but it deprived the country of his birth of an influence it can ill afford to be without. Canada needed Mr Stringer. The loss of him is irreplaceable.

Canadian authors must therefore look to themselves to remedy existing conditions, with the discriminating aid of the younger critics. It is no mere platitude to say that the future of Canadian literature is in their hands. In the interests of its development, they must stand together for mutual encouragement and support, with a view to the stimulation of artistic work, not for financial ends, not for the commercial promotion of the mediocre, of which there is too much already, but for the production of the excellent, of which there is hardly any. They must face the fact of an apathetic public at home, that gets panicky at the notion of such intellectual freedom as the writers of other countries enjoy, and every writer needs. They must meet the ingrained opposition and overcome it – bravely, manfully, not by sneaking off to avoid a clash with public taste or prejudice, but by daring to say the thing their hearts feel and their artistic consciences dictate.

In that struggle, which must take place before a literature worthy of the country can be written, it is the duty of every writer to take a real interest in what other Canadian writers are doing. As now they do not. It is rare to see one Canadian author with another Canadian author's book in his hand. They read English, American, French or German works to the almost total exclusion of those produced under the same difficulties as those under which they themselves work. Whitman has a wise line that 'poems distilled from poems pass away.' Altogether too much Canadian literature is written with an eye on an American or English book, too little with an eye on the life around the author, too little with an ear open to his own inner promptings. Neither English nor American views, habits of mind, nor tricks of pen will yield a worthy Canadian literature. It must be autochthonous, springing from this soil, evolving naturally its own forms, mental attitudes and emotional states. Therefore, new standards and criteria of values must be evolved, and for this reason, as well as mutual aid, the Canadian author must study his fellow-countrymen's books with care, even when they fall short of mastery.

The function of the critic is to be judicial among authors; but as it is the place of a judge to explain fine points to the jury, so it is the duty of the critic to be primarily interpretative as far as concerns that wider jury, which is the reading public – especially in view of the general misunderstanding in Canada of the rights and responsibilities of literature, directed, since they will the most readily realize the nature of the task, and the necessity for it. At the moment of writing, Mr D.M. De C. Legate has been appointed to relieve Mr S. Morgan-Powell of a considerable portion of the burden of his book page in the Montreal *Star*; and it is on the wide-awakeness and integrity of him, and of other very young men who will be entering this kind of work, that we must rely for the critical complement to the authors' own labours for the improving of conditions that are now far from satisfactory. The public will respond, because it is a docile and 'following' sort of public.

Canadians have demonstrated in many other walks of life that their brains are as good as anybody's. They can have a first rate national literature if they want it, and will invest the requisite intelligence and resolution. Freedom of expression is a pre-requisite. In view of a national psychological condition that is unfavourable to them, the writers will have to fight for that freedom; but they can overcome the handicap if they will stand by each other courageously, in the name of an artistic ideal.

Coming into the second century is like passing through an open door. Beyond is the open country. There are no roads. They must be made. They can be made well or ill, and may be made to lead anywhere. There is talent enough if there is dedication enough. Craven fear must be left behind, and the best intelligence must be used, if the goal is to be worth reaching. Prophecy is futile; the possibilities are infinite.

'Sh-h-h ... Here Comes the Censor!,' an address by Deacon to the Ontario Library Association on 26 March 1940, was printed as a pamphlet (Toronto: Macmillan 1940).

IT IS A PLEASURE and an honour to be the guest of the body that, more than any other, is dedicated to the preservation and spread of culture in this country. By culture, of course, I do not mean the silly affectations of drinking tea with the little finger extended, nor speaking in accents strained and weird. By culture, I mean the broad fundamentals of our way of life – those beliefs and attutudes of mind, which have shaped the behaviour of civilized man for 2,500 years and, more particularly, all that is represented in the mental evolution of our race since the introduction of printing into Europe 500 years ago, and the institutions and conventions that have grown out of these deep impulses.

Canada is today making an effort unprecedented in her history to meet a threat to those fundamentals that underlie our way of life. We know that without these treasures won for us in toil and pain by our ancestors, we cannot have any life that we care to live. Hence we mobilize our resources, human and material, – on land, at sea, in the air, and – no less – in the kingdom of the mind. We have decided solemnly that we would rather be impoverished, that we would rather die than forego this heritage of freedom.

For is not this the basis from which men, during five centuries, have been making life more worth living? By extension of knowledge, by welcome to ideas that they may be tested by experiment. In the realms of science, of theology, of politics, or social practice, we have fought battle after battle to rid the soul of man of *self-imposed shackles*, to free the mind of *fear of bogies* in order that it may approach the problems of existence *rationally*. Extension of the franchise, religious toleration, permission to explore the laws of nature – these are steps on the road. Twentieth century man is not so much struggling for control of the outer universe as he is trying to understand his own nature. But, as in other departments, nothing can be done without freedom; for the price of advance is shedding those primitive superstitions our ancestors acquired in the jungle.

Understand, there can be no compromise. The issued is joined. Forces have risen that say: 'You shall not go farther down this road of freedom.' It is one thing or the other now, once and for all. Let me quote Adolf Hitler: 'Universal education is the most corroding and disintegrating poison that liberalism ever invented for its own destruction. We must allow the great mass of the lowest order the blessings of illiteracy. We ourselves shall shake off all humane and scientific prejudices. The ideal of universal education has long been obsolete. It will not be until knowledge recovers its character of a *secret science* that it will again exercise its normal function, which is to be a means of ruling human as well as non-human nature.'

To me, these words are the supreme blasphemy. They declare an intent to use the power, which intellectual freedom has created, for the re-enslavement of man; and not, as we would use it, for further liberation of the human spirit. I repeat no compromise is possible; and that is why our armies are making war on our behalf – to preserve freedom to discover and spread knowledge. Not to use ignorance as a lever to move people; but to give them the truth that shall make them free.

You, on the home front of this world-shaking event, call on me to talk about censorship. The time for compromise there is also finished.

Either you must accept the full implications of the idea that human beings can be trusted, which is the basis of all our boasted progress; or you edge over into regulation of thought, which is the mainstay of dictatorship.

Calvin Coolidge, once returned from church, was questioned by his wife:

'What was the sermon about?'

'Sin.'

'Well, what did Dr. So-and-so say, what line did he take?'

'He was against it.'

With equal economy of phrase, that is my attitude on censorship. I am against it. Because, in my view, it is sin. The issue is a moral one; and if we are not to belie the whole of our intellectual past, we must all be against it. In my youth I wrote passionately on this subject; and now that the gray hairs have come, my conviction is more intense. Twenty years of experience with books and men confirm everything I wrote and published long ago.

In recent years we have seen Hitler make his first attack on books. He based his action on moral grounds; but as soon as he had control, moral censorship turned into political tyranny. That is exactly what John Milton, the Puritan, predicted in his speech to the Parliament of England in 1644. He was talking against the proposal to license books by a board of censors, prior to publication. He won; and ever since an author publishes what he likes, and is responsible to the courts if he has broken the law. In 1835, Joseph Howe established this right in Canada in a famous trial at Halifax. Responsible government came to Nova Scotia *only* because Howe defeated, in open court, the attempt of provincial authority to control what he printed in his paper.

Your problem is not directly the editorial freedom of newspapers (though ultimately it is the same thing). You want me to talk about the moral censorship of books, because that is a practical annoyance in your working lives. I shall neither evade nor equivocate. The real essence of this matter is not morals at all, but *manners*. The cause of offence is apt to be the insertion of coarse words – vulgarisms that perturb those of nice speech. However fittingly these words emerge from the mouths of characters in books, those of sheltered life find them alarming, improper because not used in their own homes.

For myself, I find these terse expressions far cleaner than the slimy substitutes that debase our language, but which nobody protests because they are *indirect*. And I wonder whether any here are possibly ignorant of the cathartic principle in vocabulary. Inhibitions and neuroses relative to sex and excrement can be cured, as thousands of young men have discovered, by a generous dose of the candour of Dr Rabelais – Doctor of Medicine, Doctor of Laws, Doctor of Theology, one of the wisest of writers, but generally known in Canada only as a filthy book. May I quote from that inspired interpretative critic, John Cowper Powys?

Those who suffer most from Rabelais's manner of treating sex are the incurably vicious. The really evil, libidinous people, that is to say the spiteful, the mean, the base and inhuman, fly from his presence, and for the obvious reason that he makes sex-pleasure so generous, so gay, so natural, so legitimate, that their dark, morbid, perverted natures can get no more joy out of it ... To open his book – though the steam of the grossness of it rises to heaven – is to touch the divine fingers, the fingers that heal the world.

Or we might take the evidence of Stephen Longstreet from his 1940 novel *Decade*: 'The more I read of smut the more I wonder why they print it privately and sell it under the counter. If they flooded the country with it, everybody would be bored to death with the subject in three weeks and turn to stamp collecting, the next dullest hobby in the world.'

That is profoundly true. Remove restrictions and interest lags when the novelty has worn off. The whole of the 1920's was one long effort to reflect in fiction the more flexible sexual standards of conduct that came with the Great War. Candour in dealing with the physical side of love was attractive because it had been taboo. Ten years later, bed-room scenes had become so common that they bored people. A long line of court decisions, releasing *Jurgen*, *Ulysses* and many other books, leaves the contemporary novelist very free indeed in his treatment; but your current lists of best-sellers do not feature the more sexy books as prime favourites. Mass taste is predominantly *romantic*, not erotic within the meaning of censorship advocates. The innocence of the average mind is remarkable in a generation that has seen the psychoanalysts uncovering and exploring their cesspools of imaginary emotion. The amount of reality in their revelations is questionable.

Far back in our past, conservatism of all sorts became enshrined as the means of survival in a strange world. Tribal taboos, taken as the decrees of the gods, ordained that things should be done as they always had been done; and that the old way is right and the new way wrong. Three thousand four hundred years ago, Akhnaton, Pharoah of Egypt, tried to introduce monotheism. He said that the sun was so much more important to life than was the moon that only the sun should be considered the symbol of God, and not both of them as formerly. The hullabaloo, led by the priests, backed by the rabble, compelled the king to abdicate. Thus was heresy punished; and exactly the same instinct today causes every man to hate his wife when she alters the arrangement of her hair or adopts a new style of dress. But so far has change been accepted as possibly good that the man no longer kills his wife for a new hat. He perceives under the hat he distrusts the identity of the woman he loves; and he tells her he likes the hat. It isn't true; but it is a marvellous tribute to mental progress. The husband, who has learned to tolerate conflicting forms of religion, knows that the shape of a hat is less important than the comfort of mind of a very dear person.

Book censorship plays out the same comedy. Books must have originality if they are worth anything; and whatever is new offends this ancient sense of propriety. The new is heresy; it is immoral. When it becomes familiar, that antagonism passes. How strange it is for us today to recall that Hardy was driven out of novel writing because of howls against the immorality of his stories. Many still alive had to read *Tess of the d'Urbervilles* with blushes behind locked doors. *Jude the Obscure* (1895) was universally condemned as 'Jude the Obscene,' even by those who recognized its literary merits. Now Hardy is revered as a classic – Simon pure.

We laugh over Queen Victoria being shocked by Tennyson's 'Enoch Arden' – the story of a husband, who stayed away so long that his wife married another, as she was entitled by law to do. We wonder how *Jane Eyre* ever ran foul of censorious minds, or that the novels of H.G. Wells were subject for hostile sermons and widespread bans by the libraries of England thirty years ago. The comedy goes on. Many of the books officially or unofficially frowned on as we sit here are just as surely going to take their places in the canon of accepted literature tomorrow. Today children are being forbidden to read books that their children will have to study in school and college.

Not all banned books are great. Some of trivial, and would die soon anyway – the sooner if not honoured by the public executioner. The death-rate of books is terrific. Our duty is to promote circulation of the best, not to go on lynching parties for trash.

Since I am in deadly earnest, it is not fair to withhold personal testimony from you; and I shall direct this against the argument that while books cannot hurt adults, immature minds must be guarded from contamination.

Ranging my grandfather's library as a boy, I discovered the poems cut out of the back of the one-volume Shakespeare. On enquiry, I learned he had done this to protect his daughters. In a short time I had read the poems of Shakespeare; and it would be false to attribute my ruined life altogether to their influence. Later my aunt, a woman of literary taste, asked me to name a book for my birthday. I wanted *De Profundis* by Oscar Wilde and immediately I was pronounced well on the road to hell – far gone in iniquity. So I bought *De Profundis* with my own money and found it to be the most eloquent plea for Christianity in our language. In a day of agnosticism, this book was very valuable to my education.

When I became a father, my belief in the open shelf was put into practice. My several thousand books have always been at the disposal of my children without the slightest supervision. They were not bought for infants, but were accumulated to satisfy my own curiosity about the queer manifestations of human life. They represent *my* taste at all ages. Some were banned when I acquired them. My standing instructions were: 'Read anything you like but don't bother me.' After 17 years, I can tell you precisely the result of that experiment in anti-censorship. None of my three drink, smoke, steal, use foul language, or do any of the things that the most straightlaced conscience would disapprove. Never once have their mother and I had to deal with any moral lapse more serious than forgetting to sweep the snow off the walk. I am ready to submit those three children to any form of examination – physical, mental or moral, in competition with any other trio of like age in this city. In particular, they have developed no taste whatever for pornography, though they have sampled with utmost freedom books that most parents would withhold from children. A wholesome atmosphere of open investigation has created decency of mind. I would not submit them to the course of hole-and-corner reading I had to do in my own teens.

To create taste, you must start a reader from his present taste, just as any journey must begin from where a person is. There is no use putting a wise look into the hands of a fool, nor giving a delicate one to a coarse and vulgar mind. That will only cause them to hate reading. But many an austere taste has begun, to my knowledge, at a lowly stage. I remember when we contributed one cent each to purchase the adventures of Jesse James, and kept the volumes in a hollow stump at the swimming hole because we would be whipped if we took them home. After reading three, I graduated to better stuff, but continued to pay my cent as a protest against home censorship.

Today, stuff like that – Westerns and detective yarns – is read by clergymen to get their minds off the troubles of their parishioners. Why not? I cannot stand such tripe; but that is no reason for my refusing it to those who like it. John Milton said 396 years ago: 'Evil manners are as perfectly learnt without books a thousand other ways which cannot be stopt.' There is only one thing to do with vulgar taste – feed it, glut it, so that it will turn in weariness to finer nutriment. If an individual is incapable of mental growth, the loss is precisely nothing.

We must recognize once and for all the essential prurience of the minds of censorship advocates. I carry the case now into the citadel of the enemy. They claim we have nasty minds, and I claim they have nasty minds, or they wouldn't be so obsessed with this subject. Obscenity is subjective, not objective. A club I belonged to invited the police expert on book censorship to visit us and discuss matters. He was a genial, unpretentious North-of-Ireland cop, head of the morality squad in his city. We all liked him. His chief business was to raid whore houses. When anybody complained about a book, it was submitted to him for an opinion and action if he saw fit. His first sentence to us was: 'I do not know anything about literature; I read few books; but I know dirt when I see it.' No blame attaches to this honest ignorant soul; but it may annoy you, and certainly *should* annoy you that the feeling towards books is such that authority thought it appropriate to make the same man guardian of prostitutes and judge of what sort of literature you and I may read.

But far less dangerous is it to operate under this system, with its feature of open trial, than to erect a more learned tribunal with power to suppress in a Star Chamber. Everybody knows what abuses would flourish with no publicity and no right of appeal. Ah, Milton! He said it all the first time. Hear him: 'Those books which are likeliest to taint both life and doctrine cannot be suppressed without the fall of learning.' No compromise there. Censorship spells 'the fall of learning' – even censoring the bad books. Do you see it in Germany? in Russia? in Italy? in Japan? *Yes.*

Please get immediately, because it vitally affects your profession, the new book called *The Censor Marches On* by Ernst & Lindey (Doubleday). It traces the recent history of censorship in the United States with cases and full particulars. I cannot more than mention it here – *The Censor Marches On*; but I wish to quote from the Foreword: 'The earliest manifestations of censorship under Hitler concerned sex no less than politics. No one familiar with recent attempts in the Unites States to suppress certain kinds of films and plays can doubt that the censors of the future will use sex as a pretext to crush hostile political views, nor that the full battery of tricks and expedients devised to combat obscenity will be wheeled into action anew to smash another target.'

A while back I had evidence of this in our local Customs Office. John W. Dafoe, editor of the Winnipeg *Free Press*, was sending me his latest book direct from Columbia University Press. Having learned to hold my fire until I knew the nature of the objection, I waited long while the clerk read and read and looked very doubtful. Finally I said:

'Well, what's wrong with it?'

The clerk held the book as though it were a piece of offal and replied:

'What I can't understand is why Dr. Dafoe would be writing on this subject at all – *Canada, an American Nation*.'

'What do you think he'd write about?'

'Why, the Quintuplets.'

Funny as this incident is, I ask you to realize its seriousness; and to accept it as evidence that books are feared and banned because they contain something strange, offending the tribal taboos. Lord Tweedsmuir, representing the King, had publicly announced: 'Canada is an independent, sovereign state.' But, in the view of the customs Department, this was Bolshevism. My clerk was dead against any constitutional evolution in the British Empire. Even if so famous a man as the Dionnes' physician called Canada 'a nation,' the clerk was prepared to forbid entry of the book into Canada.

Censorship is always stupid, and that is evidence that it is evil. A Russian engineer, to improve his style, wrote an essay explaining the five year plan in such simple terms that the Soviet Government distributed it free by the millions of copies. It was translated and read the world round. Here it was a best-seller for a time – *New Russia's Primer*. But a University of Toronto professor, hoping to improve his knowledge of the Russian language, tried to import a copy of the original text without success. Simultaneously, a professor in Moscow, wishing to improve his knowledge of English tried to import into Russia a copy of the Canadian edition, and his government would not allow it.

I know that, as public servants, you are restricted; and I have every sympathy with your limitations, and I know the pressure exerted against your better judgment. But I call on you to oppose this menace with all the means at your disposal, and to subscribe in your hearts to the principle, whether you are able to do anything about it or not.

Two years ago, I proudly sat on the platform of Massey Hall as part of a literary bodyguard for Thomas Mann, most distinguished of living writers. Twelve Canadians were there to attest that Canada stood with him and not with his oppressor in Berlin. It seemed right to do this. But Dr Mann's speech seemed unequal to the occasion. He said artistic creation was only possible in an atmosphere of freedom. That sounded banal and platitudinous. Tame as it sounded then, it is now a challenge.

For it is not merely aesthetic matters that are at stake as I speak; it is everything. This freedom is the pre-requisite for science, for social and political developments, for everything vital to our way of life. Only yesterday, it was a commonplace of our existence; as I speak, it is the one issue that is tearing the world apart. To me, the whole struggle is between those who believe in freedom, trusting the innate goodness of the people; and others who would enslave the race. Even they honour freedom in taking it away first, well knowing they cannot ruin men and women, who read what they like, say what they like and think what they like. Remove that keystone and the whole structure of our civilization falls.

To desert the principle of freedom now is to show cowardice in the face of the enemy. I believe that every crucial conflict of modern history is basically moral and intellectual. I believe the deciding factor in this war will be no item of military strategy, but that survival of our way of life depends on whether people like us *really believe in freedom*. If we do, great invisible powers, the dynamics of evolution, will fight for us and sustain what we have built – the open road of achievement, leading we know not where, but towards greater happiness and fuller life and closer affinity with the Divine Purpose behind the universe.

But if we do not really care about liberty, if we do not really trust our fellows, then the case is hopeless.

I am very proud of being a man in 1940. I exult in man's conquest over his environment. I bow to the explorers, the astronomers, the mathematicians, along with the surgeons and engineers and the architects of government in this complicated age. I reverence those who seek to discover the nature of man and his place in the scheme. Beyond these, again, are those who deal with ideas, who reach out to touch realities still beyond our capacity to analyse – servants of the imagination, who serve no less magnificently because they are reaching into the dimly known. This whole army marches on in faith that the goal will be worthy of the sacrifices, worthy of the sublime unselfishness of the striving.

And the condition of that progress is freedom. Beside that aspiration, and in view of the miraculous yet solid achievements in the past, what do a few vulgar words matter? – a few lewd stories? Especially when ever-changing conditions make these trumpery details of no consequence, anyhow. Edward Carpenter has written: 'The ascetics and the self-indulgent divide things into good and evil – as it were to throw away the evil; but things cannot be divided into good and evil, but all are good as soon as they are brought into subjection.'

William Blake called on us to 'build Jerusalem' here and now, on earth; and that is what many are trying to do. But it will not be built with the whip and scourge, with any sort of force. It can only be built on the willing initiative of men and women, who are free to pursue their chosen work in their own ways, and who have freed their own minds from as much prejudice as possible, and from every sort of cramping superstition and tribal taboo. The unsheathed human mind is the greatest force we know; and books are the wise, safe trainers of that force, even as Erasmus taught. When a book is refused to a reader 'for his own good,' remember John Milton's sneer at the implied claim to 'infallibility' as to what result the reading would have.

Therefore, at this moment of history, we dare not treat book censorship merely as the ridiculous antics of Mrs. Grundy, though normally it is just that. Rather now must we see this horrid thing as the spearhead of those demonic energies that are trying powerfully to destroy our civilization, in both its material and spiritual aspects. Canada wages war for the first time on her own responsibility in defence of liberties first said long ago by *our* kind to be necessary for the highest ends of individuals and of states. We are risking our newly won national existence to preserve those liberties, not for certain individuals and our own country, but for the benefit of all men – even our enemies. Marching together on this high plane, it were black treason to contravene this principle in our daily lives. Books have done more than any thing else to fit men for freedom; and we must see, at all times, that books are as free as possible to all who would use or enjoy them. The influence of books has been ennobling. On books our whole civilization rests. In guarding them from those who misunderstand them and would limit their circulation, we are aligned with the highest ideals that we know, and are preparing for the world a future more humane because more fully devoted to tolerance and reason.

Deacon reviewed A.J.M. Smith's *The Book of Canadian Poetry* (Toronto: Gage 1943) under the heading, 'A.J.M. Smith's Canadian Anthology is Both Antiquarian and Modernistic,' in *The Globe and Mail*, 30 October 1943.

algrave's Golden Treasury WAS BASED on popular taste, with the lyric predominating, and the same standard has inspired most collections of verse purporting to be nationally representative. *The Oxford Book of English Verse* represented the common denominator of educated taste, but incorporated also an ambition to demonstrate the development of poetry over several centuries. The late Professor Broadus undertook to illustrate Canada's social evolution by selections from the poets; and I never felt this was satisfactory either as history or as poetry. So there are endless approaches and combinations of approaches.

That of Professor Smith, a Canadian, who teaches in Michigan Agricultural College, is didactic. With punctilious care he has demonstrated the course of Canadian poetry in English from the British conquest to the work of a quartet, who were only born during the last war. He calls his book a 'critical and historical anthology.' Taken for what it is, this is an exceptionally fine, comprehensive and judicious piece of work. The casual reader must not expect to find here the old favorites. It is almost with a shock that one comes upon 'The Shooting of Dan McGrew,' 'The Wreck of the Julie Plante,' 'Shadow River' and 'Heat.'

On average, comparatively few lines represent each poet, as though the book had been designed for class room use. This impression is further borne out by the time periods covered. One reaches page 117, or is a quarter through the volume, before reaching the first line by Charles Mair, with whom Canada's significant poetry is generally said to begin. The Confederation poets of the Roberts-Carman school are, by contrast, confined to 70 pages, regardless of their tremendous popularity and influence.

A greater number of pages is accorded at the end to the poets of our surrealist school, including, prominently, A.J.M. Smith himself. It is a legitimate function of an anthologist to introduce younger poets. Certainly in Charles Bruce, Dorothy Livesay and Earle Birney we have writers worthy of being elevated to the canon; but the difficulty is the same as in the Gustafson anthology [*Anthology of Canadian Poetry (English)*, 1942] – an attempt to popularize a group of highly mannered writers, who make a cult of obscurity to the point that they have been unable as individuals to make any impression at all upon the reading public.

Professor Smith begins with an admirably analytic essay on the growth of poetry in Canada, in which he attempts to explain his own group by explaining their merits and presenting them as an improvement on the Confederation school, which dominated literary taste for 50 years. It is natural and legitimate that this effort should be made. Every generation needs living room and traditionally pushes its seniors in the face to enlarge its own area of occupation. Professor Smith has won a fine bridgehead for the comrades, which will permit them to infiltrate into university circles faster than they have been doing.

We needed this book very badly. It is an outright challenge to literary values in Canada, and a healthy thing to have happened. If Duncan Campbell Scott cannot hold his own in competition with A.M. Klein, Scott will have to go and the country will be the richer. But Prof. Smith must remember that it is he who joined the issue; and if it should be his friend Klein who suffers, the loss must be where it falls.

To avoid all misunderstanding, let me repeat that *The Book of Canadian Poetry* is scholarly and sound, with all the academic virtues. Its appraisals, specific and implied, are fresh, cogent and to be welcomed by the thoughtful. If there is a lack, it is on the side of the warmly human vibrations that emanate from a book of loved, familiar poems. Prof. Smith says 'maple sugar is a sickly and cloying commodity.' It is too bad that some of us still like it.

What the book presages is the teaching of Canadian poetry in schools and universities, a thing greatly to be desired. If the youngsters do not enjoy the dull poems of the early 19th century, they will certainly revel in such modern items as Pratt's 'The Cachalot' and 'Amber Lands' by Tom MacInnes. Finally, Prof. Smith has exhibited in his selections, a taste, if at times severe, yet always sound. Far more popular collections could have been made, but Canadian poetry emerges from this test extraordinarily well. The labors of Prof. Smith have given Canadians something of which they can be genuinely, if soberly, proud.

Under the heading, 'Masterly Interpretation of William Blake's Poems,' Deacon reviewed Northrop Frye's *Fearful Symmetry: A Study of William Blake* (Toronto: Saunders 1947) in *The Globe and Mail* on 17 May 1947.

WILLIAM BLAKE (1757-1827), the precursor of Aubrey Beardsley in art and an engraver of first distinction, was primarily a poet. His work is universally recognized as belonging to the canon of great English poetry. Such short lyrics as 'The Tiger' and 'The Lamb' have been sincerely admired and endlessly reprinted. The original cast of his mind and his command of gnomic and epigrammatic phrases continue to intrigue readers to this day.

He is probably the least read favorite poet of all time. Enthusiasm for a small section of his work is enormous; the bulk of his work never reached any audience of reasonable size because it was considered incomprehensible. His impatient contemporaries said Blake was mad, and this unfortunate dictum has served as excuse for the neglect of the longer prophetic poems. These form the great mass of his published writings; and he engraved them on copper as evidence of the value he attached to them.

Down the generations this genius has awaited readers until some patient scholar should study the unique symbology and mythology, which Blake invented as a proper artistic vehicle to convey his thought. There has been a good deal of writing about Blake but no big-scale attempt at comprehensive interpretation.

Northrop Frye, a young Toronto professor, has performed a major service in his large, thorough and brilliant volume, *Fearful Symmetry*. It is one of the finest pieces of interpretative criticism in the language. All lovers of poetry will rejoice that Blake can now be understood easily by the many, who have always believed these prophecies must contain noble ideas artistically expressed in cryptic form, but who never themselves sought the keys to these supposed enigmas. As Alan Anderson has well said of Dr Frye's masterly exposition: 'This book has been needed for 150 years.'

Like so much else, Blake's work ceases to be obscure after a suitable introduction and a few hints about his basic convictions and explanations of his terminology. Dr Frye insists that Blake was no mystic and did not wish to be mysterious in utterance, but rather to express precisely the world and life as he saw them. Blake was opposed to the mechanical view of the universe introduced by the philosopher Locke. He refused to accept the notion of God as a mathematician or that man was the product of impersonal natural forces.

Blake believed in the creativeness of man and therefore in his superiority to nature. This creativeness Blake called imagination. 'Man has within him the principle of life and the principle of death: one is the imagination, the other the natural man. In the natural world the natural principle will win out eventually and the man will die.' Hence Blake championed, against the materialism of his day, the human spirit and the power of mind as divine things. 'If Blake had lived a century later he would undoubtedly have taken sides with Butler and Shaw (against Darwinism) and claimed that alterations in an organism are produced by the development of the organism's imagination.'

Blake saw in civilization the triumph of mind over nature, claiming that man in his natural state was in his lowest possible state. 'The central symbol of the imagination in all Blake's work is the city,' says Dr Frye; and he aptly quotes the poet: 'Where man is not, nature is barren.' Similarly, in his theological statements Blake rejects the idea of an impersonal God:

> God appears and God is light
> To those poor souls who dwell in night,
> But does a human form display
> To those who dwell in realms of day.

Contrasting the two attitudes towards life, Blake scorns the man who sees in the sun an object 'somewhat like a guinea.' The poet, speaking imaginatively, poetically and for himself describes his own response to the spectacle of the sun: 'I see an innumerable company of the Heavenly host crying "Holy, Holy, Holy is the Lord God Almighty".'

Profound as a work of scholarship, *Fearful Symmetry* is fun to read for the simple reason that Blake himself was a lively, positive fellow – not the dreamer, but a critic of society and 'the eternal radical.' Further, Dr Frye knows that his business is to explain Blake, to make his meanings clear and the understanding of his poetry easy – not to dazzle readers with a display of his own learning, much less to inject fresh confusion of his own into a discussion of a difficult poet. His success with his subject lies precisely in the fact *Fearful Symmetry* can be grasped by any intelligent person.

Of course, there is vastly more to the book than the two or three points named. The whole of Blake's thought is reviewed and help is given with the meanings of special words. We find, for example, that hell has two meanings – one a state quite different from the orthodox place of torment, and the other is the fiery lake, but used sarcastically.

The main thing is that a major essay in literary criticism is presented with convincing logic and in a style that is lucid, graceful, even sometimes witty. In writing *Fearful Symmetry*, Dr Frye has enriched the whole literary world by rescuing the major works of a great poet from misunderstanding and obscurity. That is a notable achievement. The book will certainly lead to a Blake revival as Archibald MacMechan's discovery and recognition of *Moby Dick* gave Melville his niche in the modern Pantheon. Of the two, Blake is far more important and it is a considerable literary event that his poems in their entirety are now open to the enjoyment of all who will wisely use *Fearful Symmetry* as their guide.

Under the heading, 'A Positive Approach to Canadian Writing,' Deacon reviewed Malcolm Ross's *Our Sense of Identity: A Book of Canadian Essays* (Toronto: Ryerson 1954) in *The Globe and Mail* on 30 January 1954.

MALCOLM ROSS OF QUEEN'S set out to compile an anthology of Canadian essays. Somewhere in the process, something impelled him to abandon concentration on the traditional essay forms and neat divisions into historical eras. Instead, he has treated the prose non-fiction writers as the voices of the Canadian people and has composed a major work of interpretation, as a musical conductor would use the instruments in the hands of many players to create intelligible harmony. *Our Sense of Identity* is the first attempt at this sort of thing in this country and the book becomes immediately an important statement on the national character, variously formed by environment, history and tradition.

Stimulating to a high degree, this collection of 44 pieces by 42 writers is hearteningly positive. The concept of the bewildered, imitative Canadian with no mind of his own disappears. These writers use the most diverse inflections, talk about utterly different things; yet none apologizes for his or her country's existence. The exciting task of the reader is to decide, each for himself, the several common denominators, that, somehow, make sense of putting Susanna Moodie, W.H. Blake, Emily Carr and J.S. Woodsworth between the same covers.

Brilliant but by no means exhaustive expository remarks by Dr Ross include these valuable hints: 'We kick against the pricks of our necessity. Yet, strangely, we are in love with this necessity. our natural mode is therefore not compromise but irony – the inescapable response to the presence and pressures of opposites in tension. ... We are at once inside and outside the Plouffe family. ... Ours is not, can never be the 100 per cent kind of nationalism. ... I have been trying to suggest a motion which takes its energy in tension, a motion which is visible in unfolding spirals of irony.'

Unimaginative readers who have difficulty making a pattern of Professor Marshall McLuhan in praise of comics as the art which is keeping pace with the leaps of science, Joseph Howe's letter of 1839 to Lord John Russell on Responsible Government and Arthur L. Phelps' deft and, I hope, disturbing Christmas broadcast of 1949 may take comfort in some of the most original writing of our past 115 years. Further, little of this material is well known.

A.Y. Jackson's account of the origins of the Group of Seven is too valuable to be left as the mere memory of a broadcast. Behind the facts, of course, is the significance of a national movement of consequence. it comes as a shock to hear him say, 30 years after the event: 'Critics regarded Harris as a public menace and declared his pictures of Canada were discouraging immigration.' It is even more startling to hear Sara Jeannette Duncan explaining us to the Americans in 1887 in terms which today are commonplace and equally aplicable to the situation. That P.D. Ross, in 1884, pleaded for tolerance on behalf of Riel and the halfbreeds is news 70 years later – and good news.

Accomplishments of Canadians find their place, too. Harry Henderson explains Selye's experiments at McGill and quotes authorities as rating his discoveries as 'marking the opening of a new era in medicine' and as 'having as profound an effect' as those of Pasteur 99 years earlier. We must regard Northrop Frye's 'The Function of Criticism at the Present Time' as, itself, an achievement as well as a portent of the contributions he will make in his full maturity.

Bruce Hutchison – and who better! – has been chosen to express himself on 'The National Character,' and surely he has stated the essence of his observations and beliefs better than on any other occasion: 'We Canadians worry too much about our diversity. For it is an illusion to imagine that a nation grows strong by uniformity. ... Whereas other nations of the past grew up in a world of watertight compartments, and hardened into individual shape before other nations could touch and dilute them, we began to build a nation here only a few years ago, in a new world, in a violent world revolution, in an age when all nations were being driven together, cheek by jowl, through the new means of transport, information and propaganda. ...'

'We are among the few peoples still in the throes of collective growth. ... We have, every one of us, the feeling that we are involved in a process of perpetual expansion, development and revision, whose end we cannot see. Ours is the doubt and risk, but the unqualified satisfaction of the man who builds and makes something with his own hands. We have built here against every obstacle of geography, economics, racial division and the magnet of our American neighbor – we have built here the greatest nation of its population in all recorded history.' To explain it, he mentions: 'the unshakeable will to make a nation, a home, a life of our own, for which no inconvenience was too great, from which no temptation could swerve us.'

Humor of course there is or these would not be Canadian essays. B.K. Sandwell was in characteristically impish mood 22 years ago when he wrote his proposal that the 'Non-Voting Voter' be deprived of his vote and if total votes cast did not amount to a majority the seat would be declared vacant. It might be worth trying. Frank Underhill's caustic remarks on the Massey Report are also to the point.

A.R.M. Lower's sarcasm over R.B. Bennett's speech when leaving Canada may be the voice of history speaking a little in advance. Lister Sinclair is at his debonair happiest when dealing with the Canadian idiom as 'the result of applying British syntax to an American vocabulary. Jocularly, he suggests introducing a Mountie into every work of fiction as a trade mark. 'Perhaps one day we may reach the stage where the idea of a Canadian idiom will never be discussed; it will simply not arise in Canadian writers' minds. Then we can look again; because then we will know we have found it.' A discerning exposition.

Funniest of all is the juxtaposition of novelists MacLennan and Callaghan on the subjects of Montreal and Toronto. The author of *Two Solitudes* was never as parochial as in that piece of civic bombast. He says that Montrealers, being 'Canadians second,' have more in common with the Cantonese than with the inhabitants of other Canadian cities. Callaghan, after laughingly confessing he knows no good reason why he should live in Toronto, comes out with the simple truth: 'The English-speaking people of Montreal and Toronto think the same thoughts.'

Dr Ross, in some strange fit of illumination of which we have no details, has managed to break away from the idea that an anthology is a collection of old favorites so familiar that we don't need to read it at all –

something, certainly, that requires no pause for thought. He deserves thanks for a colossal as well as a discerning labor of research. He was fortunate in having a publisher who would permit him space adequate for a man-size demonstration of this Canadian thing, which cannot be narrowly defined but which does reflect the turbulent life of a nation consciously in action forward to a goal felt, but not yet clearly perceived.

With all its merits, *Our Sense of Identity* might have been improved by more explanatory notes, especially the identities of the writers and the circumstances. As a student of Canadian literature, I recognize 40 out of 42 contributors; but data in the back are inadequate. Howard Angus Kennedy, whom I knew, has a piece about seeing Ukrainians arrive between Battleford and Saskatoon. This is credited to *Book of the West*, 1925; but the context shows he was there in 1905. No publisher is mentioned. Nothing is said about Mr Kennedy having reported the 1885 Rebellion for the *Montreal Witness*, nor about his other books. All explanatory matter should be in one place and many readers will want more details. Reference works are few.

One deduction is that the editor probably had more items than could be included. The answer is a second volume, equally comprehensive. Nothing is sadder in our situation than the amount of first rate writing that is used once and then emptied down the drain, though a fair percentage of it would be appreciated if gathered into such collections.

'The Reviewer,' first given by Deacon as a speech to the CAA National Convention in Windsor, 1959, was printed in *The Canadian Author and Bookman* 38 (Fall 1959) .

THANK YOU FOR ALLOWING ME to celebrate my 40th anniversary as a professional reviewer by telling you about my specialty. It was in 1919 that I wrote my first review for the New York *Times*; and for the next two years I got excellent training under H.L. Mencken of the *American Mercury*; Henry S. Canby of the *Saturday Review*; and Dr Smythe of the *International*. In 1921 I rose to the dizzy height of honorary assistant literary editor of the Winnipeg *Free Press*, while continuing the practice of law. It was a fair-sized job as John W. Dafoe set aside four pages for books on the first Monday of each month. A year later I had my own department on a Toronto newspaper.

Lucky was I, who wanted to be a writer but had decided that I was not a creative writer, that there was this sudden opportunity for derivative writing. This sudden change was a direct result of a literary revolution in Canada. The lyric and pastoral poets – Roberts, Carman, Scott and Lampman – who broke into print in 1880 and dominated the scene for 40 years till 1920, were old men. New prose writers were appearing.

In 1921, Canadians were glowing with pride over their part in the First World War; this Association was founded; Louis Hémon's *Maria Chapdelaine*, published in Paris in 1913, got nowhere in French; but, when W.H. Blake translated it into English in 1921, its success was terrific. Hémon was already dead. He had been run over by a C.P.R. engine at Chapleau while riding the rods. Almost immediately, we were faced with a new race of Canadian authors – Mazo de la Roche, E.J. Pratt, Frederick Philip Grove and Laura Goodman Salverson. Readers wanted to read about the books of such writers; and so the whole-time professional reviewers were called on the scene.

Till 1921, Canadian newspapers did not regard books as important. Only about a dozen carried reviews. About the best were done by ladies of the town; Emily Murphy of Edmonton and Ruth Cohen of Winnipeg were reasonably competent. Then there was the local professor who reviewed books in his spare time.

A leading Toronto newspaper dealt out the books like cards among the reporting staff. The cub reporter would get an abstruse work of philosophy, the senior parliamentary reporter a slim volume of love poems. Each then wrote a notice of three or four inches and that was that. I remember one item of hot national interest and watched that paper for comment. One of the editorial writers went all out; he gave it 300 words.

Some newspapers had all-purpose critics – men who would review plays, movies, concerts and art shows, as well as books, for which they had not too much time. I remember one such, who was psychotic about sex. In the 1920's, novelists were claiming a new freedom in that field and this fellow could always dredge up two each Saturday. Except for title and author, all reviews, every Saturday, were interchangeable. They generally concluded: 'Unfortunately, this is a dirty book,' or words to that effect.

When a professor-reviewer, who had a short review Monday to Friday and a two-column one on Saturday, announced he would lecture in the public lecture in the public library, I was in a seat near the front. He came giggling to the front of the platform and opened:

'People are always asking me how I can read so many books. The answer is simple; I don't.' He then explained that he was an expert, and could glance at a page here and there and know all about the book. This distressed me because I was not so clever. I had to read them to find out what was in them.

At that time I was greatly interested in Edgar Lee Masters, not for the popular *Spoon River Anthology*, which I thought too much of a stunt, too much an imitation of the *Greek Anthology*, but for his shorter poems and occasional novel. On publication of *Domesday Book*, built on the pattern of Browning's *Ring and the Book*, I got it and read it immediately, though it was very long. Then I read the professor's review of it and found that, in eight column-inches, he had made eight errors of fact respecting contents of the book.

I decided to go on reading mine. The day I called on this professor and found his 14-year-old son writing the daily review, my lack of confidence was complete. However, there may be a case. Arnold Bennett's *Books and Persons*, containing his collected reviews, is clairvoyant in penetration. In a volume of reminiscences, Bennett also said: 'The fee for a review is £2. The reviewer who spends more than an hour on a book – for reading and writing his piece – simply doesn't know his business.'

Then there was an early editor of mine – a hard-boiled, efficient old newsman – who caught me reading a book and reproved me on the ground it was a waste of time. He told me to subscribe to six or eight review media, clip the reviews and when I had three or four on one book, write a bright little piece by picking something out of each. The technical word is 'scalping.' I was young and stupid enough to refuse. He threatened to fire me; and as I was serving a six-months' trial, that was serious. But my disobedience continued.

When the time was up, he gave me a $10 increase and said: 'I don't understand what you are doing. Insofar as I understand it, I don't approve of it; but the readers like it and that's all that matters. Book ads began to come in, when formerly there were none except for what one publisher called, correctly, "a sop at Christmas".'

A year ago I read a book ad that began: THE 25 LEADING CANADIAN REVIEWERS ARE AGREED THAT ... I blinked. '25 leading?' Oh, no; there can only be 25 of us altogether; they mean five leading. But I got from Walter Herbert of Ottawa a week later an analysis of how Canadian papers treated the arts. All the papers were listed vertically at the left of the page, while across the top were column-heads – drama, music, art, books, movies, radio, etc. Where the lines intersected was the name of the person in charge of each of the arts.

By actual count, there were 59 of us literary editors. I knew a great many of these people and their work. The document impressed me. The revolution in literary journalism is complete. Regina's *Leader-Post* has had its department for less than 10 years; but it's there to stay. I was glad to note that some of the best talent is working in cities of second size. London, Windsor, Saskatoon – are well served. In many places much smaller there are regular departments – not as large as in the big cities but doing their bit just as faithfully. Often pay for this is pitifully small.

All this has come about because so many more Canadians care about books and reading now than 40 years ago. This obvious trend is headed by the interest of Canadian readers in Canadian books. The appeal of Canadian authors is real; so is Canadian subject matter and Canadian settings. You may be a writer of world appeal, but your first line of readers will be the neighbors.

That is why people of Britain read mostly British books, and the Americans American books. Home products first, then a minority of imports. Canada is the only country that gets practically all British and American books – though some in tiny quantities. Our own productions are added to these; and of course the number of our new titles per annum is only a small fraction of those produced in the more populous English-speaking world beyond our borders.

The paper over whose book pages I preside and write for in company with a strong team of 25 contributing reviewers has an average capacity of 600 books a year. Analysis has shown, over a number of years that the books I select for review fall into three classes. Of British books we do 200, which is only 1% of their production; American books 200, or 1.75% of their production; Canadian books 200, being 50% of our production. That, roughly, represents the reading habits of subscribers.

There has grown up an unfortunate superstition that I love each and every Canadian author so much that I gladly slave my life away so that you may all succeed. The facts are quite different. As the new books descend on me, there is a constant sifting of the sheep from the goats. Those that get reviews are the ones which, in my opinion, are more likely to be of interest to the readers of my paper.

As a hard-headed editor, I am serving authors and publishers only incidentally. The prime aim is and must be to satisfy people who pay 10 cents for the paper. But things have come to the point where some

Canadian writers believe they are entitled to reviews as of right. I remember one furious letter by a well known Canadian author to the publisher of our paper denouncing me for not reviewing his book and demanding it be done forthwith. I just laughed. This was obviously not going to be a popular book and, at the moment, there were upwards of 50 first-rate books, of which I saw no chance of finding space for more than 25.

Why not expand? We are losing too much money now. No paper in Canada begins to meet the cost of its book department; and the bigger the paper the more its net loss on the venture. If I had my department's losses as personal income, I should regard myself as rich. Very rich. We newspapers are liberally subsidizing the book industry in Canada.

The basic truth is that the book interest in Canada is a starvling affair because 32,400 new books are published yearly in English; and 17 million people cannot consume them in economic quantities. Deduct the 30% who are less than 10 years old, and 28% who speak French – others whose time is given to movies, sports, radio and TV, immigrants unfamiliar with English, vast numbers who never read one book a year. Think of the time spent in automobiles (and the money); and/or drinking (and the money). Take away also the vast number of paperbook readers, plus the vast number who have never learned the reading habit; and it is an amazement to me that publishers remain in business. From your standpoint as authors, the serious factor is that free public libraries are patronized by hundreds of thousands of people who would rather borrow than buy. Your authors should realize that when John Smith (a rare animal) buys your $4.50 book, you get 45 cents. When a library buys it and 30 people read it, you get 45 cents. The library operates on public funds out of taxes – your taxes and mine. Why do you authors stand for being victimized in this way?

If you should ask me why all these 59 Canadian papers should sink all this money in maintaining book departments, my only guess would be the vague word 'prestige.' Among the book readers are a heavy percentage of the leaders of the learned profession and some leading industrialists – or their wives.

But, when Canada has 30 to 40 million people, books will become an economic enterprise. To a plan for expansion of my department, one of my former publishers said to me: 'We don't mind what you are losing now, but we don't want to double it.'

No system has been devised for knowing how small or large the book-review-reading public is. It will, of course, grow.

The book reviewer is engaged with the problem of informing book readers so clearly as to the contents of books that potential readers may know whether or not they should invest time and money in buying and reading the book. He or she has nothing to say to authors. Bernard Shaw and Somerset Maugham are among the famous authors who have stated that, never once have they learned anything from a review of their books.

This is quite right. The reviewer is addressing the readers. It is not his business to school-master authors. If any author reads a review of his own book, he is eaves-dropping. The remarks are not addressed to him. I, as an author in a small way, ignored the bulk of reviews of a book of mine published in 1927. Reprinted in 1954. The Victoria *Times*, reviewer cut me to pieces. I wrote my friend Bruce Hutchison, editor of the *Times*, that he should raise the salary of the reviewer for daring to attack what he evidently considered an Eastern big-shot. Bruce disappointedly replied that he regretted I had seen the first review and enclosed a clipping of a second, favorable one. This was an editorial disgrace which I deplored. Any reviewer is entitled to say anything at all about any author's book.

Long ago, the wife of one of my intimate friends approached me with humility to confess that she shared none of my outlooks. Her taste was the fiction in women's magazines. Hence, when I liked a novel, she shunned it and vice-versa. I replied that, long ago, I had gone through the same identical experience with Mencken. We were of different nationalities, of different racial stocks, of contrasting philosophies. He taught me to appreciate Dreiser; but otherwise he taught me to take his advice in reverse. It is amazing how fast the reader learns to accept advice in reverse, if it is honest in the first place.

Integrity must never be sacrificed. The reviewer should never say what he thinks he 'ought' to say; but always what he really thinks and feels. The great Hazlitt said: 'The critic's final authority is the sounding board of the critic's own soul.'

The reason for the candid confession kind of review is that the reader learns, with incredible speed, to allow for the individual reviewer's quirks, enthusiasms and prejudices, to adjust the words he is reading in the review to his own needs and tastes.

Hence the prime importance of the by-line. This puts responsibility squarely on the individual reviewer and permits the reader to know who is speaking. The unsigned review, which removes this key to comprehension, is therefore an evil.

The reviewer, who cannot stand angry complaints of readers, should take up some other form of writing. We do not get many complaints;

but when they come they are vicious because the temperament of the reviewer has clashed woundingly on the temperament of the reader. It can't be helped because the temperament of the reviewer is vital.

A reviewer's pay is not large compared to other sorts of writing; but the work is steady and pleasant and confers the benefit of constant mental growth. But no reviewer should ever forget that our trade is a utility endeavor. Publicizing and interpreting, we are the necessary links between author and publisher as producers, and the public as ultimate consumers.

The third period of Canadian literature will run from 1960 to 2000. Within the span we shall get our 40 million population; we shall attain riches and power, and the self-confidence that goes with these things. That is the sort of soil out of which the great literatures have always come. It will be a lush time for reviewers also.

The reviewer, though a specialist, is primarily a writer and should know pride of craft. If he is not a good writer himself, his articles will constantly whisper to the readers: 'This fellow doesn't know what he is talking about; he ought to be selling insurance or running an elevator.'

Every review must carry a judgment – stated or implied – but the nature of the work under discussion determines what balance there should be between description of the book and evaluation of it. On a recent Saturday it was my pleasure to print Robert Turnbull's excellent review of William Stevenson's *The Yellow Wind*. The author is the *Globe and Mail*'s Far Eastern correspondent stationed in Hong Kong; and his book is a report on his travels in China and half a dozen nearby countries. He was not writing just a travel book but, mainly, he was passing on observations about political and economic conditions. A lengthy description of Mr Stevenson's style would have been completely out of order. Besides, this aspect was covered by quotation of three paragraphs.

But when I ask Vernal House to review a book of poems, I expect and receive comment about style.

In our time there has grown up a sharp distinction between the reviewer and the critic. The reviewer is a newspaper hack. The critic is an exalted person, generally a university professor, whose own style may be dull, who may use long hard words, and who generally, but not always, is concerned with the work of long-dead authors.

Unfortunately for the validity of this distinction, the greatest critic who ever lived was a reviewer. *Sainte-Beuve* was educated as a doctor. As a hospital intern of 20 he wrote his first articles. Three years later he proclaimed the merits of Victor Hugo, forsook medicine for reviewing and, during the following 42 years, he won the title of Father of Modern Criticism.

It is said of him: 'he was creative rather than dogmatic.' For the last 20 years of his life his articles appeared every Monday morning in Paris newspapers. His column was called 'Causeries de Lundis – Monday chats.' He covered the lush mid-19th century literature of Europe. He was gifted with phenomenal insight; and it is amazing how firmly his opinions have stood up for more than a century.

Sainte-Beuve was followed 40 years later by *William Hazlitt* in England – a hack who wrote on space rate; and I am far from alone in regarding him as the greatest of English critics. I mention him here for two reasons. He preferred to be a commentator rather than a creative writer. He said: 'I would rather be a man of lesser genius, free and able to appreciate truth and beauty wherever found, rather than a man of more original and commanding genius, bound up forever in that small portion of it (truth and beauty) which I had been able to create.'

Hazlitt led what the ordinary person would call a miserable life. He was poverty-stricken. Being an opinionated, quarrelsome fellow, he lost many friends. His unhappy marriage terminated in divorce. His remaining friends, full of pity, stood beside the bed on which he lay dying at 52. Hazlitt looked up brightly and astounded them by saying: 'Well, anyway, I've had a happy life.'

The happy life of the reviewer...

The creative writer, who may produce 12 to 30 books in a working lifetime, is not only dependent materially on the commercial success of each of them, but he must have such a degree of concentration on his theme – on a particular aspect of life at a given moment in time – that he must tend to draw a distinction between 'I' and 'the world.'

When so many vital things are happening around the globe, in so many different spheres of existence, the reviewer is forever conscious of the teeming life of the human race, in all its aspects. The reviewer is daily conscious that he is a part of all happenings in a dramatic age; that he, personally, is constantly enriched by the ideas that bubble around him like champagne.

The reviewer, while he must stand apart momentarily while judging a particular book, can never stand outside the human drama. The unity of mankind is the greatest discovery of our time. That is the vital, fundamental truth of life. The reviewer is in the best position to grasp it. The reviewer is a specially privileged spectator and should be happy. I think most of us are.

CHAPTER ONE: A MAN WITH A MISSION

1 William Arthur Deacon to Sarah Annie Deacon, 18 Dec. 1927. All letters from the Deacon Collection are printed by permission of the Thomas Fisher Rare Book Library, University of Toronto, and with the approval of Lloyd Haines, W.A. Deacon's literary executor.

2 Deacon to Gary R. Huston, 31 Oct. 1965

3 Deacon to George Nelson, 16 Aug. 1961

4 *Ibid.*

5 *Ibid.*

6 *Ibid.*

7 Deacon to Nora Deacon, nd [1953?]

8 Deacon to Mrs W.A. Barnes, 24 Nov. 1934

9 Joan MacDonald, *The Stanstead College Story* (Stanstead, PQ: Stanstead College 1977)

10 Deacon to George Nelson, 13 Mar. 1962

11 MacDonald, *The Stanstead College Story* 76

12 Elizabeth Flanders to Clara Thomas, 19 Mar. 1978

13 Lloyd Haines, W.A. Deacon's son-in-law, in conversation with Clara Thomas, 1978

14 Deacon to Emily Murphy, 22 July 1924

15 Emily Murphy to Sarah Annie Deacon, 7 Aug. 1924

16 Deacon to Mrs Early, 4 May 1953; Deacon to Miss Lane, 14 July 1953

17 Deacon to Emily Murphy, 30 Nov. 1921

18 Gertrude Shulstad to Deacon, 31 Mar. 1965

19 Deacon to John Garvin, 27 Nov. 1921

20 Deacon to Laura and Charlie Townsend, 12 July 1953

21 *Ibid.*

22 Charles J. Ryan, *H.P. Blavatsky and the Theosophical Movement: A Brief Historical Sketch*, ed. Grace E.

Knocke (Pasadena: Theosophical University Press 1975)
23 Michèle Lacombe, 'Theosophy as a Canadian Intellectual Tradition' (forthcoming in *Journal of Canadian Studies*). Albert E. Smythe, journalist and itinerant lecturer, also has a claim to fame in the person of his son, Conn Smythe of Maple Leaf Gardens. *The Canadian Theosophist* continued as a monthly until the 1960s. It then became, and remains, a bi-monthly publication.

24 *The Canadian Theosophist*, I, 3 (15 May 1920) 48
25 Deacon to Thomas Henry Billings, 28 Jan. 1924
26 Deacon to Emily Murphy, 5 Sept. 1922
27 Deacon to Emily Murphy, 8 Sept. 1922
28 Deacon to Thomas Henry Billings, 25 Mar. 1931
29 Deacon to E.J. Pratt, 7 Nov. 1953
30 Deacon to Charlie and Laura Townsend , 12 July 1953
31 Deacon to Thomas H. Billings, 4 Jan. 1953

CHAPTER TWO: APPRENTICESHIP AND CHOICE

1 Deacon to George Locke, 18 Feb. 1924
2 Deacon to Isabel [Hughes?], 1 Feb. 1953
3 Deacon to Emily Murphy, 6 Sept. 1921
4 Deacon to John Garvin, 27 Nov. 1921
5 Burton Kurth to Deacon, 8 Aug. 1922. Burton Kurth's letters are printed by permission of Mr Burton Kurth, jr.
6 Deacon to Mary Deacon, 16 Oct. 1953
7 Matt Hayes to Deacon, 29 Apr. 1919
8 Deacon to Emily Murphy, 6 Sept. 1921
9 *Ibid.*
10 Deacon to John Garvin, 27 Nov. 1921
11 John Lennox, 'New Eras: B.K. Sandwell and the Canadian Au-

thors' Association, 1919-1922,' *English Studies in Canada*, VII, 1 (Spring 1981) 93-103
12 *The Canadian Bookman*, I, 1 (New Series, January 1919) 2
13 Deacon to W.A. Kennedy, 5 Dec. 1921
14 Deacon to Emily Murphy, 6 Sept. 1921
15 Deacon to *The National Pictorial*, 25 Mar. 1922. 'The Essayist' appears to have been published in September 1921, and February and March 1922. Deacon also prepared copy for October, November, and December 1921 and for May 1922. (See also Deacon to Fred Williams, 23 Mar. 1922.)
16 Deacon to *The National Pictorial*, 8 Nov. 1921
17 Complimentary dinner tendered to William Arthur Deacon by his friends, 30 May 1944, Deacon Collection

18 *The Canadian Theosophist*, I, 1 and I, 3. Sally Townsend was married to George Syme of Winnipeg and the mother of three children, Margaret, Helen, and Franklin.

19 'The Reviewer,' *The Canadian Author and Bookman*, XXXVIII (Fall 1959) 4

CHAPTER THREE: SATURDAY NIGHT 1922-8

1 Deacon to John Garvin, 27 Nov. 1921

2 *Audit Bureau of Circulations*, 29 Nov. 1977

3 Morris Wolfe, ed., *A Saturday Night Scrapbook*, introduction by Robert Fulford (Toronto: New Press 1973) ix-x

4 *Ibid.* x

5 Hector Charlesworth, 'The History of Saturday Night,' *SN* (1 Jan. 1938) 18

6 *Audit Bureau of Circulations*, 29 Nov. 1977

7 Deacon to William Allison, 19 Oct. 1927

8 Deacon to William Allison, 26 Oct. 1925

9 Hugh Eayrs to Deacon, 24 Nov. 1925. The letters of Hugh Eayrs are quoted by permission of James Eayrs.

10 Deacon to William Allison, 6 July 1923

11 Deacon to Vernon Rhodenizer, 20 Nov. 1930

12 Arthur Phelps to Deacon, 15 July 1926. The letters of Arthur Phelps are quoted by permission of Ann Phelps.

13 Deacon to Sarah Annie Deacon, 18 Dec. 1927

14 Margaret R. Sutton, secretary-treasurer and then president of Consolidated Press Ltd, the holding company for *Saturday Night* (Hector Charlesworth, 'History,' *SN* [1 Jan. 1938] 18)

15 Deacon to Miss Sutton, 12 Dec. 1926

16 Deacon Collection, *Saturday Night*

17 *Ibid.*

18 Hugh Eayrs to Deacon, 25 Sept. 1925

19 Deacon Collection, *Saturday Night*.

20 Deacon to Evelyn Tufts, 2 Nov. 1926. Edward St John has written an excellent MA thesis on the history of Graphic Press (unpublished, Carleton University 1976); see also David B. Kotin, 'Graphic Publishers and the Bibliographer: An Introduction and Checklist,' *Papers of the Bibliographic Society of Canada* XVIII (1979) 47-54.

21 Deacon to Francis Dickie, 13 Mar. 1928

22 Hector Charlesworth to Deacon, 7 Jan. 1928

23 Deacon to Charles Conroy, 5 June 1928

24 Deacon to W. Dalton, 7 May 1928

25 Deacon to C.G.D. Roberts, 30 Apr. 1928

CHAPTER FOUR: A COMMUNITY OF LETTERS I

1 Deacon to Emily Murphy, 14 Jan. 1923
2 Deacon to Laura Lee Davidson, 29 Dec. 1924
3 Deacon to Burton Kurth, 2 Apr. 1926
4 Another Canadian, H. Lovat Dickson, who was working for Macmillan in London at the time, also records in his autobiography, *The House of Words*, his sense of unworthiness at his election to the PEN Club.
5 Mrs May Abbs to Deacon, 1 Feb. 1926
6 Emily Murphy to Deacon, 22 July 1922. Emily Murphy's letters are printed by permission of Mrs Susan Creighton. E. Cora Hind was a well-known Winnipeg journalist and feminist, Madge Macbeth and Agnes Laut, writers. Lady Byng was wife of the governor-general.
7 Emily Murphy to Deacon, 14 Aug. 1924
8 Emily Murphy to Deacon, 4 May 1921
9 Deacon to Emily Murphy, 13 Sept. 1924
10 Emily Murphy to Deacon, 4 May 1921
11 Emily Murphy to Deacon, 8 Jan. 1923
12 Deacon to Emily Murphy, 14 Jan. 1923
13 Deacon to Emily Murphy, 10 Apr. 1924

14 Deacon to Emily Murphy, 21 Oct. 1924
15 *Ibid.*
16 *Ibid.*
17 Deacon to Emily Murphy, 12 Aug. 1924
18 Deacon to Emily Murphy, 16 July 1923
19 Deacon to Emily Murphy, 29 Nov. 1923
20 Deacon to Emily Murphy, 6 Dec. 1923
21 Emily Murphy to Deacon, 9 June 1924
22 W.A. Deacon, 'Emily Murphy, 1868-1933: A Memorial,' Toronto *Mail and Empire*, 4 Nov. 1933
23 Arthur Phelps to Deacon, 17 Apr. 1926
24 Arthur Phelps to Deacon, nd [1922?]
25 Arthur Phelps to Deacon, 10 Dec. 1922
26 Arthur Phelps to Deacon, 1 Mar. 1926
27 Arthur Phelps to Deacon, nd [Jan. 1926?]. Cf. Margaret Stobie, *Frederick Philip Grove* (New York: Twayne 1973) 113: '*Settlers* had not been banned.'
28 Deacon to Arthur Phelps, 5 Dec. 1925
29 *Ibid.*
30 Arthur Phelps, letter to the editor, *The Manitoba Free Press*, 29 Nov. 1925
31 Arthur Phelps to Deacon, 17 Apr. 1926

32 Deacon to Arthur Phelps, 11 Sept. 1927

33 Arthur Phelps to Deacon, 29 Oct. 1923

34 Arthur Phelps to Deacon, 17 Mar. 1925

35 Deacon to Arthur Phelps, 19 Mar. 1925

36 Arthur Phelps to Deacon, 6 Aug. 1925

37 Arthur Phelps to Deacon, 13 July 1926

38 *Ibid.*

39 Deacon to Arthur Phelps, 19 July 1926. Barker Fairley, editor of *The Canadian Forum* and Fred Jacob, literary editor of *The Mail and Empire*

40 Arthur Phelps to Deacon, nd [1926]

41 Deacon to William Allison, 17 Feb. 1926

42 Deacon to William Allison, 18 Jan. 1926

43 Deacon to William Allison, 1 Nov. 1930

44 Deacon to William Allison, 21 Jan. 1931

45 Deacon to Burton Kurth, 22 Jan. 1925

46 Deacon to Burton Kurth, 11 Nov. 1922

47 *Ibid.*

48 Deacon to Burton Kurth, 29 Aug. 1925

49 *Ibid.*

50 Tom MacInnes to Deacon, 15 Feb. 1924. Tom MacInnes's letters are printed by permission of Mr T.R. MacInnes.

51 Tom MacInnes to Lorne Pierce, 15 Feb. 1924 (copy to W.A. Deacon)

52 Deacon to Wilson MacDonald, 3 Feb. 1927

53 Wilson MacDonald to Deacon, 1 Aug. 1925

54 Deacon to Wilson MacDonald, 4 Aug. 1925

55 Charles G.D. Roberts to Deacon, 23 Oct. 1926

56 E.J. Pratt to Deacon, 19 June 1923. E.J. Pratt's letters are printed by permission of Mrs Viola Pratt.

57 E.J. Pratt to Deacon, 27 Aug. 1927

58 Francis Dickie to Deacon, 1 May 1930

59 Mazo de la Roche to Deacon, 16 Mar. 1923. Mazo de la Roche's letters are printed by permission of Mrs Esmée Rees.

60 Deacon to Mazo de la Roche, 17 Mar. 1923

61 Deacon to L.G. Salverson, 26 Apr. 1926

62 L.G. Salverson to Deacon, nd [1931?]. Mrs Salverson's letters are printed by permission of Mr. George Salverson.

63 Deacon to L.G. Salverson, 4 Apr. 1924

64 L.G. Salverson to Deacon, nd [Apr. 1926]

65 Evelyn Tufts to Deacon, 27 Jan. 1927. Mrs Tufts' letters are quoted by permission of Mrs Allison Pickett.

66 Annie Charlotte Dalton to Deacon, 7 July 1931

67 Deacon to Annie Charlotte Dalton, 21 Nov. 1925
68 Deacon to Annie Charlotte Dalton, 30 Dec. 1926
69 Deacon to Annie Charlotte Dalton, 11 Jan. 1927
70 Raymond Knister to Deacon, 18 Sept. 1923 and 10 May 1923. Raymond Knister's letters are printed by permission of Mrs Imogen Givens.
71 Deacon to Raymond Knister, 3 May 1923
72 Deacon to Raymond Knister, 30 Oct. 1923
73 Deacon to Raymond Knister, 17 Oct. 1923
74 Deacon to Raymond Knister, 19 Feb. 1925
75 Raymond Knister to Deacon, 7 Feb. 1926
76 Deacon to Raymond Knister, 4 June 1924
77 Raymond Knister to Deacon, nd, 1924

CHAPTER FIVE: WRITINGS OF THE TWENTIES

1 Deacon to Charles L'Ami, 4 Feb. 1927
2 Lorne Pierce to Deacon, 16 Oct. 1922
3 J.D. Logan and Donald French, *Highways of Canadian Literature* (Toronto: McClelland and Stewart 1924) 378
4 Alec Lucas, *Peter McArthur* (New York: Twayne 1975) 157
5 Deacon to Burton Kurth, 2 Apr. 1926
6 Deacon to Tom MacInnes, 21 Mar. 1924
7 Deacon to W. Orton Tewson, 7 Aug. 1924
8 Deacon to Sarah Annie Deacon, 24 Aug. 1924
9 Deacon to Burton Kurth, 29 Aug. 1925
10 'What a Canadian Has done for Canada' was reprinted in 1953 in Malcolm Ross's *Our Sense of Identity* and is presently being anthologized once more by Oxford University Press.
11 Ernest W. Harrold, 'Poteen,' *Saturday Night*, 25 Sept. 1926
12 Edward St John, 'The Graphic Press'
13 Henry Miller to Deacon, 5 Feb. 1928
14 Deacon to Sarah Annie Deacon, 28 Jan. 1927

CHAPTER SIX: THE FOUR JAMESES

1 Deacon to W.H. Bucknell, 30 May 1923
2 William Arthur Deacon, *The Four Jameses* (Toronto: Ryerson Press 1953)
3 Tom MacInnes to Deacon, 10 Sept. 1924
4 Deacon to Sarah Annie Deacon, 23 May 1927
5 Kate Ruttan to Deacon, nd [June

1927]. Mrs Ruttan's letters are printed by permission of Mrs Ethel Brown.
6 Kate Ruttan to Deacon, 20 June 1927
7 Kate Ruttan to Deacon, 21 June 1927
8 Kate Ruttan to Deacon, nd [June 1927]
9 Kate Ruttan, *Rhymes, Right or Wrong, of Rainy River* (Orillia: The Times Printing Company 1926)
10 *Ibid.*
11 Evelyn Tufts to Deacon, 6 June 1927
12 Deacon to Charles J. Fish, 15 July 1927
13 Deacon to Charles Conroy, 26 July 1927
14 Deacon to Hilda Kirkwood, 27 June 1958
15 Deacon to E.J. Penny, 26 May 1932
16 Deacon to J.E. Rutledge, 7 May 1932
17 Deacon to Burton Kurth, 26 June 1928
18 Deacon to Robert Weaver, 15 Feb. 1963

CHAPTER SEVEN: THE SURVIVAL GAME

1 Harrold of *The Ottawa Citizen*; Gibbon of the CPR; Rossie of *The London Advertiser*; Dalton, Vancouver poet and fellow theosophist
2 Deacon to Sarah Annie Deacon, 20 Dec. 1928
3 Deacon to Editor, *The Halifax Herald*, 20 Apr. 1928
4 Deacon to Laura Carten, 9 June 1928
5 W.A. Deacon, 'The Art of Book Reviewing,' address given in Hamilton, Ontario, 17 Nov. 1948
6 Deacon to R.L. Curthoys, 3 Jan. 1935
7 Deacon to Donat LeBourdais, 14 Sept. 1935
8 William Arthur Deacon, 'The Mail and Empire Days,' *The Inside Story* (Sept. 1961) 18
9 Deacon to Laura Carten, 9 June 1928
10 Deacon to John Scott, 13 Feb. 1931
11 *Ibid.*
12 Deacon to W.T. Allison, 10 Nov. 1933
13 John Lennox, interview with Gordon Sinclair, July 1978
14 Jack Charlesworth, 'History of the Writers' Club,' *The Shovel*, I, 3 (8 Mar. 1933) 3
15 W.A. Deacon, 'Distinction Shared through Membership in Writers' Club,' *The Shovel*, I, 3 (8 Mar. 1933) 3
16 Deacon to Sarah Annie Deacon, 12 Nov. 1932
17 Deacon to C.J. Eustace, 4 Mar. 1933
18 Roy L. Curthoys to A.C.C. Holtz, 3 Sept. 1931
19 Roy L. Curthoys to Deacon, 14 Nov. 1933; 17 Oct. 1934
20 Deacon to Roy L. Curthoys, 3 Jan. 1935

21 Murray G. Ross, *The Y.M.C.A. in Canada: The Chronicle of the Century* (Toronto: Ryerson Press 1951) 371

22 Deacon to J.V. McAree, 14 Sept. 1935

23 Deacon to Sarah Annie Deacon, 28 Aug. 1936; Deacon to R.A. Farquharson, 11 Aug. 1936

24 Deacon to George Sutton Patterson, 17 Aug. 1936

25 Deacon to R.A. Farquharson, 11 Aug. 1936; 15 Aug. 1936

26 R.A. Farquharson, telegram, William A. Deacon's retirement dinner, 11 Jan. 1961

27 'Deacon's Annual,' 1937, biographical material, Deacon Collection

28 *Ibid.*

29 E. George Smith to Deacon, 12 June 1939

CHAPTER EIGHT: A COMMUNITY OF LETTERS II

1 Deacon to D.C. Scott, 20 July 1931

2 D.C. Scott to Deacon, 2 Aug. 1931. D.C. Scott's letters are printed by permission of Mr John S. Aylen.

3 Deacon to D.C. Scott, 5 Aug. 1931

4 Leslie MacFarlane to Deacon, 28 July 1931. Leslie MacFarlane's letters are printed by permission of Brian MacFarlane.

5 Deacon to Leslie MacFarlane, 4 Aug. 1931

6 Laura Goodman Salverson to Deacon, 7 Apr. 1931

7 Deacon to Laura Goodman Salverson, 20 Nov. 1933

8 Deacon to George Salverson, 18 Jan. 1934

9 Deacon to E.J. Pratt, 6 April 1935

10 E.J. Pratt to Deacon, 8 Apr. 1935

11 Georges Bugnet to Deacon, 30 Jan. 1930. Georges Bugnet's letters are printed by permission of M. Jean-Marcel Duciaume.

12 Deacon to Georges Bugnet, 6 Feb. 1930

13 Georges Bugnet to Deacon, 17 Feb. 1930

14 H. Lovat Dickson, *Wilderness Man* (Toronto: Macmillan Company of Canada 1973)

15 Deacon to Grey Owl, 19 Jan. 1935

16 Grey Owl to Deacon, 30 Jan. 1935 (Beaver Lodge, Prince Albert National Park, Saskatchewan). Grey Owl's letters are printed after consultation with his executors, The Canada Permanent Trust Company, and by permission of Lloyd Haines, literary executor of William Arthur Deacon.

17 Deacon to Grey Owl, 24 Apr. 1935

18 H. Lovat Dickson, in conversation with Clara Thomas, 1978

19 Grey Owl to Deacon, 10 May 1935

20 Deacon to Grey Owl, 9 June 1935

21 Grey Owl to Deacon, 13 May 1937

22 Deacon to Morley Callaghan, 14 Sept. 1932

23 Deacon to Morley Callaghan, 20 Feb. 1934

24 Deacon to Morley Callaghan, 10 Sept. 1935

25 John Mitchell to Deacon, 28 July 1930. John Mitchell's letters are printed by permission of Mrs Dorothy Sisco.

26 Deacon to John Mitchell, 12 Dec. 1933

27 John Mitchell to Deacon, 14 Mar. 1934

28 John Mitchell to Deacon, 16 July 1934

29 Deacon to John Mitchell, 30 Aug. 1935

30 John Mitchell to Deacon, 4 Sept. 1935

31 Deacon to Gordon Pook, 2 Sept. 1932

32 Bill Deacon, in conversation with Clara Thomas, 1978

33 Deacon to Carlton McNaught, 26 Dec. 1933

34 Carlton McNaught to Deacon, 21 Apr. 1934. Carlton McNaught's letters are printed by permission of Professor Kenneth McNaught.

35 Deacon to Carlton McNaught, 27 Apr. 1934

36 Deacon to J.S. Woodsworth, 30 June 1934

37 J.S. Woodsworth to Deacon, 2 July 1934. J.S. Woodsworth's letters are printed by permission of Mrs Grace MacInnis; for references to 'the Toronto affair' see Kenneth McNaught, *A Prophet in Politics* (Toronto: University of Toronto Press 1959) 266.

38 Deacon to J.S. Woodsworth, 5 July 1934

39 Deacon to John W. Holmes, 4 Apr. 1932

40 John W. Holmes to Deacon, 17 June 1932. John W. Holmes's letters are printed by permission of Dr John W. Holmes.

41 Deacon to John W. Holmes, 21 Sept. 1932

42 Harold A. Innis to Deacon, 6 Jan. 1934. Harold A. Innis's letters are printed by permission of Mrs Anne Dagg, Mrs Mary Cates, and Messrs Hugh and Donald Innis.

43 A.R.M. Lower to Deacon, 29 Jan. 1935. A.R.M. Lower's letters are printed by permission of Professor A.R.M. Lower.

44 A.R.M. Lower, *My First Seventy Years* (Toronto: Macmillan Company of Canada 1967) 205-6

45 A.R.M. Lower to Deacon, 28 Sept. 1936

46 Deacon to George M. Wrong, 22 Feb. 1934

47 George M. Wrong to Deacon, 23 Feb. 1934. George M. Wrong's letters are printed by permission of Mrs Agnes Armstrong.

48 George M. Wrong to Deacon, 29 Apr. 1935

49 George M. Wrong to Deacon, 11 May 1939

50 Deacon to B.H. Liddell Hart, 19 May 1934

51 Deacon to B.H. Liddell Hart, 13 June 1934

52 B.H. Liddell Hart to Deacon, 17 Sept. 1934

53 Deacon to B.H. Liddell Hart, 13 Oct. 1934

54 B.H. Liddell Hart to Deacon, 4 Dec. 1934

CHAPTER NINE: WRITINGS OF THE THIRTIES

1 William Arthur Deacon, *My Vision of Canada* (Toronto: Ontario Publishing Company 1933) 273

2 W.A. Deacon and W. Reeves, ed. *Open House* (Ottawa: Graphic Press 1931) 17

3 Deacon to W.R. Dent, 17 Mar. 1931

4 Deacon to Donat LeBourdais, 26 May 1931

5 John Garvin, 'Open House,' *The Canadian Bookman*, XIII, 12 (Dec. 1931) 239

6 'Open House,' *The Canadian Magazine*, LXXVI, 5 (Nov. 1931) 42

7 Frank Underhill, 'Speaking Up in Toronto,' *Saturday Night*, Autumn Literary Supplement (10 Oct. 1931) 4

8 Deacon to Sarah Annie Deacon, 18 Dec. 1927

9 J.S. Ewart, *The Kingdom of Canada ... and Other Essays* (Toronto: Morang and Company 1908) 370

10 Hugh Keenleyside, *Canada and the United States* (New York: Knopf 1929) 383

11 John Mitchell, *The Kingdom of America* (Brampton, Ontario: The Banner and Times 1930) 38

12 *The Canadian Theosophist*, VIII, 5 (15 July 1927)

13 Deacon to Burton Kurth, 26 Dec. 1933

14 Deacon to Col. Edward House, 12 Feb. 1934

15 Deacon to Henry Weekes, 25 Dec. 1934

16 Deacon to Carlton McNaught, 4 Dec. 1933

17 Carlton McNaught, 'A Challenge to Colonialism,' *The University of Toronto Monthly*, XXXIV, 4 (Jan. 1934) 107

18 Carlton McNaught to Deacon, 30 Nov. 1933

19 Frank Underhill, 'The Importance of Being Earnest,' *The Canadian Forum*, XIV, 158 (Nov. 1933) 74

20 Mary Vipond, 'National Consciousness in English-Speaking Canada in the 1920s: Seven Studies' (unpublished PHD thesis, University of Toronto 1974) 266-328

21 Deacon to N.T. Carey, 23 Feb. 1934

22 W.A. Deacon, 'First Epistle to Canadians,' 15 Feb. 1934, Native Sons of Canada, Deacon Collection

23 Deacon to N.T. Carey, 1 Apr. 1934

24 Frederick Philip Grove to Deacon, 24 Sept. 1936. Frederick Philip Grove's letters are printed by permission of Mr Leonard Grove.

25 Deacon to Phyllis Attwood [William Tyrrell Ltd], 27 Oct. 1952

26 Deacon to George McCrossan, 31 July 1942

27 Deacon to Bruce Hutchison, 19 Jan. 1954

28 *My Vision of Canada*, Deacon Collection

CHAPTER TEN: THE CANADIAN AUTHORS' ASSOCIATION

1 Deacon to Gordon Sinclair, 19 Dec. 1946

2 For a detailed history of the CAA, see John Lennox, 'A Sense of Belonging: The Canadian Authors' Association,' 95 pp, unpublished ms. Scott Library, York University; see also Mary Vipond, 'The Canadian Authors' Association in the 1920s: A Case Study in Cultural Nationalism,' *Journal of Canadian Studies*, xv (Spring 1980) 68-79.

3 Deacon to Isabel LeBourdais, 2 Apr. 1954

4 Deacon to H.A. Kennedy, 5 Jan. 1935

5 'Our Forward March,' *The Canadian Author and Bookman*, XII, 2 (Dec. 1934) 6

6 If reorganization of *The Canadian Poetry Magazine* was one remedy, the donations of different members of the Association provided essential assistance as well and helped keep the magazine on the thin margin of solvency. Pratt's editorship continued until August 1943. Sir Charles G.D. Roberts was named editor, but he died shortly before his first issue of the magazine went to press. The magazine continued with the March 1944 number under the acting editorship of Amabel King and the associate editorship of Leo Cox. They were in charge until Watson Kirkconnell took over in September 1944. Earle Birney became editor in 1946; subsequently the magazine went through a series of editors and was eventually absorbed by *The Canadian Author and Bookman* in the autumn of 1968.

7 *The Canadian Author and Bookman*, XIV, 2 (Dec. 1936) 6

8 *Ibid.* 7-8

9 Deacon to Leslie Gordon Barnard, 24 Apr. 1939

10 Deacon to Eric Gaskell, 7 May 1939

11 W.A. Deacon, 'Governor General's Awards Board Report,' *The Canadian Author and Bookman, Supplement*, XXIII, 3 (Fall 1947) 16

12 Watson Kirkconnell, *A Slice of Canada: Memoirs* (Toronto: University of Toronto Press 1967) 298

13 It was not until 1959 that Governor General's Awards were given for Canadian works in French and even now the awards do not carry the same prestige or recognition in French Canada as in English Canada.

14 The following year, the second award – by now known as the 'Tweedsmuir Award' – was given posthumously to Annie Charlotte Dalton of Vancouver for her poem, 'Wheat and Barley,' judged the best of the poems published in Volume II of *The Canadian Poetry Magazine*. With this presentation, the awarding of dual prizes terminated, as *The Canadian Poetry*

Magazine reverted to its original policy of conferring cash prizes for the three best poems in each issue.

15 Deacon to V.H. Rhodenizer and E.J. Pratt, Jan.-Feb. 1939

16 W.A. Deacon, 'History of Literary Awards, 1936-43,' CAA, Deacon Collection

17 *The Canadian Author and Bookman*, xv, 4 (July 1938) 22

18 *The Globe and Mail*, 13 June 1939

19 Deacon to Madge Macbeth, 4 May 1939

20 Deacon to Eric Gaskell, 7 May 1939

21 *The Canadian Author and Bookman*, Supplement, xxi (Dec. 1945) 16

22 Keith Edgar, 'A Tree Grows in Toronto,' *The Canadian Author and Bookman*, xxi, 3 (Sept. 1945) 16

23 Deacon to Charles Clay, 9 Dec. 1945

24 CAA minutes, 16 Mar. 1946, National Executive Committee

25 *The Canadian Author and Bookman*, Supplement, xxiii, 3 (Sept. 1946) 41. I was present at that banquet, bedazzled and bemused because Deacon had not only been instrumental in having Longmans publish my MA thesis, *Canadian Novelists, 1920-1945*, but had also decided to present leatherbound copies of the book to the governor-general and retiring members of the executive on this occasion. The evening was glorious, formal, and hot – an unseasonable heat-wave which may well still be a record. (CT)

26 *The Canadian Author and Bookman*, Supplement, xxii, 3 (Sept. 1946) 18, 21

27 Deacon to Gordon Sinclair, 19 Dec. 1946

28 Philip Child to Deacon, 3 Nov. 1947

29 'The President's Valedictory,' *The Canadian Author and Bookman*, Supplement, xxiv, 4 (Fall 1948) 12

30 Deacon to Jean Bruchési, 11 July 1946

31 Deacon to Scott Young, 5 July 1950

32 Mary Vipond, 'The Canadian Authors' Association in the 1920s'

CHAPTER ELEVEN: THE GLOBE AND MAIL YEARS

1 W.A. Deacon, 'The Art of Book Reviewing,' radio broadcast, Hamilton, 17 Nov. 1948

2 Deacon to Earle Birney, 6 Aug. 1947

3 Deacon to Dorothy Dumbrille, 8 Dec. 1953

4 Deacon to Joan Walker, 15 Jan. 1953

5 W.A. Deacon, 'A Poet on the Height of land: The Significance of Duncan Campbell Scott's Career' (Stanstead, PQ: Stanstead College 1948)

6 Deacon to Yvonne Stevenson, 5 Mar. 1965
7 W.A. Deacon, Ryerson lectures, preface
8 *Ibid.*, introduction
9 *Ibid.*
10 *Ibid.* The continuing reputation of Wilson's work has amply vindicated Deacon's opinion of it.
11 *Ibid.* 'Hugh MacLennan'
12 *Ibid.* 'Four French-Canadian Novelists'
13 *Ibid.*, 'Frederick Philip Grove'
14 Deacon to Lorne Pierce, 15 Apr. 1952
15 Deacon to Nora and Bill Deacon, 1 Feb. 1952
16 Deacon to Lorne Pierce, 22 Feb. 1953
17 Deacon to Miss Park, 6 Apr. 1961
18 Deacon to Louis Blake Duff, 20 Sept. 1951
19 In 1945 the Foundation was incorporated under the revised title, The Canadian Writers' Foundation. For a report on the history and development of the Foundation, see Michèle Lacombe, Canadian Writers' Foundation, Report, 2 Oct. 1979, Deacon Collection. See also Walter Dawson, *The Foundation and the Man* (Ottawa 1959). In this pamphlet, a history of the CWF, Deacon's part in its instigation is not given the credit that his letters clearly demonstrate.
20 Deacon to Hugh MacLennan, 4 July 1948
21 He was entirely right in this. I was teaching for Western at the time. (CT)
22 Deacon to George Nelson, 18 Oct. 1961
23 Lorne Pierce to Deacon, 15 Dec. 1956. Printed by permission of Mrs Beth Pierce Robinson
24 Deacon to Lorne Pierce, 8 Jan. 1957
25 W.A. Deacon, 'The Reviewer,' *The Canadian Author and Bookman* XXXVIII (Fall 1959) 6-7

CHAPTER TWELVE: A COMMUNITY OF LETTERS III

1 Germaine Guèvremont to Deacon, [15? Apr.] 1946. Germaine Guèvremont's letters are printed by permission of Mme Louise Guèvremont-Gentiletti. (our translation)
2 Germaine Guèvremont to Deacon, 22 Mar. 1950
3 Germaine Guèvremont to Deacon, 8 Dec. 1953
4 Deacon to Germaine Guèvremont, 13 Dec. 1953
5 Germaine Guèvremont to Deacon, 8 Dec. 1953
6 Colleen Thibaudeau to Deacon, 15 Sept. 1950 (enclosure). Printed by permission of Roger Lemelin
7 W.A. Deacon, notes of address by Roger Lemelin, Feb. 1951

8 Miss Sybil Hutchison to Deacon, [Spring, 1947?] (enclosure). Printed by permission of Marjorie Bonner Lowry

9 Deacon to J.S. Ross, 4 Apr. 1946

10 J.S. Ross to Deacon, 15 Apr. 1946

11 Deacon to W.O. Mitchell, 5 Mar. 1947

12 Margaret Coulby to Deacon, 17 Apr. 1947. Margaret Coulby's letters are printed by permission of Dr Margaret Whitridge.

13 Deacon to Margaret Coulby, 18 Apr. 1947

14 Hugh MacLennan to Deacon, 9 Sept. 1945. Hugh MacLennan's letters are printed by permission of Hugh MacLennan.

15 Hugh MacLennan to Deacon, 24 May 1961

16 Hugh MacLennan to Deacon, 8 Apr. 1945

17 Dorothy Duncan to Deacon, 21 Apr. 1945. Dorothy Duncan's letters are printed by permission of Hugh MacLennan.

18 Hugh MacLennan to Deacon, 7 Mar. 1946

19 Hugh MacLennan to Deacon, 5 Dec. 1948 [1947?]

20 Deacon to Hugh MacLennan, 8 Jan. 1948

21 Hugh MacLennan to Deacon, 5 Dec. 1948 [1947?]

22 Hugh MacLennan to Deacon, 12 Jan. 1948

23 Deacon to Hugh MacLennan, 4 July 1948

24 Hugh MacLennan to Deacon, 7 July 1948

25 Deacon to Hugh MacLennan, 11 July 1948

26 Deacon to Hugh MacLennan, 13 July 1948

27 Hugh MacLennan to Deacon, 18 July 1948

28 Thomas Raddall to Deacon, 2 Dec. 1944. Thomas Raddall's letters are printed by permission of Thomas Raddall.

29 Ibid.

30 Ibid.

31 Thomas Raddall to Deacon, 13 Nov. 1950

32 Deacon to Thomas Raddall, 23 Oct. 1950

33 Thomas Raddall to Deacon, 1 Nov. 1950

34 Thomas Raddall to Deacon, 7 Oct. 1953

35 Thomas Raddall to Deacon, 24 Mar. 1953

36 Deacon to Thomas Raddall, 28 Mar. 1953

37 Thomas Raddall to Deacon, 2 Aug. 1953

38 Hugh MacLennan to Deacon, 7 Mar. 1946

39 Hugh MacLennan to Deacon, 28 Apr. 1946

40 Deacon to Gabrielle Roy, 16 Feb. 1946

41 Deacon to Gabrielle Roy, 2 Mar. 1946

42 Gabrielle Roy to Deacon, 11 Mar. 1946. Gabrielle Roy's letters are printed by permission of Gabrielle Roy.

43 Deacon to Gabrielle Roy, 24 Mar. 1946
44 *Ibid.*
45 Deacon to Gabrielle Roy, 29 Apr. 1947
46 Gabrielle Roy to Deacon, 9 Apr. 1949
47 Gabrielle Roy to Deacon, 22 Oct. 1950
48 Gabrielle Roy to Deacon, 16 Mar. 1954
49 Deacon to Gabrielle Roy, 18 Mar. 1954
50 Gabrielle Roy to Deacon, 30 Oct. 1955
51 Deacon to Gabrielle Roy, 10 Dec. 1955

CHAPTER THIRTEEN: THE RETIREMENT YEARS

1 Deacon to Sherwood Fox, 29 Dec. 1960
2 Deacon to Bill and Nora [Deacon], 16 Jan. 1954
3 W.A. Deacon, retirement speech, 11 Jan. 1961
4 *Ibid.*
5 Deacon to Peter Newman, 8 Nov. 1963
6 Deacon to Lady Eaton [Flora McCrea] 29 Jan. 1961
7 Deacon to Lloyd Haines, 3 Apr. 1967
8 Jessie L. Beattie was one of the old friends to whom he confessed his anxieties in writing. She has incorporated many of his letters to her in *William Arthur Deacon: Memoirs of a Literary Friendship* (Hamilton: Fleming Press 1978).
9 Deacon to Lloyd [Haines], 27 Sept. 1967; Deacon to Bill [Deacon], 19 Sept. 1967
10 Deacon to Lloyd Haines, 1 Dec. 1967
11 Leslie Fiedler, 'Literature as an Institution,' *The New Republic*, xxx (May 1981) 24
12 Two senior Canadian sociologists, one who grew up in Montreal and one in Owen Sound, Ontario, recently told me that as young people, MacDonald was the only poet they ever saw and heard in the flesh. They remember his school performances with pleasure. Growing up in Strathroy, Ontario, I had the same experience. (CT)
13 Gabrielle Roy to John Lennox, 13 Jan. 1979

INDEX

This book
was designed by
WILLIAM RUETER
and was printed by
University
of Toronto
Press